Dollars and Sense

An Introduction to Economics

SEVENTH EDITION

Marilu Hurt McCarty
Georgia Institute of Technology

HarperCollinsCollegePublishers

Senior Editor: Bruce Kaplan
Project Editor: David Nickol
Design Supervisor: Mary McDonnell
Cover Design: Mary McDonnell
Photo Researcher: Michelle Ryan
Production Administrator: Jeff Taub
Compositor: Better Graphics, Inc.
Printer and Binder: R. R. Donnelley & Sons Company
Cover Printer: The Lehigh Press, Inc.

Dollars and Sense: An Introduction to Economics, Seventh Edition

Photo Credits
Page 15, Andy Sacks/Tony Stone Images; page 44, Michael Dwyer/Stock Boston; page 64, Jean-Claude Lejeune; page 82, Cameramann International; page 110, Cameramann International; page 129, Robert E. Daemmrich/Tony Stone Images; page 157, Scott, Foresman and Company; page 181, Scott Foresman and Company; page 205, Paul Hosefros/The New York Times; page 234, Scott, Foresman and Company; page 261, Jean-Claude Lejeune; page 280, Paul Menzel/Stock Boston; page 299, Jean-Claude Lejeune; page 321, Jean-Claude Lejeune; page 352, Bob Daemmrich/Sygma.

Library of Congress Cataloging-in-Publication Data

McCarty, Marilu Hurt.
Dollars and sense : an introduction to economics / Marilu Hurt McCarty. —7th ed.
p. cm.
Includes bibliographical references and index.
ISBN 0-673-46806-2
1. Economics. I. Title.
HB171.5.M46 1993
330—dc20 93-28159
CIP

93 94 95 96 9 8 7 6 5 4 3 2 1

Contents

Chapter 9
Government Finance and Fiscal Policy 191

Chapter 10
Financial Institutions and Monetary Policy 217

Chapter 11
Inflation 248

Chapter 12
Unemployment 269

Preface

The fundamental objective of *Dollars and Sense* is to help students develop the reasoning power necessary for analyzing the economic issues and evaluating the policy proposals they will encounter as citizens in a rapidly changing world. To this end, the text emphasizes a set of basic economic tools and applies these tools to such topics of current interest as economic growth, minimum-wage legislation, environmental pollution, inflation and unemployment, poverty and public assistance, fiscal policy and taxation, and the trade deficit and international competitiveness. The continuing goal of this seventh edition is to make the subject matter and methods of economics more meaningful and comprehensible to today's college students.

Dollars and Sense is intended for use in the one-term economics courses for students with little or no background in the subject. The text's emphasis on current issues should help students from all disciplines acquire habits of systematic thought that they can carry with them to their own fields of study. At the same time, the text provides the kind of analytical foundation that will enable interested students to proceed to more advanced study in economics with a greater understanding of its scope and methods.

ORGANIZATION AND COVERAGE

Each chapter is divided into two parts. The first, *Tools for Study,* presents both verbally and graphically the basic analytical tools of economics. Economic behavior is described and analyzed, and economic behavior is discussed within the context of existing social, political, technological, and environmental conditions. The second part of each chapter, *Theory in Practice,* includes practical applications of the topics discussed in the first part, examining recent events, debates over current policy, and business practices.

Chapter 1 introduces the student to the economic problem and the function of an economic system as a means of allocating resources. The concepts of scarcity, opportunity costs, and marginal analysis are discussed and applied. Problem solving through marginal analysis is introduced at the level of the family unit and local government.

Chapters 2 through 5 provide the core of microeconomics: how price and output decisions respond to supply and demand in free markets and how imperfectly competitive markets fail to respond efficiently to supply and demand. Chapter 6 deals with supply and demand in markets for productive resources, with emphasis on labor resources and the labor movement. Chapters 7 through 10 provide the core of macroeconomics: the definition and measurement of gross domestic product, the equilibrium level of GDP, and the use of fiscal and monetary policy to affect equilibrium.

Chapters 11 through 13 focus on current domestic problems and issues: inflation, unemployment, and poverty. Recent policy applications include wage and price controls, collective bargaining procedures, and the crisis in Social Security. Chapters 14 and 15 consider the broader long-range problems of economic growth and international economic relations. Current applications include population growth and the food crisis, exchange instability, and multinational firms.

CHANGES IN THE SEVENTH EDITION

The Seventh Edition of *Dollars and Sense* incorporates some significant changes suggested by users of earlier editions. For example, some sidebars have been incorporated in the text for improved continuity. Some examples have been trimmed and updated. Graphs and tables have been added or improved for greater computation ease. Chapter 6 on labor markets has been reorganized to focus more clearly on resource productivity. Chapters 7 and 8 on macroeconomics have been changed to integrate international economics more fully into the discussion. Chapter 10 on monetary theory and policy has been revised to stress the increased competition and reduced specialization among financial intermediaries. Chapter 11 on inflation has been revised to focus on the aggregate-demand and aggregate-supply origins of inflation. Chapter 14 continues its strong emphasis on the importance of economic growth.

New selections in the series *Contemporary Thinking about Economic Issues* include Jeffrey Sachs on privatization in Eastern Europe; Bernd Horne on labor problems in the reunited German state; David Aschauer on the potential stimulative effects of infrastructure investment; Dertouzos, Lester, and Solow on regaining the competitive edge; Robert Eisner on the true cost of the S&L bailout; Sar Levitan on enterprise zones; Thomas DiLorenzo on environmental pollution in command economies; and William Nordhaus on the economics of the greenhouse effect. It is hoped that these selections will spark students' interest in objective research into current economic problems.

SPECIAL FEATURES

This text incorporates a number of special features to make it more attractive and useful to instructors and students alike:

- **Level and method of presentation.** A determined effort has been made to use familiar language and to enliven explanations with humor, personal experiences and observations, and invitations for the student to relate topics to his or her own life. Simple equations and graphs are used judiciously to reinforce verbal descriptions and for further development of basic principles in applied situations.
- **Tools for independent study.** Three features of the text encourage independent, self-paced instruction by the student. *Learning Objectives* at the start of each chapter give the student a set of goals to accomplish, and *Current Issues for Discussion* provide thoughtful questions to answer (or analyze intelligently) while reading. *Test Yourself* questions require students to apply concepts they have just learned. The *Self-Check,* a set of multiple-choice questions separating the two parts of each chapter, allows students to test their mastery of the concepts presented in *Tools for Study* before they go on to the applications. Answers and explanations for the self-checks are found at the end of the text.
- **Terms to remember.** Important terms and concepts in each chapter are set off in boldface type and are formally defined at the end of the chapter.
- **Problem-solving tools.** The *Theory in Practice* section of Chapter 1 presents a six-step model for analyzing and solving economic problems that can be used throughout the

book as well as independently outside the course.

- **Viewpoints.** Short *Viewpoint* essays throughout the text discuss topics of special interest and show how economics operates within a historical, social, and political framework.
- **Topics for Discussion.** Discussion questions at the end of each chapter include review questions requiring definitions or factual information as well as "brain teasers" that ask students to apply the tools they have recently learned to current issues. The seventh edition includes new questions in almost every chapter.
- **Supplementary Materials.** Although the text itself includes many features of a workbook, a *Study Guide* for students is available to reinforce and expand the material covered in each chapter. An *Instructor's Manual* is also available.
- **Reading lists.** Each text chapter includes a list of recent articles in news magazines and professional journals, selected for their clear, straightforward language and relevance to fundamental economic principles.

ACKNOWLEDGMENTS

I am especially indebted to my good friends and colleagues who reviewed portions of the original manuscript and offered worthwhile suggestions and comments: Carl Biven, Jack Blicksilver, Sherman Dallas, Eva Galambos, Virlyn Moore, Beverly Schaffer, and my father, A. Raymond Hurt. I also appreciate the help and advice of the reviewers who aided in the preparation of the seventh edition: Fritzic V. Allen, Contra Costa College; Kathleen K. Bromley, Monroe Community College; Robert R. Ebert, Baldwin-Wallace College; John B. Egger, Towson State University; Ken Harrison, Stockton State College; Stephen B. Packer, St. Peter's College; and John C. Wassom, Western Kentucky University.

Marilu Hurt McCarty

Chapter 1

Scarcity and Choice

Tools for Study

LEARNING OBJECTIVES

After reading this chapter, you will be able to:

1. Explain the problem facing all economic systems.
2. List the three questions every economic system must answer.
3. Explain the concept of opportunity cost and show how opportunity costs affect choices.
4. Construct and interpret a graph.
5. Use a graph to illustrate a nation's production possibilities.
6. Use a method of problem solving to plan budgets for a family and for a government.

CURRENT ISSUES FOR DISCUSSION

What factors affect a nation's capacity to produce goods and services?

How can a nation use its resources more efficiently?

We Americans love a challenge. Our ancestors readily took up the challenge of settling a wild and remote continent. They cleared the land, suffered the winters, and raised the cities. They fought for the right of self-government, and they took up the responsibility of using the nation's resources to satisfy national goals.

The tradition of pursuing noble goals has continued with each new generation of Americans, and our efforts have succeeded beyond our forefathers' grandest dreams. We have prospered greatly, and we have extended our prosperity to more and more segments of our own population, as well as to populations abroad. Our material prosperity has brought improved health and living conditions, better education and job opportunities, and—most important—the potential for fullest personal development to us all.

Challenges did not end with the pioneer era. In fact, the problems faced by today's generation have more frightening possibilities than any we have faced before. More of the world's people want more things. At the same time, more of the world's resources are becoming depleted or are concentrated in the hands of people whose preferences regarding resource use are different from ours. There are more conflicts over access to the "good life," both in our own nation and in the world as a whole. And, regrettably, our capacity to inflict harm on each other has grown faster than our capacity to do good.

Today's Americans must make difficult choices and decide complex issues that impose costs now for the sake of benefits far in the future.

Many of our choices involve economics. Economics is both the basis for our prosperity and the reason for our struggle. Through understanding economics, we—as individuals and as a nation—can make the decisions, shoulder the responsibilities, and find the solutions to the problems that confront us.

That is our challenge!

ECONOMICS AS A SCIENCE

The study of economics evolved along with people's everlasting drive to make sense of our environment. As human beings, we do not like to think of ourselves as mere combinations of cells with specialized functions enabling us to consume food, grow hair, and so forth. We become uneasy at the thought that we are, after all, only engaged in some collective "milling around" during our stay here on planet Earth. We want to understand the order in our surroundings and to find a place for ourselves in our universe.

The drive to understand and explain our environment began in the fourteenth century during the period of European history known as the Renaissance. More plentiful food supplies and a gradual improvement in living conditions made it possible for some people to use their time for tasks other than for producing the food and shelter necessary for life. Instead, they could devote their energies to investigating the mysteries of the world environment.

In the beginning, the emphasis was on understanding the physical environment. Astronomers made the rather comforting discovery that heavenly bodies are subject to physical laws governing their orderly movement through space. Biologists discovered the circulation of the blood and the fact that we are ourselves orderly systems controlled by understandable biological laws. Through investigations like these, scientists developed a body of natural laws to explain the order in our physical world.

In due course, scholars turned to the *social* world in search of the natural laws that explain people's relationships with one another. The year 1776 was important for two new social sciences—political science and economics. That was the year the American nation began its experiment in political democracy. And it was the year Adam Smith published the first complete explanation of how an economic system works.

The title of Adam Smith's book was *An Inquiry into the Nature and Causes of the Wealth of Nations*. The book is often spoken of as simply *The Wealth of Nations*; but the full title is important because it invites the reader to explore the processes through which nations create wealth. The ability to create wealth depends on a nation's economic system.

What is an economic system? And why is an economic system necessary? How does our economic system work for you? Answering those questions will be an important part of your study of economics.

ECONOMICS AND THE HISTORY OF IDEAS

The social science of economics developed along with the natural and physical sciences; but social sciences suffer from certain disadvantages relative to the other sciences. Although investigations of the world of nature can be carried out systematically and without bias, investigations of the social world might not. Social scientists are a part of the system they are investigating. They may bring to their investigations their own prejudices and self-interests, with the result that their conclusions might be biased.

Another disadvantage is that the social world itself changes, giving social scientists new information and forcing them to change their explanations. Much of our world has changed since the Industrial Revolution, when modern economic theory began. In those times, competition was vigorous, and competition prevented a single firm from dominating the entire market for a particular good or service. The advantages of competition produced the economic theory known as "laissez-faire," from the French expression for "let alone." According to laissez-faire, an economic system functions best if individuals are left alone to pursue their own self-interest, with minimum interference by government.

The world depression of the 1930s brought a change in economic conditions. With minimum government involvement in the economic system, production in our nation's economy fell by almost half. A British economist, John Maynard Keynes, proposed that government use its power to help put farms and factories back to work. Increased government involvement in the U.S. economy was given the force of law with the Employment Act of 1946.

In recent years some critics of government involvement have complained that government has grown too powerful. Some economists favor a return to laissez-faire; others recommend still greater government involvement.

Economic issues change. Economic theory and policy evolve in response to changing social, political, and economic conditions. (Then there's the story of the old economics professor who asks the same exam questions year after year but keeps changing the answers.) Economics is an evolving course of study. Students of economics must always question the theories and policies of the past and look to the changing needs and opportunities of the future.

TEST YOURSELF

What economic issue currently dominates the nation's agenda? What political interest groups favor alternative solutions? How do economic conditions in other nations affect our own economic prosperity?

THE FUNDAMENTAL PROBLEM OF ECONOMICS

Throughout the history of life on this planet, people have faced the economic problem of scarcity: scarce land, mineral, and labor resources for producing the things we want. At the same time growing numbers of people have wanted more things—goods and services for making work easier and life more pleasant. With scarce resources and increasing human wants, we must *choose* the things we want most. Choosing to have some of the things we want requires us to give up other things we might have had.

If all resources were free—that is, if all of us could have as much as we wanted of everything—we wouldn't need an economic system. There are, in fact, some **resources** we tend to think of as **free**. Fresh air and sunshine, for example, may be free on a tropical island. Each person can have as much as he or she wants, and there will still be enough for everyone else. In a crowded city, on the other hand, fresh air and sunshine may be very much a scarce resource. We must pay a price in order to obtain it. The price of pollution control (or an airline ticket to a tropical island) is an example of the price we might pay. Unfortunately, as we soon discover, most resources are scarce.

Because resources are scarce, they must be used carefully. Every community, whether of cave dwellers or high-rise apartment dwellers, must establish a system for allocating its scarce resources toward production of those goods and services the people want most. How much of the scarce land should be used to produce wheat and how much to produce strawberries? How much of the scarce mineral resources should be used for autos and how much for airplanes? How much of the scarce labor should be used to build dams and how much to teach college students?

We can't have all we want of everything. So we must choose the things we want most. That is why we have an economic system. An economic system provides a way of choosing.

The problem of scarce resources and unlimited wants is called the **economic problem**. We have said that every nation faces limits on its ability to satisfy its ever-increasing wants. With scarce resources there are limits to the quantities of goods and services we can produce during a particular period of time. The economic problem requires that a nation use its scarce resources efficiently to produce the goods and services its people want most.

The Four Kinds of Resources

Resources are classified in four groups: land, labor, capital, and management or entrepreneurial ability.

Land

Land may be thought of as "natural resources." Land includes all the original and nonreproducible gifts of nature: fertile soil, mineral deposits, fossil fuels, and water. All are fixed in amount but, when combined with human ingenuity, may be used to produce wanted goods and services.

In years past the vastness of the earth's natural resources tempted us to regard them as inexhaustible and, therefore, free. Threats of future shortages, however, remind us that we must use our scarce land resources efficiently.

Labor

Labor may be thought of as "human resources." Labor is the productive activity of human beings: teachers, psychiatrists, lathe operators, roustabouts, statisticians. Failure to use productively a single willing hour of labor results in a permanent sacrifice of the good or service that resource might have produced.

Capital

Capital may be thought of as "manufactured resources." Capital includes the tools and equipment that strengthen, extend, or replace human hands in the production of goods and services: hammers, sewing machines, turbines, bookkeeping machines, and component parts of finished goods. Even the specialized skills of trained workers can be thought of as a kind of human capital. Capital resources permit "roundabout" production: thus, capital resources enable us to produce goods indirectly through a kind of tool rather than directly by physical labor.

To construct a capital resource requires that we postpone the production of other goods and services today so that we can produce a tool that will enable us to produce more goods and services in the future. To postpone production of wanted goods and services is sometimes a painful decision, particularly when people are poor and in desperate need of goods and services for use today.

Economists do not think of money as capital, because money by itself cannot produce anything at all. However, money is a convenient means of "storing" resources today for use in production of goods and services tomorrow. Later in this text we will have more to say about the process of "storing" resources for future production.

Management or Entrepreneurial Ability

Management or entrepreneurial ability may be thought of as the "creative resource." It is the human initiative that combines other resources to produce a certain good or service. Entrepreneurial ability is provided by the owner or developer, creator, or administrator of a productive enterprise.

The entrepreneur plays another important role in our economic system. Because the future is not known, the developer or creator of a new enterprise must accept the risk of losing it. Entrepreneurs will accept the risk of loss only if they believe there is also the strong possibility of gain. It takes a certain kind of person to be a risk-taker, and the entrepreneur is that type of person.

The first three resources are certainly necessary. But the fourth may be even more essential for producing the largest possible quantity and quality of desired goods and services.

THE THREE QUESTIONS: WHAT? HOW? FOR WHOM?

A nation's stock of resources is limited. Those resources can be combined in a variety of ways to produce goods and services. To decide how to allocate its scarce resources, a society must answer three basic questions:

The society must first decide **What?** to produce. "How much military equipment?" and "How many consumer goods?" might be the major choice facing a nation preparing for war. "How many new houses?" and "How many machines?" may be the critical choice for a newly industrializing nation. "How many agricultural products?" and "How many manufactured goods?" the most important choice for a nation entering international trade.

Whatever goods and services the society chooses to produce, it must at the same time sacrifice other goods and services it might have chosen.

Second, a society must decide **How?** resources should be combined to produce the desired goods and services. If the society is rich in land, it may decide to emphasize the use of land in production. This was true in our own country in the nineteenth century and is true in Argentina and Australia today. If workers are plentiful, the society may emphasize the use of labor, as in populous China. If the society is rich in capital resources, it may emphasize the use of machinery, as in today's Japan. A country without fertile land and with few human resources may choose to develop and encourage entrepreneurial ability through training in business management.

Whatever resources the society decides to use in production, it must at the same time sacrifice other goods and services those resources might have produced.

Finally, any society must decide **For Whom?** output is to be produced. Who is to be rewarded at the time goods and services are distributed? Brain surgeons or ballet dancers? Poets or industrial designers? Teachers or soldiers? Often, a person's reward reflects the value the society places on the good or service that person produces. A generous reward will encourage greater production of a good or service the society wants most.

Needless to say, whatever persons the society decides to reward generously, it must at the same time reward others less well.

ORGANIZING PRODUCTION

An economic system is the way a nation organizes itself to answer the three basic questions. Nations differ according to the kinds of

Contemporary Thinking About Economic Issues

THE COLLAPSE OF AN ECONOMIC SYSTEM

After the Communist Revolution of 1917, the Union of Soviet Socialist Republics (USSR) set up a command economic system to allocate resources and plan production. Central planning worked well in the Soviet Union for establishing heavy industry, recovering from two world wars, and maintaining strong military power. However, central planning worked badly for increasing productivity in agriculture and light industry and for encouraging technological innovation.

Under the Soviet command system, Soviet farmers were forced to deliver agricultural products to the central government for distribution at low prices to urban factory workers. Low food prices did not provide farmers the incentive to increase output. By the mid 1980s food supplies had shrunk to the point that the Soviet people lost confidence in their government and their system of central planning.

Even worse than shortages of food was the problem of a technologically backward manufacturing sector. In spite of the dictates of the Soviet planning committee, production of manufactured goods fell farther and farther behind production in other nations. In 1985 Soviet Communist Party leader Mikhail Gorbachev proposed to restructure the nation's economy to include some of the incentives that encourage production in free market economies. The Russian word for restructuring is "perestroika."

Perestroika has proved to be very difficult, and shortages have grown even worse. In 1991, Gorbachev was forced to step down from his leadership role, and Boris Yeltsin was elected the first President of the Russian Republic. Many of the other Soviet republics withdrew from the Union to form separate nations, each with the freedom to choose its own economic system.

Today all the former Soviet republics

resources they own and according to the value systems of their people. Value systems have evolved over years and years of history and influence a nation's choice of goods and services. Differences in resources and value systems lead to differences in economic systems. In fact, there are three basic kinds of economic systems, with many variations and combinations of the three in different times and places. As you read the descriptions that follow, think about the nations with which you are familiar and compare their systems for organizing production. What resource supplies and what value systems have influenced their choice of economic system?

The Traditional Economic System

Very primitive societies generally answer the three basic questions through traditional means—repeating within the family, generation after generation, old, familiar patterns of production. Farming families continue to till the land. Hunters, carpenters, and tailors pass face similar economic problems. One problem is that to increase incentives in farming will require higher food prices. Higher food prices will encourage food production and increase farm incomes, making it possible for prosperous farmers to buy the products of manufacturing firms. Increased production and sales in the manufacturing sector will ultimately increase the wages of urban workers and provide higher standards of living for all the people.

Creation of a market system doesn't happen overnight, however. Before market incentives can bring prosperity to farms and factories, many urban workers will suffer rising food prices and falling living standards. Their complaints will reflect increasing opposition to perestroika and will bring increasing political problems to the leaders of the former Soviet Republics.

Many observers of the former Soviet Union hope the people of the newly independent republics will have the patience to work toward a prosperous market economy in the future rather than revert to the backwardness of central planning.

Can you suggest measures that might help the leadership of the new republics accomplish the change to a market economy while reducing the current sacrifices of their people? What additional problems must the people overcome if they are to create an efficient market economy?

Marshall I. Goldman, *The USSR in Crisis: The Failure of an Economic System,* Norton, New York, 1983.

Marshall I. Goldman, *Gorbachev's Challenge: Economic Reform in the Age of High Technology,* Norton, New York, 1987.

on their skills within their families, who continue to produce the same goods and services in the same old ways.

A traditional economic system may be the only option for a community where resources are few and the margin between life and death is narrow. The community may barely be able to feed itself, with little surplus left over for trying new ways. As a result, there may be little room for experimenting and few opportunities for economic growth or development.

Traditional economies continue to exist today in remote parts of Africa, Asia, and Latin America. The Amish community in the northeastern United States is an example of a people who still organize production in the same ways as their ancestors did many years ago.

The Command Economic System

In some societies new resources may be discovered and better production techniques de-

Thinking Seriously About Economic Issues

ORGANIZATIONS AND ECONOMIC EFFICIENCY

The efficiency of an economic system may depend on the strength and character of its political and social organizations. Mancur Olson is an economist who studies such organizations and the ways they contribute to healthy economic growth or economic weakness and decline.

According to Olson, organizations are difficult to construct. Because the benefits enjoyed by members can often be enjoyed by nonmembers as well, there may be no incentive to join. For this reason, forming organizations requires a long period of social stability, during which incentives build up to join and strengthen existing organizations. When a society has been stable for a long time, there is greater likelihood that there will be many organizations representing many special interest groups within the society.

Some examples of organized interest groups in the United States are associations of businesses, workers, and professions: trade associations like the American Dairy Association, labor unions like the International Ladies Garment Workers Union, and legal and medical organizations like the American Bar Association and the American Medical Association. The important point about such organizations has to do with their incentives with respect to production and distribution in the economy as a whole. Because each organization represents a relatively small fraction of the total economy, the gain its members would enjoy from increasing the nation's economic efficiency is relatively small. Similarly, the loss members would suffer from decreasing efficiency is relatively small. For both these reasons, organizations have little incentive to increase the nation's economic efficiency and—even worse—few disincentives to decrease inefficiency.

Without incentives to increase efficiency, individual interest groups concentrate

veloped, so that it becomes possible to produce more goods and services than the minimum necessary for life. When a nation can produce a surplus, it must decide what additional goods and services to produce. Such a nation might answer the three questions through a system of command.

In a command economic system a central authority decides what is to be produced, makes plans accordingly, and sees that the plans are carried out. Often the plan focuses on some national goal, such as military power or industrial development. A central authority can ensure that the necessary sacrifices are made for producing military equipment or building new capital resources. The Soviet Union used a command economic system to build its industrial capacity after the Communist revolution. Even the United States uses some forms of command—when it collects taxes and uses tax revenues to finance public projects.

You can imagine how difficult a command economic system would be in a modern, complex economy. It would be particularly difficult without computers for planning produc-

instead on gaining a larger share of existing production for themselves. The result is increasing conflicts over shares of output, conflicts that consume energy better used to increase efficiency. If the nation is to grow and prosper, says Mancur Olson, it must reduce the power of organized interest groups and develop policies to enhance economic efficiency.

There are a number of ways to accomplish this result, some more pleasant than others. A particularly unpleasant way—but one that was ultimately successful in Germany and Japan—is war. War destroys many existing organizations and requires a united effort to rebuild productive capacity in the most efficient way possible. A more pleasant way to reduce the power of organizations is through free trade. Free trade opens the nation to competition from other nations and forces organized groups to compete with highly motivated groups from abroad. Another way is to strengthen the nation's political parties. Large political parties can absorb and combine small interest groups and improve their incentive systems. Because each of the two major political parties in the United States represents almost half the nation, increases in efficiency that are achieved by one party or the other do indeed benefit their members. Thus, there is greater incentive to cooperate toward improving efficiency and increasing total production.

Understanding economics is important. Along with your study of economics, however, you should understand the organizations that operate within our economic system and affect its performance. Consider also your own participation in organizations and how these organizations affect the nation's economic efficiency.

Mancur Olson, *The Rise and Decline of Nations*, Yale University Press, New Haven, Conn., 1982.

tion and without rapid communication and transportation facilities for carrying out the production plan.

The Free Market Economic System

Adam Smith described a third kind of system for organizing scarce resources: the market system, which was developing in the newly industrializing nations of Western Europe at the time Smith was writing *The Wealth of Nations*. The market system differs from either the traditional or command system in that, under the market system, decisions about production are made freely, without government control, by the people of the society themselves.

A free market system represents a kind of economic democracy. Just as political democracy allows people to vote for the candidates they prefer, the market system allows people to vote—with their dollars—for the goods and services they want most. Business firms try to satisfy people's wants and receive profits as their reward. Profits give successful firms the funds they need to invest in new capital resources—machinery, factories, and transportation facilities—and for research to develop new products and new kinds of production. According to Adam Smith, when a society organizes production through a free market system, the people live better and enjoy higher standards of material wealth than are possible in traditional or command societies.

ECONOMIC EFFICIENCY

We began this text with a description of the challenges our nation has faced. The fundamental challenge of our past, present, and future is this—to use our scarce resources to produce the goods and services we want most.

The United States has chosen the market system as the basis for making economic decisions (although we have elements of tradition and command, as well). We believe the market system is the most efficient system for answering the questions **What? How?** and **For whom?**

Efficiency is an important concept in economics. It means we are producing the maximum quantity of output from our scarce resource inputs: maximum output/input. An economic system is efficient if it produces the maximum possible quantities of the goods and services its people want with its limited quantities of land, labor, capital, and entrepreneurial resources.

In fact, we can describe two kinds of efficiency: **technical efficiency** and **allocative efficiency.** Technical efficiency refers to the total quantities of goods and services that are produced with available resources and technology. Our free market system provides the incentives that encourage farms and factories to produce the largest possible quantity of goods and services with the smallest possible quantity of scarce land, labor, capital, and entrepreneurial resources. Technical efficiency helps us enjoy rising material standards of living and improved quality of life.

Allocative efficiency refers to production of the particular goods and services the people want. Our free society guarantees each of us the right to choose the way we want to live, including how we work and how we spend what we earn. The right to choose enables us to allocate our nation's resources toward producing the particular goods and services we want.

We can sum up our study of economics this way: Because resources are scarce, production is limited. Deciding to use resources in one way requires the sacrifice of other things we might have had. We want our economic system to be efficient: to produce the most of what we want with the least sacrifice of what we might have had. Understanding economics helps us make these choices efficiently.

OPPORTUNITY COSTS

Economics is about choosing. The sad fact is that every time we make a choice we pay a cost. The cost to use a resource to produce one good or service is the next most desired good or service we might have produced instead. Economists refer to the alternative uses of a resource as **opportunity costs.**

We all experience opportunity costs every day. For example, the cost of playing a tennis match is the golf game we might have played instead (or the nap in the shade). The cost of baking a loaf of bread (in addition to the flour, eggs, and other ingredients) is the picture we might have painted. The cost of intensive study for one subject is the "A" we might have earned in another.

We are most conscious of opportunity costs when we choose how to spend our money. With limited financial resources, deciding to spend a dollar for one good requires the sacrifice of another good we might have bought instead. The purchase of a new sweater may require the sacrifice of a pair of concert tickets.

Producers suffer opportunity costs, too, when they employ limited productive resources. When a business firm employs an hour of labor, a piece of machinery, or an acre of land, its managers must consider the alternative uses of these resources. Labor and materials can be used to build schools or bridges, ice rinks or pizza parlors, airplanes or trains. The cost of each is the other good or service not produced. An acre of land used for tennis courts is not available for use as a parking lot.

If a society allocates its resources to produce the most wanted goods and services with the least sacrifice of other goods and services, we say the society is efficient. By choosing efficiently, we reduce opportunity costs and enjoy the largest possible quantities of wanted goods and services.

Self-Check

1. The economic problem is concerned primarily with:
a. Relieving poverty.
b. Redistributing wealth.
c. Motivating people to work more productively.
d. Choosing how to use society's scarce resources.
e. Gathering data for economic analysis.

2. Whenever society chooses to produce one type of output:
a. It must sacrifice some other type of output.
b. Resources will be fully employed.
c. It avoids opportunity costs.
d. It may also increase all other types of output.
e. It avoids the problem of decision making.

3. The philosophy of laissez-faire:
a. Favors the free pursuit of self-interest.
b. Recommends government involvement in the economy.
c. Was born in the Great Depression of the 1930s.
d. Was developed by John Maynard Keynes.
e. All of the above.

4. Which of the following is *not* a true description of a capital resource?
a. Construction of capital allows us to produce more goods in the future.
b. Capital is money.
c. Capital allows roundabout production.
d. Production of autos requires more capital than production of hamburgers.
e. Nations differ in the quantities of capital owned.

5. Which of the following correctly describes a free market economy?
a. It is not necessary to make sacrifices in a free market economy.
b. Under the market system a central authority plans economic growth.
c. A market economy provides little opportunity for technological advance and growth.
d. A market economy responds to dollar "votes" of consumers.
e. The market system is based on preserving past methods of production.

6. Which of the following statements is false?
a. Even simple day-to-day decisions involve opportunity costs.
b. If there were no scarcity, there would be no opportunity costs.
c. Opportunity costs are foregone alternatives.
d. Opportunity costs are always measured in dollars.
e. Consumers often compare opportunities at the margin.

PRACTICE IN CONSTRUCTING AND INTERPRETING GRAPHS

Economists use graphs to illustrate important relationships. Graphs are like symbols in that they express ideas quickly with few words of explanation. There are many symbols we recognize instantly without explanation. You will have no problem recognizing these symbols.

With a little practice you will have no problem understanding graphs. You will find graphs useful in your study of economics and in your work after you leave school. In this economics course you will use graphs to measure such things as production, costs, prices, incomes, and employment.

Figure 1.1 is a graph of the quantity of production at Country Kitchen Bakery when various quantities of labor resources are employed. The graph is drawn on two axes or perpendicular lines. The horizontal axis shows hours of labor employed per day; the vertical axis shows daily production of bread. If 10 hours of labor are employed, 25 loaves can be produced. Follow the dotted line from 10

Figure 1.1 Daily Bread Production at Country Kitchen Bakery

The graph illustrates a direct relationship between the two values. As hours of labor increase, bread production also increases.

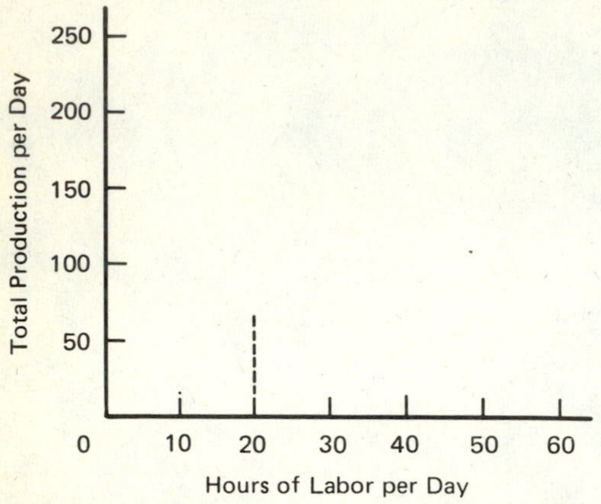

hours up to a point representing 25 loaves. If 20 hours are employed (two workers for 10 hours each), 75 loaves can be produced. Again follow the dotted line from 20 hours to the point representing 75 loaves.

Points representing every combination of labor hours and bread production were plotted on the graph. Then a line was drawn connecting all the points. Because some quantity of bread can be produced if, say, 5, 23.75, or 51.33 hours of labor are employed, the line was drawn as a continuous curve. The zero point (0) on the graph is called the origin. The line representing bread production begins at the origin because when zero hours of labor are employed, zero bread can be produced.

Over the range of employment shown in Figure 1.1, there is a **direct,** or positive, **relationship** between hours of labor and bread production: that means that as labor increases, bread production also increases. Likewise, as labor decreases, bread production decreases. On other graphs the **relationship** between the two values might be **inverse,** or negative: as one value increases, the other decreases.

The data in the table accompanying Figure 1.2 describe grain production from one acre of land when various quantities of fertilizer are applied. Use the information in the table to construct a graph on Figure 1.2. Label the horizontal axis "pounds of fertilizer applied during the growing season." Label the vertical axis "bushels of grain harvested per growing season." On the horizontal axis mark off spaces representing 10, 20, 30, 40, and 50 pounds of fertilizer. On the vertical axis mark off spaces representing 50, 100, 150, 200, 250, and 300 bushels of grain. Plot points representing the combinations shown in the table.

Even if no fertilizer is used, the field produces 100 bushels of grain during the growing

Figure 1.2 Constructing a Graph

Pounds of Fertilizer	0	10	20	30	40	50
Bushels of Grain	100	150	175	200	200	175

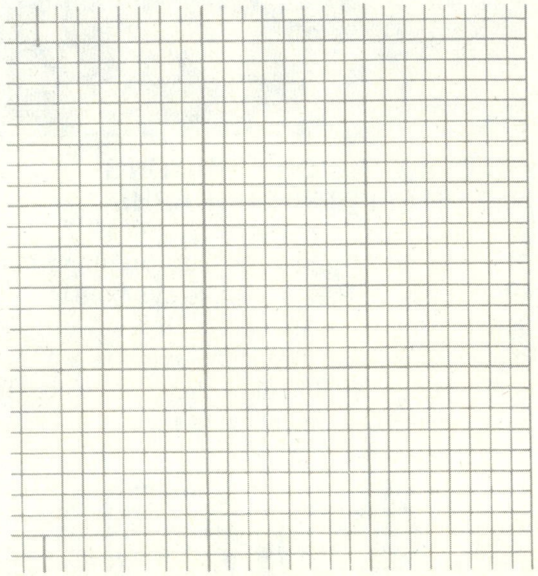

season. Therefore, your first point should lie on the vertical axis at 100 bushels. Follow a line up from 10 pounds of fertilizer to 150 bushels for your second point. Plot all the remaining points and connect them with a continuous line.

What can you learn from your graph? Describe its shape. Why do you think it has this shape? Based on your graph, what would you estimate total production to be if 25 pounds of fertilizer is applied during the growing season? Is there a direct relationship between the use of fertilizer and grain production? Over what range? A portion of your graph illustrates an inverse relationship between the use of fertilizer and total production. Can you explain this result?

CHOOSING AT THE MARGIN

We have said that economics is about choosing. Understanding economics helps us develop habits of thought that enable us to choose better—to compare the benefits of every choice against its opportunity cost and to make the most efficient choices.

In this section we will use a graph to illustrate the economic act of choosing. Choosing is necessary to every one of us in our roles as consumers and as producers. As consumers we compare the benefits of every spending decision against the cost. We compare the benefits of a new car with those of a family trip to the beach, a night on the town with a new sports jacket, or a motorcycle with a year's membership in a health club. We want to get the greatest possible benefit out of every dollar of our limited budgets.

As producers we compare the benefits of every production decision with the cost of resources for carrying it out. We know that our resources are scarce. So we produce the goods we want most with the resources we have in greatest abundance: boats from plentiful fiberglass, wheat from vast Western plains, and clothing from abundant cotton.

Most of our economic choices are made at the margin. The margin is the edge or border where we must decide whether to take one more step, whether to purchase one more unit of a particular good or whether to use one more unit of a particular resource.

We use **marginal analysis** unconsciously every day. We use marginal analysis when we allocate our time, continuing one activity until the benefits gained from spending one more minute are less than the benefits from spending that minute doing something else. Marginal analysis helps students allocate study time and workers allocate work time among a number of tasks. (Even a fun-seeker allocates pleasure time by comparing the benefits gained from spending one more minute playing with the benefits of spending that minute resting.)

We also use marginal analysis when we allocate our money. We spend for one item until the benefits gained from spending one more dollar are less than the benefits from spending that dollar on something else. A music fan buys compact discs only up to the point where he or she believes a paperback novel would be more enjoyable. Have you recently used marginal analysis to make a spending decision?

Business firms use marginal analysis to decide the level of production. An auto manufacturer produces autos until production of one more auto brings in less revenue than it costs to produce. A barber keeps his shop open until one more hour brings in less revenue than the cost of staying open.

Business firms also use marginal analysis when they decide how many units of a particular resource to use in production. They hire salespeople until hiring one more salesperson adds less to sales revenue than his or her wage. They buy land for shopping centers until one more acre of space adds less to revenue than it costs.

In effect, our entire economic system makes decisions at the margin. We increase production until one more unit of output is worth less than the resources required to produce it. In this way we help ensure that our scarce resources are used to produce the things we want most.

PRACTICE USING THE MODEL OF PRODUCTION POSSIBILITIES

We can illustrate the process of choosing with the **model of production possibilities.** An economic model is a simplified view of economic reality. It includes certain fundamental features of the economic environment but omits unnecessary details. Models permit us to focus on the problem as a whole and to understand the opportunity costs associated with alternative choices.

Remember the fundamental problem of economics. Then suppose a nation owns a particular quantity of land, labor, capital, and entrepreneurial resources and that it enjoys a particular level of technical knowledge. With its resources and level of technology, the nation can produce a range of combinations of particular goods and services. It can choose to allocate all resources toward one product—food, for example, or industrial machinery or military equipment. Or it may own such a wealth of resources that it can choose to produce more frivolous products—sports cars, compact disc recorders, and whirlpool baths.

Figure 1.3 is a graph of the model of production possibilities for a nation that can produce two kinds of goods: wheat and coal. Table 1.1 shows the possible combinations of wheat and coal the nation can produce in a year, and the two axes on Figure 1.3 represent quantities of the two goods. Thus, the vertical axis represents wheat, measured in bushels on a scale from 0 to 800. The horizontal axis represents coal, measured in tons on a scale from 0 to 50.

Figure 1.3 Production Possibilities Curve

Given its limited resources and state of technology, a society can produce any combination of goods up to its production possibilities curve. Point *E* is beyond this society's present capabilities; point *F* underutilizes the society's resources.

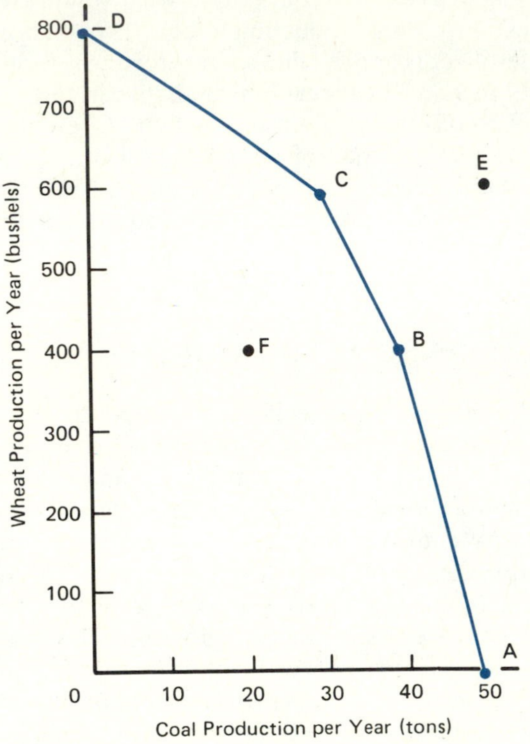

If all resources are devoted to producing coal, the maximum quantity the nation can produce per year is 50 tons. Follow the horizontal axis in Figure 1.3 to 50 tons and notice the point *A*, which represents the maximum quantity of coal this nation can produce. If 50 tons of coal are produced per year, the nation can produce no wheat. Thus, the opportunity cost of 50 tons of coal is the amount of wheat the nation might have produced instead. (Can you look at Table 1.1 and determine the pre-

Table 1.1 Production Possibilities Curve.

Wheat (bushels per year)	0	400	600	750	800
Coal (tons per year)	50	40	30	10	0

cise opportunity cost of 50 tons of coal? What is the opportunity cost of each ton?)

If the nation allocates all its resources instead to producing wheat, the maximum output is 800 bushels. Follow the vertical axis to 800 bushels and notice the point *D*, which represents the maximum production of wheat per year. If 800 bushels of wheat are produced, the nation will produce no coal. The opportunity cost of 800 bushels of wheat is 50 tons of coal. (What is the opportunity cost of each bushel?)

Now let us suppose that the nation wants to produce some combination of the two goods. (Without coal for heat, it's difficult to use wheat for making bread.) The maximum combinations of wheat and coal per year are: (*A*) zero wheat and 50 tons of coal, (*B*) 400 bushels of wheat and 40 tons of coal, (*C*) 600 bushels and 30 tons, and (*D*) 800 bushels and zero tons. Locate these points on Figure 1.3 by moving along the horizontal axis the appropriate distance and then moving up the vertical axis.

A line connecting the points of production possibilities has been called just that—the **production possibilities curve;** it is the frontier beyond which this nation cannot produce. A society can choose any combination of output that lies on its production possibilities curve. If it chooses to move along the curve to produce more of one good in any particular year, it must be willing to give up some quantity of the other good. This is its opportunity cost.

A nation cannot choose a combination of products outside its production possibilities curve. Point *E* on Figure 1.3, for example, represents quantities of coal and wheat (50 tons and 600 bushels) that are impossible to produce with the nation's limited resources and existing technology. On the other hand, point *F* is a combination of goods that underutilizes the nation's scarce resources. At point *F*, some miners and farmers are out of work, resulting in a permanent loss of the coal and wheat they might have produced. In the next section you will read about one time when the United States was operating inside its production possibilities curve and another when the nation attempted to operate outside the curve.

TEST YOURSELF

How much coal and how much wheat would be produced at *F*? How much more coal could be produced? How much more wheat? Explain how the production possibilities curve can be used to illustrate choosing at the margin.*

UNEMPLOYMENT AND INFLATION

When the United States entered World War II, observers in this country and abroad were amazed at how fast we were able to begin producing tanks, planes, guns, and ammunition. The reason we were able to move so quickly into war production was because many of our resources had been out of work. The period before the war was the period of the Great Depression. In the depths of the Depression, 12 million workers or one-quarter of the labor force were unemployed, and many others were working at jobs beneath their full capacity. The U.S. economy had been operating at a point inside our production possibilities curve, producing smaller quantities of coal, wheat, autos, and other goods than our resources and technology were capable of pro-

* Suggested answers to these and other specific Test Yourself questions can be found following Topics for Discussion.

ducing. The wartime emergency shifted idle workers, idle machines, and empty factories into useful work without the sacrifice of other kinds of production.

Conditions were quite different in the 1960s when the United States entered the war in Vietnam. Except for a relatively small number of workers who would normally be changing jobs, all of the nation's resources were already employed. To increase production of military equipment for the war would require a sacrifice of the civilian goods and services that were currently being produced. The Vietnam War was unpopular, however, and President Lyndon Johnson hoped that more military goods could be produced for the war without forcing civilians to pay the war's opportunity costs.

Economists reminded the President of the model of production possibilities. They pointed out that when all of a nation's resources are already employed, increasing production of one product requires the sacrifice of another. The U.S. economy could move along its production possibilities curve but not beyond it.

If the United States were a command economic system, it would be a simple matter to cut back civilian production by changing the central plan. Then the required resources could be moved out of civilian production and into military production. Even our free market system has ways to force consumers to reduce their purchases of civilian goods so that resources can be moved out of civilian goods production and into purposes decided by government. In fact, a tax increase was proposed to do just that.

It was several years before the tax increase was finally passed, however. In the meantime, consumers continued to spend for civilian goods and services in the same amounts as before the war, while government increased its purchases of military goods. With the increase in total spending, the nation was spending beyond its production possibilities, at point *E* outside the production possibilities curve.

When total spending is greater than the maximum quantity of goods and services being produced, the ultimate result is rising prices. With consumers and government bidding against each other for the limited quantities of goods, the result is to push prices up. A general increase in prices is called **price inflation**.

Price inflation prevented consumers from buying all the civilian goods and services they wanted, so the U.S. economy did remain on its production possibilities curve after all. In fact, price inflation acted as a kind of tax. Because each dollar of consumer spending bought fewer goods and services, production of civilian goods fell, and scarce resources did move into military production for use in fighting the war.

RESOURCE SPECIALIZATION

Have you noticed that the production possibilities curve is bowed out in the middle? The largest combinations of total output are near the center, where some resources are used to produce wheat and some to produce coal. Why is this? The reason is the character of particular resources. Not all resources are equally suited to the production of coal or wheat. When workers can choose among two or more types of jobs, they will generally choose to work where they are more productive, and they will become more skillful as they work. Furthermore, if too much labor is employed in one type of production, each worker will have less of other needed resources—land and capital equipment—with which to work. Total production will not grow very much as more workers are added. To use all resources in one type of production or the other pulls the production possibilities curve down at the ends and causes a bulge in the middle.

It is not practical to draw a model of production possibilities with more than two axes. But we might imagine a multidimensional figure in which the possible combinations of all goods and services are shown. Then the nation must choose a particular combination for which its resources will be used. Producing a combination on the production possibilities curve achieves technical efficiency. Producing the precise combination that the people want achieves allocative efficiency.

CHANGES IN PRODUCTION POSSIBILITIES

In Figure 1.3 we used the model of production possibilities to illustrate a nation's maximum possible production of goods and services. The model is useful also for illustrating the effects of changes in economic conditions over time.

First, suppose the nation discovers new resources: new mineral deposits or, perhaps, untapped labor skills. New supplies of productive resources increase production possibilities and cause the production possibilities curve to shift to the right. Advances in technology have the same effect, changing the shape of the production possibilities curve to show increased capacity for producing the good favored by the new technology. The production possibilities curve in Figure 1.4a shows a nation with relatively greater technical progress in the production of wheat. Figure 1.4b shows relatively greater technical capacity for producing coal.

Now consider the effect of a decrease in available resources, perhaps combined with a failure to develop new technologies. The result may be lower production possibilities and a backward shift of the production possibilities curve. Figure 1.4c shows a backward shift of production possibilities, with reduced capacity for producing both goods.

Changes in the shape of the production possibilities curve occur when there are changes in the costs of production of the two goods, measured in terms of opportunity costs. Look again at Figure 1.4a. Technologi-

Figure 1.4 Changes in Production Possibilities

Increased capacity for producing wheat (*a*), or coal (*b*), is shown by a shift of the production possibilities curve to the right. Reduced capacity for producing both goods (*c*) is shown by a shift of the curve to the left.

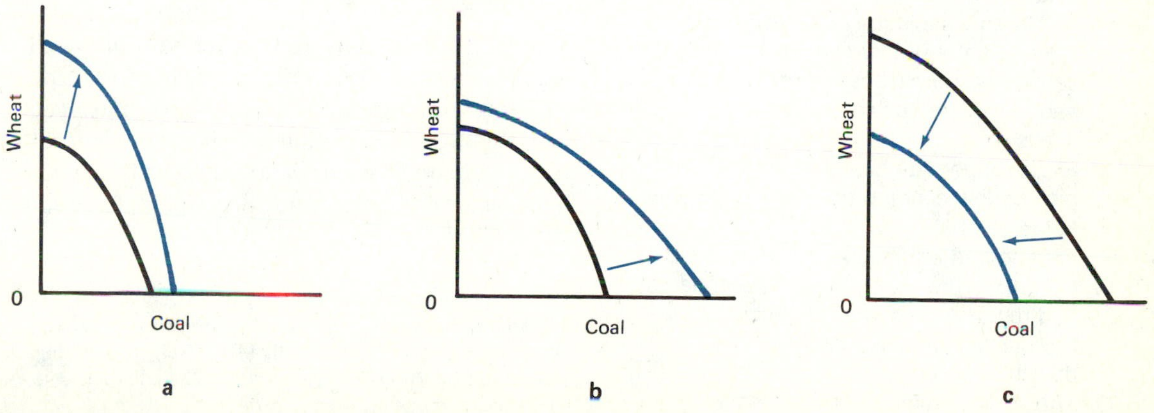

cal progress favoring wheat production has reduced its cost, such that fewer units of coal must be sacrificed for each additional unit of wheat. Indeed, our nation's success as an industrial power is largely a result of advances in the technology of agriculture. As fewer workers and machines have been needed to produce food, more resources have been shifted into construction of factories and capital equipment for producing other kinds of consumer goods.

America has prospered also because of our large, integrated national market. Our rich and varied resources allow regions to specialize in particular types of production. There are no barriers to free trade among regions: no customs duties, no currency exchanges, no restrictions that might slow the free movement of goods in trade. When regions specialize and sell to a wider consumer market, it is practical to develop advanced technology for increasing production. The result for our nation has been a continued shift to the right of production possibilities, with rising standards of living for our people.

TEST YOURSELF

How will each of the following affect the position and shape of a nation's production possibilities curve:

1. A war that devastates much of the farmland and kills many young workers?
2. A "Green Revolution" in agriculture that increases the use of chemical fertilizers, pesticides, herbicides and genetic engineering for producing disease-resistant seeds?
3. State-supported vocational schools to provide low-cost job training to disadvantaged youths?
4. Widespread emphasis on "doing one's own thing," rejecting society's standards, and refusing to conform to accepted behavior? (A number of answers are possible here.)
5. The "Puritan ethic" with its disapproval of conspicuous wealth and its emphasis on hard work and thrift?
6. The formation of an "Economic Community" of nations, within which barriers to free trade are gradually removed?
7. Environmental legislation forbidding certain uses of a region's air, water, and landscape?
8. A trade embargo that reduces imports of a commodity necessary in certain other kinds of production?

USING ECONOMICS TO MAKE CHOICES

You make choices every day that involve economics. Should you buy a second pair of shoes or a pair of slacks or, perhaps, save your money? Should you buy a car or rely on public transportation? Should you take a new job that offers a higher salary or stay at your old job within walking distance of your home? Should you do your own repairs around the house or hire a professional?

These simple examples illustrate a number of economic concepts you have already learned: scarcity, opportunity cost, production possibilities, marginal analysis. Making personal economic choices is not always easy, but a knowledge of economics can help you make choices efficiently.

How can you learn to think "economically"? You may learn to use economic reasoning automatically only after you are well acquainted with economics. (It is hard to think in a foreign language until you have mastered the language.) Following the six steps to problem solving below can help you learn to apply economic concepts and principles to your daily life:*

* For more on problem-solving methods, see Fels and Uhler, *Casebook of Economic Problems and Policies* (West Publishing Co., St. Paul, MN, 1974), and Elbing, *Behavioral Decision in Organizations,* 2nd edition (Scott, Foresman and Co., Chicago, 1978).

1. Define the problem.
2. State your goals or objectives.
3. Identify the economic concepts involved in the problem.
4. List the alternative choices available to you.
5. Evaluate each alternative.
6. Decide which alternative is best in light of your evaluation and goals.

In this section we will use the six problem-solving steps to solve some common economic problems.

A Problem in Family Budgeting

The Wilcoxes live in a one-bedroom apartment for which they pay $335 a month, including utilities. Both the Wilcoxes work, and together they earn a yearly income of $15,000 after taxes. Lately they have been complaining of not knowing where their income is going. For the past year, it seems, they have been unable to save any of their income, even though they believe that saving is necessary for emergencies or for future needs.

The Wilcoxes know that certain regular expenditures cannot be cut back to allow for saving. Their regular expenditures include housing costs (rent and utilities), food and other household needs, and transportation to and from work (they do not own a car and must use public transportation). According to their calculations, the minimum they must spend on these necessities is as follows: $4,000 a year for housing, $2,000 a year for food, and $1,000 a year for transportation.

Other purchases the Wilcoxes want to make include additional units of housing (in the form of new home furnishings, electrical appliances, etc.), food (an occasional dinner out), and transportation (a day at the seashore). They also want to use some of their income for recreation, health care (including health insurance), and clothing. However, the regular expenditures for housing, food, and transportation must come first—that is, the Wilcoxes must allocate a total of $7,000 a year to cover regular expenses before deciding on other uses of their income.

The Wilcoxes need a plan for using their income more efficiently: to achieve the maximum possible benefits from their limited income. Let us see how the six problem-solving steps can help.

1. *Define the problem.* The problem, as the Wilcoxes put it, is that they do not know "where the income is going." There may be unnecessary or improper expenditures, and there is never enough income left to save.
2. *State the goals or objectives.* The Wilcoxes' goal is similar to that of our economic system as a whole: to use their limited resources efficiently to achieve the largest possible quantities of the things they want.
3. *Identify the economic concepts involved in the problem.* The concepts include: living with scarcity (the Wilcoxes must decide how to allocate their limited income), opportunity cost (money spent on one good is not available for spending on another and money spent is not available for saving), and marginal analysis (the family must decide how to make use of each additional dollar of income).
4. *List the alternative choices.* Once the Wilcoxes have allocated a total of $7,000 for regular expenditures, there are a number of ways they might use the remaining $8,000: purchase additional units of housing, food, or transportation; purchase other things such as health, recreation, and clothing; save the money; or a combination of these.
5. *Evaluate each alternative.* To simplify the

decision, the Wilcoxes break down their income into units of $1,000. They now have 15 units of income each year to allocate among the choices available to them.

In order to evaluate their choices, the Wilcoxes must have some way of measuring the benefits from each. After some thought, they come up with a measure they decide to call utility points, or utils. They assign a value of 100 utils to each unit of spending on their regular purchases of housing, food, and transportation. Then they assign fewer than 100 utils to less essential purchases, depending on the urgency of their need for each. Table 1.2 shows the benefits in utils the Wilcoxes expect to enjoy from each single purchase. The first four units of housing provide benefits worth 100 utils each, for a total of 400 utils; the first two units of food provide a total of 200 utils; the first unit of transportation provides 100 utils. Other purchases yield the benefits shown in the table.

The Wilcoxes' regular purchases of housing, food, and transportation yield total benefits of 700 utils. How should they use their next $1000 of income? An additional $1000 spent for housing or food is not an efficient choice, because the next purchase of housing yields only 85 utils and the next purchase of food yields only 70 utils. However, a unit of health care yields 95 utils, the largest amount available among the remaining choices. Thus, the Wilcoxes obtain the maximum total benefits by using their next $1000 of income to purchase one unit of health care.

The Wilcoxes should save the next unit of income, since the first unit of saving yields benefits worth 90 utils. (The high value reflects the importance the Wilcoxes have attached to saving.) The next choice could be a first unit of clothing or a fifth unit of housing, both of which yield 85 utils. The following choice is the 85-util item they did not choose.

6. Decide which alternative is best in light of the evaluation and goals. The Wilcoxes repeat step 5 until they have allocated all 15 units of income. For each successive unit, they consider all the alternatives and choose the one alternative that yields the greatest benefits. Their final budget is shown in Table 1.3. Total benefits from the final decision are 1,370 utility points, the maximum total benefits possible with their income of $15,000.

Most families do not (consciously!) go through such a detailed process when planning a budget. The usual practice is quite similar in principle, however, to the Wilcoxes' plan. A family planning a budget considers alternative uses of family income and allocates each dollar according to the benefits they expect to receive from its use. They do not choose, for

Table 1.2 Utility Points from Spending Each $2000 of Money Income (measured in utils).

	Housing	*Food*	*Transportation*	*Recreation*	*Health Care*	*Clothing*	*Saving*
1st unit	100	100	100	80	95	85	90
2nd unit	100	100	80	75	60	70	80
3rd unit	100	70	40	60	25	55	70
4th unit	100	50	0	60	0	30	40
5th unit	85	25		45		0	0
6th unit	70	0		35			
7th unit	40			20			
8th unit	20			0			
9th unit	0						

Table 1.3 Wilcox Family Budget.

Good or Service	*No. of Units Purchased*	*Income Spent for Each Good or Service*	*Utility Points from Each Purchase*
Housing	5	$ 5,000	485
Food	2	2,000	200
Transportation	2	2,000	180
Recreation	2	2,000	155
Health care	1	1,000	95
Clothing	1	1,000	85
Saving	2	2,000	170
Total income		$15,000	
Total utility points			1,370

example, to use $1,000 for recreation if they need that money to pay the rent!

TEST YOURSELF

Explain how the Wilcox budget demonstrates decision making at the margin. What are the opportunity costs of each alternative choice? How would the Wilcoxes use $3,000 of additional income?

Using Economics to Choose Public Projects

Governments, like families, allocate their budgets among public projects according to priorities, comparing the benefits and costs of expenditures at the margin. Unlike families, however, a government's primary concern may be to create social benefits rather than private benefits. Governments may aim to choose projects that provide the greatest benefits for the community as a whole.

Another difference is that many government projects are not divisible into small units. Government projects involve large lump sums. A road must go from somewhere to somewhere. A baseball field must be of a certain size. You can't build three-fourths of a gymnasium. For this reason, government spending decisions are not typical marginal decisions.

Moreover, the benefits of government projects are difficult to measure. The value of a public service is the amount its users would pay for it if it were provided by private business. How much would you pay for the use of public roads or public education, for community protection against smallpox, or for a swimming pool in the city park? Your willingness to pay depends on your own expected benefits, which you may not be able to measure.

Total costs are also difficult to measure. The cost of land, labor, and materials is easy to calculate. (Remember that these costs measure the opportunity cost of using these resources in certain ways.) However, there are broader social costs that government should consider as well. The disruption and dislocation of homes and businesses during construction imposes costs on the community that may be impossible to measure precisely.

Table 1.4 gives hypothetical benefit and cost data for three groups of public projects. Estimated benefits and costs are expressed in thousands of dollars. For example, a new school costs $6.5 million to build but will yield

Table 1.4 Benefit and Cost Data for Public Projects. (Figures are in thousands of dollars.)

	Benefits	*Costs*	$\frac{Benefits}{Costs}$ = *Benefit-Cost Ratio*
Education			
New school	$19,500	$6,500	________
Gymnasium	1,000	800	________
Driver-training course	750	500	________
Transportation			
Highway	$ 4,000	$2,000	________
Rapid-transit service	6,000	8,000	________
Bus service	1,750	500	________
Recreation			
Stadium	$ 1,200	$ 900	________
Golf course	1,000	2,000	________
Pool	1,200	500	________

benefits to the community estimated at $19.5 million.

TEST YOURSELF

See if you can go through the six problem-solving steps to choose the allocation of resources that yields the maximum social benefit for the dollars spent. First, calculate the expected benefits per dollar of cost for each project. (Divide benefits by costs.) Assume the government's budget for the year is limited to $10 million. What projects should be undertaken? What is the total cost of this year's public projects?

A ratio of expected benefits to dollar cost is called a **benefit/cost ratio**. A benefit/cost ratio greater than one means that benefits outweigh costs; a ratio less than one means that costs outweigh benefits. What would a ratio of exactly one mean? What projects in Table 1.4 have benefit/cost ratios less than one? What projects are economically efficient, even though they do not fit within this year's budget?

SUMMARY

1. Scholars of the past sought to understand the natural laws that govern physical and social environments. The economic theory of the market system and the political theory of democracy developed together. Both depend on the free exercise of individual choice.
2. Economics deals with the economic problem: scarce resources and unlimited wants. Land, labor, capital, and management or entrepreneurial ability are scarce resources.
3. An economic system is necessary for organizing scarce resources for producing the goods and services the community wants most. An economic system answers the questions *what* to produce, *how* to produce it, and *for whom* to produce it.
4. An economic system may be based on tradition, command, or free markets. Adam Smith's *Wealth of Nations* described the operation of a free market economic system.
5. The U.S. economy is based primarily on free markets. We believe a free market economy is most efficient, in terms of both technical and allocative efficiency.
6. However a society chooses to answer the three economic questions, it will suffer opportunity costs. Opportunity costs are the sacrifice of other choices that might have been selected. Economics helps us

compare the benefits of each choice with its costs.

7. Graphs are useful in economics. The graph of production possibilities illustrates the problem of scarce resources and the inevitability of opportunity costs.

TERMS TO REMEMBER

economic problem: the problem of scarce resources and unlimited wants

free resources: resources in such abundance that their price is zero

land: the original and nonreproducible gifts of nature

labor: the productive activity of human beings

capital: produced means of production, such as buildings, tools, and machines

management or entrepreneurial ability: the resource that combines other resources in production

what? how? for whom? the three basic questions of resource allocation

economic system: an arrangement through which a society chooses the allocation of its resources

technical efficiency: using resources to produce the maximum possible output with scarce resources and available technology

allocative efficiency: using resources to produce the goods and services people want

opportunity costs: the things we give up when we choose to use our resources in one way rather than another

direct relationship: for two values, when one increases, the other increases; when one decreases, the other decreases

inverse relationship: for two values, when one increases the other decreases

marginal analysis: a way of making decisions based on comparing the costs and benefits of one more unit of something

production possibilities model: a simplified view of reality for explaining the economic environment

production possibilities curve: a graph showing the maximum quantities of output a society can produce, given its scarce resources and available technology

price inflation: a general increase in prices; a rise in some prices that is not offset by a fall in other prices

benefit/cost ratio: a ratio of the sum of all benefits from a project relative to the sum of all costs; a ratio of at least one represents an efficient use of funds

TOPICS FOR DISCUSSION

1. The following terms were used frequently in this chapter. They are not strictly economic terms but are used in everyday conversation. Explain how they are involved in the study of economics.

   Law or principle
   Costs and benefits
   Efficiency and model

2. Explain how the three fundamental economic questions are involved in a nation's decision to reduce production of military equipment and increase financial support for education.
3. A famous soprano can earn $100 an hour recording operatic arias. However, she has a taste for home-grown tomatoes and spends many hours cultivating her garden when she could be performing. How would you determine the cost of her tomatoes?
4. Use a production possibilities curve to illustrate limited time for study. Suppose you must prepare lessons in mathematics and Spanish, and you have only 10 hours to work. If you devote the entire time to mathematics, you can work 50 problems. If you devote the entire time to Spanish, you can translate 25 pages. Other possibilities are:

Spanish (in pages)	0	8	15	20	25
Mathematics (problems)	50	45	40	25	0

Construct a production possibilities curve using these quantities. Label the horizontal axis "Spanish" and the vertical axis "mathematics" and graph the appropriate quantities. (Remember to move along the horizontal axis first, then up the vertical axis.)

Is your curve bowed out in the center? Why do you suppose it has this shape? What is the opportunity cost of the first 8 pages of translation? The first 25 problems? What is the maximum total work you could accomplish in the limited time? Based on your experience, can you make a reasonable decision how to allocate your time? If you need a good grade in Spanish to pass the course, will this influence your decision?

Suppose you purchase an electronic calculator and your production possibilities increase as shown below:

Spanish	0	8	15	20	25
Mathematics	75	70	65	40	0

Show your new production possibilities curve on the same graph. You have experienced technological progress!

5. Most married women now work outside the home. Their decision to accept a job involves marginal analysis. They must compare the benefits with the costs of their jobs. Some benefits and costs are listed below. Can you add others?

BENEFITS	*COSTS*
Salary	Income taxes
Opportunities for advancement	Transportation costs
Intellectual stimulation	Home-cleaning costs
New social contacts	Loss of social contacts
	Loss of time for cultural or physical development

What social and technological changes in recent years have changed the nature of benefits and costs? What personal changes may have changed the relationships between benefits and costs for particular women?

6. Consult current newspapers or magazines for information regarding the attempts of the former Soviet Union and Eastern European nations to change their economic systems from central planning to a market system. Report on your findings.
7. Demographers predict that the average age of the U.S. labor force will rise in the next 20 years. How will this affect our production possibilities curve?

ANSWERS TO TEST YOURSELF

(p. 19) Twenty tons and 400 bushels; any combination on the production possibilities curve represents such a choice.

(p. 22) 1. A backward shift of production possibilities.
2. Increased production possibilities for food and other agricultural products.
3. Increased production possibilities for goods and services using relatively large quantities of labor.
4. Whether production possibilities decrease or increase depends on whether rebellious attitudes result in lower or higher worker productivity.
5. Increased production possibilities.

6. Incentives to expand production to satisfy the larger market.
7. Reduced production possibilities for goods requiring relatively large quantities of restricted resources.
8. Reduced production possibilities for goods and services using the restricted resource.

(p. 25) The Wilcoxes allocate units of income in steps, always making sure that each step yields the largest possible benefits. With three additional units of income, the Wilcoxes could purchase one additional unit of housing, food, and clothing, each of which would yield 70 additional utils for the largest possible increase in benefits. The opportunity costs of this decision are lower than the added benefits.

(p. 26) Ratios are as follows: Education—3, 1.25, 1.5; transportation—2, 0.75, 3.5; recreation—1.33, 0.5, 2.4. The community should choose the school, the driver-training course, the highway, the bus service, and the pool. The gymnasium and the stadium are also worthwhile. The rapid-transit service and the golf course are definitely not recommended.

FURTHER READING

Avineri, Sclomo, "The Return to History: The Break-up of the Soviet Union," *Brookings Review,* Spring, 1992.

Bergson, Abram, "The Economics of Perestroika: An Inauspicious Beginning," *Challenge,* May/June, 1989.

Coombs, H.C., *The Return of Scarcity,* Cambridge University Press, Cambridge, 1990.

Cox, Robert W., *Production, Power and World Order,* Columbia University Press, New York, 1987.

DeIulio, John J., Jr., and Anne Morrison Piehl, "Does Prison Pay?" *Brookings Review,* Fall, 1991.

Etzioni, Amitai, "Eastern Europe: The Wealth of Lessons," *Challenge,* July/August, 1991.

Gramlich, Edward M., "Setting National Priorities: 1992," *Journal of Economic Perspectives,* Spring, 1992.

Heilbroner, Robert L., *The Worldly Philosophers,* Simon and Schuster, New York, 1967.

North, Douglass C., "Institutions," *Journal of Economic Perspectives,* Winter, 1991.

Rumer, Boris, "New Capitalists in the U.S.S.R.," *Challenge,* May/June, 1991.

Sawhill, Isabell, ed., *Challenge to Leadership,* Urban Institute Press, Washington, D.C., 1988.

Sen, Amartya, *On Ethics and Economics,* Basil Blackwell, Inc., New York, 1987.

Stigler, George J., *Memoirs of an Unregulated Economist,* Basic Books, New York, 1988.

Ward, Barbara, *5 Ideas That Changed the World,* Norton, New York, 1959.

Chapter 2

Demand and Supply: The Basics

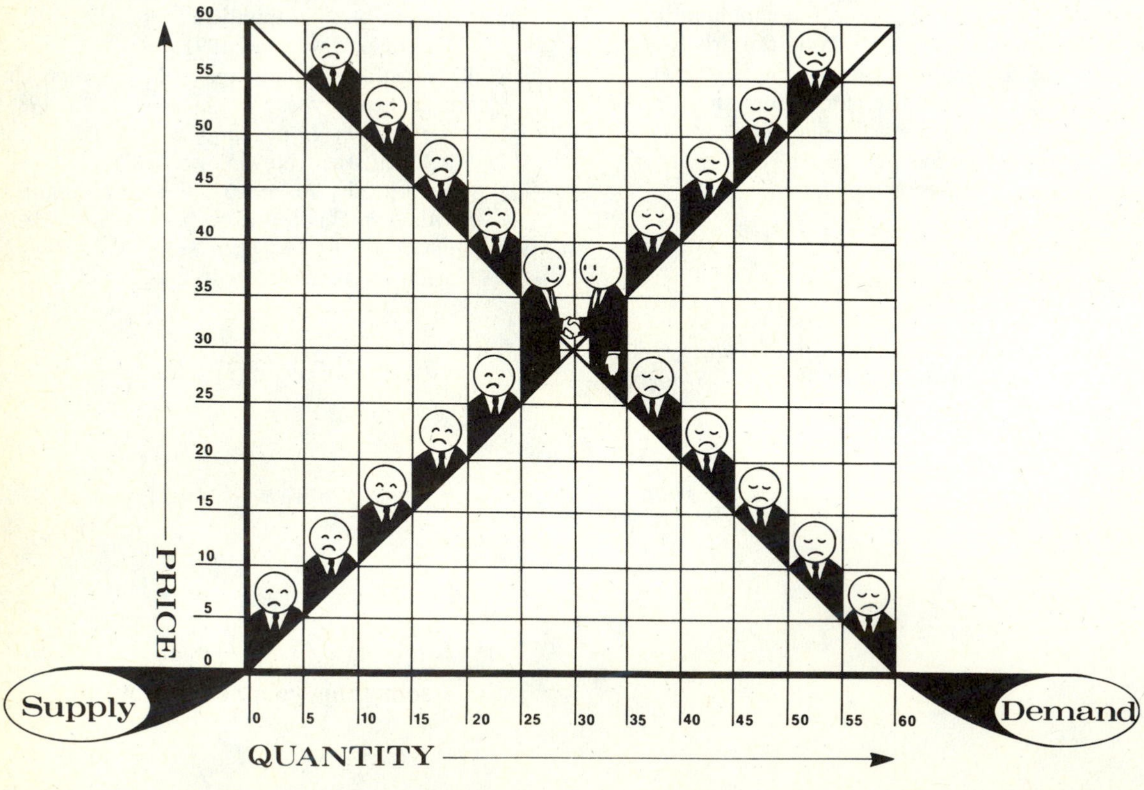

Tools for Study

LEARNING OBJECTIVES

After reading this chapter, you will be able to:

1. Describe the four characteristics of competition.
2. Explain and illustrate the laws of demand and supply.
3. List factors affecting demand and supply and explain their effects.
4. Explain market equilibrium.

CURRENT ISSUES FOR DISCUSSION

What are the advantages and disadvantages of government involvement in markets?

How do changes in market conditions affect the allocation of resources?

People "in the ordinary business of life."

That was how early economists described the subject matter of economics. Producing goods for exchange, responding to market incentives, and adjusting to changing market conditions became the subject of the social science of economics.

THE INVISIBLE HAND

The economist Adam Smith was a great admirer of the market system. In *The Wealth of Nations* Smith described how free markets answer the question **What?** and produce the things consumers want. Free markets provide the highest levels of living possible with the community's scarce resources and available technology.

All this is accomplished by what Smith called the "invisible hand." Buyers and sellers seek their own individual self-interest, without the need for any form of government control. In doing so, they are led, as if by an "invisible hand," to decisions that yield the maximum possible output of desired goods and services.

To understand this, suppose you want something that your neighbor produces. In exchange for your neighbor's product, you must produce something your neighbor wants. Both of you give up something of less value to yourself than what you receive in return; therefore, both gain. By pursuing your own self-interest, you increase total welfare in the community as a whole.

Indeed, Adam Smith had a certain reverence for the system that he believed promotes the highest possible living standards for all people.

COMPETITION IN THE MARKET

If Adam Smith's free market is to work, there must be perfect competition in the marketplace. Perfect competition rarely exists in the real world, as you will realize when you read the description that follows. Still, the model of perfect competition is useful as a standard for comparing circumstances and results in the real world.

Perfect competition has four characteristics:

1. There must first be *many buyers and sellers,* all seeking their own advantage. Furthermore, buyers and sellers must be small relative to the size of the market. Small buyers and sellers cannot affect market price by buying more or less or by offering to supply more or less for sale. Many small buyers and sellers ensure that, in competition, every buyer and seller is a "price taker."
2. There must be *perfect information* regarding selling conditions throughout the market. No single buyer should unknowingly pay a higher price or a seller charge a lower price than prevails throughout the market.
3. There must be *ease of mobility* to the most favorable market for buying or selling. Buyers must be able to seek the lowest prices, and sellers the highest prices for their goods. Owners of productive resources must be willing and able to move their resources into markets where they are most scarce and where they can be employed most efficiently.
4. Finally, in perfect competition the goods or services of one seller must be *just like those of all other sellers* in the market. If a particular supplier's product is in some way different from the others' comparable product, buyers might be willing to pay a premium price for that product. Then we would not have perfect competition. In perfect competition, autos, soft drinks, and cigarettes, for example, would have no real or apparent differences to make one seller's product more desirable than another's.

There is a story that illustrates the characteristics of perfect competition. It concerns a gentleman who wanted to play a joke on the clerk in the pet shop.

The gentleman asked to purchase a canary, and while the clerk was ringing up the sale, she chatted about what a nice pet the bird would be. The gentleman smiled and explained that he really didn't need a pet, already owning a nice cat. But occasionally the cat liked to have a little fun and exercise, and he needed the canary for . . . well, you get the idea. The clerk drew back in indignation and ordered the gentleman from the premises—without the canary.

Chuckling inwardly at the success of his joke, the gentleman headed for the door where an elderly lady had been listening to the entire conversation. She tugged at his sleeve to get his attention and whispered, "They're fifty cents cheaper down the street."

TEST YOURSELF

Explain how this story illustrates the four characteristics of competition. How do you know competition is not really perfect in the story? Can you suggest other markets where competition is more nearly perfect?

BUILDING A MARKET MODEL

Adam Smith's "invisible hand" guides buyers and sellers as they exchange goods and services in perfectly competitive markets. The study of how individual markets work is called

microeconomics. Consumers enter markets to purchase particular goods and services. Business firms respond by producing the goods and services consumers want. Microeconomics, therefore, is the study of individual markets, where many small sellers respond to many small consumers' desires for goods and services.

The quantities that all consumers are willing and able to buy at various prices constitute **market demand.** The quantities that all business firms are willing and able to sell at various prices constitute **market supply.** Combining market demand and market supply for a particular good or service yields a model of the market. As we consider demand and supply in this chapter, we assume that markets are perfectly competitive—that the four characteristics of Adam Smith's free market are true. In Chapter 5, we relax the assumption of perfect competition and describe the operation of markets when competition is not perfect.

Market Demand

Consumers buy goods and services because of their own tastes or preferences and their income or ability to pay the price. Given an individual consumer's tastes and income, there are certain quantities he or she would want to buy at various prices during any particular period of time. An individual consumer's own wants are shown in his or her **demand schedule** for a good or service. The wants of all consumers in a market combine to form the market demand schedule for that good or service.

Table 2.1 gives demand schedules for two hypothetical consumers and for all consumers taken together in the market for compact discs. Columns (2) and (3) show that at lower prices consumers Andy and Barbra would purchase larger quantities than at higher prices. Column (4) shows the market demand schedule. It is the sum of the quantities all consumers want to buy during the year at the prices shown in Column (1).

Figure 2.1a is a graph of consumer Andy's demand schedule. The line on the graph is Andy's demand curve. The demand curve shows that Andy would buy 3 compact discs at a price of $16 and 10 at a price of $6. Figure 2.1b is a graph of consumer Barbra's demand schedule. Note that Barbra's tastes or income permit her to purchase more compact discs than Andy, whatever the price.

Figure 2.1c is a graph of market demand. A market demand curve shows the quantities all consumers in the market would be willing and able to buy at various prices during the year. At a price of $16 consumers would buy a total of 13,000 compact discs per month, and at $4 consumers would buy a total of 36,000.

TEST YOURSELF

It is possible to show on Figure 2.1c the total expenditure (or total revenue) from the sale of CDs at any price. This is done by drawing a rectangle whose northeast corner touches the demand curve. Can you explain why?

Table 2.1 Hypothetical Demand Schedules for Compact Discs (per year).

(1) Price	*(2) Consumer Andy's Demand*	*(3) Consumer Barbra's Demand*	*(4) Sum of Consumer Demands = Andy + Barbra + . . . + n = Market Demand*
$16	3	6	13,000
12	5	8	21,000
8	8	10	29,000
4	12	14	36,000

Figure 2.1 Demand for Compact Discs

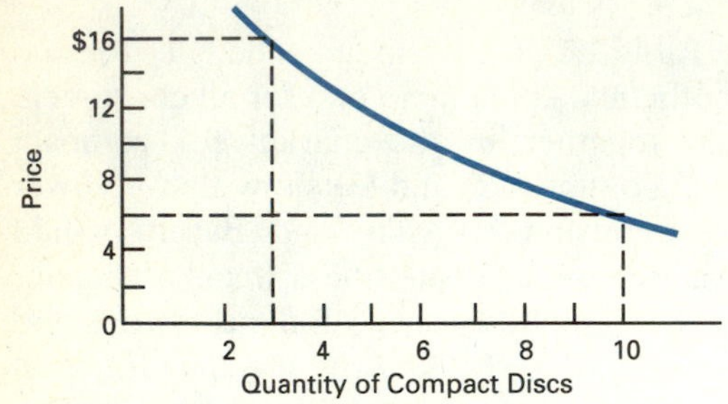

a. Consumer Andy's Demand This Year

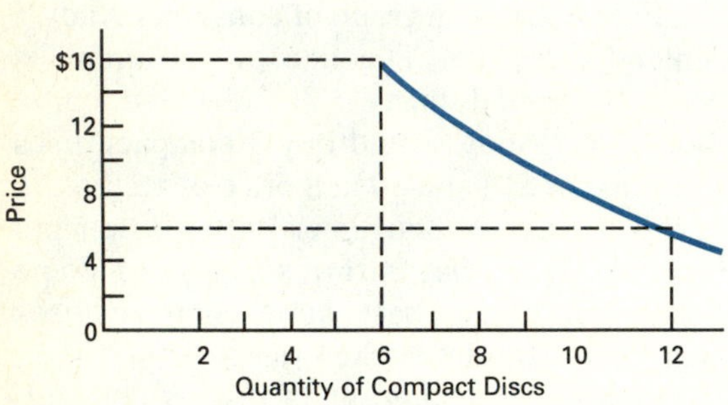

b. Consumer Barbra's Demand This Year

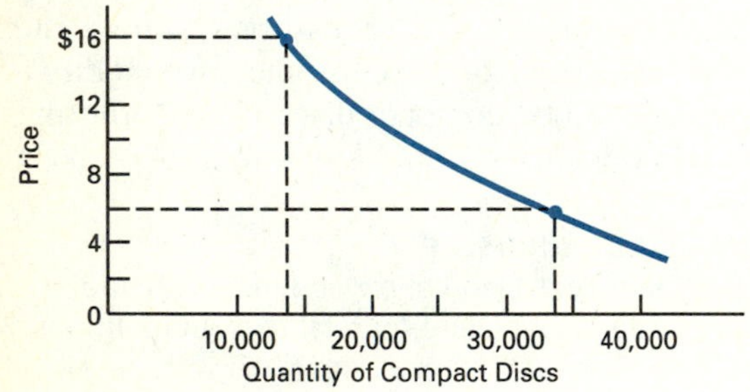

c. Market Demand This Year

The Law of Demand

Consumer demand helps answer one of society's basic economic questions: What should be produced? An individual consumer's demand curve shows the quantities of a good or service the consumer would buy at various prices during a particular period of time. A consumer is normally willing to pay a high price to acquire one unit, and perhaps even the first few units, of a good or service. Eventually, however, additional units are not as useful as the first. This means that the consumer will buy more units only if the price is lower.

A consumer's demand for compact discs (and pizzas and most other goods and services) is said to be *inversely* related to price. At high prices a consumer wants to buy fewer units than at low prices. The inverse relationship between price and quantity demanded is known as the **law of demand.**

The Difference Between "Quantity Demanded" and "Demand"

Economists mean quite different things when they say "quantity demanded" and "demand." Remember that a demand curve shows the quantities consumers are willing and able to buy at various prices. A change in the price of a good causes a **change in quantity demanded.** A change in quantity demanded is shown as a movement along the demand curve for that good. In Figure 2.1c a change in price from \$16 to \$4 causes a movement along the demand curve from point A to point B. A reduction in price typically causes an increase in quantity demanded: in this case, from 13,000 units at a price of \$16 to 36,000 units at a price of \$4.

Factors other than price affect consumers' decisions to buy. Other factors affecting consumer choice are held constant while drawing a particular demand curve. Changing the other factors that affect consumer demand would cause a change in the entire demand curve. Economists say there is a **change in demand.** The next section describes the factors that cause a change in demand, shown as a shift in the entire demand curve.

Determinants of Demand

Some factors that can cause a change in demand are changes in:

1. The incomes of buyers.
2. The number of buyers in the market.
3. Consumers' tastes and preferences.
4. The prices of related goods.
5. Consumers' expectations about the future: future prices, income, and government policies.

1. To understand how changes in other factors can change demand, first suppose Andy's income doubles. Now Andy is willing and able to buy twice as many compact discs as before at every price. Andy's old and new demand schedules are shown in Table 2.2, and both schedules are graphed on Figure 2.2. Notice that Andy's new demand curve lies to the right of the old one. There has been a change in demand. In this case, there has been an increase in demand, as shown by a shift of the demand curve to the right. At

Table 2.2 Consumer Andy's Demand Schedule for Compact Discs (per year).

Price	*Old Demand Schedule*	*New Demand Schedule*
$16	3	6
12	5	10
8	8	16
4	12	24

each and every price, Andy is willing and able to buy a larger quantity than before. (If Andy's income had been cut in half, we would expect his demand to fall. At each and every price, he would be willing and able to buy fewer CDs than before. A decrease in demand is shown as a shift of the demand curve to the left. Pencil in a decrease in demand on Figure 2.2.)

Remember that we described a change in quantity demanded as a movement along a demand curve caused by a change in the price of a good. In contrast, a change in demand is a shift of the entire demand curve caused by a change in a factor other than the price of the good. An

Figure 2.2 Change in Demand

An increase in income causes an increase in Consumer Andy's demand for compact discs. An increase in demand is shown by a shift of the entire demand curve to the right. At a price of $10 Andy is willing to purchase 12 compact discs for the year.

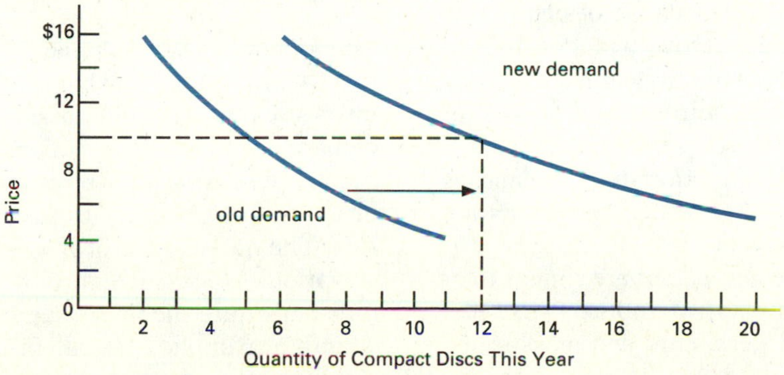

increase in demand shifts the demand curve to the right; a decrease, to the left.

TEST YOURSELF
In 1992, certain auto manufacturers offered cash rebates to car buyers in the hope of increasing car sales. Do rebates cause a change in quantity demanded or a change in demand?

2. The other factors that affect demand have similar results. If the *number of buyers* in the market should increase, for example, we can expect demand for a particular good to increase. Merchants are generally pleased when a new highway is built, bringing more tourists into their shops and shifting demand curves to the right. On the other hand, when a major local manufacturing plant closes, fewer workers and their families remain in the area, and many merchants are distressed to see their demand curves shift to the left.
3. A change in *consumer tastes* also affects demand. Suppose consumers decide that reading or going to the movies is a better way to spend their leisure time than listening to compact discs. The demand curve for CDs would shift to the left. (On the other hand, demand for books or movie tickets would shift to the right.) Can you think of other goods that have enjoyed an increase in demand (or suffered a decrease in demand) because of changes in consumer tastes? How will consumers' growing concerns about health and the environment affect their demand curves for particular goods and services?
4. The fourth factor affecting demand is *prices of related goods*. Some goods are **substitute goods** in consumers' budgets. Substitutes are goods that are similar to or can be used in place of another—like pizza and hamburgers, cars and mass transportation, rock concerts and sporting events. An increase in the price of one good normally reduces quantity demanded for that good. Consumers purchase less of the good whose price has increased and more of its substitute. (What would you expect to happen to the demand for compact discs if the price of concert tickets should fall?)

   Some goods are *complementary* in consumers' budgets. **Complementary goods** are goods that "go together"—like cars and gasoline, compact discs and CD players, beer and pretzels. If the price of CD players should rise, we might expect the demand curve for CDs to shift to the left.
5. Finally, consumers' *expectations* about future events affect demand. For example, expected price increases encourage consumers to "buy now to beat the price rise." Expected price reductions discourage current purchases. Expected changes in income or in certain government policies may also cause changes in demand for particular goods.

TEST YOURSELF
What would you expect to happen to market demand curves for air travel during the week before announced rate reductions are scheduled to take effect?

Market Supply

Many people say it is impossible to wash one hand without also washing the other. Economists say it is just as impossible to think about demand without also thinking about supply. Supply describes the willingness and ability of business firms to offer goods and services for sale. The quantities a firm would offer for sale at various prices over a particular period of time constitute the firm's **supply schedule.** The quantities supplied by all firms in a market combine to form the **market supply** schedule for that good or service.

Table 2.3 Hypothetical Supply Schedules for Compact Discs (per year).

(1) Price	*(2) Metro Music's Supply*	*(3) Tune Town's Supply*	*(4) Sum of Firm Supply = Metro + Tune + . . . + n = Market Demand*
$16	8500	11,000	55,000
12	6500	9000	35,000
8	4500	7000	15,000
4	2500	5000	10,000

Table 2.3 gives supply schedules for a year for Metro Music and Tune Town and for all firms taken together in the market for compact discs. Columns (2) and (3) show that at higher prices both firms would offer a larger **quantity supplied** than at lower prices. Column (4) shows the market supply schedule, the sum of quantities all firms would supply at the prices shown in Column (1).

Figure 2.3a is a graph of Metro Music's supply schedule. The line on the graph is Metro Music's supply curve. It shows that Metro Music would supply 5500 compact discs at a price of $10 but only 3500 if the price is only $6. Figure 2.3b is a graph of Tune Town's supply schedule. Note that Tune Town has resources or technology that enable that firm to produce more compact discs than Metro Music at every price.

Figure 2.3c is a graph of market supply. The market supply curve shows the quantities all firms in the market would offer for sale during the year at various prices. At a price of $16 all firms in this market would supply a total of 55,000 compact discs, and at a price of $6 all the firms would supply a total of 12,000.

The Law of Supply

When we drew our demand curves, we saw an *inverse* relationship between price and the quantity that would be demanded by consumers. Now we see that there is a *direct* relationship between price and the quantity that would be supplied by producers. At low prices, few units would be supplied. At high prices, larger quantities would be supplied. The direct relationship between price and quantity supplied is known as **the law of supply.**

The Difference Between "Quantity Supplied" and "Supply"

As with demand, it is important to distinguish between quantity supplied and supply. A change in the price of a good causes a change in "quantity supplied," shown on a graph as a movement along the supply curve. In Figure 2.3c a price change from $16 to $6 causes a movement down the market supply curve from point *A* to point *B*. The change in quantity supplied is from 55,000 to 12,000 units.

Factors other than price also affect firms' decisions to supply goods for sale. Other factors affecting supply are held constant while drawing a particular supply curve. Changing the other factors causes a change in supply, shown as a shift in the entire supply curve.

Other factors that can cause a change in supply are changes in:

1. The *costs* of resources used in the industry.
2. The *number of firms* in the industry.
3. The *state of technology* used by firms in the industry.

Figure 2.3 Supply of Compact Discs

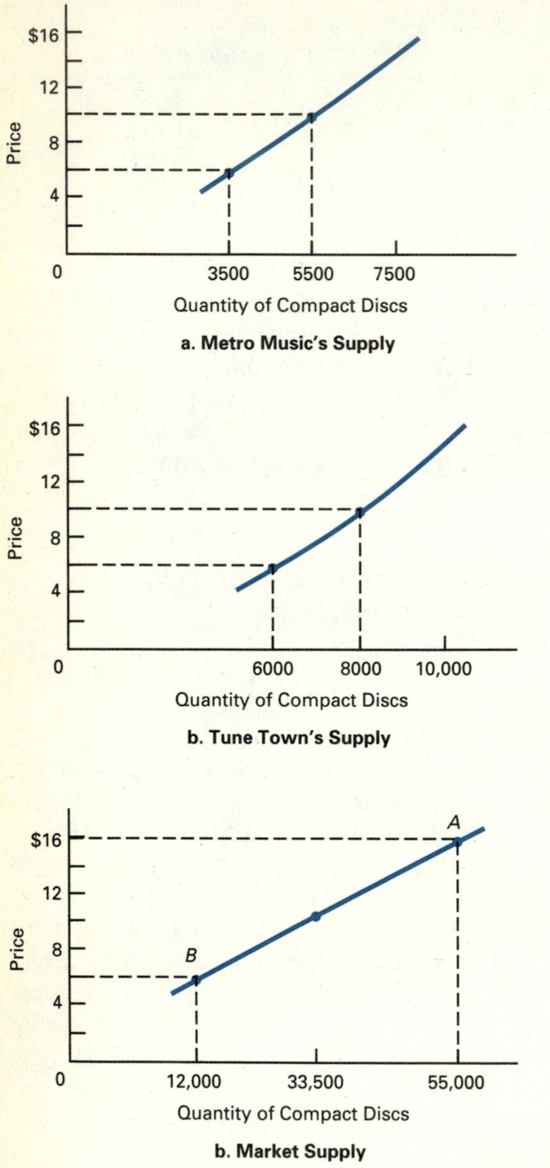

4. *Prices of related goods.*
5. *Expectations of future events,* including price changes.

How do these other factors affect supply? First, suppose the cost of resources used in production increases. As a result, the cost of producing all units increases, so that Metro Music produces fewer units at every price level. (Another way of saying this is that higher prices are required for every quantity.) The old and new supply schedules are shown in Table 2.4, and both schedules are plotted on Figure 2.4. The graph shows that there has been a change in supply. The new supply curve lies to the left of the old curve because there has been a decrease in supply. (An increase in supply would be shown by a shift to the right.) At every price Metro Music supplies fewer compact discs than before.

Now suppose the number of firms in the industry changes. If the number of producing firms increases, we might expect the supply of a good or service to increase. A recent example is the market for home computers. Growing demand for home computers has encouraged many new firms to move into the industry. As a result the market supply curve for home computers has shifted to the right. A change in technology also affects supply. The improved technology of producing videocassette recorders has reduced their costs of production and increased supply.

TEST YOURSELF

Can you give examples of industries in which a decrease in the number of firms or a change in technology has caused supply to fall? What has happened to the market supply curve?

Table 2.4 Metro Music's Supply Schedules for Compact Discs (per year)

Price	*Old Supply Schedule*	*New Supply Schedule*
$16	8500	7500
12	6500	5500
8	4500	3500
4	2500	1500

Figure 2.4 Change in Supply

An increase in the cost of electric power reduces Metro Music's supply of compact discs at every price level. A decrease in supply for the year is shown by a shift of the entire supply curve to the left.

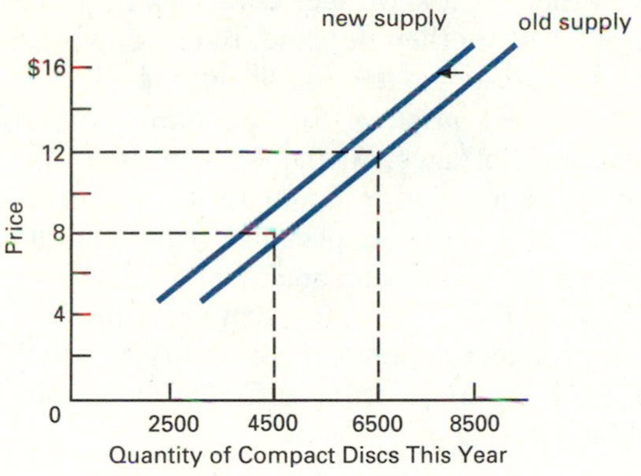

What are the effects on the supply of one good when there are changes in prices of other goods or expectations of price changes? Changes in other prices affect producers' decisions to supply similar or related goods. For example, falling wheat prices generally cause the supply of soybeans to increase, as farmers replant their fields with the higher-priced crop. On the other hand, expectations of falling wheat prices generally cause the supply of wheat to increase, as farmers try to sell their existing stocks before prices fall. Can you illustrate each of these market changes graphically?

To summarize: A change in "quantity supplied" is a movement along the supply curve, brought about by a change in price. A change in "supply" is a shift of the entire supply curve to a new position, brought on by a change in a factor other than price.

TEST YOURSELF

A rise in the price of American grain increases the cost of producing beef cattle. Do higher grain prices cause a change in the supply or a change in the quantity supplied of beef?

MARKET EQUILIBRIUM

In free, competitive markets the interaction of demand and supply determines the price of a good. In our hypothetical market for compact discs, many consumers (demanders) enter the market to purchase CDs. Many producers (suppliers) respond by offering CDs for sale. Consumers and producers must agree on a market price. When a price is established at which all the CDs offered for sale are bought, we say the **market** has reached **equilibrium.**

Through a process of bargaining, buyers and sellers agree on a price that just "clears the market." At the agreed-on price, all the quantity offered for sale will be bought.

Figure 2.5 is a model of the market for compact discs. Demand and supply are shown together just as if all consumers and all producers were meeting together to bargain for

Figure 2.5 Market Equilibrium

At a price of $10, quantity demanded equals quantity supplied for the year. There are no surpluses or shortages, and the market is in equilibrium.

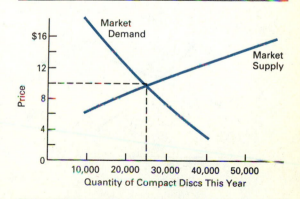

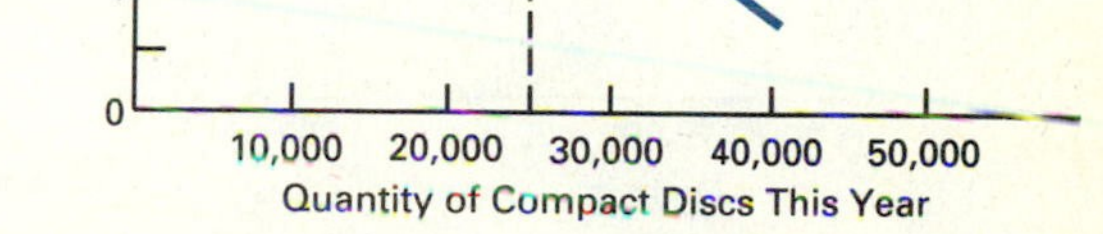

prices and quantities. The price that clears the market is $10, shown where the market demand curve intersects market supply. At a price of $10, consumers want to buy 25,000 CDs and producers want to sell 25,000 CDs. Buyers of the 25,000 CDs are satisfied with the price of $10; firms producing CDs are willing to supply 25,000 tapes at a price of $10. Thus, the equilibrium price and quantity are, respectively, $10 and 25,000 units.

Surpluses and Shortages

What would happen at a price higher or lower than the equilibrium price? As shown on Figure 2.6, at a price of $14, quantity supplied is 45,000 CDs, and quantity demanded is only 17,000. At a price higher than equilibrium there is a **surplus,** in this case a surplus of 45,000 − 17,000 = 28,000 CDs. When there is a surplus, competing suppliers will attempt to increase their sales, reducing price until price reaches the equilibrium level.

When price is below equilibrium, there is a **shortage.** Figure 2.6 shows that at a price of $8, quantity supplied is 15,000 CDs, and quantity demanded is 29,000. The shortage amounts to 29,000 − 15,000 = 14,000 CDs. When there is a shortage, consumers will attempt to satisfy their demand, bidding up price until price reaches the equilibrium level.

Only at a price of $10 are there no surpluses or shortages. At the equilibrium price, quantity demanded is equal to quantity supplied. Each consumer purchases the quantity at which his or her personal desire for CDs is high enough to justify the equilibrium price. Each producer supplies the quantity at which the equilibrium price is sufficient to justify producing it.

Figure 2.6 Surpluses and Shortages

If price is higher than the equilibrium price, quantity supplied is greater than quantity demanded, and there is a surplus for the year. If market price is lower than the equilibrium price, quantity demanded is greater than quantity supplied, and there is a shortage for the year.

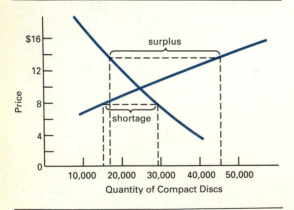

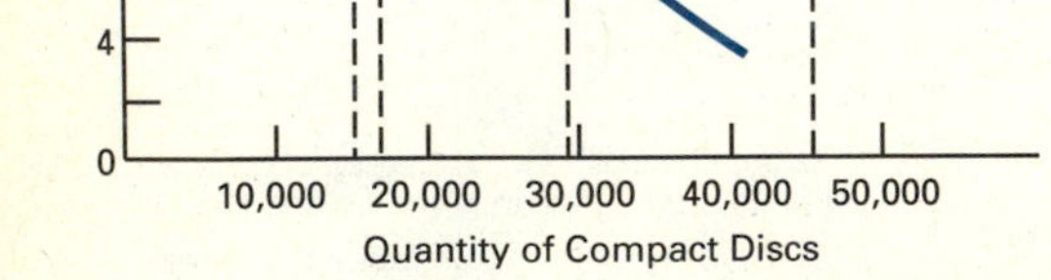

Changes in Equilibrium

When conditions change in any market, demand and supply can change, too. Changes in consumer tastes or incomes can shift demand curves to the right or left. Changes in production costs or technology can change supply. Changes in the number of firms or consumers can shift supply and demand curves. When curves shift, the market moves toward a new equilibrium price.

Changes in equilibrium prices and quantities change production plans for the nation's business firms, increasing production of some goods and services and decreasing production of others. Changing production plans require resources to move out of some kinds of production and into others. In this way, the invisible hand moves a nation's economy along its production possibilities curve, producing the things the people want at prices they are willing to pay.

Figure 2.7 shows how changes in demand or supply have affected equilibrium prices in

Figure 2.7 Changes in Equilibrium Price and Quantity

a. Wheat The demand for wheat increased as Russian and Chinese buyers entered the U.S. market for grain. Producers attempted to satisfy the increased demand, but production costs rose, and prices rose also.

b. Pocket Calculators Improved technology reduced the cost of producing pocket calculators and increased supply. Consumers moved down their demand curves and purchased more calculators at lower prices.

c. Chemical Fertilizers The increased price of imported oil raised the cost of producing chemical fertilizers and reduced supply. Farmers moved up their demand curves and purchased less at higher prices.

d. Bowling Consumers' tastes changed and they preferred roller skating to bowling. The demand for games of bowling dropped and the price fell.

e. Ski Lodges Higher incomes allowed more Americans to take vacation trips. The demand for rooms in ski lodges increased and the price increased.

f. Fish The high price of beef caused consumers to shift to diets including more fish. Increased demand for fish pushed its price up, too.

g. Haircuts Changing hair styles reduced the profitability of barber shops. Many barbers left the market, causing a decrease in supply. Consumers purchased fewer haircuts at the higher price.

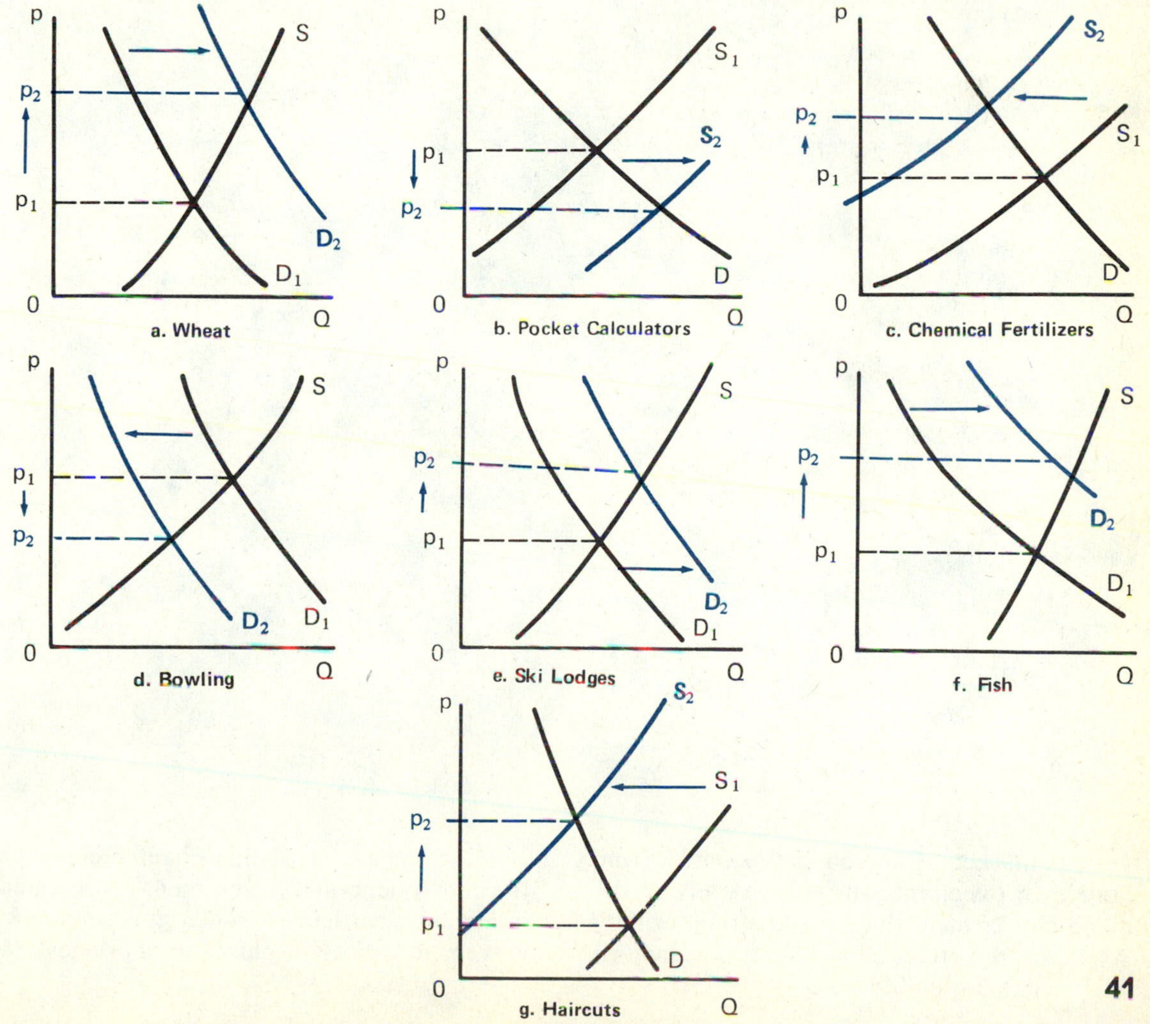

Thinking Seriously About Economic Issues

HAVE YOU EVER WONDERED WHAT THINGS COST WHEN YOU WERE BORN?

Compare these prices. Some have risen or fallen substantially. Some have hardly changed at all. Can you suggest reasons for the difference?

	1974	1992
Ford's smallest-model car	$2,600	$4,600–$7,200
One-way air ticket to Montreal	105	199
Alka-Seltzer (25 tablets)	.44	3.59
Right Guard deodorant (7 oz)	.79	2.19
9-volt transistor battery	.14	3.49
Aqua Net hairspray	.39	1.29
One-quart thermos bottle	1.99	4.99
Nylon bikini	16	35
Ladies' sandals	1.99	9.99
Pantyhose	.50	3.59
Central air conditioning	1,199	1,300
Ground beef (1 lb)	.68	1.79
Sliced bacon (1 lb)	.78	1.39
Top round steak	1.48	3.59
Watermelon	.98	3.89
Pocket calculator:		
Add, subtract, multiply, divide	34.95	4.96
Reciprocals, squares, square roots	89.95	9.96
19.9 cubic foot refrigerator-freezer with ice maker	499	679
Small room air conditioner	134	199
Bahamas trip (per person, double occupancy):		
5 days, from West Palm Beach	89	
4 days from Atlanta		359

various markets. Can you cite examples from your own experience in which supply or demand curves have shifted to the right or left? What was the effect of each shift on equilibrium price and quantity?

The remainder of this chapter considers the consequences of government involvement in markets, particularly when government involvement causes surpluses or shortages.

Self-Check

1. Perfect competition does *not* depend on:
 a. A large number of buyers and sellers.
 b. Information about market conditions.
 c. Distinguishing characteristics of the product.
 d. Ease of movement among markets.
 e. Small size of firms relative to size of the market.

2. For most goods and services:
 a. Quantity demanded is low at low prices.
 b. Quantity demanded is high at high prices.
 c. Demand is based on costs of production.
 d. Quantity demanded is inversely related to price.
 e. Quantity demanded is directly related to price.

3. Which of the following is not an example of a change in supply?
 a. Improved technology of sound reproduction reduces the equilibrium price of recordings.
 b. A falling price for natural gas encourages existing firms to produce less.
 c. Cereal manufacturers shift from producing corn flakes to producing oat bran.
 d. Foreign car manufacturers sell their products in the United States.
 e. Competition from Brazilian farmers causes U.S. farmers to stop producing soybeans.

4. Which of the following is an example of a change in quantity demanded?
 a. Consumer tastes shift away from Kentucky Fried Chicken and toward Mexican dinners.
 b. All consumers who want CB radios already have them.
 c. A major discount firm conducts a "One-Third Off Sale."
 d. High gasoline prices reduce automobile sales.
 e. Unemployed auto workers must reduce their living standards.

5. Which of the following is not true of market equilibrium?
 a. The price "clears the market."
 b. Everyone who wants the product can buy it.
 c. There is no surplus or shortage.
 d. Price is high enough to satisfy those who supply the equilibrium quantity.
 e. Quantity supplied is equal to quantity demanded.

6. Which of the following pairs does not belong with the others?
 a. Paper and pen.
 b. Turkey and liverwurst.
 c. Hammer and nails.
 d. Bread and jam.
 e. Shoes and stockings.

Theory in Practice

PRICE CEILINGS AND PRICE FLOORS

We have seen how the invisible hand works to allocate our nation's scarce resources to produce the variety of things we want to buy. Individual consumers' demand curves and producers' supply curves combine to answer the question: What is to be produced, in what quantities, and at what prices?

In the real world, most markets are not entirely free to operate in precisely the way Adam Smith described. Our economic system is not entirely a free-market system but a mixed system: with some elements of a command system and even some tradition. Our government intervenes in the market in a number of ways. Often, government involvement affects the prices and quantities of goods and services.

One reason for government involvement in markets results from changes in demand or supply that yield abnormally high or low prices for particular goods or services. Abnormally high prices may unfairly reward and punish particular groups in our society. To avoid abnormally high prices, government may set a **price ceiling,** above which market price may not rise. Abnormally low prices unfairly punish other groups. To avoid abnormally low prices, government may set a **price floor,** below which price may not legally fall. In both cases, government fixes prices at a level that satisfies voters' view of fairness, or equity, in the distribution of goods and services.

A disadvantage of price ceilings and price floors is that they can prevent markets from moving to equilibrium. They may cause surpluses and shortages, and surpluses and shortages may linger longer than when the market is allowed to push prices up or down to the equilibrium level.

To illustrate the problem of government price-fixing, we consider the markets for natural gas and farm commodities.

Price Ceilings for Natural Gas

More than thirty years ago, the U.S. government became concerned about conditions in the market for natural gas produced in the south-central United States. Increasing demand for natural gas had caused the market demand curve to shift to the right; increasing production costs had caused the supply curve to shift up to the left. The result was rising prices, with worsening hardships for households and industrial users of this clean fuel. To satisfy some voters' preferences for fairness, government put in place a price ceiling to hold the price of all natural gas traded in interstate markets to $.50 per thousand cubic feet.

The market for natural gas is shown in Figure 2.8. According to Figure 2.8 the equilibrium price that clears the market is $1.50 per thousand cubic feet. Under government regulation, however, price could not rise above the $.50 ceiling. At the artificially low price, consumers and business firms wanted to buy larger quantities of natural gas to heat their homes and to operate manufacturing processes. Quantity demanded at the low ceiling price was as high as *Ob*. Meanwhile, at the artificially low price, producers of natural gas were willing to supply only *Oa*. With a government-imposed price ceiling, the market could not move toward equilibrium, and there was a shortage of natural gas. The shortage is shown on Figure 2.8 as *ab,* the difference between quantity demanded (*Ob*) and quantity supplied (*Oa*).

Figure 2.8 The Market for Natural Gas

A price ceiling creates a shortage of natural gas.

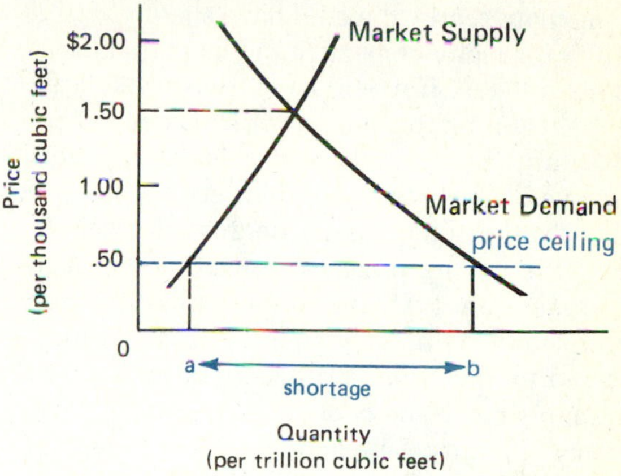

Some Americans grew accustomed to a cheap supply of natural gas and used it wastefully. Others could not buy any natural gas at all and turned to other fuels, increasing the demand for other energy resources and causing their prices to rise. The artificially low price pushed some producers of natural gas out of business, and the country faced a potential crisis of supply. The effects of price ceilings can be disastrous shortages.

TEST YOURSELF

Are natural gas and other fuels substitutes or complements?

When government fixes prices below the equilibrium level, the smaller quantity supplied may have to be rationed by some device other than price among the large numbers of would-be buyers. Rationing requires a large bureaucracy and raises additional questions regarding fairness.

In 1978 Congress and President Carter began removing the ceiling price on natural gas. Immediate removal would have sharply raised prices for many consumer and industrial users of natural gas. It would have transferred large amounts of purchasing power from consumers of natural gas to owners of existing supplies. To avoid disruptions in markets for natural gas, the president and Congress decided to raise the ceiling price by some amount each year until in 1985 the ceiling was removed completely. Gradually rising prices were expected to encourage producers of natural gas to supply more and consumers to use less until finally quantity supplied would be equal to quantity demanded at the market equilibrium price.

Figure 2.9 The Market for Corn

A price floor creates a surplus of corn.

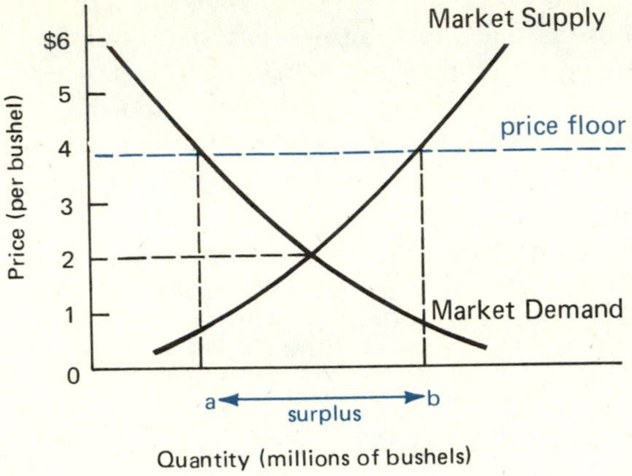

Price Floors for Farm Commodities

Another example of government price-fixing began during the Great Depression of the 1930s. American farmers were suffering severe hardships because of low farm prices. New scientific techniques and advanced agricultural equipment had increased food production faster than the American public wanted to buy. As a result, supply curves for farm commodities had shifted to the right faster than the rightward shift of demand, and farm prices and incomes had dropped dramatically.

The voting power of the farming sector was strong. In response to farmers' demands, Congress passed laws setting price floors for certain farm commodities, including corn, wheat, rice, cotton, tobacco, and peanuts.

The market for corn is shown in Figure 2.9. According to Figure 2.9 the market equilibrium price is $2.00 per bushel, but price was not allowed to fall below the government-supported price of $4.00. At the artificially high price, consumers wanted to buy less corn for cooking; ranchers wanted to buy less corn for livestock feed. At the artificially high price, quantity demanded was only *Oa*, but farmers were willing to supply as much as *Ob*. In fact, many farmers converted their fields from other crops to increase their production of corn. The result of the government-supported price was a surplus of corn, shown on Figure 2.9 as *ab*, the difference between quantity supplied and quantity demanded.

U.S. farmers grew accustomed to government-supported prices for their products. They continued to expand output or, at least, failed to cut production or to leave farming for occupations that would earn sufficient income at free-market prices. The U.S. government made crop loans to farmers based on the artificially high support price. Farmers who were unable to sell their grain at that price defaulted on their loans and turned their crops over to the government. The effects of a price floor can be embarrassing surpluses.

Farm legislation expires every five years, and Congress decides on new policies appropriate to current conditions. Recent farm legislation has as its objective to reduce government involvement in markets for farm products, while improving stability of farm incomes. Today's farm legislation sets "target prices," which are designed to be just below equilibrium prices in normal crop years and to cover farmers' basic costs of seed, fertilizer, labor, and machinery. In years of high demand relative to supply, farmers can sell their grain at free-market prices, pay their costs, and earn a profit. In years of low demand relative to supply, the free-market price tends to fall below the target price; then government pays farmers the difference between the market price and the target price. Government payments allow farmers to stay in business, while enabling consumers to enjoy low food prices at the supermarket.

A second part of the current farm law is aimed at stabilizing the supply of farm commodities. Under the "set aside" provision of the current law, farmers are asked not to cultivate a portion of their land when particular crops are expected to be in surplus. A grain storage program purchases farmers' surplus grain in years of plenty for resale in years of shortage.

Has Government Price Setting Been a Blessing or a Curse?

We might agree that government involvement in markets for natural gas and farm products began with the best intentions. Our political system helps ensure that government policies reflect the wishes of voters. Often, however, price ceilings and price floors have benefited particular interest groups while at the same time reducing the efficiency of the economy as a whole.

Look again at the market for natural gas in Figure 2.8. A higher free-market price for natural gas would have discouraged nonessential uses of this valuable resource and conserved our nation's supplies. Moreover, the higher price would have encouraged new and existing firms to seek out and develop new sources of natural gas. An increase in supply would have helped bring prices down in the future. The result of free-market pricing might have been more balanced use of all available fuels in American homes and business firms.

In the farming sector, lower free-market prices for farm commodities would have meant temporary hardships for farmers. Some would have left farming to seek better jobs in manufacturing firms. With fewer farmers in the market, the supply of farm commodities would have shifted to the left. Prices would have risen until finally the remaining farmers were earning enough income from their crops to pay the full costs of farming.

Other examples of government price fixing have had other harmful effects. Throughout most of the 1970s the price of crude oil produced in the United States was controlled by a low ceiling price. The price ceiling made gasoline cheap to American drivers and encouraged the use of private automobiles. In addition, the price of parking in downtown areas is often held below equilibrium by downtown department stores, and the cost of building highways is often paid by the federal government at low cost to local taxpayers. Artificially low prices for all these complementary goods and services have contributed to the rise of automobile traffic in the United States.

Remember that the opportunity cost of using land as a highway or parking lot is the other things for which the land could have been used: department stores, restaurants, factories, homes, wildlife reserves, and so forth. It is correct to say that the artificially low price for gasoline has cost our nation the

Thinking Seriously About Economic Issues

PRIVATIZATION IN EASTERN EUROPE

When World War II ended in 1945, the nations of Eastern Europe came under the influence of the Soviet Union and adopted a command economic system. Under the command system most production was controlled by government, and a central committee was set up to decide output and prices and allocate resources. With the collapse of the Soviet Union, Eastern European nations are now free to establish market systems more like that of the United States.

One of the first tasks of the new market systems is "privatization": that is, placing in private hands the farms, factories, and mines that formerly were controlled by government.

Private ownership will allow private entrepreneurs to decide how best to satisfy consumer demand and how to produce at lowest cost. Small and medium-sized factories may be auctioned off or sold to employees, with the help of government loans. Larger factories may be organized as corporations and shares of stock sold to private investors. To ensure fairness in the distribution of corporate stock, governments may issue "vouchers" to all citizens, allowing them to choose stock in particular enterprises.

Harvard economist Jeffrey Sachs has contributed to the reform programs of Eastern Europe and understands the difficulties of privatization.

Privatization is difficult in part because the absence of market prices makes it impossible to know what factories are worth. Moreover, privatization will require years to accomplish, years during which standards of living in these nations may stagnate and public discontent grow. Western nations can help ease the process by opening their borders to trade with newly privatized farms and factories. Help in the form of loans—from individuals, nations, or institutions—will also be welcome. Loans or grants can help Eastern European nations build transportation and communication facilities and purchase technical assistance for modernizing production.

Jeffrey D. Sachs, "Crossing the Valley of Tears in East European Reform," *Challenge,* September/October 1991.

opportunity to use land for homes, businesses, and recreational areas.

Most economists believe that free-market prices help ensure technical and allocative efficiency in the use of our scarce resources: that is, production of the largest quantities of what we want with the smallest quantities of land, labor, capital, and entrepreneurship. Free-market prices avoid the shortages and surpluses associated with price ceilings and price floors. Occasionally, government may need to intervene in certain markets to ease temporary hardships for particular groups. Over the long run, however, the free market generally provides a better answer to the question What?

SUMMARY

1. Adam Smith developed the body of theory that explains how buyers and sellers behave in perfect competition. When markets are free and competitive, the economy will achieve the greatest possible output from its scarce resources.
2. Perfect competition requires many small buyers and sellers, perfect knowledge of market conditions, ease of mobility to favored locations, and products that are identical.
3. The free-market system is based on the preferences of consumers who evaluate the usefulness of goods and services. The result is many consumer-demand schedules that are added together to form market demand. Demand curves typically slope downward because larger quantities are bought only at lower prices.
4. Changes in income, tastes, number of buyers, prices of related goods, and expectations of future changes cause changes in market demand.
5. The quantities of a good or service that a business firm would offer for sale at various prices constitute the firm's supply schedule. Adding together the supply curves of all firms in a market yields market supply. Supply curves slope upward because larger quantities will be supplied only at higher prices.
6. Changes in the number of firms in the industry, the costs of resources used in the industry, the state of technology, related prices, and price expectations cause supply curves to shift to the right or left.
7. Market equilibrium is the price at which the quantity demanded by consumers is just equal to the quantity supplied by producers. At prices higher than the equilibrium price, quantity supplied is greater than quantity demanded, and there is a surplus. At prices lower than the equilibrium price, quantity demanded is greater than quantity supplied, and there is a shortage.
8. Government may intervene in free markets to ease temporary hardships created by shifts in demand or supply. It may establish a price ceiling or price floor when market price is believed to be too high or too low. A price ceiling is likely to cause a shortage; a price floor, a surplus.

TERMS TO REMEMBER

microeconomics: the study of how individual economic units help answer the questions What? How? and For whom?

market demand: the quantities all consumers together would buy at various prices

market supply: the quantities all suppliers together would sell at various prices

demand schedule: the quantities a particular consumer is willing and able to buy at various prices

the law of demand: the relationship between price and quantity demanded is inverse; that is, as price increases, quantity demanded decreases, and as price decreases, quantity demanded increases

change in quantity demanded: a movement along a demand curve in response to a change in price

change in demand: a shift in a demand curve in response to a change in some factor other than price

substitute goods: goods that can easily be used in place of one another (hamburger or pizza); as the price of one good changes, demand for the substitute changes in the same direction

complementary goods: goods that are normally used together (beer and pretzels); as the price of one good changes, demand for the complementary good changes in the opposite direction

supply schedule: the quantities a particular firm is willing to supply at various prices

market supply: the quantities all firms together would supply at various prices

quantity supplied: the quantity that would be supplied at a particular price

the law of supply: the relationship between price and quantity supplied is direct; that is, as price increases, quantity supplied increases, and as price decreases, quantity supplied decreases

market equilibrium: the point on the demand and

supply curves at which quantity supplied is equal to quantity demanded

surplus: the difference between quantity supplied and quantity demanded when price is above the equilibrium price

shortage: the difference between quantity demanded and quantity supplied when price is below the equilibrium price

price ceiling: a price set by government, above which market price is not allowed to rise

price floor: a price set by government, below which market price is not allowed to fall

TOPICS FOR DISCUSSION

1. Which of the following markets are likely to be most competitive? Explain your answer.

Barber shops	Hairstylists
T-shirts	Polo shirts
Electric power	Concrete

2. What are the characteristics of a competitive market? Which characteristics of competition are present or absent in each of the following markets: personal computers, weight machines, avocados, education, home-delivered milk?
3. Explain why it is important to draw a demand curve for a particular period of time. Then explain how demand curves are likely to change as the period of time lengthens.
4. List substitutes and complements for each of the following: movies, motorcycles, gold chains, wallpaper.
5. Demonstrate graphically the effect of high gasoline prices on demand curves in markets for other goods and services: tickets to theme parks, airline tickets, tires.
6. A certain auto manufacturer reduced the price of its compact model because of a bad safety record, but still sales fell. Does this result contradict the law of demand? Explain.
7. During a period of rising food prices, I went to the supermarket for a head of lettuce. The lettuce bin was not sporting its customary price sign. Because lettuce prices had been fluctuating between 69 and 99 cents, I asked the produce manager what the price was that day. He whispered the answer: 69 cents. Of course, I took advantage of the low price to buy several heads. Then the produce manager explained the reason he hadn't put a sign over the bin.

   "If I put out a sign saying '69 cents' I'd be all out of lettuce before noon," he said. "If I had plenty and the price was 99 cents, I'd put out a big sign. But this way I can save what I've got and make it last all day."

   Was this grocer using the price system to allocate a scarce commodity among his customers? Why do you think he acted the way he did? Can you suggest a better approach to his problem?
8. Consumer boycotts are occasionally used to protest high food prices. An effective boycott can be shown as a backward shift of the demand curve. Our understanding of free markets should give us some clues as to the reaction of suppliers to lower demand (and lower prices). How do you think a boycott will affect food prices after several months, during which farmers have had time to adjust to the new conditions? How will the "invisible hand" change farm output? Show your answer graphically.
9. Changing life-styles and the changing age mix of the U.S. population have brought on an increase in wine sales. As a result, prices have risen from 25 to 200 percent (depending on the quality of the wine). California vintners have expanded cultivation of grapes, and wine lovers hope that prices will soon stabilize.

   Comment on the information given above. Use a series of graphs to illustrate changes in consumer demand and equilibrium price. Then show how producers are adjusting to changes in market conditions.
10. Some local governments in the United States have imposed rent controls on city apartments. Discuss the purpose of this kind of price ceiling and list as many consequences as you can.
11. National concerns regarding the harmful effects of alcohol consumption are contributing to a shift in demand curves. Describe the con-

sequences for equilibrium prices, total expenditures for alcoholic beverages, and resource allocation. How would a famous eighteenth-century economist have described these changes?

ANSWERS TO TEST YOURSELF

(p. 32) Other sellers, information about prices, buyer's ability to walk down the street, and identical canaries. In perfect competition, the prices would be equal.

(p. 33) Total revenue is price times quantity. The area of a rectangle is height times base. A rectangle formed under the demand curve has price for its height and quantity for its base. Therefore, the area of the rectangle = height × base = price × quantity = total expenditure or total revenue.

(p. 36) A change in quantity demanded.

(p. 36) A shift to the left.

(p. 38) Black and white television sets; luxury autos; a shift to the left.

(p. 39) A change in supply.

(p. 45) Substitutes.

FURTHER READING

Flavin, Christopher, "Beyond the Gulf Crisis: An Energy Strategy for the 90s," *Challenge*, November/December, 1990.

Mokyr, Joel, *The Lever of Riches*, Oxford University Press, New York, 1990.

Relman, Arnold S., "What Market Values Are Doing to Medicine," *Atlantic*, March, 1992.

Romm, Joseph J., and Amory B. Lovins, "Fueling a Competitive Economy," *Foreign Affairs*, Winter, 1992/1993.

Sandler, Todd, et al, "Economic Analysis Can Help Fight International Terrorism," *Challenge*, January/February, 1991.

Stobaugh, Robert, and Daniel Yergin, eds., *Energy Future*, Random House, New York, 1979.

Chapter 3

More About Demand: Price Elasticity

Tools for Study

LEARNING OBJECTIVES

After reading this chapter, you will be able to:

1. Explain differences in consumers' responsiveness to price changes for different goods or services.
2. Describe demand curves in terms of their responsiveness to price changes.
3. Explain how consumers' responses to price changes affect a firm's total revenue from sales.
4. Describe the basis for price discrimination.

CURRENT ISSUES FOR DISCUSSION

What difference does price elasticity make:
to consumers?
to business firms?
to government?

Most people are interested in prices. "What is the price?" is one of the first things we learn to say when studying a foreign language. We want to pay the lowest possible price for the things we want.

Prices are often confusing, however. Even when price is clearly stated, the basis for the price may not be obvious. For example, it is not obvious why air fares between the same two cities are different for different passengers or at different times of the day or week. It is not obvious why a textbook should cost more than a popular novel!

In Chapter 2 we constructed a model of supply and demand in a perfectly competitive market. We saw how the interaction between demand and supply curves determines the equilibrium price. The **equilibrium price** is the price at which the quantity offered for sale is just equal to the quantity consumers want to buy. At the equilibrium price there is no surplus or shortage.

In this chapter we look more closely at demand and the factors that influence demand curves. We show how the shapes of demand curves differ and how their differences affect the seller's total revenue from sales. Finally, we see that achieving the maximum possible revenue from sales requires a particular pricing strategy. Then we try to clear up some of the confusion regarding air fares and textbook prices.

PRICE ELASTICITY OF DEMAND

In Chapter 2 we saw that the positions of demand curves differ according to incomes

Viewpoint

PRICE ELASTICITY OF DEMAND IN THE MARKET FOR PETROLEUM

Price elasticity of demand measures the responsiveness of quantity demanded to changes in price. Price elasticity of demand for some goods depends strongly on the physical circumstances necessary for consuming it; that is, the buildings and equipment or the social arrangements surrounding the goods' use. Physical surroundings change slowly, with the result that quantity demanded may respond slowly to price changes.

Consider the response of U.S. consumers to changes in the price of energy. In 1973 an embargo of oil shipments to the United States raised the price of a barrel of crude oil from $2.50 to $12.50. In spite of rising oil prices and fears of increasing scarcity, most Americans continued to drive their automobiles, heat and cool their homes and office buildings, and purchase petroleum-based products and synthetic materials. (Given their existing social arrangements, changing their patterns of consumption would have been extremely costly.) Quantity demanded remained high, and consumers' total expenditure for imported petroleum and petroleum products rose from $8.4 billion in 1973 to $26.6 billion in 1974. In fact, total U.S. purchases of petroleum increased from 12 percent to 26 percent of the nation's total import bill.

For several years the cost of imported petroleum increased at an average rate of more than 12 percent a year. Not only were demand curves for petroleum relatively price inelastic over the period, but fairly strong economic growth was pushing demand curves to the right. Then in 1979, oil exporters again increased the price of petroleum—to almost $30 a barrel. The U.S. oil import bill leaped by 43 percent, and prices of goods and services related to petroleum rose sharply, too. In 1980 the

and numbers of buyers, consumer tastes, prices of related goods, and expected future events. The shapes of demand curves differ also. The shape of a demand curve depends on price elasticity of demand.

Price elasticity of demand is sometimes reflected in the slope of the demand curve.* Because the usefulness of some goods diminishes quickly, their demand curves slope downward rather steeply as we acquire more units during a particular period of time. Salt, for example, is a good of which the first unit purchased is useful, even essential. Further purchases in any one time period, however, could become a nuisance. Consumers would not buy larger quantities of salt even if the price should fall drastically, and they would not buy smaller quantities if the price should rise.

Economists describe the demand for such goods as **price inelastic:** They mean that the quantity demanded is not very responsive to price changes. Necessities with few substitutes generally have relatively inelastic de-

*The slope of a demand curve does not always reflect price elasticity of demand. In fact, the slope of a demand curve depends also on the horizontal scale of the graph. Can you demonstrate how changing the horizontal scale can change the slope of a demand curve?

nation suffered a recession, and growth was slow until 1981, when a new recession took hold that became the most severe (in terms of unemployment) since the Great Depression of the 1930s.

By 1983, a decade of high petroleum prices had encouraged changes in many of the physical facilities and social arrangements that are associated with the consumption of petroleum products. The most noticeable change was a shift in buying habits from large, gas-guzzling "luxury" automobiles to smaller, more fuel-efficient compact cars. Another was a change in building construction to use natural sources of heat, light, and shade more effectively. Finally, many U.S. families moved closer to their places of work or school, and some organized car pools.

Business firms also made changes in response to high petroleum prices. Many firms reorganized their production processes to use less energy. Some eliminated product lines that consumed large amounts of energy, and some went out of business.

How have all these developments affected the price elasticity of demand for petroleum and petroleum-related products? From relatively price inelastic demand in the 1970s, demand curves for petroleum gradually became more price elastic in the 1980s. New physical facilities and social arrangements became more flexible, so that today consumers can change the quantities of petroleum they buy as the price of petroleum changes. (By the 1990s, however, more plentiful supplies and lower prices for petroleum were encouraging increased consumption, and some consumers were returning to their high energy consumption of the 1970s.)

mand. These are things that we must buy in some certain quantity, but we have little use for more than that quantity.

The demand for many other goods is *price elastic*. For goods with **elastic demand:** The quantity demanded is quite responsive to price changes. Luxuries and goods with many substitutes often have relatively elastic demand. Consumers can decide to buy or not, depending on price.

Can you think of other goods or services with elastic and **inelastic demand?** How do you think consumers respond to changes in the price of dental care, meat, doughnuts, airline tickets, wallpaper, and gasoline? (As is often true in economics, an acceptable answer is "It depends.")

Price elasticity of demand affects consumers' total expenditure for a good. If market demand is relatively price elastic, consumers respond significantly to price changes. A price rise will cause a substantial drop in sales, so that expenditure falls. On the other hand, a price reduction will cause a substantial increase in sales, so that total expenditure increases. Henry Ford discovered this result in the early days of the automobile industry. Mr. Ford found he could increase his firm's total revenue from sales by reducing the price of his autos. (Can you explain this result in terms of price elasticity of demand?)

If market demand is price inelastic, consumers do not respond very much to price changes. They buy roughly the same quantities regardless of price. In this case, a price increase does not cause sales to fall very much, so that total expenditure increases. On the other hand, a price decrease does not cause sales to increase very much, so that total expenditure falls. The oil-producing nations of the Middle East understand this result quite well. During the 1970s they discovered they could increase their countries' total revenue from oil sales by increasing oil prices. (Explain this result in terms of price elasticity of demand.)

What Determines Price Elasticity of Demand?

Price elasticity of demand depends on these three characteristics:

1. The availability of substitutes.
2. The importance of the item in the consumer's budget.
3. The time it takes to develop or discover a substitute.

When there are many substitutes, consumers can change buying plans freely. A small increase in the price of pineapples will cause a large decrease in quantity demanded, as consumers substitute similar but lower-priced fruits. Likewise, a small decrease in the price of meat will cause a large increase in quantity demanded, as consumers purchase meat rather than relatively higher-priced cheese. In general, we can say that goods with many substitutes have price elastic demand. Essential goods with no substitutes have price inelastic demand.

When purchasing a particular good requires a relatively large part of a consumer's budget, quantity demanded responds readily to a change in price. In contrast, if the good is a small item in a consumer's budget or if its price is very low, consumers do not change their buying plans very much. Hence, a large item generally has elastic demand, and a small item, inelastic demand. Which good would you expect to have more elastic demand: automobiles or auto parts?

Finally, demand is generally more price elastic over longer periods of time. Over time, consumers can find substitutes to take the place of goods whose prices have risen, and they can find new ways to use goods whose prices have fallen. After years of struggling to adjust to higher gasoline prices during the 1970s, U.S. consumers finally cut their purchases of gasoline in the 1980s. Many consumers turned to public transportation, and their demand curves became more price elastic. (Consumers faced a different sort of budget crisis in the mid 1980s when a bad crop year pushed up the price of peanut butter. For peanut butter lovers who refuse to accept substitutes, demand curves remained price inelastic for a very long time!)

Different consumers may have different price elasticities of demand for the same good. A particular consumer's price elasticity of demand depends on whether he or she considers the good essential (few substitutes) and how important the good is in the consumer's own budget.

CALCULATING PRICE ELASTICITY OF DEMAND

Business firms devote much effort to estimating price elasticity of demand for their products. Consumers' responsiveness to price changes has a lot to do with total expenditure for a good and, ultimately, a firm's **total revenue** from sales.

Thinking Seriously About Economic Issues

HAVE YOU EVER WONDERED HOW YOUR FAMILY'S INCOME AND EXPENDITURES COMPARE WITH THOSE OF OTHER FAMILIES?
AVERAGE ANNUAL INCOME AND EXPENDITURES

	All Families	*Under Age 25*	*Between Ages 45 and 54*
Income before taxes	$31,889	$14,089	$43,451
Food	4,296	2,761	5,490
Alcoholic beverages	293	318	324
Housing: Shelter	5,032	3,025	6,130
Fuel, utilities, and public services	1,890	906	2,357
Household appliances and furniture	1,557	736	1,748
Apparel and service	1,617	1,034	2,165
Vehicles	2,129	1,591	2,967
Gas and motor oil	1,047	722	1,391
Other transportation	1,946	1,185	2,692
Health care	1,480	403	1,597
Personal insurance and pensions	2,592	972	3,847
Other	4,080	2,687	5,804
Personal taxes	2,952	843	4,070

Statistical Abstract of the United States, 1992.

Figure 3.1a Elastic Demand (per day)

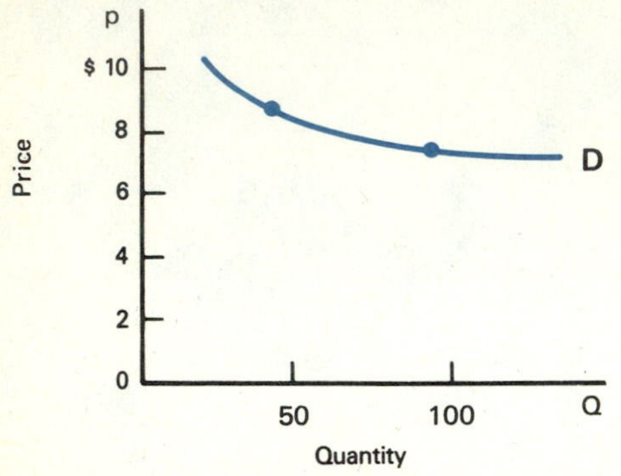

Figure 3.1b Inelastic Demand (per day)

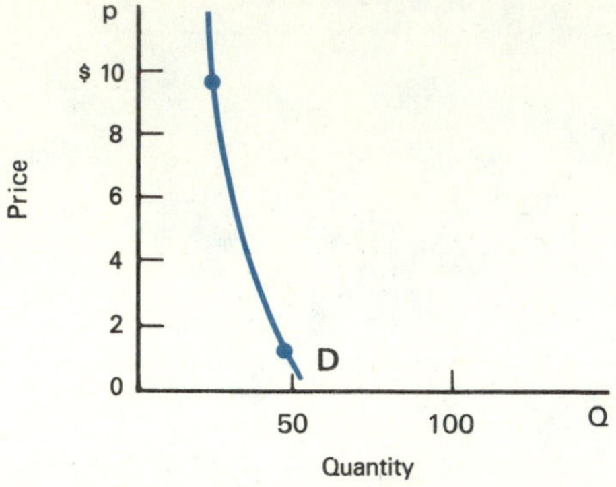

We measure price elasticity of demand as the percentage change in quantity demanded relative to the percentage change in price:

$$\frac{\%\Delta Q_d}{\%\Delta p}.*$$

If $\%\Delta Q_d$ is greater than $\%\Delta p$, consumers respond significantly to price changes; the value of the **elasticity ratio** is greater than 1, and with price elasticity of demand greater than 1, we say that demand is price elastic. If $\%\Delta Q_d$ is less than $\%\Delta p$, consumers respond only slightly to price changes; the value of the ratio is less than 1, and with price elasticity of demand less than 1, we say that demand is price inelastic. If $\%\Delta Q_d$ is precisely equal to $\%\Delta p$, price elasticity of demand is equal to 1, or unity. Consumers respond to price changes with equal percentage changes in quantity.

We have suggested that differences in price elasticity may be reflected in the shapes of demand curves. Look at Figure 3.1a, in which a small percentage change in price (from $9.00 to $8.00) causes quantity demanded to change by one-half. Demand is relatively price elastic over this range of the demand curve, and the curve is relatively flat. Now look at Figure 3.1b, in which a large percentage change in price (from $10.00 to $1.00) causes quantity demanded to change only slightly. Demand is relatively price inelastic over this range, and the curve is relatively steep.

In some markets, quantity demanded responds in extreme ways to price changes. This is true of the demand curves in Figures 3.2a and 3.2b. Figure 3.2a is described as infinitely price elastic because quantity can change in infinite amounts with no change in price. Figure 3.2b is described as perfectly price inelastic because quantity does not change at all with infinite changes in price.

Most demand curves reflect different price elasticities at different price levels. Look at Figure 3.3. The demand curve in Figure 3.3 is called a linear demand curve because its slope is constant over its entire length. Along any small segment of the curve, price elasticity is equal to the following ratio:

$$e_d = \%\Delta Q_d/\%\Delta p.$$
= percentage change in quantity demanded/percent change in price

*The symbol Δ (delta) is used to denote "change in."

Figure 3.2a Infinitely Elastic Demand (per day)

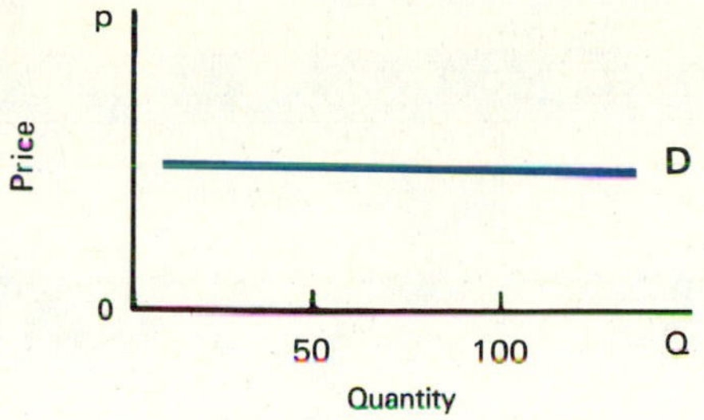

Figure 3.2b Perfectly Inelastic Demand (per day)

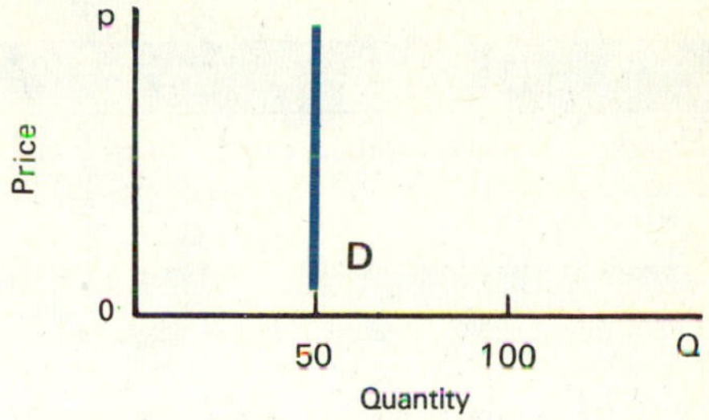

Notice that both numerator and denominator are in percentage terms. To calculate a percent change it is necessary first to measure the actual change and then compare the actual change with a total, or base, value. Because the total value changes with a movement along the demand curve, it is appropriate to use as a base the average of the two values before and after the change. For example, a price reduction from \$500 to \$400 represents an absolute change of $(p_1 - p_2) = \$500 - \$400 = \$100$. In percentage terms a \$100 price reduction is

$$\%\Delta p = (p_1 - p_2)/\left(\frac{P_1 + P_2}{2}\right)$$

$$= (500 - 400)/\frac{(500 + 400)}{2}$$

$$= 100/450 = 0.22 = 22 \text{ percent.}$$

Thus, $\%\Delta p = 22$ percent. Again from Figure 3.3, a price reduction of \$100 causes quantity demanded to increase from zero to 100 units. In percentage terms the change in quantity is

$$\%\Delta Q_d = (Q_1 - Q_2)/\left(\frac{Q_1 + Q_2}{2}\right)$$

$$= (0 - 100)/\frac{(0 + 100)}{2}$$

$$= -100/50 = -2.00 = -200 \text{ percent.}$$

Thus, $\%\Delta Q_d = -200$ percent.

With $\%\Delta p = 22$ percent and $\%\Delta Q_d = -200$ percent, price elasticity of demand along this segment of the demand curve is

$$e_d = \%\Delta Q_d/\%\Delta p = -200/22 = -9.09.$$

This value has been written alongside the linear demand curve in Figure 3.3.

Other price elasticity computations were performed similarly and the results added to

Figure 3.3 Price Elasticity of Demand Along a Linear Demand Curve

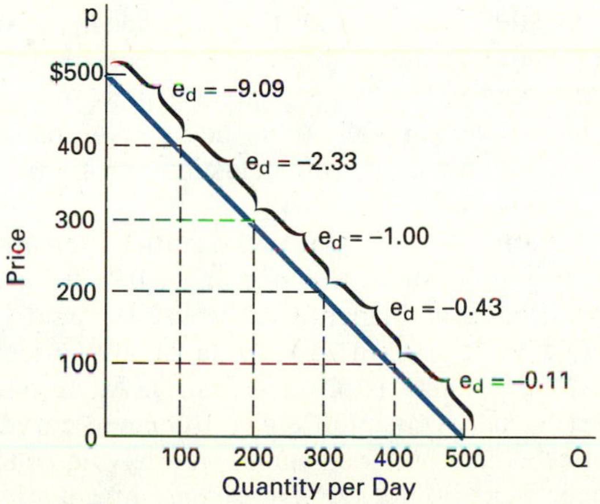

Table 3.1 Calculating Price Elasticity of Demand

p	Q	$\%\Delta p = \frac{(p_1 - p_2)}{\frac{(p_1 + p_2)}{2}}$	$\%\Delta Q = \frac{(Q_1 - Q_2)}{\frac{(Q_1 + Q_2)}{2}}$	$e_d = \frac{\%\Delta Q_d}{\%\Delta p}$	*Total Expenditure* = $p \times Q$
500	0				\$0
		$\frac{(500 - 400)}{\frac{(500 + 400)}{2}} = \frac{100}{450} = .22$	$\frac{(0 - 100)}{\frac{(0 + 100)}{2}} = \frac{-100}{50} = -2$	$\frac{-2}{.22} = -9.09$	
400	100				\$40,000
		$\frac{(400 - 300)}{\frac{(400 + 300)}{2}} = \frac{100}{350} = .29$	$\frac{(100 - 200)}{\frac{(100 + 200)}{2}} = \frac{-100}{150} = -.67$	$\frac{-.67}{.29} = -2.33$	
300	200				\$60,000
		$\frac{(300 - 200)}{\frac{(300 + 200)}{2}} = \frac{100}{250} = .40$	$\frac{(200 - 300)}{\frac{(200 + 300)}{2}} = \frac{-100}{250} = -.40$	$\frac{-.40}{.40} = -1$	
200	300				\$60,000
		$\frac{(200 - 100)}{\frac{(200 + 100)}{2}} = \frac{100}{150} = .67$	$\frac{(300 - 400)}{\frac{(300 + 400)}{2}} = \frac{-100}{350} = -.29$	$\frac{-.29}{.67} = -.43$	
100	400				\$40,000
		$\frac{(100 - 0)}{\frac{(100 + 0)}{2}} = \frac{100}{50} = 2$	$\frac{(400 - 500)}{\frac{(400 + 500)}{2}} = \frac{-100}{450} = -.22$	$\frac{-.22}{2} = -.11$	
0	500				\$0

the figure. (We performed the computations as if price is to be reduced and quantity increased, but the results would be the same if we reversed the direction of price and quantity changes.)

Notice that all the values for price elasticity of demand have a negative sign. Price elasticity of demand is almost always negative, because price increases almost always cause decreases in quantity demanded. Likewise, price reductions almost always cause increases in quantity demand. Because price and quantity demanded typically move in opposite directions, the numerator and denominator of the elasticity ratio will typically have opposite signs, making the ratio negative. In general, the sign of the elasticity ratio is less important to business planners than its magnitude, so we generally omit the minus sign and just remember that price elasticity of demand is almost always negative.

Notice also that price elasticity of demand varies along the linear demand curve from a high value at high prices (where demand is price elastic) to a low value at low prices (where demand is price inelastic). Along one very small segment of a linear demand curve, price elasticity of demand is precisely equal to one. That is, the percent change in quantity demanded is precisely equal to the percent change in price, and price elasticity of demand is unity.

Variations in price elasticity of demand affect consumers' total expenditures and business firms' total revenue from sales. The linear demand curve in Figure 3.3 has been reproduced as Figure 3.4a to illustrate the effect of price changes on total revenue. Figure 3.4b shows total revenue at combinations of price and quantity taken from the demand curve. The horizontal axis of Figure 3.4b corresponds to that of Figure 3.4a and represents quantity sold at various price levels. The vertical axis represents total revenue, calculated by multiplying price times quantity at various points on the demand curve:

$$\text{Total Revenue} = TR = p \times Q.$$

Look first at the demand curve at a price of \$500, where quantity demanded is zero. Then look at a price of \$0, where quantity demanded is 500 units. Total revenue associated with both points is zero, plotted accordingly on Figure 3.4b. Now select other points on the demand curve, calculate total revenue, and plot the point: At p = \$400 and $Q = 100$, TR = \$400 × 100 = \$40,000; at p = \$300 and $Q = 200$, and TR = \$60,000; at p = \$200 and $Q = 300$, TR = \$60,000; at p = \$100 and Q = 400, TR = \$40,000.

Note carefully the shape of the Total Revenue curve in Figure 3.4b. The Total Revenue curve in Figure 3.4b is typical of *TR* curves associated with linear demand curves. All such *TR* curves have maximum total revenue in the midrange of price and quantity and declining total revenue outside that range. Compare the *TR* curve with the values for price elasticity of demand shown on Figure 3.3 and note that maximum total revenue occurs when price elasticity of demand is equal to one: $e_d = 1$. Along the corresponding small segment of the demand curve the percentage change in price causes an equal percentage change in quantity demanded, so that total revenue neither rises nor falls.

The result is different along other segments of the demand curve. To see why, begin high on the demand curve, where we found price elasticity to be $e_d = 9.09$. With $e_d > 1$, price reductions cause greater percentage increases in quantity demanded; therefore total revenue increases as we move to the right on the quantity axis. Similarly, price increases cause greater percentage decreases in quantity demanded, so that total revenue falls as we move to the left on the quantity axis. The

Figure 3.4a A Linear Demand Curve

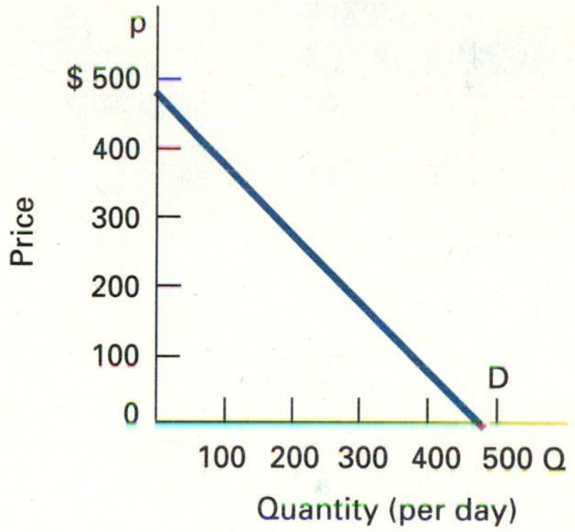

Figure 3.4b Total Revenue from Daily Sales Associated with a Linear Demand Curve

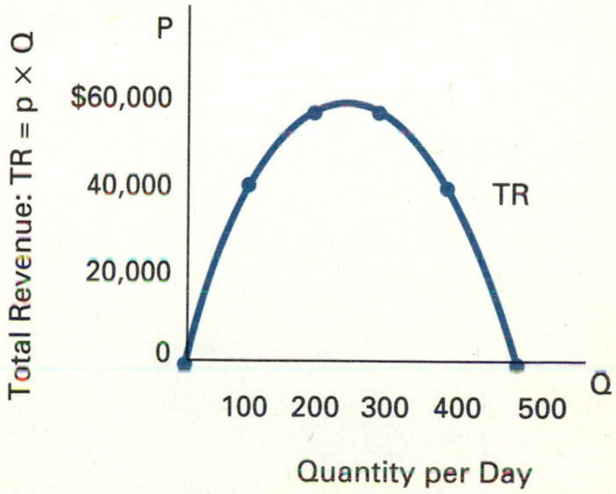

behavior of total revenue reflects the relatively greater responsiveness of quantity demanded to price changes along this segment of the demand curve.

Now look at the lower segment of the demand curve, where $e_d = 0.11$. Percentage price reductions cause smaller percentage increases in quantity demanded, and total revenue falls as we move to the right on the quantity axis. Price increases cause smaller percentage decreases in quantity demanded, so that total revenue increases as we move to the left. The behavior of total revenue reflects the relatively smaller responsiveness of quantity demanded to price changes along this segment of the demand curve.

These results suggest certain conclusions. If a firm has the power to set its own price, it might seek a revenue-maximizing price, with quantity determined at the point on its demand curve where $e_d = 1$. Reducing price to this level will cause greater percentage increases in quantity demanded and increase *TR*. Or, alternatively, raising price to that level will cause smaller decreases in quantity demanded and increase *TR*. Most firms do not have the power to set price, of course. In fact, in this chapter we have assumed that competition exists in the market so that no firm can affect price at all. (We relax that assumption in Chapter 5.) Moreover, for most firms maximum revenue is not itself an appropriate goal. Firms must consider production costs, too (the subject of Chapter 4), and the profit remaining after all costs are paid. This makes maximum profit a more appropriate goal than maximum revenue. We have more to say about a firm's profit later.

Self-Check

1. **Consumer A's demand for pizza is relatively price inelastic. This means that A:**
   a. prefers hamburger to pizza.
   b. buys all the pizza she or he could afford.
   c. will not buy pizza if its price increases.
   d. buys roughly the same amount regardless of price.
   e. responds significantly to price changes for pizza.
2. **Most consumers probably have relatively inelastic demand for:**
   a. Oranges.
   b. Gasoline.
   c. College textbooks.
   d. Filet mignon.
   e. Magazines.
3. **Which of the following has no effect on price elasticity of demand:**
   a. The availability of substitutes.
   b. Total expenditure for the good.
   c. The importance of the good in the consumer's budget.
   d. The time required to develop a substitute for the good.
   e. Whether the good is essential or a luxury.
4. **Price elasticity of demand of −0.5 suggests that:**
   a. Decreasing price would cause total revenue to increase.
   b. The item has many substitutes.
   c. Quantity demanded changes by half the percentage change in price.
   d. Percentage change in price is less than percentage change in quantity.
   e. All are correct.
5. **Which of the following is incorrect:**
   a. A linear demand curve has a price elasticity of one.
   b. A horizontal demand curve is infinitely price elastic.
   c. A vertical demand curve is perfectly price inelastic.
   d. Price elasticity may differ at different points on a demand curve.
   e. Equal percentage changes in price and quantity yield a price elasticity of one.
6. **Total revenue from sales:**
   a. Increases as you move down a linear demand curve.
   b. Decreases as you move down a linear demand curve.
   c. Can be represented by a rectangle drawn beneath a demand curve.
   d. Is zero when the price elasticity is one.
   e. None of the above.

Theory in Practice

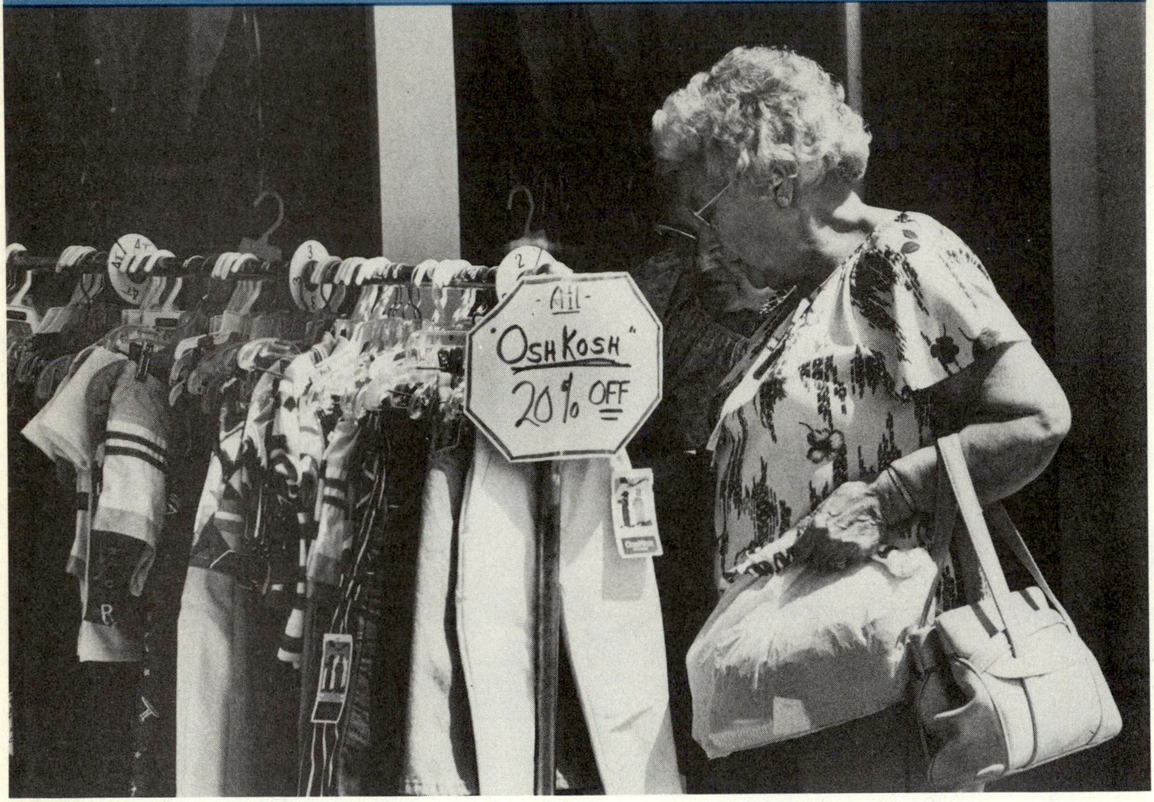

PRACTICE WITH PRICING

We have described how a firm's pricing policy affects its total revenue from sales. Competitive firms normally lack the power to set price. However, there are circumstances where a firm can separate its markets and set different prices according to price elasticity of demand in the separate markets. Imagine a clothing merchant who owns shops in two different parts of town. Currently she sells 200 sweaters a day at a unit price of $25, for total revenue of $TR = p \times Q = \$25 \times 200 = \$5{,}000$. However, she suspects that consumers differ in the two neighborhoods with respect to tastes, incomes, portion of income spent for clothing, and willingness to accept substitutes for her sweaters. In fact, the retailer suspects that consumer demand in one neighborhood is relatively price inelastic: consumers will continue to buy substantially the same quantities regardless of price, so that price elasticity of demand at a unit price of $25 is only $e_d = 0.5$. On the other hand, consumer demand in the other neighborhood is relatively price elastic: Consumers respond significantly to price change, so that price elasticity at a price of $25 is $e_d = 1.5$.

Demand curves representing the two neighborhoods are shown in Figures 3.5a and

Figure 3.5a Price Discrimination; First Market for Clothing

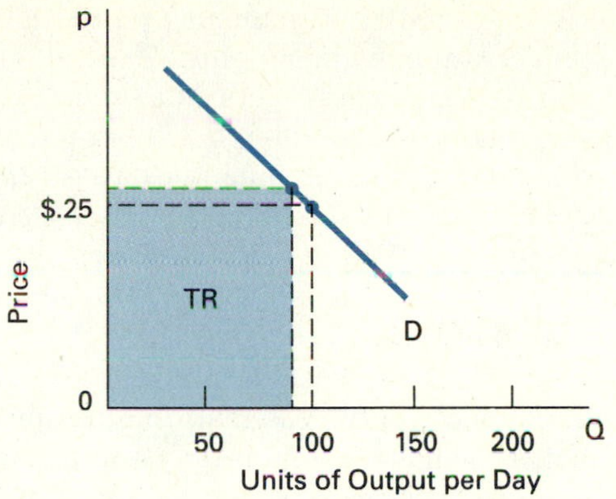

Figure 3.5b Price Discrimination; Second Market for Clothing

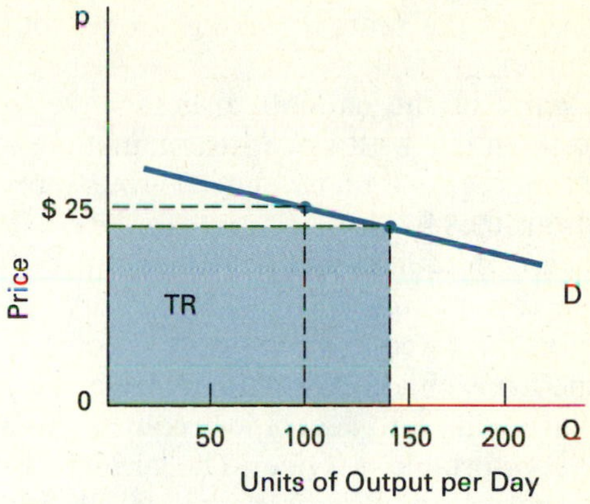

3.5b. For simplicity, we have assumed that half of daily sales are currently being made in each shop at the $25 price, for equal revenues of $2,500.

Now let us change the prices in the two neighborhoods and calculate the effect on total revenue. In the first market, price is below the level of maximum total revenue. (We know this because price elasticity of demand is less than one.) With $e_d = 0.5$, increasing price by 10 percent in this market should reduce quantity demanded by only 0.5(10 percent) = 5 percent. Total revenue in this market would increase to $TR = p \times Q =$ 1.10($25) × 0.95(100) = $2,612.50.

In the second market, price is above the level of maximum total revenue. We know this because, with $e_d = 1.5$, reducing price by 10 percent should increase quantity demanded by 1.5(10 percent) = 15 percent. Total revenue in this market would increase to $TR = p \times Q =$ 0.90($25) × 1.15(100) = $2,587.50.

The shaded rectangles in Figures 3.5a and 3.5b show how total revenue increases when markets are separated and prices are set according to price elasticity of demand. The merchant's new price policy earns total revenue of $2,612.50 + $2,587.50 = $5,200, for an increase of $200 every day. The decrease in quantity demanded in the first market is less than the increase in the second, so that the merchant's total quantity increases to 210 units.

TEST YOURSELF:
What does this example suggest about pricing policies for textbooks versus novels? Explain the difference.

PRICE DISCRIMINATION

The practice we have described is known as **price discrimination.** Merchants frequently practice price discrimination, reducing price in markets with relatively elastic demand and increasing price in markets with relatively inelastic demand. In this way, they approach the point of maximum total revenue in every market.

There is another form of price discrimination when firms separate consumers even more precisely and set different prices for different segments of a single demand curve.

Price differentials of this sort are common for tickets to cultural and sporting events. The basis for separating consumers may be the location of the seats or the age or sex of the consumer.

Many of the nation's airlines have been experimenting with price discrimination as a way to increase total revenue. Throughout the 1980s airlines faced rising costs for labor, fuel, and capital equipment. Revenues did not increase fast enough to pay a satisfactory return on funds invested in the industry. Today many airline firms charge lower fares for passengers who are willing to accept less convenient and less comfortable service. The airlines hope that enough new passengers will buy the lower-priced tickets to offset the lower price each passenger pays.

Figure 3.6 shows a hypothetical demand curve for seats on an airplane for a typical day. There are 200 seats, and the airline would like to "sell" the seats at prices that will yield the most revenue per day. Let 50 seats be designated "First Class," and provide First Class passengers with plenty of comfortable leg room, champagne and lobster for dinner, and attentive stewards. Some passengers will be willing to pay $100 for First Class service. Designate the remaining seats "Tourist Class" and serve Tourist Class passengers baked chicken for a price of $75. Total revenue is *TR* = $100 × number of First Class passengers (maximum 50) plus $75 × number of Tourist Class passengers (maximum 150), for maximum revenue of $16,250 per day.

Maximum total revenue per day is represented by the shaded rectangles under the demand curve in Figure 3.6. Total revenue is price times quantity sold, shown by the height and width of the two rectangles.

Unless all the seats are sold each day, total revenue will be less than the maximum. In fact, if demand is relatively price inelastic over this price range, only a certain number of tickets will be sold regardless of the difference in ticket prices. In Figure 3.7 only 30 First Class passengers and 100 Tourist Class passengers yield total revenue of ($100 × 30) + ($75 × 100) = $10,500. Notice the smaller shaded area when only 130 seats are sold per day.

Consider the situation if demand is relatively price elastic at lower prices. Let the First Class and Tourist passengers fly at the stated rates and then open the remaining seats to "No Frills" passengers at a price of only

Figure 3.6 Airline Revenues with "First Class" and "Tourist" Fares

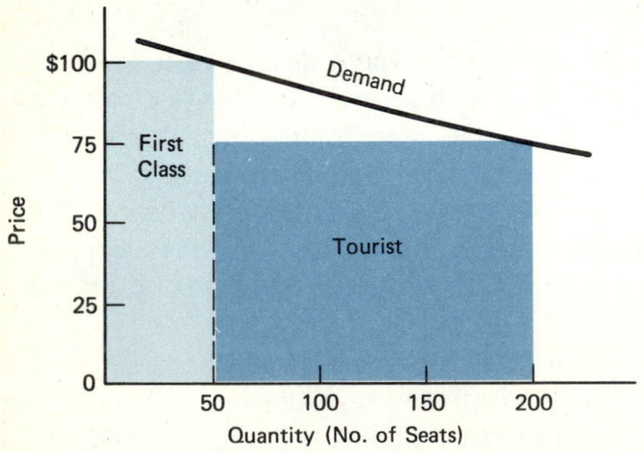

Figure 3.7 Airline Revenues with "First Class" and "No Frills" Fares

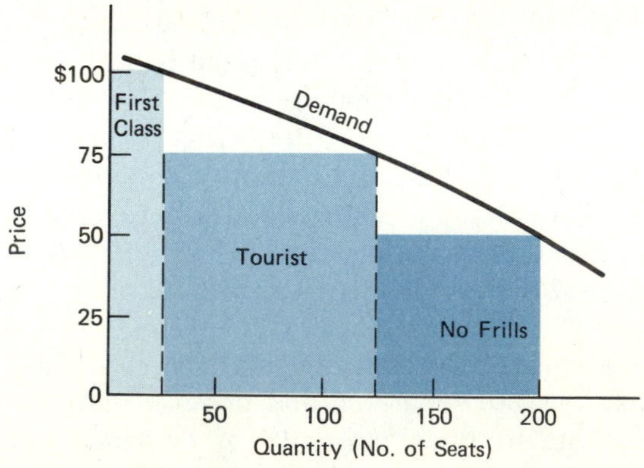

$50. No Frills passengers are unceremoniously dispatched to the rear of the plane and served no food or drink at all. If the remaining seats are filled at the lowest rate, revenue increases by $50 × 70 = $3,500, for a total of $10,500 + $3,500 = $14,000 per day. Unless the firm can fill its planes with First Class and Tourist passengers, it would seem to be an advantage to offer No Frills tickets. Total revenue will increase by the added rectangle in Figure 3.7.

The experiment in pricing turned out well for some airlines. The results seemed to show that demand for air travel is relatively price inelastic at high prices and price elastic at low prices. Regular travelers had to purchase tickets regardless of price, but many new passengers decided to take a trip just because air fares were reduced. (Why? Remember the factors that determine elasticity.) The airlines were able to fill more of their seats with passengers paying various rates, and total revenue increased.

Experiments with elasticity can be profitable!

PRACTICE DECIDING TAX POLICY

Governments consider price elasticity of demand when they add an excise tax to the price of a consumer good. Generally, the taxed item should have price inelastic demand. Otherwise, consumers will not buy nearly as much at the higher price, and the government will not collect much revenue.

How would you describe price elasticity of demand for cigarettes? Are smokers likely to respond to price changes by buying either substantially more or fewer cigarettes?

Apparently governments believe that the demand for cigarettes is relatively price inelastic. The demand curve in Figure 3.8 is drawn on the assumption that smokers will not respond very much to price changes. At a price of $20 per carton, quantity demanded is 4,000 cartons. Notice the rectangle representing total expenditure at $20: total expenditure = quantity demanded × market price = 4,000 × $20 = $80,000.

Figure 3.8 Hypothetical Demand Curve for Cigarettes

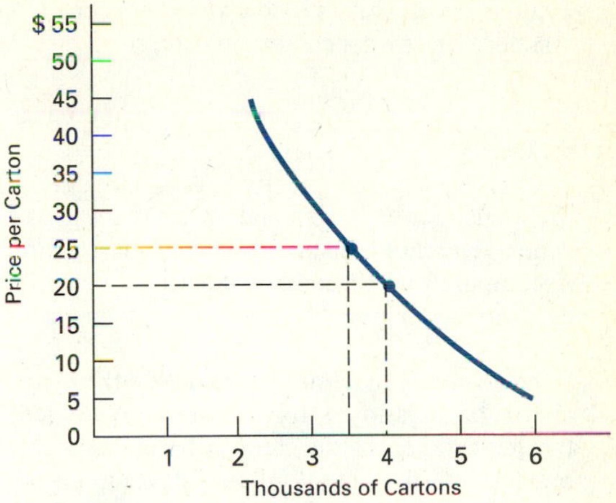

Now suppose government imposes a tax that adds $5 per carton to price. At the new price of $25, quantity demanded is 3,500 cartons. Notice the rectangle representing total expenditure: 3,500 × $25 = $87,500. Mark off the rectangle that represents government's **cigarette tax revenue:** tax revenue = quantity demanded × tax = 3,500 × $5 = $17,500.

With the excise tax, consumer expenditures for cigarettes increase from $80,000 to $87,500, but producers' share of revenue falls. Producers still receive $20 per carton, but they sell only 3,500 cartons for revenue of 3,500 × $20 = $70,000. Mark off the rectangle representing producers' revenue before the tax and the rectangle representing consumer expenditures after the tax.

TEST YOURSELF

Compare government tax revenues from a cigarette tax with tax revenues from a tax on a good with relatively price elastic demand (like cheese). How might the demand curve for cheese differ from the demand curve for cigarettes? How would you describe the tax collections rectangle?

SUMMARY

1. Price elasticity of demand measures the responsiveness of consumers to price changes. It is computed as percentage change in quantity demanded divided by percentage change in price.
2. Price elasticity of demand depends on the availability of substitutes for the good or service, the importance of the item in the consumer's budget, and the time it takes to develop a substitute.
3. A horizontal demand curve has zero percentage change in price; therefore, its price elasticity of demand is infinite. A vertical demand curve has zero percentage change in quantity; therefore, its price elasticity is zero, or perfectly elastic.
4. On a linear demand curve, price elasticity varies from high (at high prices) to low (at low prices). Maximum total revenue occurs at the price and quantity where $e_d = 1$. A revenue-maximizing firm observes the following rule: If $e_d > 1$, reduce price for greater total revenue; if $e_d < 1$, increase price for greater total revenue.
5. Some firms practice price discrimination in separate markets to take advantage of differences in price elasticity. In markets where price elasticity of demand is less than one, firms increase price to increase total revenue; in markets where price elasticity is greater than one, firms reduce price to increase total revenue.
6. Some firms increase total revenue by setting not one single price but a series of prices. Their objective is to collect all (or almost all) of the revenue represented by the area beneath the demand curve.
7. Governments consider price elasticity of demand when imposing a tax. Because demand for cigarettes is relatively price inelastic, cigarettes are often taxed.

TERMS TO REMEMBER

price elasticity of demand: the responsiveness of quantity demanded to changes in the price of a good or service

elastic demand: having a quantity demanded that responds to change in price; percentage change in quantity demanded is greater than percentage change in price

inelastic demand: having a quantity demanded that responds very little to change in price; percentage change in quantity demanded is less than percentage change in price

price elastic: condition in which percentage change in quantity is greater than percentage change in price

price inelastic: condition in which percentage change in quantity is less than percentage change in price

total revenue: price times quantity sold; or the sum of all prices times quantities sold at various prices

elasticity ratio: $\%\Delta Q_d / \%\Delta p$

price discrimination: the practice of setting different prices in different markets, generally on the basis of differences in price elasticity of demand

cigarette tax revenue: number of units sold times tax levied on each unit

TOPICS FOR DISCUSSION

1. The data below describe a linear demand curve. Construct a table that enables you to calculate price elasticity of demand at four intervals along the demand curve. Then locate the price at which total revenue would be maximized. Explain your answer.

PRICE	*QUANTITY*
10	10
8	14
6	18
4	22
2	26

2. What characteristics of each of the following

would determine its price elasticity of demand:

insulin
automobile tires
fresh fruit
house paint
soft drinks
a visit to the dentist's office
vintage wine
sports cars

3. Explain the basis for the distinctive shape of the total revenue curve associated with linear demand curves.
4. Make a list of items whose purchase is generally taxed. What economic characteristic do such items share? Illustrate your answer graphically and explain.
5. Old Reliable Air Service reduced its intercity fare from $37.50 to $35.00 and increased ticket sales from 120 to 160 for the week. Compute Reliable's price elasticity of demand. Was the price change a wise move? Explain. Should Reliable continue to reduce price? Why or why not?
6. What circumstances must be true for price discrimination to benefit a retailer? Why?
7. What considerations might affect a city's decision to levy a sales tax? Why might the city decide to exempt food from the tax? Medicine?
8. Compare price elasticity of demand for various kinds of restaurant meals: fast foods, ethnic foods, elegant dining. What steps do restaurants take to affect price elasticity of demand?
9. Would universities benefit from the practice of price discrimination? Explain the advantages and disadvantages.
10. This chapter has focused on price elasticity of demand. Economists are also interested in income elasticity of demand. Construct a definition and a formula for income elasticity of demand. Then discuss the implications of income elasticity of demand for particular industries and employments.

ANSWERS TO TEST YOURSELF

(p. 65) Because textbooks are typically assigned for the course, students' demand curves are relatively price inelastic. Price may be set higher than the price of a comparable novel, which consumers can buy or not as they choose.

(p. 67) If demand for cheese is relatively price elastic, the higher price causes a greater percentage decrease in quantity demanded. The result is lower total expenditures for cheese and lower tax collections for the government.

FURTHER READING

Akerlof, George A., "The Market for 'Lemons'," in *An Economic Theorist's Book of Tales,* Cambridge University Press, Cambridge, 1984.

Becker, Gary S., "The Economic Approach to Human Behavior," in *The Economic Approach to Human Behavior,* Chicago University Press, Chicago, 1976.

Brunner, Karl, and William H. Meckling, "The Perception of Man and the Conception of Government," in *Readings in Public Sector Economics,* Catherine Elliot and Sam Baker, eds., Heath, 1990.

Chaloupka, Frank, "Rational Addictive Behavior and Cigarette Smoking," *Journal of Political Economy,* April, 1991.

Heyne, Paul, *The Economic Way of Thinking,* 6th ed., Macmillan, 1991.

Medoff, Marshall H., *Economic Inquiry,* April, 1988.

Nardinelli, Clark, and Curtis J. Simon, "Customer Racial Discrimination in the Market for Memorabilia: The Case of Baseball," *Quarterly Journal of Economics,* August 1990.

Veblin, Thorstein, *The Theory of the Leisure Class,* 1899.

Chapter 4

More About Supply: Costs of Production and Price Elasticity of Supply

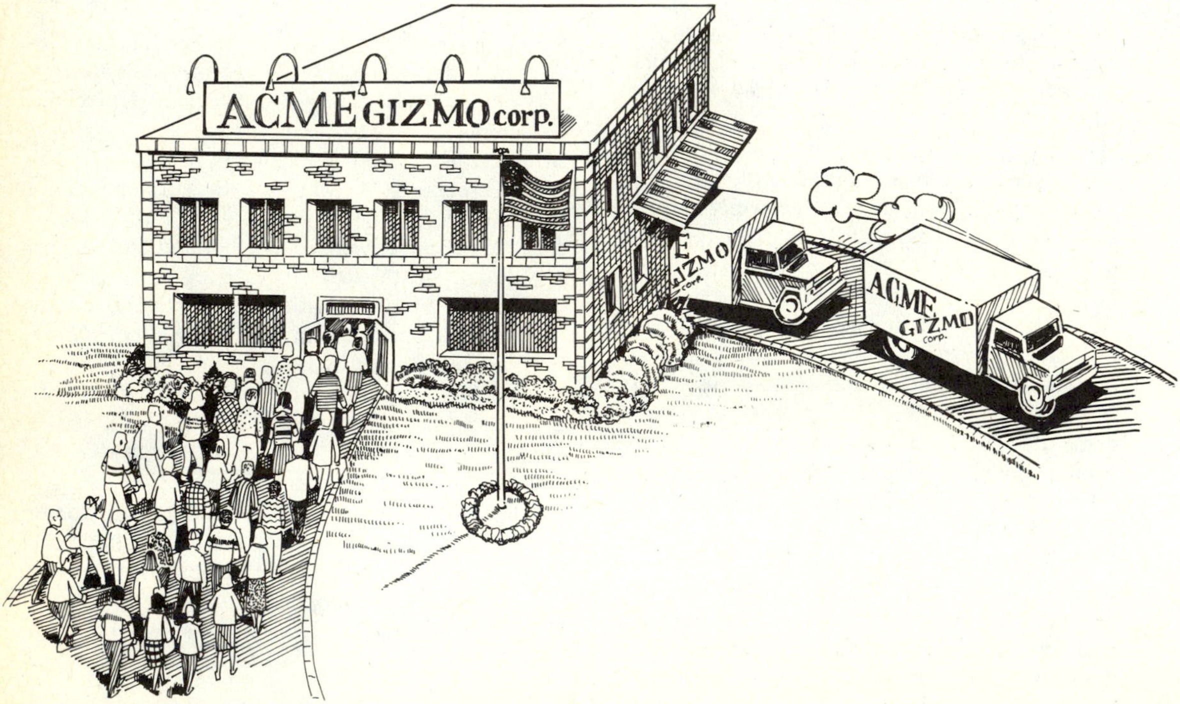

Tools for Study

LEARNING OBJECTIVES

After reading this chapter, you will be able to:

1. Define and describe the behavior of costs of production.
2. Show how costs of production determine the position and shape of supply curves.
3. Distinguish between normal profit and economic profit.
4. Explain how firms in competition decide the profit-maximizing quantity to supply.

CURRENT ISSUES FOR DISCUSSION

How can firms justify continuing to supply output for prices that yield losses?

In Chapter 3 we examined demand curves in detail. We described the circumstances that affect the shape and position of demand curves. In this chapter we focus on the circumstances that affect supply curves and, in particular, the forces that make the invisible hand work.

The invisible hand guides business firms to produce the things consumers want with the least expenditure of scarce resources. (We have called that result *efficient*.) In order to do its job, the invisible hand must have information about costs of production. A firm's costs of production reflect its use of scarce resources and define the price the firm must receive for its product if it is to remain in business.

MARKET SUPPLY

A producer's response to consumer demand is shown by his or her supply schedule. A *supply schedule* shows the quantities of a good or service that would be offered for sale at various prices during a particular period of time. Every firm in the industry may be expected to have a supply schedule which, when added to the supply schedules of all other firms, constitutes *market supply*. When a supply schedule is plotted on a graph, the result is a supply curve for the designated period of time.

DERIVING A FIRM'S SUPPLY CURVE

Understanding costs of production is essential for understanding a firm's supply curve. (Production cannot be carried on for long unless the firm earns enough revenue from sales to pay its costs of production.) Business firms employ accountants, whose job is to calculate the costs that must be paid to the firm's suppliers, workers, and owners. These costs are included in the firm's accounting costs, but they are not quite the same as the costs that concern economists. When viewed from the standpoint of economics, costs of production include the opportunity costs of all resources used to produce the firm's product, whether or not the cost is actually paid to a supplier, worker, or owner. In this section we look at **economic costs** in detail.

To begin, we will note that economic costs behave differently according to the time spans in which they occur: the **short run** or the **long run.** The short run is a period of time in which certain resources are fixed in quantity and quality and cannot be changed. Buildings and equipment are generally considered fixed in the short run. They are fixed, but they can be combined with various quantities of other resources that are not fixed—such as labor, materials, and electric power—to produce various quantities of output. The resources that can be varied in the short run are called variable resources. The long run is a period of time in which all resources are variable. The quantities of buildings and equipment are variable in the long run, when they can be increased or decreased along with the quantities of labor, materials, and electric power.

In the following sections, we discuss the behavior of economic costs in the short run. Then we look at the long run and the differences in the behavior of costs when all resources are variable.

Economic Costs and Economic Profit

Economic costs can be measured in terms of the opportunity cost of resources provided for use in production:

The opportunity cost of labor is measured in terms of wages or salaries.

The opportunity cost of land is measured in terms of rent.

The opportunity cost of capital is measured in terms of interest.

The opportunity cost of entrepreneurship is measured in terms of profit.

The last cost item requires further explanation. To understand profit we must distinguish between the necessary profit that measures the opportunity cost of an entrepreneurial resource and a payment over and above the necessary profit. Some level of profit is necessary to compensate entrepreneurs for the opportunity cost of the entrepreneurial resource. The necessary profit is called **normal profit,** and an extra profit over and above the necessary amount is what economists call **economic profit.** Because normal profit is a necessary payment to the entrepreneurial resource, it is considered a part of economic costs. Thus, when we speak of economic costs, we are speaking of wages and salaries, rent, interest, and normal profit:

$$\text{economic costs} = \text{wages} + \text{rent} + \text{interest} + \text{normal profit}$$

If a firm's revenue from sales exceeds the sum of its economic costs, we say that the firm has received economic profit:

$$\text{total revenue} - \text{economic costs} = \text{economic profit}$$

Most firms have as an objective to maximize economic profit or, in other words, to maximum the difference between total revenue and the sum of economic costs. Maximum economic profit occurs when the firm follows the profit-maximizing rule:

TO MAXIMIZE PROFITS A FIRM MUST EXPAND PRODUCTION UNTIL PRODUCTION AND SALE OF THE LAST UNIT INCREASES TOTAL REVENUE BY JUST ENOUGH TO OFFSET THE INCREASE IN TOTAL COST.

To understand the profit-maximizing rule, we look more closely at economic costs. We have said that economic costs measure the opportunity cost of resources used in production. Economic costs can be classified in two ways, depending on their behavior as output increases. The two kinds of costs are **fixed costs** and **variable costs**, and they depend on the firm's use of fixed resources and variable resources. Fixed costs are the costs of the firm's fixed resources, and fixed costs stay the same in the short run regardless of how many units of output are produced. Variable costs are the costs of variable resources, and variable costs change as quantity of output changes.

Fixed Costs

Fixed costs occur only in the short run. Remember that the short run is a period of time in which certain of a firm's resources are fixed—resources that include buildings and equipment and even managerial personnel. Buildings and equipment are owned or leased for a particular period of time, and managerial personnel have contracts for work over a particular period. Whether or not the firm produces any output at all during this period of time, the costs of its fixed resources must be paid. Increasing the quantity of output above zero during the short run permits the firm to spread its fixed costs over larger and larger quantities of output. The result is that average fixed cost (or fixed cost for each unit of output) falls with quantity of output.

The concept of fixed cost is illustrated in Figure 4.1, using Metro Music, producer of compact discs, as an example. For the short run Metro Music has fixed resources for which charges of $1000 must be paid, whether or not the firm produces any output at all. Fixed cost is shown on Figure 4.1a. For any quantity of compact discs produced during this period of time, average or unit fixed cost is AFC = FC/Q, as shown on Figure 4.1b. Average fixed cost is high for small quantities and diminishes for larger quantities of output (Q).

Figure 4.1a Fixed Costs

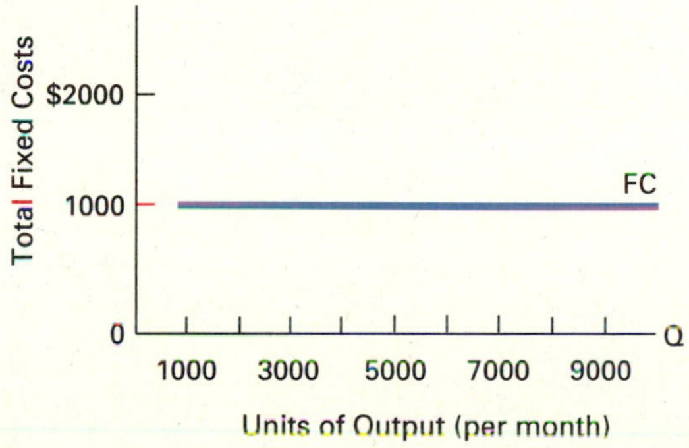

Figure 4.1b Average Fixed Costs

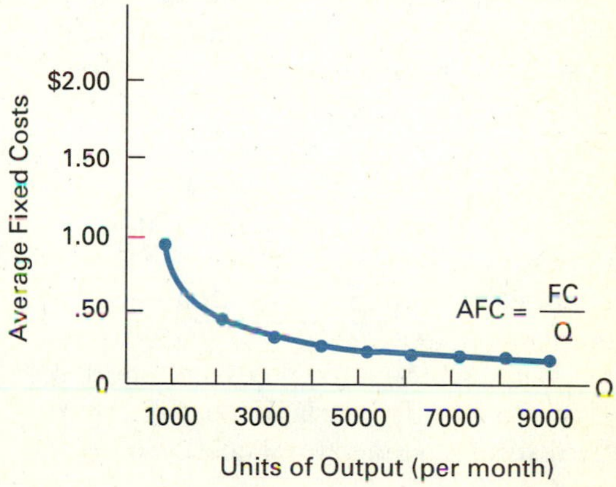

Variable Costs

Variable costs are payments for the variable resources that are used along with the firm's existing fixed resources. Examples of variable resources are labor, materials, electric power, and water. Increasing production above zero in the short run requires the firm to employ additional quantities of variable resources and pay additional variable costs.

Generally, there is some range over which producing additional units of output requires proportionally smaller additional quantities of variable resources. The reason has to do with the technical design of the firm's fixed plant and equipment. Most manufacturing plants are designed to produce a certain quantity or range of quantities over a particular period of time. For this range of production, variable resource requirements per unit of output tend to fall. When average variable resource requirements fall, average variable cost will fall as well. If production is expanded beyond this range, variable resource requirements will tend to increase more than proportionally to output. With rising average variable resource requirements, average variable cost will also increase.

The typical behavior of average variable cost in the short run is shown in Figure 4.2. Variable cost per unit tends to fall in the short run as quantity of output increases. We say that production becomes more efficient. The most efficient, lowest-cost level of production for Metro Music's plant and equipment appears to be around 3000 compact discs per month. If quantity of output increases beyond 3000 units in the short run, variable cost per unit tends to increase. Beyond the lowest-cost level of production, production becomes less and less efficient.

When average fixed cost in Figure 4.1b is added to average variable cost in Figure 4.2, the result is average total cost, shown on Figure 4.3.

Figure 4.2 Average Variable Cost

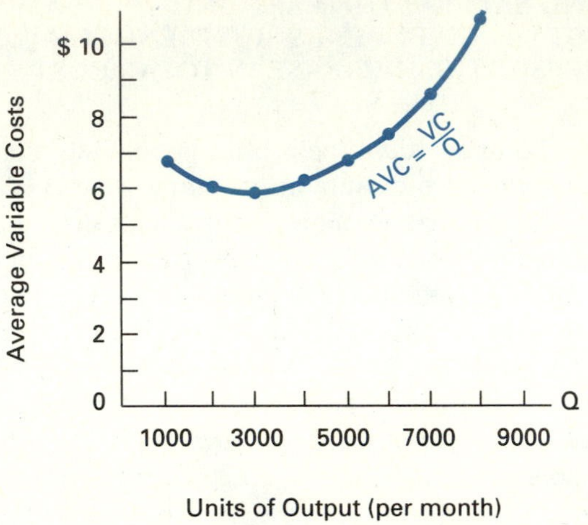

Figure 4.3 Average Total Cost

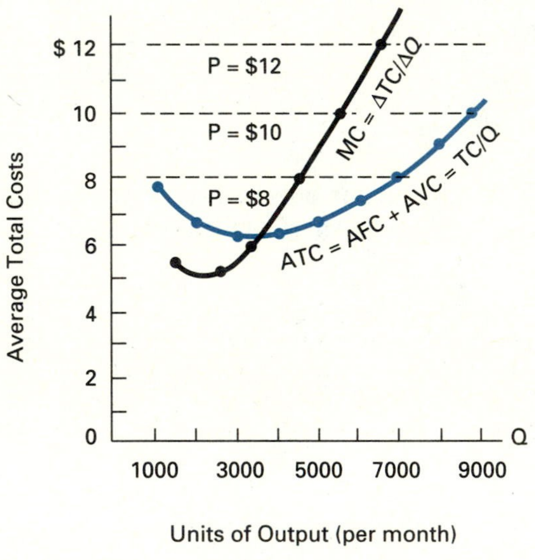

Cost Data

The data for drawing Figures 4.1, 4.2, and 4.3 are listed in Table 4.1. Column (2) lists Metro Music's constant fixed cost for all quantities

Table 4.1 Metro Music's Cost Data.

(1) Q Output per Month	*(2) FC* Fixed Cost	*(3) AFC* Average Fixed Cost	*(4) VC* Variable Cost	*(5) AVC* Average Variable Cost	*(6) TC* Total Cost	*(7) ATC* Average Total Cost	*(8) MC* Marginal Cost
1000	1000	1.00	6800	6.80	7800	7.80	
2000	1000	.50	12,000	6.00	13,000	6.50	5.20
3000	1000	.33	17,000	5.67	18,000	6.00	5.00
4000	1000	.25	23,000	5.75	24,000	6.00	6.00
5000	1000	.20	31,000	6.20	32,000	6.40	8.00
6000	1000	.17	41,000	6.83	42,000	7.00	10.00
7000	1000	.14	53,000	7.57	54,000	7.71	12.00
8000	1000	.125	67,000	8.38	68,000	8.50	14.00
9000	1000	.11	91,000	10.11	92,000	10.22	24.00

of compact discs (Q) in the short run. Column (3) shows how average fixed cost declines for larger quantities of CDs shown in Column (1). Column (4) shows total variable cost for various levels of CD production, and Column (5) shows average variable cost $AVC = VC/Q$, as production becomes more efficient, most efficient, and less efficient.

Study the cost data carefully. Notice that average variable cost declines as production increases to 3000 CDs. The technical design of Metro Music's fixed plant and equipment makes production most efficient at about 3000 CDs per month. Beyond production of 3000 CDs, production becomes less efficient, and average variable cost rises. Total cost in Column (6) is the sum of Columns (2) and (4).

Average total cost in Column (7) is $ATC = TC/Q$ or $AFC + AVC$. Notice the behavior of average total cost. The decline and eventual rise of *ATC* is a result of the continuous decline in *AFC* and the eventual rise in *AVC*. Understanding average total cost is necessary for determining a firm's economic profit (or loss) per unit of output. By subtracting average total cost from the product's selling price, a firm calculates its average, or unit, economic profit. Thus:

$$p - ATC = \text{average economic profit (or loss)}$$

Make certain you understand fixed and variable resources and their costs before you go on to the next section.

Marginal Cost

Column (8) in Table 4.1 introduces a new cost concept that is necessary for determining supply in the short run: **marginal cost.** Marginal cost is the *change in* total cost associated with producing a single additional unit of output: $MC = \Delta TC/\Delta Q$. The values in Column (8) are calculated by subtracting successive *TC* values in Column (6) and dividing by $\Delta Q = 1000$ units from Column (1). Since *MC* is associated with *changes in* quantity of output, the data are entered between the lines in the table.

The behavior of *MC* reflects changes in variable resource requirements associated with production at less than or greater than the most efficient operation of the firm's fixed plant and equipment.

To illustrate changes in total costs, we have added a marginal cost curve to Figure 4.3. Notice that *MC* declines as the level of production increases from zero to some relatively small quantity. The declining *MC* curve tells us that smaller additional quantities of variable resources are needed to produce additional units of output. As production approaches the most efficient, lowest-cost quantity of output at $Q = 3000$, MC begins to rise. Larger additional quantities of variable resources are needed to produce additional output. Still, until production reaches $Q = 3000$, MC is less than ATC and pulls ATC down. When production expands beyond the most efficient level, even larger additional quantities of variable resources are needed to produce additional units of output. Beyond the most efficient level of production, MC rises above ATC and begins to pull ATC up.

Marginal Revenue and Quantity Supplied

Now we are ready to derive Metro Music's supply curve for compact discs. Remember the profit-maximizing firm's rule for determining supply:

TO MAXIMIZE PROFIT A FIRM MUST EXPAND PRODUCTION UNTIL PRODUCTION AND SALE OF THE LAST UNIT INCREASES TOTAL REVENUE BY JUST ENOUGH TO OFFSET THE INCREASE IN TOTAL COST.

Because marginal cost represents additions to costs as output increases, following the profit-maximizing rule requires information about marginal cost. Any unit of output that adds less to total cost than it adds to total revenue increases Metro Music's profit in the short run and should be produced. In fact, a profit-maximizing firm like Metro Music should increase production as long as the marginal cost of one more unit is less than the added revenue it brings in.

Now we want to compare increases in total costs with increases in total revenue. We define a firm's additional revenue from sales as **marginal revenue.** Marginal revenue is the change in total revenue associated with production and sale of an additional unit: Marginal Revenue = $MR = \Delta TR/\Delta Q$. For firms in competition, the additional revenue from additional sales is the current market price. This is because in competition price is set by the market, and no firm is large enough to affect price. Understanding this allows us to say:

$$\begin{aligned} \text{additional revenue} &= \text{marginal revenue} \\ &= \text{price and} \\ MR &= p \end{aligned}$$

Comparing marginal cost with marginal revenue enables Metro Music to make its supply decision. In fact, if $MR > MC$, Metro Music should follow the profit-maximizing rule and increase production. This is because marginal revenue greater than marginal cost indicates that the next unit sold adds more to revenue than it adds to costs. Therefore, producing the next unit causes the firm's economic profit to increase. On the other hand, if $MR < MC$, Metro Music should follow the profit-maximizing rule and reduce production. Marginal revenue less than marginal cost indicates that the next unit adds less to revenue than it adds to costs. Therefore, producing the next unit causes the firm's economic profit to fall. And finally, only if $MR = MC$ is Metro Music producing the profit-maximizing quantity of output. Marginal revenue equal to marginal cost indicates that the last unit sold adds just enough revenue to cover its additional cost. This is the profit-maximizing quantity of output in the short run.

We can summarize the profit-maximizing conditions this way:

If $MR > MC$, increase production.
If $MR < MC$, reduce production.
If $MR = MC$, continue to produce at this level.

Look again at Figure 4.3 and Metro Music's MC curve. Horizontal lines drawn at \$8, \$10, and \$12 indicate possible selling prices for compact discs when the CDs are sold in competitive markets. The profit-maximizing quantity at each price is the quantity shown on the *MC* curve where $p = MR = MC$. Thus, at a price of p = \$8.00 Metro Music should supply Q = 4500 compact discs; when p = \$5.00, Q = 5500; when p = \$6, Q = 6500; and so forth. For any other price not indicated by a horizontal line (p = \$6.50, \$5.75, \$4.25, etc.) the profit-maximizing quantity may be read from the *MC* curve.

The Shutdown Point

Reading quantity from the *MC* curve allows us (almost) to treat *MC* as Metro Music's short-run supply curve. Points high on the *MC* curve indicate a firm's willingness to sell at high prices with, most probably, economic profit for the supplying firm. At some point on the *MC* curve, price would be just high enough to cover the firm's average total costs, including normal profit but no economic profit. Points low on the *MC* curve indicate prices below the firm's *ATC*, but such prices may not discourage the firm from offering goods for sale. Such points may still be on the firm's supply curve even though they yield negative economic profit (or loss): $p - ATC$ = average economic profit < zero. Whether or not a below-cost price appears on a firm's supply curve depends on the nature of the costs included in that price.

To understand this point, consider a point low on Metro Music's marginal cost curve, with production of 2500 units at a price of p = \$5.00. With price less than *ATC* = \$6.25, the firm would experience negative economic profit, or loss, of \$5.00 − \$6.25 = − \$1.25 for each unit produced and sold. Losses may be acceptable in the short run under certain conditions.* The important condition is that price must be high enough to cover average variable cost.

Remember that fixed cost must be paid in the short run, regardless of whether the firm earns economic profit. For Metro Music to produce no output at all would involve short-run losses amounting to the entire fixed cost: *FC* = \$1000. However, production of any quantity of output for which price at least covers *AVC* would yield some revenue for reducing the loss associated with Metro Music's fixed cost. Therefore, a price of \$5.00 is not necessarily unacceptable in the short run. The question is whether p = \$5.00 does, in fact, cover Metro Music's average variable cost.

Look at Table 4.1 at about Q = 2500, where *MC* = \$5.00. Production of 2500 units per month would involve variable cost of between \$5.67 and \$6.00. This means that in addition to short-run losses of *FC* = \$1000, Metro Music would incur losses of between \$.67 and \$1.00 for each unit produced, attributable to average variable costs. With price less than average variable cost, every unit produced and sold increases the firm's negative economic profit (or loss). In fact, the lowest price for which Metro Music should produce CDs in the short run would be \$5.67, a price that just covers variable cost at its lowest point. At a price of \$5.67 the firm's maximum economic loss would be its fixed cost of *FC* = \$1000 per month.

We might identify p = \$5.67 as Metro Music's **shutdown point** in the short run. Production will be carried on in the short run only if price is at least as great as \$5.67, and the profit-maximizing quantity is shown on the *MC* = supply curve. Prices greater than \$6.00 would enable Metro Music to earn economic profit. Prices between \$5.67 and \$6.00 would involve economic loss, but short-run losses would not exceed *FC* = \$1000. We have said that Metro Music's *MC* curve is (almost) its short-run supply curve. Now we see that Metro Music's supply curve is the portion of *MC* that lies above Metro Music's shut-down point at its minimum acceptable price.

At the end of Metro Music's short run, for

* A number of firms experienced short-run losses in the 1990s: Chrysler, Ford, the former Pan American Airlines.

which certain resources are fixed, the firm would want to reconsider its participation in this market. If short-run losses have occurred and are expected to continue, Metro Music should consider leaving this business. Continuing losses would indicate that the firm's resources might be better employed elsewhere. On the other hand, if production has yielded economic profit, Metro Music might want to expand its capacity to produce even greater output.

Decisions to expand or contract a firm's productive capacity are called **long-run decisions.** Long-run decisions involve increasing or decreasing the firm's fixed resources, and they depend on the firm's expectations of market conditions in the long run. We have more to say about long-run decisions later.

The Short-Run Supply Curve

Metro Music's short-run supply curve has been drawn again as Figure 4.4. At prices lower than \$5.67 the firm will produce zero output and suffer losses equal to fixed cost of \$1000. At a price of \$5.67, the firm will produce and sell 3000 CDs per month. It will produce and sell as many as 6000 CDs if price is at least \$10.00.

Figure 4.4 Metro Music's Supply Curve

Metro Music's supply curve is its marginal cost curve above the shutdown point.

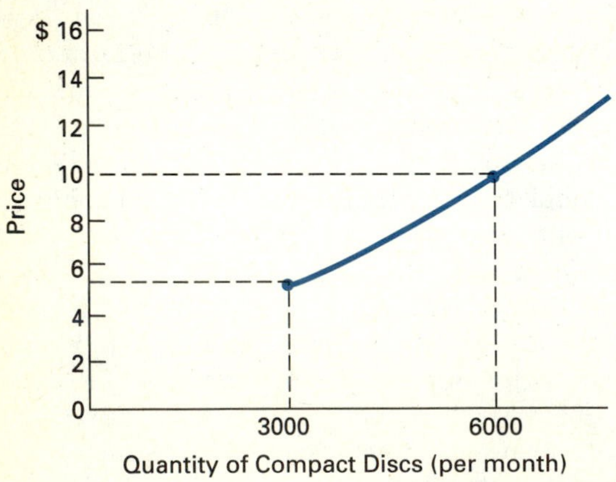

PRICE ELASTICITY OF SUPPLY

In Chapter 3 we described demand curves in terms of price elasticity of demand. As you might have expected, it is also possible to describe supply curves in terms of price elasticity.

Price elasticity of supply measures the responsiveness of suppliers to changes in the price of a good or service. It is defined as the percentage change in quantity supplied relative to a percentage change in price:

$$\text{price elasticity of supply} = e_s = \%\Delta Q_s \,/\, \%\Delta p$$

Because quantity supplied in the short run depends on marginal cost, the responsiveness of suppliers to price changes depends strongly on the behavior of marginal cost. For some goods, marginal cost rises fairly quickly as more units are produced. This means that larger quantities can be offered for sale only if price rises substantially, and supply is not very responsive to small price changes. In such cases, percentage change in quantity is low relative to percentage change in price. Economists describe supply for such goods as price inelastic: quantity supplied is not very responsive to price changes. When supply is price inelastic, supply curves slope upward rather steeply.*

For other goods, quantity supplied can be increased with little increase in marginal cost

* Remember we pointed out in Chapter 3 that the slope of a demand curve depends also on the horizontal scale. The same is true of the slope of a supply curve.

THINKING SERIOUSLY ABOUT ECONOMIC ISSUES

HYPERMARKETS

What's bigger than a supermarket? Would you believe a hypermarket?

About a dozen U.S. cities now have markets as large as eight ordinary supermarkets—stores so big they could hold almost six football fields. (A typical supermarket would hold only about two-thirds of a football field.)

Hypermarkets offer their customers tremendous variety in fresh vegetables, meat and seafoods, prepared foods, baked goods, and desserts. On the other hand, they are tremendously expensive to build, staff, and stock. To pay its high fixed cost a hypermarket requires a large volume of business: At least 500,000 customers within a 20-minute drive are necessary to push average fixed cost down to a level that permits the firm to earn a profit. Most metropolitan areas lack the potential market to make a hypermarket profitable.

To offset its many food items that contribute little to profit, a hypermarket must stock many items for which price is substantially greater than average total cost. It must also turn over its low-profit items frequently, so that a large volume of sales creates large total profits.

How would the cost curves of a hypermarket differ from the typical cost curves shown in this text? Why might it profit a hypermarket to have a restaurant, even if the restaurant operates at a loss?

and correspondingly smaller increases in price. Percentage change in quantity supplied is large relative to percentage change in price. When suppliers respond readily to small price changes, supply is said to be price elastic. Supply curves slope upward less steeply for goods whose supply is price elastic.

What Determines Price Elasticity of Supply?

Price elasticity of supply depends on how quickly firms can change quantity when price changes. We have seen that the responsiveness of suppliers to price depends strongly on marginal cost; that is, the additional cost of increasing production with the firm's existing fixed plant and equipment. Here are some other factors that affect price elasticity of supply:

1. Price elasticity of supply also depends on the time required to increase or decrease fixed resources or to enter or leave the industry. It takes longer to expand production of steel than fast-foods, for example. Therefore, we would expect firms producing fast foods to respond more readily to price changes than firms producing steel.
2. Price elasticity of supply depends strongly on the storability of the item. A product's storability determines whether it can be stockpiled when price is low and brought to market later when price is high. There-

fore, storability determines how quickly firms can change quantity when price changes.

TEST YOURSELF

Consider the following groups of items. How would you describe the responsiveness of supply to changes in price? Ask yourself: Can firms produce much more if price rises or less if price falls? How flexible are production plans of suppliers? Is the product easily storable?

1. Strawberries, milk, eggs, beef.
2. Sweaters, autos, potato chips.
3. Gold, coal, lumber.
4. Transistors, screwdrivers, stained-glass windows.
5. Autos in the 1920s and autos in the 1990s.

Self-Check

1. Economic costs include all but which one of the following?
a. Charges for repairing the firm's truck.
b. Interest on a loan from the company president's father.
c. Rent on a warehouse owned by the company president.
d. A required payment to the entrepreneur who set up the company.
e. An extra return resulting from abnormally high product prices.

2. Which of the following statements is correct?
a. If $MC > MR$, the firm should expand production.
b. As long as $MR > MC$, the firm should expand production.
c. Production should not be carried on if $p < ATC$.
d. Shutdown will occur if p falls below AFC.
e. A firm may decide not to pay fixed costs in the short run.

3. Fixed costs
a. Occur only in the long run.
b. Decrease with quantity of output.
c. Depend on quantity of output in the short run.
d. All of the above.
e. None of the above.

4. XYZ Pizza Parlor's supply of pizza is price elastic. This probably means:
a. It has facilities for producing large quantities.
b. Supply is responsive to price changes.
c. It would cut back production significantly if price fell.
d. Increasing production would not significantly affect unit costs.
e. All of the above.

5. Average economic profit or loss
a. Is equal to $AVC - p$.
b. Is equal to $p - MC$.
c. Is the change in profit associated with a unit change in output.
d. Increases with quantity of output.
e. Is the difference between price and average total cost.

6. Maximum profit occurs where $MC = MR$ because
a. Additions to total revenue are greater than additions to total cost.
b. Average total cost is lowest.
c. Marginal cost is lowest.
d. Total revenue is greatest.
e. Additions to total cost are equal to additions to total revenue.

Theory in Practice

PRICE ELASTICITY AND PRICE FIXING

When government sets prices, it considers price elasticity of demand and supply. Recall our two examples of price controls from Chapter 2: natural gas and farm commodities. How has price elasticity affected markets under price controls? How would removal of price controls affect quantities demanded and supplied in these markets?

In the market for natural gas, the artificially low price ceiling caused buyers to move down their demand curves. They responded to lower prices by purchasing substantially larger quantities. We would say that demand was relatively price elastic. When demand is price elastic, removal of a price ceiling sharply curtails quantity demanded, limiting sales of natural gas to only the most urgent users.

TEST YOURSELF

What characteristics of natural gas help make demand relatively price elastic? Refer to the determinants of price elasticity of demand if you need help.

Price elasticity of supply has affected quantities supplied. Price ceilings on natural gas have clearly reduced incentives to increase production of this clean, efficient fuel.

Would a free market price have encouraged greater production?

No one really knows for certain how much natural gas remains in underground reservoirs or how much it will cost to get it out. This makes a clear answer impossible. To the extent that convenient sources of natural gas exist, supply may be price elastic, and a free-market price will not be substantially higher than a government-controlled ceiling price. However, as sources become depleted, supply will eventually become less elastic, and price could rise sharply. At higher prices, little additional fuel will be available, and only the most urgent needs will be satisfied.

TEST YOURSELF
Illustrate graphically the market for natural gas under the assumption of relatively elastic demand and inelastic supply. Show government's price ceiling. Then discuss the consequences of removing the price ceiling.

Price elasticities are different in the markets for farm commodities. Demand for farm products is relatively price inelastic: consumers' response to small price changes is not as great as for natural gas. This is because families must buy food items in roughly constant quantities regardless of price. Artificially high price floors do not substantially reduce quantity sold—at least in the immediate period. Nor would lower free market prices increase food purchases very much.

Price elasticity of supply of farm commodities varies, depending on the length of time for responding to price change. Over short periods supply is relatively price inelastic. But modern technology has made supply of farm products relatively price elastic over time periods long enough for grain to ripen, calves to mature, and so forth. Under these circumstances, artificially high price floors encourage excess production. On the other hand, a small drop in prices from high support levels might reduce farm production sharply. Many farmers would leave the farm for jobs in industry. The fewer remaining farmers would have to supply the nation's entire food requirements in good years and bad. Widespread crop failures in any one year would make supply curves quite price inelastic and lead to significant price increases.

All these considerations and more are involved in government's decision to control prices—or to remove controls. The issue of government price fixing is not a simple one.

TEST YOURSELF
Illustrate graphically the market for farm commodities under the assumption of fairly inelastic demand and elastic supply. Show government's price floor. Then discuss the consequences of removing price controls.

Price Elasticity of Supply Over Time

The prices we pay for the essential things of life depend strongly on supply. The location and shape of supply curves depend on decisions to produce goods and services. Many firms assemble the resources and organize production for the market. In the short run they offer goods for sale as long as market price is high enough to cover average variable cost of production.

Production costs behave differently over the long run. This is particularly true in the home building industry. Most homes are built by small, privately owned construction firms. For such firms, capacity to increase production is limited in the short run. Substantially increasing production would stretch their managerial staff too thin and require their skilled workers to work overtime; it would overwork capital equipment and make it more subject to breakdowns. As a result, an increase in the market price for housing would bring forth little increase in quantity supplied in the short run. With inelastic supply, prices in the housing market are subject to wide swings.

Over a longer time, conditions are likely to be different. If higher prices continue, more firms and more resources will enter the housing industry. More new homes will be offered for sale, with little increase in price. We would say that supply is more price elastic over the long run.

What about supply over a very long time? The housing industry is a good example of what can happen to supply curves if there is plenty of time for responding to price changes.

In recent years, wide swings in housing prices have brought major changes to the housing industry. The structure of the industry has been changing from a fragmented industry of many small firms to one of fewer, larger firms. Larger firms can use modern production techniques and equipment for producing more houses at lower costs. For example, a large firm can assemble wall sections and roof panels at a centrally located factory. On an ordinary assembly line, low-skilled workers can nail building sections together according to a standard pattern. Even electric wiring and plumbing can be installed at a central location. Then flatbed trucks can carry the preformed parts to building sites in a particular neighborhood. Only a few skilled workers may be needed to complete the construction. Finally, a large firm can deliver appliances to an entire tract of houses at one time.

Technological change of this sort can make supply curves more price elastic over the very long run. Figure 4.5 shows a range of hypothetical supply curves for the immediate time period, a longer time period, and a very long time period. Explain the effect on price as the time for adjusting to increased housing demand lengthens.

Could a supply curve ever slope downward to the right? Under what conditions

Figure 4.5 Hypothetical Supply Curves in the Market for Housing

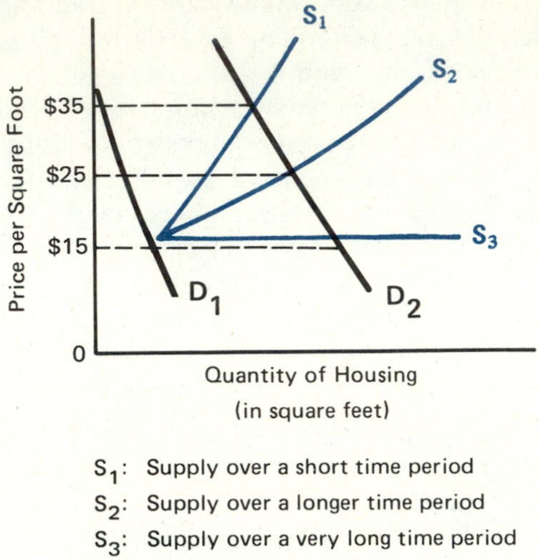

might this occur? (Refer to the discussion of factors that determine price elasticity of supply in the first part of this chapter.)

FINANCING A NEW BUSINESS

Many Americans have as their goal to start their own businesses supplying a particular good or service. To organize a business firm requires, first, the acquisition of funds. Funds can be acquired in several ways: by borrowing or by selling stocks and bonds. Most firms begin by selling stocks and bonds to interested investors.

When a firm sells common or preferred stocks, it is essentially selling shares of ownership. Common stockholders understand that, as part owners, they will participate in the fortunes (whether good or bad) of the firm. That is, they will receive a share of economic profit in the form of dividends when times are good. When times are bad, they may receive no dividends at all. They have the right to vote to select the firm's managers, and they may sell their shares at any time. If the firm has paid large dividends (or is expected to in the future), stockholders may find the value of their stock increasing. Unfortunately, the reverse is also true.

Whereas holders of common stock experience the ups and downs of business along with the fortunes of the firm, holders of preferred stock experience somewhat less risk. Preferred stockholders are guaranteed a certain dividend, if any dividends are paid at all. But preferred stockholders are normally not entitled to vote to select the firm's managers.

Bonds differ from stocks in that they are essentially loans from savers, with a definite schedule of interest payments and a definite date of maturity when the principal of the loan is to be repaid. In general, the assets of the firm are used as collateral (a pledge for the fulfillment of the loan contract). If the firm is very profitable, bondholders will receive no more than the agreed amount. If the firm is not profitable, bondholders must be paid before dividends are paid to preferred or common stockholders. Bondholders may also sell their bonds to other investors before maturity.

A new firm may also acquire funds by borrowing from banks or other financial institutions, subject to the credit policies of particular institutions.

Most new business firms seek a combination of funding through stocks, bonds, and borrowing that satisfies their particular objectives. Bond sales and borrowing have the advantage that interest payments are deductible from the firm's income before calculating taxes owed. They have the disadvantage that agreed interest and principal payments must be paid, even if the firm's income is low. Stock sales have the advantage that dividends may or may not be paid, depending on the profits of the firm. They have the disadvantage that dividends are paid from income that has already been taxed and are taxed a second time as part of stockholders' income. Another disadvantage of selling stocks is that as more stocks are issued, the share of the firm's profits that can be paid to a single stockholder decreases.

In the 1980s a popular way to set up a business was to purchase an existing business through a leveraged buyout (LBO). "Leverage" refers to borrowed funds. Thus, an LBO was the purchase of a firm's stock using borrowed funds. In general, the assets of the purchased firm were used as collateral for the loan. Interest and principal payments on the loan were financed by operating the acquired firm profitably or by selling off some of its assets.

Some LBOs turned out to be very profitable, as the firm's new owners reduced costs and operated the firm more efficiently than the previous owners. Other LBOs ran into difficulty when profits or asset sales produced insufficient funds to make the heavy interest and principal payments on the firm's large debt. For some firms, interest payments amounted to more than half the firm's profits, versus an average of only 2 percent 25 years ago.

Why do you suppose LBOs are feared by managers of many business firms? What are the possible effects on the nation's productivity when business firms face the threat of an LBO?

SUMMARY

1. A firm's supply schedule is based on economic costs, which include all necessary payments to owners of resources used in production. Economic profit is profit above the necessary normal profit paid to people who supply entrepreneurial ability.
2. Payments to fixed resources must be paid in the short run, regardless of quantity of production; payments to variable resources depend on quantity of production.
3. Quantity supplied can be read from a firm's

marginal cost curve, because $MC = MR = p$ defines the profit-maximizing quantity for a firm in competition. The shutdown point occurs where price is equal to average variable cost in the short run.

4. Price elasticity of supply measures the responsiveness of producers to price changes and reflects the behavior of marginal costs. Other determinants of price elasticity of supply include the time required to increase fixed resources or to enter or leave the industry, and the storability of the product.
5. Price elasticity of demand and supply influences the range of price and quantity changes when government price controls are removed.

TERMS TO REMEMBER

economic costs: necessary payments to owners of productive resources

short run: time period in which the quantity and quality of certain resources (such as buildings and equipment) are fixed, not subject to change

long run: time period in which all resources are variable

normal profit: a necessary payment for the use of entrepreneurial ability

economic profit: a payment greater than normal profit

fixed costs: costs that are constant in the short run regardless of quantity of output

variable costs: costs that vary with quantity of output in the short run

marginal cost: the change in total cost associated with a change in quantity of output

marginal revenue: the change in total revenue associated with a change in quantity of output; in competition marginal revenue is the same as price

shutdown point: the point on the marginal cost (supply) curve at which price is equal to average variable cost

price elasticity of supply: the responsiveness of quantity supplied to changes in price

TOPICS FOR DISCUSSION

1. Explain why it is important to draw a supply curve for a particular period of time. Then explain and demonstrate market changes that could cause changes in the position and/or slope of market supply.
2. Complete the table below. Then perform the exercises that follow.

Q	FC	AFC	VC	AVC	TC	ATC	MC
1	100	100	10	10	110	110	10
2	___	___	18	___	___	___	___
3	___	___	24	___	___	___	___
4	___	___	34	___	___	___	___
5	___	___	48	___	___	___	___
6	___	___	66	___	___	___	___
7	___	___	90	___	___	___	___
8	___	___	118	___	___	___	___
9	___	___	150	___	___	___	___
10	___	___	186	___	___	___	___

a. The firm's shutdown price is ______.
b. The firm receives economic profit for any price greater than ______.
c. When price is $14, the profit-maximizing quantity is ______. Economic profit is ______.
d. When price is $32, the profit-maximizing quantity is ______. Economic profit is ______.
e. Draw the firm's supply curve.

3. Since World War II, the electronics industry has produced many exciting and innovative products. One of the most recent has been the video recorder for recording television programs. Initially, only two Japanese firms supplied the entire market. How would you describe price elasticity of supply in the short run, over a 5-year period, and over a 25-year period? What would you expect to happen to price as supply changes?
4. Some local governments in the United States have imposed rent controls on city apartments.

Discuss the purpose of this kind of price ceiling and list as many consequences as you can.

5. Oil spills near the U.S. coast are increasing pressure for corrective actions by firms operating oil tankers. Describe the likely chain of events that will follow such actions and the ultimate consequences for U.S. consumers.
6. Often it is suggested that firms continue to produce goods even though less than a normal profit is being earned. They justify this behavior as a means of maintaining "market share." What economic conditions might warrant such behavior?

ANSWERS TO TEST YOURSELF

(p. 80) The time for responding to price changes is probably shortest for eggs, sweaters, potato chips, transistors, screwdrivers, and autos in the 1990s. The technology is fairly simple and flexible for these items, making their supply curves relatively price elastic. Beef requires longer to produce, and stained-glass windows require specialized craftsmanship, making their supply curves less elastic. Milk, gold, coal, and lumber can be stored, so that supply is relatively elastic. Strawberries cannot be stored or quickly produced, making supply extremely inelastic.

(p. 82) There are substitutes. It is a relatively large part of consumers' budgets.

(p. 83) Removing the price ceiling will cause a significant reduction in quantity demanded but little increase in quantity supplied.

(p. 83) Removing price floors for farm commodities will cause little increase in quantity demanded and a substantial decrease in quantity supplied.

FURTHER READING

Blair, Margaret M., "Who's in Charge Here?" *Brookings Review,* Fall, 1991.

Brooks, Karen, et al, "Agriculture and the Transition to the Market," *Journal of Economic Perspectives,* Fall, 1991.

Drucker, Peter F., *The Concept of the Corporation,* New York American Library, New York, 1964.

Fleming, Harold M., *Gasoline Prices and Competition,* Meredith, New York, 1966.

"Grotesque: A Survey of Agriculture," *The Economist,* December 12, 1992.

Heilbroner, Robert, et al, *In the Name of Profit,* Doubleday, Garden City, N.Y., 1972.

Renshaw, Edward, "Paying for Oil Security," *Challenge,* November/December, 1990.

Trager, James, *Amber Waves of Grain,* Arthur Fields, New York, 1973.

Chapter 5

Imperfect Competition and Inefficient Outcomes

Tools for Study

LEARNING OBJECTIVES

After reading this chapter, you will be able to:

1. Describe how competition eliminates economic profit and increases efficiency.
2. Define monopoly, oligopoly, and monopolistic competition and give examples of each.
3. Explain why imperfect competition brings economic profit and inefficiency.
4. Discuss the laws that enforce competition.

CURRENT ISSUES FOR DISCUSSION

How does monopoly affect us?
How do some natural monopolies set prices?
Is competition or monopoly more likely to bring technological progress?

Adam Smith and the Classical economists that followed him described how markets work when there is perfect competition. As you learned in Chapter 2, perfect competition depends upon:

Many buyers and sellers, each too small to affect market price.
Products so similar that no one producer can insist on a price higher than the equilibrium price.
Complete information about market conditions.
Ease of movement out of the least favorable markets and into the most favorable markets.

In perfect competition, many firms compete for the consumer's dollar. An invisible hand guides firms to produce the goods and services consumers want.

In Chapters 2, 3, and 4 we described the market model that illustrates the Classical theory of free, competitive markets. In the Classical theory, consumer demand schedules for a particular period of time combine to yield a market demand curve. Firms' decisions to supply goods and services combine to yield market supply. The interaction between market demand and supply determines market equilibrium for the particular time period. At equilibrium, price is such that quantity demanded is equal to quantity supplied, and there is no surplus or shortage.

In the short run, the competitive price may yield economic profit or loss. Economic profit or loss occurs because of the existence of fixed resources and because in the short run it is impossible to expand or contract fixed plant and equipment. Thus, quantity supplied may not increase or decrease significantly when demand rises or falls, and price may be greater or less than average total cost. In the long run, however, an industry can expand or contract its fixed plant and equipment. When new firms enter an industry or existing firms leave, supply curves will shift to the right or left.

In this chapter, we consider how changes in supply can cause price to rise or fall to the level of average total cost, eliminating economic profit or loss. This result occurs only in competition, however. Without competition, firms may choose not to increase supply, so that economic profit continues. The existence of economic profit indicates that quantity supplied is less than quantity demanded at a price that just covers average total costs. Fewer resources are allocated to produce the product that would be justified by consumer wants—an indication of inefficiency in the allocation of the nation's scarce resources.

DECIDING PRICE AND OUTPUT IN COMPETITION

Adam Smith described how competitive markets are guided by a kind of invisible hand. The invisible hand encourages new firms to enter markets where they can earn economic profit. As new firms add their supply curves to those of existing firms, market supply increases, pushing price down until it just covers full economic costs, including wages and salaries, rent, interest, and normal profit. At the lower price there is no excess return, or economic profit.

Figure 5.1 illustrates the invisible hand at work in a competitive market. New firms entering the market cause an increase in market supply, shown as a rightward shift in the sup-

Figure 5.1 An Increase in Supply in a Competitive Market

Where there is economic profit, new firms enter the market. Market supply increases and price falls until economic profit is eliminated.

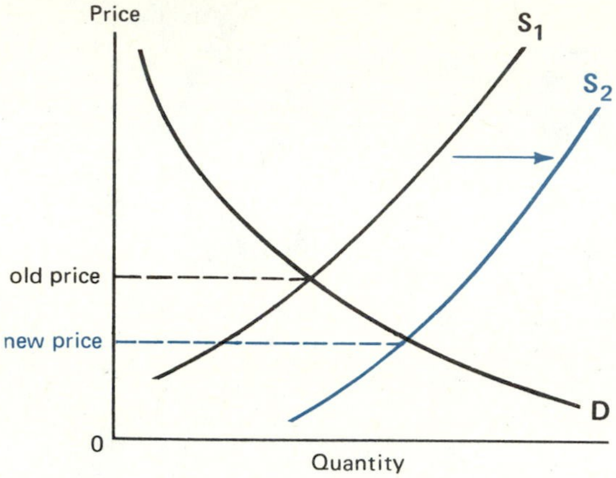

ply curve and creating a surplus at the current price. As all the firms in the market compete to sell their surplus, they push price down. If the new price includes economic profit, still more firms will enter the market, continuing to push price down until price is equal to average total cost. When $p = ATC$, there is no economic profit and no further incentive for new firms to enter the market. After all these adjustments have taken place, the new price is just high enough to cover full economic costs, including normal profit but not economic profit.

In the long run, competition ensures technical as well as allocative efficiency. Competitive markets are technically efficient because they force price down to the lowest possible level for which the good or service can be produced. Why is this so? Firms in competition must construct their plants according to the most efficient design, and they must operate their plants at the best possible rate for holding down average total cost. Otherwise, they will suffer losses at the competitive price and must ultimately go out of business.

Competitive markets achieve allocative efficiency, too, because they satisfy consumers' wants at prices just high enough to pay the minimum necessary cost of scarce resources.

Economic loss calls for the opposite kind of adjustment. When the market equilibrium price is below average total cost, total revenue from sales is less than total cost, and firms suffer loss. Economic loss also acts like an invisible hand, in this case encouraging firms to leave the market. As firms leave, supply falls, and price rises to cover average total cost.

Figure 5.2 shows how competitive markets adjust to loss. Firms leaving the market cause a decrease in supply and a leftward shift of the supply curve, which creates a shortage at the current price. Buyers bid against each other for the limited supply and force price up. Finally, a new equilibrium is reached with a higher price and a smaller quantity sold. The new equilibrium price is just high enough to cover average total cost, including normal profit but not economic profit. Again, the new equilibrium price is the minimum price for which this product can be produced.

Figure 5.2 A Decrease in Supply in a Competitive Market

Where there is negative economic profit, firms leave the market. Market supply falls and price rises until negative economic profit (loss) is eliminated.

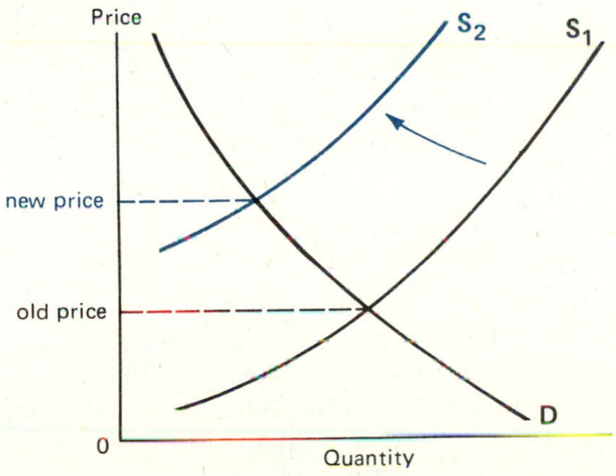

We say that firms in competition are **price takers**. Competitive firms face an equilibrium price which they are too small to affect. They can sell any quantity at the market equilibrium price, but they can sell nothing at a higher price. Competitive firms will continue to supply output as long as market price is at least as great as average total cost. When all firms follow this rule, they force price to a level that includes neither economic profit nor loss.

Now do you see why Adam Smith had such respect for free markets? In free markets, consumer demand curves act as signals, informing producers of the preferences of buyers for particular goods and services. Free markets drive producers, in turn, to seek the lowest-cost way to satisfy consumer wants. The result is efficient production: the minimum expenditure of scarce resources and the maximum production of the goods consumers want. When production is efficient, the opportunity costs of production are the lowest they can be.

Although Adam Smith had great respect for free competitive markets, he realized that competition might not be perfect in the real world. In the real world, some business firms might try to control the output of particular goods and services. They would look for ways to maintain high prices so that they could continue to receive economic profit. They might prefer not to "flood the market" with increased quantities but instead to limit supply and keep price high. Without competition, firms are not forced to produce the maximum quantities of the things consumers want with the minimum expenditure of scarce resources.

Thinking Seriously About Economics

CONCENTRATION RATIOS

A way to measure imperfect competition is to compare the percent of the market served by the largest firms in an industry. An industry in which 4 firms supply 92 percent of the market, for example, would be regarded as imperfectly competitive. An industry in which the largest 50 firms supply only 56 percent of the market is much closer to the competitive model.

The percent of the market supplied by the largest firms is called a concentration ratio. It is a measure of the extent to which production is concentrated in a few large firms. The table of Concentration Ratios in Manufacturing provides concentration ratios for a number of industries, based on the 4 largest, 8 largest, 20, and 50 largest firms in the market. Can you identify the industries described in the preceding paragraph? Would you agree that the first industry is highly concentrated and the second more nearly competitive?

CONCENTRATION RATIOS IN MANUFACTURING

		Percentage of shipments, ranked by company size			
Industry	*Number of Companies*	*4 Largest*	*8 Largest*	*20 Largest*	*50 Largest*
Petroleum refining	282	28	48	76	93
Motor vehicles and car bodies	284	92	97	99	99+
Meat-packing plants	1658	20	43	61	75
Electronic computing equipment	1520	43	55	71	82

Thus, to the extent that competition is imperfect, our market system is not efficient.

MONOPOLY

Remember that one of the characteristics of competition is many small sellers producing identical products. In the real world, few markets fit this description. Few markets have many small sellers, and few products are identical to all other products in the market. In fact, many real-world markets have only a few large sellers. Others have many sellers, but the products of all the sellers are different. In such markets, the efficient results of Adam Smith's competitive model may not occur.

If there is only one large seller in a market, the firm is said to be a **monopoly**. Except for monopolies achieved through patents,

Industry	Number of Companies	Percentage of shipments, ranked by company size: 4 Largest	8 Largest	20 Largest	50 Largest
Radio and TV communications equipment	2083	22	35	57	73
Aircraft	139	64	81	98	99+
Pharmaceutical preparations	584	26	42	69	90
Photographic equipment and supplies	723	74	86	91	94
Bottled and canned soft drinks	1236	14	23	39	56
Telephone, telegraph apparatus	259	76	83	92	97
Bread, cake, and related products	1869	34	47	60	73
Cigarettes	8	Withheld to avoid disclosure			
Construction industry	817	42	52	69	81
Tires and inner tubes	108	66	86	98	99+
Soap and other detergents	642	60	73	83	90

Compare the percent of shipments made by the 50 largest companies with the total number of firms in the industry to get an idea of the structure of the industry.

Statistical Abstract of the United States, 1989.

trademarks, franchises, or government regulation, monopolies are forbidden under the U.S. antitrust laws. Still, there are many markets where a few large firms behave like a monopoly and achieve results like a monopoly. When we speak of monopoly in this text, we are referring to groups of firms that behave like a single firm and have the power to affect market price. Such groups of firms are sometimes called **shared monopolies**.

A monopoly can be achieved in several ways. The monopoly may be the first firm (or group of firms) in the market; it may buy out smaller rival firms; or it may drive weaker competitors out of business. A monopoly must keep out competitors in order to limit supply and keep price from falling; and it will try to increase demand so that there will be buyers at profitable prices.

A country fellow in the rural South had

learned this lesson quite well—without ever attending business school! Some tourists were driving along a detour far off the main road when they became hopelessly mired in the mud. A humble shack was the only sign of civilization, and the farmer's tractor was available (at a price) to pull their car from the ditch. As he handed the fellow a fifty-dollar bill, the tourist observed, "I'll bet you're busy night and day pulling cars from this mud, aren't you?"

"Nope," replied the farmer. "Night's when we haul the water."

(In what sense is the farmer a monopolist? How would you describe the tourists' price elasticity of demand for the farmer's service?)

Gentlemen's Agreements

In years past, achieving monopoly often occurred through gentlemen's agreements. When only a few large firms occupied an industry, the firms might agree among themselves to behave like monopolists. They would agree not to reduce prices, and they would sometimes establish market shares for each firm. In this way, each firm would enjoy control over supply in a protected market. Firms like these are said to be **price makers**. As distinguished from **price takers**, price makers have power to affect market price.

(You can illustrate gentlemen's agreements with a cartoon showing two donkeys tethered at the ends of a strong rope. Each donkey is struggling to eat a bale of hay just beyond his reach at the end of the rope. But when the donkeys agree to cooperate, they are able to eat first one bale and then the other, and both are satisfied.)

Horizontal and Vertical Monopolies

There are two kinds of monopolies, both offering good opportunities for economic profit. One kind of monopoly is a combination of firms that provide the same good or service and is called a **horizontal monopoly**:

supermarket—supermarket—supermarket
auto plant—auto plant

The second kind of monopoly is a combination of firms that process a single product from start to finish—from its raw form to its distribution to the final consumer—and is called a **vertical monopoly**:

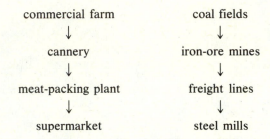

commercial farm	coal fields
↓	↓
cannery	iron-ore mines
↓	↓
meat-packing plant	freight lines
↓	↓
supermarket	steel mills

It is easy to see the opportunities for economic profit that come from controlling production of a product from raw material to finished good.

OLIGOPOLY

True monopoly is rare in U.S. markets, but oligopoly is fairly common. An **oligopoly** is a market in which a few large firms supply most of the output but some small firms may produce for certain small segments of the market. Oligopolies typically occur in industries that require a large capital investment. In such industries, initial capital costs may be too high for small firms to get started, or market demand may not be high enough for many firms to operate efficiently.

When a few large firms dominate a market, the results are similar to monopoly. Oligopoly firms may not actually agree to limit output and raise prices; our antitrust laws would forbid that. Still, because their costs are similar, oligopolists often arrive at similar price and quantity decisions without actual agreements. Like monopolists, they become price makers.

Some examples of markets long dominated by a few large firms are automobiles (dominated by General Motors, Ford, and Chrysler), steel (dominated by U.S. Steel, Bethlehem, and Republic), rubber tires (dominated by Goodyear, Uniroyal, Firestone, Goodrich, and General), and meat packing (dominated by Swift, Armour, Wilson, and Cudahy).

The large capital requirements for making autos, steel, and tires discourage new firms from competing with the giants. Even in oligopoly, however, an occasional small firm can carve out a special market niche, with customers that seek particular variations of the basic product. Custom-made automobiles and specialty steel are some examples.

Oligopoly is associated with some of the same kinds of inefficiences we associate with monopoly: price is higher than average total cost, and supply is less than would be produced in perfect competition. There is another problem with oligopoly that results from the firms' pricing decisions. Oligopolistic firms do not want to compete on the basis of price; therefore, they avoid reducing price, even if technological change or lower material costs would call for a price reduction. This means that oligopoly firms are unlikely to see or to welcome technological change. Moreover, when demand for their product falls, oligopoly firms are more likely than competitive firms to reduce quantity than to reduce price. This makes oligopoly firms a frequent source of layoffs and plant closings.

MONOPOLISTIC COMPETITION

Many markets in the United States are neither monopolistic nor competitive and are described by a term that suggests characteristics of both: **monopolistic competition**.

Monopolistic competition is similar to monopoly because each firm claims to produce a distinctly unique product: the only socially accepted shampoo, the only truly tasty soft drink, the only fully nutritious frozen dinner. Even though their products are similar, monopolistically competitive firms try to make them seem different so as to achieve a monopoly in a particular market. They achieve the appearance of uniqueness through differences in style or packaging or simply through clever advertising. Monopolistically competitive firms can raise price above the competitive level and still hold on to customers who are persuaded of the product's uniqueness. Thus, a monopolisitcally competitive firm is a price maker, but in a more limited sense than a true monopolist or oligopolist.

Monopolistic competition is also similar to competition because there are often many firms in the industry. Capital requirements are low, and so many firms enter the market that each firm produces a smaller quantity than is technically efficient. A clear example of inefficiency in monopolistic competition is when four fast-food restaurants crowd into a single block. Each one promises unique "service with a smile," but together they divide a market that might be served more efficiently by two larger restaurants.

Monopolistic competition occurs often in retail trade and personal services such as delicatessens, fabric shops, laundries, and barber shops. Monopolistically competitive firms give entrepreneurs a chance to operate their own businesses, and they provide consumers a wide variety of products from which to choose. These advantages are achieved at a cost in efficiency, however; more of society's resources are allocated to production than are necessary to produce the particular good or service. Resources allocated to packaging, advertising, and designing, for example, might better be allocated to real production. On the other hand, opportunities for entrepreneurs and variety for consumers might be worth some sacrifice of efficiency.

The three kinds of imperfect competition can be summarized as follows:

Monopoly
- One seller
- Difficult to enter
- Unique product
- Control over price
- Higher price, lower quantity than competition

Oligopoly
- Few sellers
- Somewhat difficult to enter
- Identical or differentiated product
- Similar prices
- Somewhat higher price and lower quantity than in competition
- Tendency to respond to changes in demand by reducing quantity rather than by cutting price

Monopolistic Competition
- Many small sellers, relative to the size of the market
- Easy to enter
- Variety of products, each regarded as somewhat unique
- Some control over price
- Slightly higher price than in competition and probably higher costs of production

Can you name local examples of the three kinds of imperfect competition?

DECIDING PRICE AND OUTPUT IN IMPERFECT COMPETITION

When competition is imperfect, markets do not operate as efficiently as the free markets that Adam Smith described. Without competition, firms are not forced to supply maximum quantities of goods at prices just high enough to cover average total cost. If imperfectly competitive firms can prevent the entry of new competition, they can continue to collect economic profit.

Remember that firms in perfect competition are price takers, free to sell any quantity but unable to affect the market equilibrium price. In imperfect competition, a firm becomes a price maker. Facing the entire demand curve for its product, a firm in imperfect competition can set any price on the demand curve and sell the corresponding quantity. To sell a larger quantity requires a movement down the demand curve to a lower price. Setting a higher price requires a movement up the demand curve to a smaller quantity.

What price will the imperfectly competitive firm set? The answer depends, first, on the effect of price changes on the firm's total revenue and, second, on the effect of quantity changes on the firm's total costs. (These topics were the subjects of Chapters 3 and 4, respectively.) Changes in total revenue and total cost affect the firm's profit and determine its profit-maximizing quantity and price.

Let us look first at the effect of price changes on a firm's total revenue. Suppose an imperfectly competitive firm is selling 5 shirts a day at a unit price of \$15. Total revenue is $TR = Q \times p =$ \$75 per day. Suppose the firm can sell 6 shirts if it reduces price to \$14 (for $TR =$ \$84) or 4 shirts if it raises price to \$16 (for $TR =$ \$64). In this case, the firm can increase total revenue by reducing price and increasing the number of units sold. In fact, if demand is elastic at the current price, reducing price will always yield an increase in total revenue. (Remember that price elasticity of demand greater than one means that a percentage reduction in price will cause a greater percentage increase in quantity demanded.)

Table 5.1 shows an imperfectly competitive firm's total revenue from sales at various prices.

Figure 5.3 is the demand curve associated with the prices and quantities in Table 5.1. The imperfectly competitive firm can select

Table 5.1 Total Revenue at Various Prices (per day).

Quantity Demanded	*Price*	*Total Revenue*
5	$15	$ 75
6	14	84
7	13	91
8	12	96
9	11	99
10	10	100

any price on the demand curve and sell the corresponding quantity. What price will the firm set?

Before we can answer that question, we must look at the effect of quantity changes on total costs. Like a firm in competition, the imperfectly competitive firm seeks to achieve maximum economic profit. Because economic profit is the difference between total revenue and total cost, the imperfectly competitive firm looks for the price and quantity on its demand curve that maximizes the difference between total revenue and total cost.

Figure 5.3 A Demand Curve in Imperfect Competition

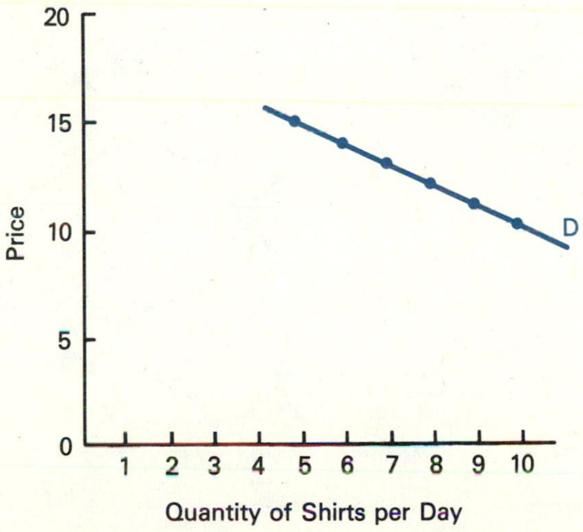

Selecting price and quantity in the imperfectly competitive firm is similar to competition in another respect. Like the competitive firm, the imperfectly competitive firm follows the profit-maximizing rule and selects quantity where marginal revenue is equal to marginal cost: $MR = MC$. The reason is that when $MR = MC$, the last unit sold adds just enough to revenue to cover what it adds to cost. When the last unit sold adds the same to revenue as it adds to cost, economic profit is maximum.

Now we come to the significant difference between pricing with and without competition. The difference has to do with marginal revenue. Although marginal cost of production may be the same whether or not there is competition, marginal revenue is not the same. Unlike the firm in competition, the firm in imperfect competition is the only firm in its market. Therefore, the imperfectly competitive firm faces the entire market demand curve for its product. Facing the entire market demand curve means that in order for the firm in imperfect competition to sell an additional unit it must reduce price. Selling all units at the lower price means that marginal revenue for the firm in imperfect competition is less than price.

Consider again the imperfectly competitive supplier of shirts described in Table 5.1. Selling 5 shirts for $15 yields total revenue of $75. Selling 6 shirts for $14 yields total revenue of $84. The increase in revenue associated with a one-unit increase in quantity is $MR = \$84 - \$75 = \$9$. With $p = \$14$ and $MR = \$9$, marginal revenue $MR = \$9$ is less than price $p = \$14$.

Table 5.2 is the same as Table 5.1 with an additional column showing marginal revenue. Because marginal revenue is associated with changes in the number of units sold, marginal revenue has been written between the lines in the table.

Table 5.2 Total Revenue and Marginal Revenue in Imperfect Competition (per day).

Quantity Demanded	*Price*	*Total Revenue*	*Marginal Revenue*
5	$15	$ 75	
6	14	84	$9
7	13	91	7
8	12	96	5
9	11	99	3
10	10	100	1

Figure 5.4a shows points for marginal revenue associated with the prices and quantities shown in Table 5.2. For every price and corresponding quantity, marginal revenue is less than price. Now look at Figure 5.4b, which includes a typical marginal cost (*MC*) curve. Use the profit-maximizing rule to locate the price and quantity where $MR = MC$. Note that marginal revenue is equal to marginal cost when $Q = 6$ shirts per day. Find the selling price for $Q = 6$ by looking at the demand curve where $p = \$14$.

Now we can see the significant difference between pricing in competition and pricing in imperfect competition. In perfect competition, price and marginal revenue are the same: $p = MR$. Therefore, the profit-maximizing quantity occurs where $p = MR = MC$. In imper-

Figure 5.4a Marginal Revenue in Imperfect Competition

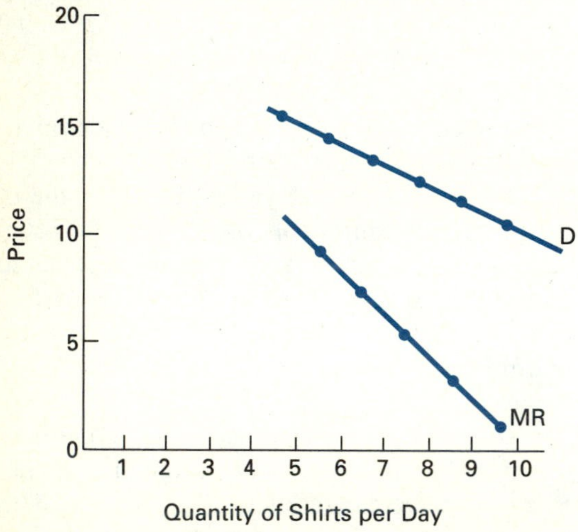

Figure 5.4b The Profit-Maximizing Price and Quantity in Imperfect Competition

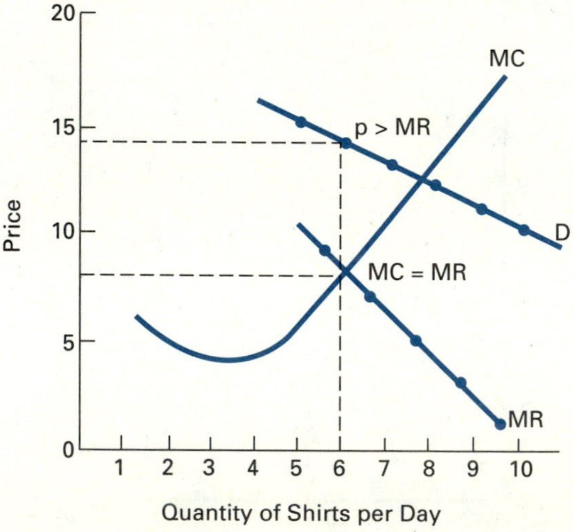

Viewpoint

TWO MONOPOLIES IN AMERICAN HISTORY

During the earliest stages of industrialization in the United States following the Civil War, there was cutthroat competition among American business firms. (The donkeys were still struggling to get to the hay.)

In the building of the railroads, early industrialists like Cornelius Vanderbilt fought ruthlessly to drive their competitors out of business. Where a competing railroad served the same route as Vanderbilt's line, Vanderbilt would reduce his fares below average total cost. He would make up the loss by raising fares on other routes where he faced no competition. When the competing railroad was forced into bankruptcy, Vanderbilt would buy it cheaply. Eventually Vanderbilt's railroad controlled freight service over most of the Northeastern United States.

In the petroleum industry, John D. Rockefeller began with several small oil refineries. However, Rockefeller realized that he could increase his market power if he controlled the oil from well to final distributor. Rockefeller's Standard Oil Company bought up the major oil pipelines and established a monopoly in the transport of crude oil. As the only buyer of oil from well owners, Standard Oil would offer a low price. Then the oil would be transported over Rockefeller's pipelines. Finally, as the only seller of delivered oil to refiners, Standard Oil would insist on a high price.

Low prices for crude oil, on the one hand, and high prices for delivered oil, on the other, forced well owners, refiners, and distributors out of business. Then Rockefeller bought them up and was able to bring a major part of the petroleum industry under the control of a single firm. Whenever Rockefeller's rivals could not be forced out of business or could not be merged with the dominant firm, they could often be persuaded to enter into a gentlemen's agreement. (The donkeys agreed to share the hay.)

These two cases illustrate vertical and horizontal monopoly. Can you identify each?

fect competition, marginal revenue is less than price: $MR < p$. Therefore, the profit-maximizing quantity occurs where $MC = MR < p$. The result is price greater than marginal revenue and marginal cost, providing the imperfectly competitive firm the opportunity to collect economic profit.

To Summarize

The result of imperfect competition is inefficiency, both in the failure to produce what people want (allocative inefficiency) and in the failure to produce at lowest possible cost (technical inefficiency). The significant characteristic of monopoly, oligopoly, and monopolistic competition is the firm's power to set price.

A firm's power to set price depends on the shape of the firm's demand curve and, in particular, price elasticity of demand at the current price. Firms with greater market power face demand curves that are relatively price inelastic: percentage increases in price yield smaller percentage decreases in quantity demanded. A price inelastic demand curve indicates that some consumers want the product so badly they are willing to pay a higher price than the price in competition. (Remember our story about the tourists.) Firms in competition have less market power. They face demand curves that are relatively price elastic: percentage increases in price yield larger percentage decreases in quantity demanded. A price elastic demand curve indicates that consumers have greater choice and can decide to buy or not, depending on price.

THE RESULTS OF IMPERFECT COMPETITION

Imperfect competition in industry has harmful effects, both for today's consumers and for the consumers of the future. With monopoly, oligopoly, or monopolistic competition, prices tend to be higher than in competition, and quantity tends to be lower. Barriers to entry prevent new firms from responding to market signals. When consumers must pay more of their incomes for products produced by imperfectly competitive firms, they have less to spend for other things, thus slowing the development of other industries.

Often, firms that sell to imperfectly competitive firms are harmed as well. They must accept low prices for their products. Workers and suppliers of materials and component parts may have no choice but to accept low wages and low prices from the imperfectly competitive firm.

Higher prices and smaller quantities of finished goods make our economy less efficient than it would be in competition. Remember that in competition, economic profits serve as a signal to expand production. Without competition, it is doubtful that a firm will use its economic profit to improve its production techniques or its product. The result of imperfect competition may be slower growth of production and lower resource productivity.

The harmful effects of imperfect competition are especially damaging in international trade. Higher prices and lower quality have caused U.S. auto and steel manufacturers to lose markets to foreign suppliers. Monopolistically competitive firms have used scarce resources to make trivial packaging or design changes and have neglected to make major innovations that would advance our nation's technology. For all these reasons, imperfect competition may have reduced the U.S. capacity to compete against technically advanced firms abroad.

ANTITRUST LEGISLATION

Imperfect competition was not a serious problem early in our nation's economic development, but toward the end of the 1800s a great merger movement swept the nation's economy. Mergers were made simpler by the development of a new form of business: the **corporation**.

In the corporate form of business, firms sell shares of stock to large numbers of investors. Buyers of stock become part owners of the corporation and receive a share of corporate profits. In theory, stockholders have the power to select managers and decide company policy. In fact, few stockholders exercise their voting rights, leaving actual power in the hands of a few active stockholders. This makes it possible for a few people to control several firms just by buying a few shares of the

HOW SHOULD WE THINK ABOUT ANTITRUST?

Robert Katzmann is worried about current thinking on antitrust.

It used to be that the emphasis in antitrust was on the power that monopolies could wield over small business and consumers. "Trust busters" like President Theodore Roosevelt were concerned that powerful monopolies could squeeze small businesses and stifle "entrepreneurialism, individualism, and economic self-reliance." Not only would powerful monopolies damage the efficiency of the nation's economy; through their concentration of economic power, they would "undermine democratic government."

Over the past decade, the emphasis has changed, and today antitrust activity concentrates more on economic efficiency as a guide to enforcement of antitrust laws. With the emphasis on economic efficiency, antitrust activity has diminished. One reason is that large businesses are frequently *more* efficient than small businesses. Economists at the University of Chicago point out that large firms are better able than small firms to take advantage of economies of scale; and the large profits of such firms may be a result not of exploitation of small firms but of greater efficiency.

Another reason for the decline in antitrust is the seriousness of other problems facing the nation today. The problems of inflation, unemployment, and international competition call into question the allocation of resources to fight business firms that are only trying to do a good job in the market. The dominance of this philosophy in the Reagan administration led to a decrease in the budget of the antitrust enforcement division of the Federal Trade Commission (FTC). As a result, the FTC now allows more vertical and conglomerate mergers and is more lenient regarding horizontal mergers, as well.

Katzmann worries about these developments. Giving such emphasis to the economic aspects of mergers, he says, implies neglect of the social and political consequences of economic power. Although it is correct to consider economic efficiency in ruling on merger activity, we should not forget all those fundamental values associated with competition: the stimulus to economic growth and employment and the pressures toward price stability and technological progress. To fail to enforce the antitrust laws would be to abandon our founding fathers' "social and moral vision of America."

Robert A. Katzmann, *Regulatory Bureaucracy: The Federal Trade Commission and Antitrust Policy*. 1979, MIT Press, Cambridge, MA.

outstanding stock of each. In the 1800s such arrangements were called **trusts***,which were established to monopolize production in certain key industries: sugar, meat packing, steel, rail transport, tobacco, and petroleum.

With a monopoly in the production of a good or service, a trust could pay low prices to its suppliers and charge high prices to its customers. The sugar trust, for example, could pay farmers low prices for sugar while a monopolistic railroad was charging farmers high prices to transport it. In the late 1800s, midwestern farmers pressured Congress for legislation to outlaw trusts, and in 1890 Congress passed the Sherman Antitrust Act.

The Sherman Antitrust Act

The Sherman Antitrust Act forbids any "contract, combination . . . or conspiracy, in restraint of trade." Any act to "monopolize, or combine or conspire . . . to monopolize" a market is prohibited.

The Sherman Act is so broad, however, that it is difficult to decide precisely what actions are forbidden. The law's vagueness has left plenty of room for interpretation by the courts. Also, while the act prohibits cooperative agreements among firms, it does not prohibit outright purchase of firms.

Except for court action against the Standard Oil Company and the American Tobacco Company, the Sherman Act has been used primarily against labor unions, which were once regarded as monopolies in labor markets.

The Clayton Antitrust Act

In 1914, Congress passed the Clayton Antitrust Act to outlaw specific business practices that are harmful to competition. For example, the Clayton Act forbids price discrimination where the effect is to reduce competition. Price discrimination involves setting prices below costs in markets where there is competition. Low prices tend to force competing firms out of business, and the loss can be made up by setting higher prices in markets where there is no competition. The Clayton Act also forbids tying contracts, which require the buyer of one of a firm's products to buy a full line of products—thus shutting competing suppliers out of those markets. And the law forbids interlocking directorates, in which a single individual would serve on the board of directors of several related corporations, thus allowing the firms to coordinate their price and output policies and avoid competition.

Finally, the Clayton Antitrust Act forbids a firm to acquire voting stock in related corporations in order to operate them as one large firm. The act has been amended to forbid outright purchase of competing firms. Today firms wishing to purchase or to merge with a related firm must request permission from the Antitrust Division of the U.S. Department of Justice.

Difficulties of Enforcement

Enforcement of the antitrust laws has been uneven and has depended largely on the particular philosophy and loyalties of the U.S. president. Over the first seventy years of the antitrust laws, not one businessman was sent to jail for a violation. Some fines were imposed, but fines were small compared to the expected profits from a "gentlemen's agreement."

In 1959, for the first time, business executives were sent to jail under the antitrust laws. Again in 1961, respected managers of major firms were sent to jail for conspiring to fix prices on electrical generating equipment.

In the 1970s executives of large corporations were found guilty of making illegal con-

* Similar arrangements today are called holding companies.

Thinking Seriously About Economic Issues

THE DEBATE OVER BIGNESS

Economists disagree as to whether bigness in business is good or bad. On one side of the argument, John Kenneth Galbraith sees some benefits from large business firms. Since average total costs tend to fall as output increases, large firms could mean lower prices for consumers. Moreover, Galbraith believes that large firms allocate more funds to research and development than small firms. Galbraith would allow large firms to operate, but he recommends government regulation of their price and output policies.

On the other side of the argument, Milton Friedman worries about market power, however it is used. He believes that large concentrations of financial (and political) power threaten individual freedom. Friedman recommends vigorous enforcement of the antitrust laws. He favors breaking up established market power and preventing further concentrations of power from developing.

For several decades early in this century, the U.S. government relaxed its prosecution of the antitrust laws. The philosophy was: bigness is not necessarily bad if market power is used fairly. As a result, monopolistic behavior increased in many markets.

In mid-century a new philosophy took over. In 1945 the Justice Department forced Alcoa Aluminum Company to separate some of its operations into competing firms. Alcoa was not accused of monopolistic behavior—just growth through good management. The new philosophy seemed to be to stop monopoly before it develops.

The case of the Brown Shoe Company is another example of the Justice Department's new philosophy. When Brown Shoe Manufacturing Company applied for permission to merge with Kinney Shoe Stores, the combined firms would have made up only a very small part of the shoe market. Still, the Justice Department decided that the merger would be a dangerous start down the road to monopoly, and it was not permitted.

Recent antitrust cases have focused on parallel practices: cooperative industry policies that shut potential competitors out of the market. The breakfast cereal industry, for example, includes three large firms whose combined market power acts to deny shelf space to small cereal manufacturers. The Justice Department would like to break up the firms into competing divisions, but the cereal firms are resisting the effort.

tributions to political campaign funds. It was suspected that the contributions were aimed at forestalling prosecution for antitrust violations. The most publicized case involved the purchase of several companies by the International Telephone and Telegraph Company. Following a large campaign pledge, ITT was allowed to keep the largest of its new acquisitions.

Recently the Antitrust Division has moved more vigorously to examine the pricing policies of highly concentrated industries. In

1981 executives of firms producing certain kinds of transparent paper were found guilty of price-fixing and sentenced to jail terms. In 1984, American Telephone and Telegraph Company complied with a court order and broke up into a number of regional telephone companies, while retaining control over subsidiary long distance and research and manufacturing operations.

CONGLOMERATES

Antitrust prosecution of horizontal and vertical monopolies has led business firms to develop new ways of building market power. In recent years corporations have formed **conglomerates**, in which the combining firms are from totally unrelated industries. A conglomerate may include firms producing such diverse products as dog food, whiskey, aerospace equipment, and Chinese food. Because the combining firms are in different industries, a conglomerate does not technically reduce competition. Still, it may represent a dangerous concentration of financial and political power.

NATURAL MONOPOLIES

We have seen that competitive markets tend to be more efficient than imperfectly competitive markets, but this is not always true. Some markets are more efficient when production is carried out by only one large firm. Such firms are called **natural monopolies**. A single firm may be able to produce electric power and transportation and communications services more efficiently, for example, than could many competing firms. Firms that produce electric power and transportation and communications services for local markets are called **public utilities**. Most public utilities are privately owned, but their prices are set by regulatory commissions to prevent them from behaving like ordinary monopolies.

A utility must invest millions of dollars in capital equipment. However, once its plant and equipment are in place, a utility can provide larger and larger quantities of service without much additional cost. This is because large-scale production allows a utility to spread its fixed costs over many units of service, so that average fixed cost is quite low.

A regulatory commission must decide what price and quantity of output would be fair to consumers and also fair to the stockholders of the utility. It is important to be fair to the stockholders or they will refuse to reinvest their funds in the firm. Then the utility cannot increase its productive capacity along with the needs of the community.

Consider the hypothetical market demand curve for electric power, shown on Figure 5.5. Market demand for power includes demand from households, retail stores, and factories.

Figure 5.5 Market Demand for Electric Power

Some users are willing to pay as much as 10 cents per KWH for electric power. If the rate falls to 2 cents per KWH, quantity demanded is much greater.

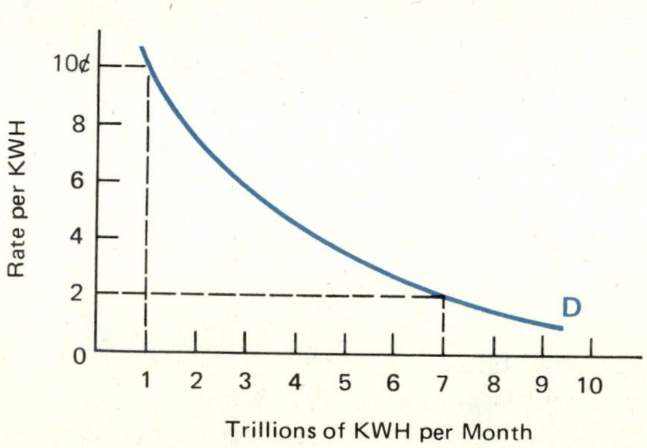

Buyers whose demand for electric power is most urgent may be willing to pay as much as 10 cents per kilowatt hour (KWH). These buyers might include some homeowners and many manufacturing firms. According to Figure 5.5, the total quantity demanded at a price of 10 cents would be 1 trillion KWH per month.

Many homeowners and businesses would be willing to pay in the range of 5 cents per KWH for larger quantities of power. If the rate were as low as 2 cents, they would use even more. The result is a market demand curve for electric power that slopes downward like a typical demand curve.

Charging all consumers a single rate for power yields total revenue equal to a rectangle formed under the demand curve at the single rate. (Can you explain why?) The utility can increase revenue, however, by pricing according to a rate schedule. A rate schedule charges different rates to different groups of consumers, based on the amount of power they use. With a rate schedule the utility can collect all the revenue under the demand curve for each group of consumers.

This is an example of price discrimination, and it would be illegal for an ordinary monopoly. However, the regulatory commission may permit price discrimination if it enables the utility to cover full costs while increasing the quantity of power it offers for sale.

Figure 5.6 shows total revenue collected with (a) a single rate for all consumers and (b) a rate schedule. On Figure 5.6b the rate schedule ranges from 2 cents to 10 cents per KWH. Notice the substantial increase in quantity and revenue with a rate schedule. Another advantage of a rate schedule is that it allows consumers far out at the right of the demand curve to enjoy the service even if the rate they pay is less than the cost of production. In effect, consumers at the left of the demand curve are helping pay for power used by those at the right.

The power company uses its revenue to pay operating costs and to compensate all those who help finance the utility's investment

Figure 5.6 Total Revenue

A rate schedule allows the company to collect all the revenue under the demand curve within the rate schedule.

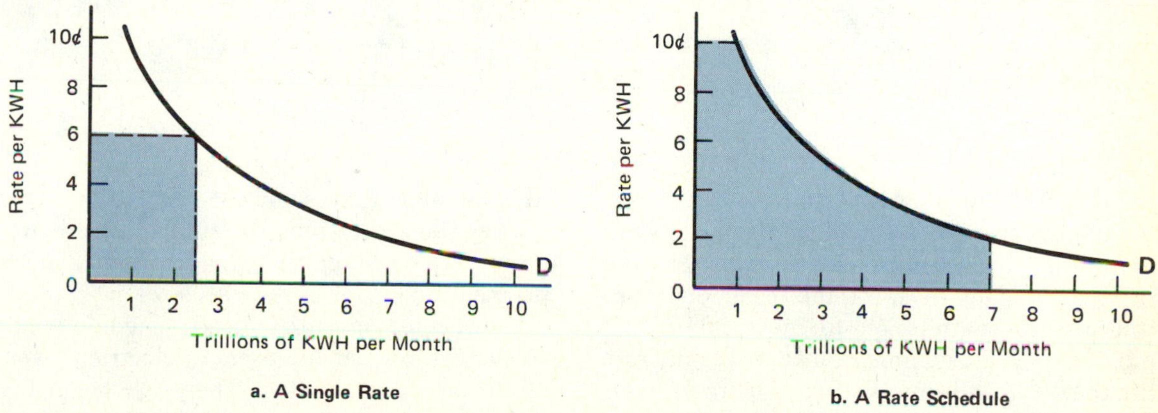

Viewpoint

DEREGULATING THE AIRLINES

For half a century the U.S. air travel industry was regulated by the Civil Aeronautics Board (CAB). Air fares and routes were controlled to guarantee service to consumer markets at prices that would cover costs of production.

Many airlines operate on the "hub-and-spoke" principle. A major city is designated a hub, with short spokes coming in to feed the long spokes going out to other hubs. Costs per passenger-mile are higher on the short spokes because fixed costs are spread over fewer units of output. The CAB allowed the airlines to set fares higher than average total cost on long spokes so that fares could be lower than average total cost on short spokes.

Under CAB regulation, competition in the air travel industry was limited to airline "frills": attractive flight attendants, food and beverage service on flights, and advertising gimmicks. By the late 1970s, U.S. consumers were becoming concerned about high costs, excess capacity, and general inefficiency in air travel. Congress directed the CAB to begin deregulating the industry and put itself out of business.

Competition brought tremendous changes in air travel. The major coast-to-coast lines focused their efforts on their long flights, cutting fares sharply to expand sales volume and keep their large planes filled. Some large airlines were unable to survive the fare wars and went out of business or cut back service. Small "commuter" airlines sprang up to serve short-haul passengers. Small airlines could operate with limited terminal facilities and nonunion labor, so their costs were low and profits high. However, some small markets were found to be unprofitable, and air service to those areas was discontinued.

Many economists believe that the air travel industry is becoming more efficient. Competition is pushing air fares to the level of average costs (including normal profit) in each of a wide variety of consumer markets. Finally, total investment in the airline industry is beginning to reflect more accurately the actual requirements for service in air travel markets.

in plant and equipment: that is, banks and owners of the firm's stocks and bonds. When operating and capital costs increase, the power company must ask the regulatory commission for permission to increase its rate schedule. If the commission approves the rate increase, all consumers will pay more for their electric power. Some consumers will move up their demand curves and use less power. If the power company has calculated correctly, however, it will collect greater total revenue to meet its higher costs.

Agreeing on a "fair" rate schedule is not easy. There are many users of electric power, all seeking lower rates. There are relatively few owners of stocks and bonds, seeking

Viewpoint

THE END OF A NATURAL MONOPOLY

For almost a century, American Telephone and Telegraph Company was regarded as a natural monopoly. Although small, independent companies provided telephone service in some communities, the giant utility generally controlled local and long-distance calls, equipment manufacture, and research in electronic communications. Pricing policies were regulated by public service commissions to enable the company to cover its costs and to guarantee an acceptable level of profits for paying stockholder dividends. Regulated prices were set higher than full costs for business and long-distance calls so that prices for local residential users could be set lower than full costs. To finance one type of service through profits earned on another type is called **cross-subsidization**.

Probably the most significant event for breaking up AT&T's communications monopoly was the development of communications satellites and microwave radio transmissions. The new technologies enabled new firms to enter the market for long-distance calls and provide services more cheaply than AT&T. The Justice Department and MCI Communications Company filed antitrust suits against AT&T, and in 1982 a consent decree was signed in which AT&T agreed to divest itself of its local operating companies. The operating companies were reorganized into seven regional companies, still to be regulated by local public service commissions. AT&T Information Systems was established to provide telephone equipment and services. Western Electric, Bell Labs, and long-distance calling remained with AT&T, and AT&T was given permission to enter new businesses, including businesses involving computers.

With deregulation, competition in long-distance calling was expected to bring those rates down. Computerized communications introduced new services, including electronic mail, video transmission, and data communication. New equipment manufacturers produced an array of new communications equipment.

Perhaps the breakup of AT&T was inevitable. Small, new firms were demanding the right to enter AT&T's markets, and AT&T needed authorization to explore and develop new markets. It appears no longer practical to allow a regulated monopoly to subsidize customers in competitive markets with profits earned in nonregulated markets. Still, there are problems. Without subsidies for local rates, many low-income households may be excluded from the communications network. Some form of government subsidy may be required for these households.

higher returns on their investments. The voting strength of the first group may influence elected commissioners to hold rates down. Or power companies may seek to ensure rate increases by making campaign contributions to commissioners.

If rates are held down so that the return on invested capital falls, owners of the firm's stocks and bonds may decide to use their savings instead for other investments. New power plants and equipment will not be built, and service will deteriorate. With revenues insufficient to cover full costs, a utility may need government help in the form of tax credits, subsidies, or outright government ownership.

Government involvement in the power industry has several disadvantages. If utility managers expect government to cover their costs, they may be less concerned about holding costs down. Also, a tax-supported subsidy must be financed by all the taxpayers while the benefits go only to users of the service. Most economists believe it is more efficient and more equitable for users of electric power to pay for higher costs through higher rates for the power they use.

Self-Check

1. **Firms in perfect competition:**
   a. Produce identical products.
   b. Enter an industry in which there are economic profits.
   c. Expand or contract supply until price is equal to average total cost.
   d. Produce output at the lowest unit costs in the long run.
   e. All of the above.

2. **Monopolization is likely to result from:**
   a. Gentlemen's agreements.
   b. Repeal of the patent laws.
   c. Economic theory.
   d. Low initial capital requirements.
   e. Growing numbers of consumers in the market.

3. **Which of the following is not characteristic of an oligopoly?**
   a. A few large firms in the industry.
   b. Generally high capital requirements.
   c. Similar cost patterns.
   d. Ease of entry of new firms.
   e. Similar pricing policies.

4. **A product sold by a monopolistically competitive firm:**
   a. Has a lower price than under competition.
   b. Is identical with others in the industry.
   c. Is produced by a few large firms.
   d. May experience frequent model changes.
   e. Has characteristics similar to oligopoly.

5. **Antitrust laws forbid:**
   a. Tying contracts.
   b. Interlocking directorates.
   c. Price discrimination, if the effect is to reduce competition.
   d. Mergers harmful to competition.
   e. All of the above.

6. **When there is a monopoly in industry:**
   a. Excess economic profit serves as a signal attracting new firms.
   b. Price is the minimum for which the good can be produced.
   c. Output is greater than under competition.
   d. A larger volume of sales may mean a smaller total revenue.
   e. New firms can enter the industry with ease.

Theory in Practice

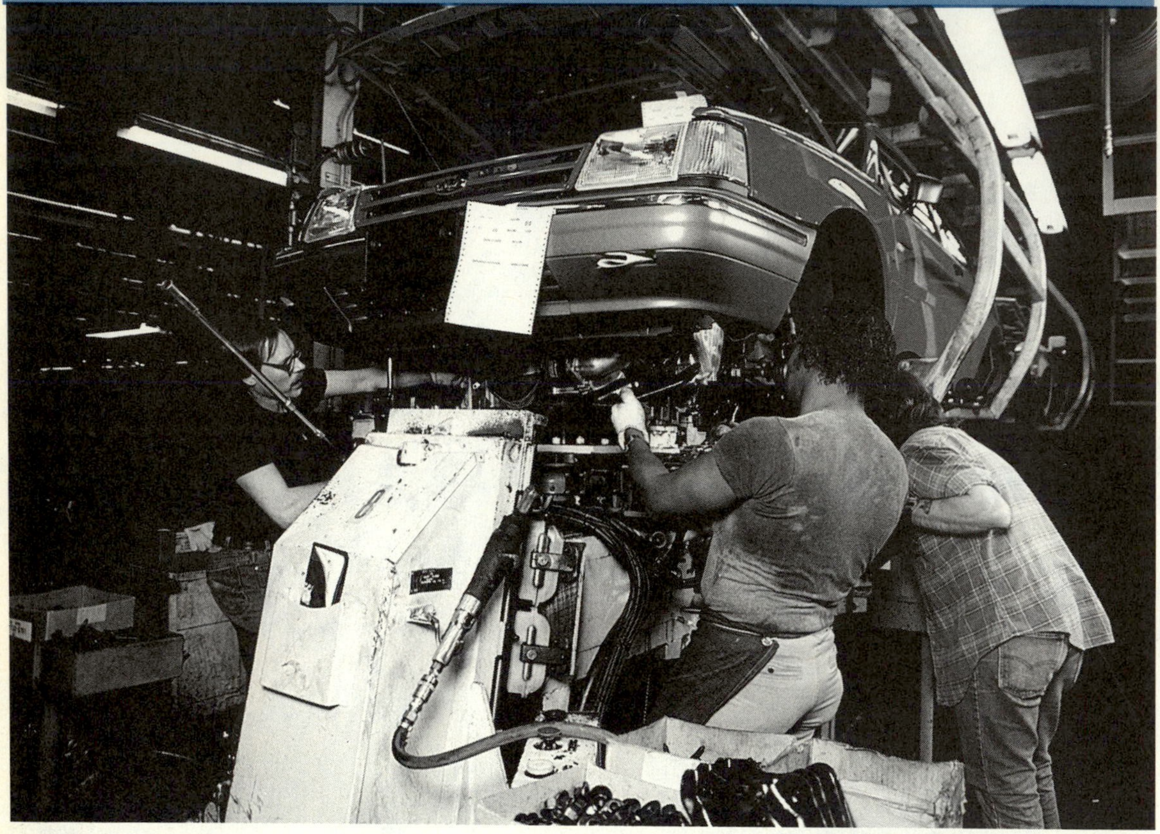

PRICING IN IMPERFECT COMPETITION

Probably the least competitive industry in the United States is the automobile industry. More precisely, the automobile industry is an oligopoly, in which three large firms supply more than 90 percent of domestic production. Antitrust laws prevent the three firms from cooperating to raise price, limit output, or establish market shares. Still, after long years in the same business, each firm knows pretty well how the other firms will behave under current market conditions. As a result, their pricing and output decisions are often similar.

How does imperfect competition affect price and quantity in the market for automobiles?

Figure 5.7a shows a hypothetical demand curve for Super Cruisers for the year. In a free, competitive market, many sellers would supply Cruisers, producing a market supply curve like the one shown in Figure 5.7b. Each seller would be forced by competition to charge the market price of $8000. The market price would be just high enough to cover all

Figure 5.7 The Market for Super Cruisers

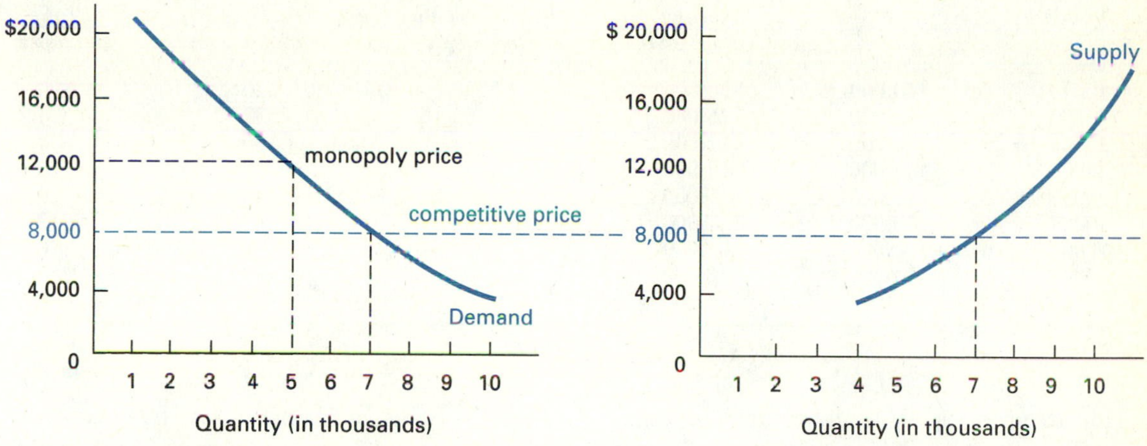

a. Market Demand for Autos per Year

b. Competitive Market Supply per Year

costs of production, including normal profit, and quantity supplied would be equal to quantity demanded.

TEST YOURSELF
What would be the equilibrium quantity of autos at a price of $8000?

If a single firm (or cooperating group of firms) has a monopoly in the market for Super Cruisers, there is no market equilibrium price. The imperfectly competitive firm (or firms) can charge any price on its demand curve and sell the corresponding quantity. Suppose the profit-maximizing price is $12,000. At a price of $12,000 the quantity of autos demanded is less than it would be at the competitive price, and production is lower in the automobile industry.

TEST YOURSELF
What is the quantity demanded at a price of $12,000?

Furthermore, the imperfectly competitive price may include economic profit over and above the average total cost of producing automobiles. Without competition, economic profit cannot serve as a signal to attract new firms into the industry.

Look at Table 5.3. Columns (1) and (2) provide hypothetical data about market demand. If Super Cruisers are selling for $20,000, only 1000 units will be sold, for total revenue of $20 million. At a price of $6000, 8000 Cruisers will be sold, for total revenue of $6000 × 8000 units, or $48 million. Column (3) contains hypothetical cost data. Producing 1000 Cruisers costs an average of *ATC* = $20,000. Total cost to the firm is $20,000 × 1000 units, or $20 million. Producing 8000 Cruisers costs an average of $10,000, for a total cost of $80 million.

Columns (4), (5), and (6) in Table 5.3 allow us to compare total revenue at every level of output with the cost of production. The difference between total revenue and total cost is economic profit.

Suppose you are the manager of an imperfectly competitive firm producing Super Cruisers. What quantity of output would you

Table 5.3 Hypothetical Demand and Cost Schedules for Super Cruisers (per year).

No. of Units Demanded per Year	*Price*	*Average Total Cost*	*Total Revenue (millions)*	*Total Cost (millions)*	*Economic Profit (millions)*
1000	$20,000	$20,000	$20	$20	$ 0
2000	18,000	16,000	36	32	4
3000	16,000	12,000	48	36	12
4000	14,000	10,000	56	40	16
5000	12,000	8000	60	40	20
6000	10,000	8000	60	48	12
7000	8000	8000	56	56	0
8000	6000	10,000	48	80	−32
9000	4000	14,000	36	126	−90

decide to produce? You could achieve maximum economic profit by producing 5000 units and selling them for $12,000 each. (How much economic profit would you earn on each Cruiser?)

Now suppose this is a competitive industry. The existence of economic profit would encourage other firms to enter this market. Production and sale of Super Cruisers would increase. New firms would set lower prices in order to sell larger quantities.

TEST YOURSELF

What is the lowest price for which competitive firms would profitably produce and sell Cruisers? What quantity would be sold at that price? Why is it not a good idea to produce a larger quantity than this?

PRACTICE IN OLIGOPOLY PRICING

The four largest tobacco companies in the United States were once a single monopoly firm: the American Tobacco Company. In 1911 the Supreme Court dissolved the American Tobacco Company and formed four separate firms: American Tobacco, Reynolds Tobacco, Liggett and Myers, and Lorillard. Sales of tobacco grew steadily after that, and by the 1970s per capita consumption of tobacco was twenty-five times what it had been in 1911. Sales of all the major tobacco companies increased with the increase in demand, so that by the 1980s they controlled more than 80 percent of the U.S. cigarette market.

Today's tobacco industry is described as an oligopoly. Like most oligopolies, the major tobacco companies avoid price competition. They decide price through a system of price leadership, with Reynolds Tobacco Company acting as the price leader. Reynolds is big enough to discourage price cutting by the other firms. If another firm were to reduce price, Reynolds would cut below and gain a larger share of the market. If another firm were to raise price, Reynolds would refuse to follow the increase, again gaining a larger share of the market. Thus, the other tobacco firms realize it does not pay to set different prices, and they follow the price set by the leader.

Price leadership is possible because the major cigarette brands are regarded as good substitutes. Customers can easily switch from one brand to another if prices are different. (What does this tell you about price elasticity of demand for particular brands?) Price leadership enables all the firms to enjoy economic profits. Moreover, if average total costs were to rise and profits fall for the four tobacco companies, the three other firms would wait for Reynolds to make the first move. As soon

Thinking Seriously About Economic Issues

MONOPOLY IN MONOPOLY

It's not whether you win or lose, it's how you name the game! That's the problem in the antitrust dispute over the game of Monopoly.

You will find few Americans who aren't familiar with the game of Monopoly. Legend has it that Monopoly was devised around the turn of the century by a Virginia Quaker, Elizabeth Magee. It was known as "The Landlord's Game." For years, several versions were played on painted oilcloth.

In 1933 a retired hotel manager from Georgia became interested in the game and bought rights to the idea. After updating and standardizing the rules, he sold the patent and trademark to Parker Brothers. Today Parker Brothers is one of the world's largest producer of games, and Monopoly is its most profitable product. More than 80 million games of Monopoly have been sold worldwide.

Such success could not forever go unchallenged. Many other manufacturers have come up with ideas for similar games, hoping to share some of this market's profits. Parker Brothers has fought them all and has generally been successful in preventing other firms from selling any games similar to the original, one-and-only Monopoly. It was successful, that is, until 1973, when an economics professor from California came out with a new game he called Anti-Monopoly.

Professor Ralph Anspach is a specialist in antitrust law. His new game is similar to the original Monopoly, but instead of building monopoly its objective is to break it up. His idea caught on, and in the first two years he sold 280,000 games for total revenue of about a million dollars—all this after investing only $5000 to set up his own company.

By law the Monopoly trademark belongs exclusively to Parker Brothers. Theirs is a legal monopoly. Therefore, Parker Brothers sued Professor Anspach for illegal use of their property. In turn, Professor Anspach sued Parker Brothers over the validity of the trademark itself. He pointed out that some trademarks eventually become a part of the language itself and are free to be used by any firm. Kleenex, Kodak, aspirin, and even checkers are examples of terms that used to be brand names exclusively but now are widely used to refer to whole classes of products. And besides, said Anspach, Anti-Monopoly does not involve competition with Monopoly at all.

Apparently the Court agreed. Anspach won his case.

as Reynolds increases price, the other firms would quickly follow.

Because of their control of supply, oligopoly firms tend to react differently to changes in demand than would competitive firms.

Remember that competitive firms respond to an increase in demand by moving up their supply curves and supplying a larger quantity at a higher price. They respond to a decrease in demand by producing a smaller quantity at a lower price. The advantage in competition is that price changes help moderate changes in quantity so that production and employment in the competitive industry remain fairly stable.

Oligopolistic firms react differently to changes in demand, and the result may be damaging to total production and employment. In oligopoly, price tends to remain constant, so that a change in demand primarily affects quantity of output. Thus, production tends to rise or fall by the full amount of the change in demand. The result for the economy as a whole is wider swings in production and employment. Workers in oligopolistic industries are subject to alternating periods of heavy overtime work followed by layoffs.

SUMMARY

1. Economic profit is a return over and above the full cost of resources used in production. In competition, economic profit serves as a signal attracting new resources into an industry. Negative economic profit, or loss, signals resources to leave an industry. As firms enter (or leave), price falls (or rises) until economic profit is finally eliminated.
2. The free movement of resources is difficult to achieve in the real world. Some industries become monopolized when conditions prevent the entry of new firms.
3. Pure monopolies are rare in U.S. industry. However, several firms have occasionally made gentlemen's agreements not to compete against each other.
4. Other forms of imperfect competition are oligopoly (dominated by a few large firms) and monopolistic competition (where many small firms produce differentiated products).
5. A monopoly may reduce output and raise price above the competitive level. If there are no competitors to force price down, a monopoly can continue to collect economic profit.
6. In the late 1800s political pressure was put on Congress to outlaw vertical and horizontal monopolies. The Sherman Antitrust Act of 1890 and the Clayton Antitrust Act of 1914 forbid certain practices aimed at reducing competition. More recently, competition has been threatened by conglomerates, combinations of firms in unrelated industries.
7. Very large firms may have an advantage in some types of production because of the low average total cost associated with a large volume of output. Firms in these industries are called natural monopolies.
8. Public commissions regulate price and output policies of natural monopolies. However, the job of regulating prices and profits is not an easy one.

TERMS TO REMEMBER

price takers: firms that can sell any quantity at the market price but no quantity at a higher price

monopoly: a market supplied by one firm or by a group of firms acting as one

price makers: firms that can raise their prices by reducing their output

horizontal monopoly: a combination of firms, all producing the same type of output

vertical monopoly: a combination of firms, each involved in one stage of production of a particular good or service

oligopoly: a market mainly supplied by a few large firms

monopolistic competition: a market supplied by many small firms, each producing a slightly different product

corporation: a business firm owned by holders of stocks, or shares of ownership and managed by hired managers

conglomerate: a combination of firms, each producing an entirely different good or service

natural monopoly: a market that is more efficient if production is carried out by one large firm

cross-subsidization: the practice of financing one type of service through profits earned on another type

TOPICS FOR DISCUSSION

1. Explain the difference between the following pairs of terms:

   Vertical monopolies and horizontal monopolies.
   Competitive pricing and monopoly pricing.
   Price takers and price makers.

2. How is each of the following involved in enforcing the antitrust laws:

   Natural monopolies
   Price leadership
   Conglomerates

3. One area in which monopoly power may be of particular concern in the United States is the news media. The situation is especially threatening in towns where there is single ownership of newspaper, radio, and television facilities. The Antitrust Division of the Department of Justice has been pressuring the Federal Communications Commission to draw up rules to deal with monopolization of the news media. One proposal would require owners to sell or swap properties in order to increase competition in the local market.

   Can you suggest any advantages in single ownership of the news media? What are the disadvantages? What position would you take with respect to the proposal before the regulatory commission?
4. In the late 1800s, farmers of the midwestern states complained they were being squeezed between monopoly suppliers and monopoly buyers. They had to pay high prices to suppliers of agricultural machinery, freight service, and fuel, and they had to accept low prices from meat packers, grain dealers, and the sugar trust.

   Do such problems exist today? How can the courts help reduce them? How are U.S. consumers affected?
5. Public utilities often face the problem of "peak loads" at particular times of the day or year. Power usage is greatest during the day (industrial plants) and in the summer (air conditioning). Telephone usage is greatest on weekdays (business calls). Mass-transit usage is greatest in the morning and evening rush hours. A public utility must invest in additional capital resources to fill exceptionally high demand, but its resources may be idle during other times of the day or year. Costs may also be higher during peak times if old, obsolete equipment is brought into service to satisfy higher demand.

   How might a public regulatory commission deal with this problem? Would you favor price discrimination in such situations? How would price discrimination work?
6. Explain how the goal of technical and allocative efficiency is served under competition and without competition.
7. During the 1980s, federal regulations allowed cities to control entry into the cable television market. Use your understanding of economic theory to predict the consequences of these restrictions for the cable television market. What are the potential dangers of cooperation between local governments and cable monopolies? Can you suggest an economically efficient arrangement for this market?
8. The McCarran-Ferguson Act of 1945 exempts insurance companies from the antitrust laws. Why do you suppose insurance companies were singled out for exemption? What are the possible consequences?

ANSWERS TO TEST YOURSELF

(p. 111) 7000 units.
(p. 111) 5000 units.
(p. 112) The lowest price is determined by minimum average total cost: $ATC = \$8000$ with production of about 5500 units. Producing more units would force price below *ATC*. Firms might produce for a price lower than *ATC* in the short run only if price at least covers average variable cost.

FURTHER READING

Adams, Walter, ed., *The Structure of American Industry; Some Case Studies,* Macmillan, New York, 1955.

Adams, Walter and James W. Brock, "Gigantomania Follies," *Challenge,* March/April, 1992.

Borenstein, Severin, "The Evolution of U.S. Airline Competition," *Journal of Economic Perspectives,* Spring 1992.

Bradley, Joseph F., "Antitrust Law and Innovation Cooperation," *Journal of Economic Perspectives,* Summer 1990.

Crandall, Robert W., "Regulating Communications," *Brookings Review,* Summer 1992.

Jorde, Thomas and David J. Teece, "Innovation and Cooperation: Implications for Competition and Antitrust," *Journal of Economic Perspectives,* Summer 1990.

Josephson, Matthew, *The Robber Barons,* Harcourt Brace and World, New York, 1962.

Mason, Edward S., *Economic Concentration and the Monopoly Problem,* Atheneum, New York, 1964.

Morrison, Steven and Clifford Winston, *The Economic Effects of Airline Deregulation,* Brookings, Washington, 1986.

Rose, Nancy L., "Fear of Flying? Economic Analysis of Airline Safety," *Journal of Economic Perspectives,* Spring 1992.

Scitovsky, Tibor, "The Benefits of Asymmetric Markets," *Journal of Economic Perspectives,* Winter 1990.

Symposium: Horizontal Mergers and Antitrust, *Journal of Economic Perspectives,* Fall 1987.

Temin, Peter, *The Fall of the Bell System,* Cambridge University Press, Cambridge, 1987.

Chapter 6

Labor Markets and the Labor Movement

Tools for Study

LEARNING OBJECTIVES

After reading this chapter, you will be able to:

1. Apply the laws of supply and demand to resource markets.
2. Explain the rule for deciding the number of workers to hire and at what wage.
3. Discuss the history of the labor movement.
4. Distinguish between craft unions and industrial unions.
5. Define closed shop and secondary boycott.

Current Issues for Discussion

How might labor unions interfere with efficiency in labor markets?

How does the collective bargaining process work?

How are labor unions changing in response to changes in resource markets?

A first-grade teacher struggled through a long, rainy day to keep her squirmy dears quietly and constructively occupied (with no recess period for the children to release energies while the teacher regained hers). At last, it was dismissal time, and appropriate mittens, hoods, and galoshes (last year's small sized) had to be fitted, then exchanged, and often exchanged a second time. This was all accomplished amid great hilarity and confusion. One little boy amused himself in the hubbub by exploring the contents of the teacher's desk, where he found the brown window envelope containing her paycheck. He asked what it was, and upon hearing the answer, he queried, "Oh, do you work someplace?"

THE NATURE OF WORK

Most of us "work someplace"—whether or not we receive a paycheck. Indeed, in Western society the nature of a person's work is probably the clearest indication of his or her social status. Our work is essential to our emotional health and to the progress of our society. In a more immediate sense, work is essential to our material well-being and even survival. Lacking sufficient banana trees beneath which to recline as ripened fruit continuously satisfies our hunger, we are compelled to "rise and shine" and "put our shoulders to the wheel." We must cooperate to produce the goods and services we need for life. Someone must cultivate our grain, weave our cloth, build our homes, and yes, even bury us.

The change from self-sufficiency to coop-

Viewpoint

A DISADVANTAGE OF SPECIALIZATION AND DIVISION OF LABOR

There was a parlor game making the rounds several years ago in which the players were asked to answer the question "Who are you?" with three responses. Supposedly, deep psychological insights could be gained from the answers and their sequence. For example, a man who answers, "I am a teacher, I am a father, I am a Democrat," reveals much of his personal sense of self.

How frightening it would be to have no answers to the question! Without a sense of self, one almost ceases to exist. And most of us in Western nations achieve our sense of self through our work. We do, therefore we are.

When modern manufacturing adopted assembly lines and simplified jobs, workers began to lose some of the sense of self they once associated with their work. Repeating one simple task over and over tends to reduce a worker's pride and responsibility for the finished product. At one time it may have been possible to reply in answer to the parlor question, "I am an automaker." But it is not very satisfying to admit "I am a lever operator," "a wrench twister," or a "windshield lifter."

Karl Marx called this problem alienation. Worker alienation is the separation of a worker from the product of his or her work. Alienation diminishes a worker's sense of self and reduces opportunities for creative expression and personal growth. Alienation often leads to boredom on the job, deteriorating product quality, and reduced worker productivity.

The harmful effects of worker alienation have caused some firms to change their manufacturing processes entirely, to change from making jobs more simple to making them more complex. Some automobile manufacturers allow teams of workers to organize the manufacturing process as it was in the "old days" before the assembly line. They reward worker teams according to the quantity and quality of the finished product. The daily output of automobiles may be somewhat less than under the assembly-line method, but there have been benefits in improved worker morale and, frequently, improved product quality and lower supervisory costs as well.

eration in work marked the beginning of economic development. When communities divided the necessary work and workers specialized in particular tasks, they could produce more than they could working alone. To illustrate the benefits of division of labor and specialization, Adam Smith told a famous story of a pin factory. When all of the workers concentrate on producing finished pins, he said, they can produce fewer pins than if workers are assigned specific tasks on an assembly line.

Two early American businessmen, Frederick Taylor and Frank Gilbreth, studied division of labor and specialization. They called their work **task management**: the separation of jobs into simple tasks requiring little special training or effort. Henry Ford used task management in the world's first auto assembly lines, and today Apple Computer uses assembly lines to produce PCs.

The effect of specialization and division of labor is to increase dramatically the output produced per unit of work. Through specialization and division of labor, modern societies can produce not only the necessities but also some of the luxuries that enrich life. Thus, modern consumers can enjoy an abundance of VCRs, computers, ice makers, and what-have-you.

LABOR SUPPLY AND DEMAND

This chapter focuses on labor as a productive resource. Productive resources are bought and sold in markets similar to the markets for finished goods and services. We begin our discussion of labor markets with the assumption that resource markets are perfectly competitive; that is, that the four characteristics of competition prevail. Later, we relax this assumption and describe the effects of imperfect competition in resource markets. Although our discussion focuses on the market for labor resources, we should note that the principles that govern supply and demand for labor apply as well to supply and demand for land and capital resources.

Resource supply shows the quantities of a resource that would be offered for sale at various prices. Like any other supply curve, a resource supply curve is drawn for a certain period of time during which factors other than price are assumed to remain constant. Thus, the resource supply curves of labor define the quantities of labor that would be offered at various wage rates over a certain period of time. When the individual supply curves of all workers are added together, the result is a market supply curve of labor.

In general, the supply of labor obeys the law of supply: that is, workers tend to offer larger quantities of labor at higher wages.

Likewise, the demand for labor obeys the law of demand: firms tend to employ larger quantities of labor at lower wages. Market demand for labor is the sum of all individual firms' labor demand curves. As we found in product markets, the intersection of demand and supply curves determines the equilibrium price and quantity: the wage rate and the quantity of labor that will be employed during the time period for which the supply and demand curves are drawn.

The supply curve in Figure 6.1 shows the quantities of labor that will be offered for em-

Figure 6.1 A Market for Labor

As the wage rate increases, hours of labor supplied increase, and hours of labor demanded fall.

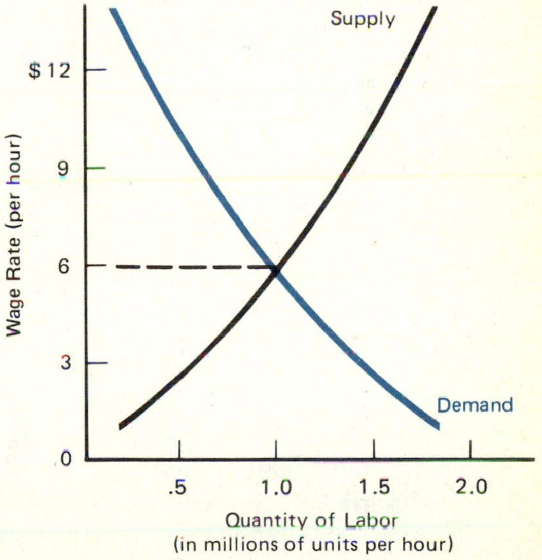

ployment in a particular market at various wage rates. The supply curve slopes upward to show that larger quantities will generally be offered at higher wage rates. The demand curve slopes downward because larger quantities will be employed only at lower wages. The equilibrium wage rate in Figure 6.1 is $6 per hour. At a wage of $6, a total of one million hours of labor will be employed in this market.

The Opportunity Cost of a Productive Resource

In a perfectly competitive resource market, the equilibrium price reflects the opportunity cost of using the resource in a particular way. The equilibrium price is higher when there are many possible uses for a resource and lower when the resource is useful for producing only one product. Likewise, the equilibrium price is higher when the resource is relatively scarce and lower when the resource is plentiful.

In labor markets, the equilibrium wage determines another result. For an individual firm the market wage determines the most efficient quantity of labor to employ with the firm's own fixed resources.

A Firm's Demand for Labor

Remember that a firm employs two kinds of resources: fixed resources and variable resources.

Fixed resources are resources the firm cannot easily change in the short run. In the short run the firm cannot easily change the size of its plant and equipment, but the firm can vary the use of variable resources and, thus, the quantity of output it produces. **Variable resources** are such things as labor, raw materials, and the electric power necessary for operating the fixed plant.

The Law of Variable Proportions (or the Law of Diminishing Marginal Product)

As the proportion of variable resources to a firm's fixed resources changes, quantity of output tends to change in particular ways. Adding the first units of a variable resource generally causes quantity of output to increase by larger and larger amounts. We say that total product increases at an increasing rate. Eventually, however, increasing the proportion of variable to fixed resources increases quantity of output by smaller and smaller amounts. We say that total product increases at a decreasing rate. At some quantity of variable resources, adding still more variable resources to existing fixed resources may even cause total product to fall.

This principle is known as the **law of variable proportions** (or the **law of diminishing marginal product**). It states that there is some proportion of variable resources to fixed resources that yields maximum increase in total product. When total product increases at its maximum rate, we say that marginal product is at the maximum. Beyond this quantity (or range) of variable resources, additional units of the variable resource add less to total product than the one before. When total product increases at a decreasing rate, we say that marginal product diminishes.

The Equilibrium Wage and Employment

Given a firm's quantity of fixed plant and equipment, there appears to be some quantity (or range) of variable resources that yields maximum marginal product. If the firm employs too many or too few variable resources relative to its existing fixed resources, additions to total product are lower.

The firm does not normally employ precisely the quantity of variable resources that yields maximum marginal product. In fact, a more important consideration for determining employment and, ultimately, output is prices. The firm must consider two kinds of prices when making its employment decision:

1. The price of the finished product.
2. The price of the variable resource used to produce it.

Thus, in the short run, a profit-maximizing firm decides employment according to the following rule:

TO MAXIMIZE PROFIT A FIRM SHOULD EMPLOY UNITS OF A VARIABLE RESOURCE UP TO THE POINT WHERE THE VALUE OF THE OUTPUT OF THE LAST RESOURCE UNIT HIRED IS JUST OFFSET BY THE RESOURCE'S PRICE.

As long as the firm follows this rule, it maximizes profits from the use of its fixed and variable resources.

To understand the profit-maximizing rule, consider this simple example. Table 6.1 provides hypothetical data for a grumpet firm that sells grumpets at a market price of $3. The firm owns a certain quantity of fixed plant and equipment and can employ various quantities of labor at an hourly rate of $6. Column (1) lists quantities of labor, and Column (2) lists quantities of grumpets per hour when various quantities of labor are employed. Notice that increasing employment of variable resources causes hourly production to behave just as we have described it. In fact, as resource employment increases, total product increases, first at an increasing rate, and then at a decreasing rate. Finally, if more than 6 workers are employed, total product decreases.

Column (3) lists the market value of hourly production at various levels of employment when grumpets sell for $3. Column (4) lists changes in the value of hourly production at various levels of employment, and Column (5) lists the hourly wage.

How many workers should the firm hire? To hire 1, 2, or 3 workers would enable the

Table 6.1 Resource and Production Data (per hour).

(1) Number of Workers Q_L	*(2) Total Product* TP	*(3) Value of Total Product* $TP \times p$	*(4) Value of Additional Production* $\Delta(TP \times p)$	*(5) Wage Rate* w
1	2	$ 6	$ 6	$6
2	5	15	9	6
3	9	27	12	6
4	12	36	9	6
5	14	42	6	6
6	15	45	3	6
7	14	42	−3	6

firm to sell its grumpets and pay all the workers' wages. However, by hiring only 1, 2, or 3 workers the firm sacrifices the gain from hiring the fourth worker at $6 and selling his or her additional output for $9. In fact, the firm should hire the fifth worker, whose additional production is worth just enough to pay his or her hourly wage. This is the profit-maximizing level of employment.

Now, suppose the wage rate falls to $3. At a wage of $3 a sixth worker adds just enough to total product to pay his or her wage. The lower wage rate has the effect of increasing the profit-maximizing level of employment.

TEST YOURSELF

What is the profit-maximizing level of employment if the wage rate is $9?

Have you noticed that, given the behavior of production in the short run when certain resources are fixed, the profit-maximizing level of employment depends on the wage rate? In fact, the profit-maximizing level of employment determines 3 points on the grumpet firm's demand curve for labor: w = $9 and $Q_L = 4$; w = $6 and $Q_L = 5$; w = $3 and $Q_L = 6$. These points have been plotted on Figure 6.2 and connected to form the grumpet firm's demand curve for labor.

We can summarize resource demand as follows. A firm wants to employ the quantity of a resource that maximizes profit. By adding variable resources to a certain quantity of fixed resources, the firm causes total product to increase, first at an increasing rate, and eventually at a decreasing rate. The firm calculates its own demand for a variable resource by measuring the value of the resource's contribution to total product. Then the firm employs the quantity of the resource at which the value of the added product of the last resource unit employed is just enough to pay the resource price. The firm's demand curve slopes downward because of the law of variable proportions (or the law of diminishing marginal product). Because additions to total product diminish, additional resources will be employed only if the value of added output is greater than the resource's price.

Figure 6.2 A Firm's Demand for Labor

A firm's demand curve for labor slopes downward because of the law of variable proportions (or the law of diminishing marginal product).

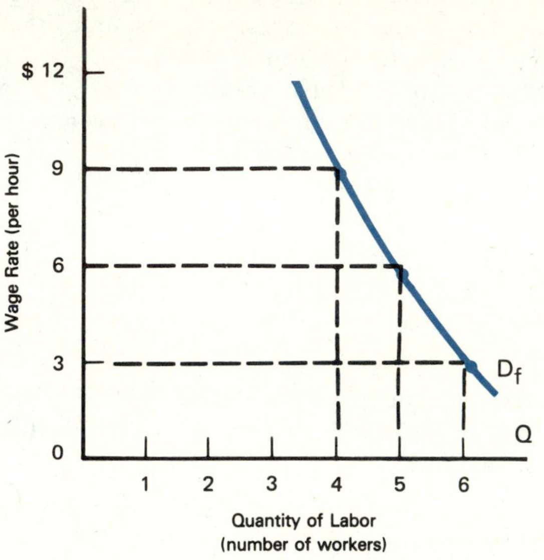

Money Wages and Real Wages

We have described the relationship between wage rates and the quantity of workers hired. It is important to distinguish between money wages paid by employers and real wages. Money wages refer to the dollar amount of wages. Real wages refer to the purchasing power of wages: the real goods and services a worker can buy with his or her wages.

Some workers may concentrate on increases in money wages and fail to notice decreases in real wages. Real wages fall when prices rise and reduce the purchasing power of the dollars workers receive. Increases in real wages depend on increased worker productivity: increased output of goods and services consumers want to buy. Higher productivity increases total quantities of goods and services and increases the real income available to pay suppliers of all resources.

PRODUCTIVITY AND PRODUCTIVITY GROWTH

Increasing real wages requires increasing worker productivity. We define worker productivity as output per unit of labor input.

Increasing worker productivity is important for two reasons. First, it enables us to enjoy larger quantities of goods and services; and second, it holds down production costs and helps keep prices from rising.

Over the years, increases in worker productivity have varied among industries, chiefly because of differences in the level of mechanization and standardization of production. The greatest growth of worker productivity has occurred in communications, electric power, gas, and sanitary services. Utilities like these are described as **capital-intensive** because each worker has a relatively large amount of capital equipment for increasing output. Industries with few opportunities for mechanizing production are described as **labor-intensive**. Services such as finance, real estate, and insurance are generally labor-intensive. However, the increased use of computers is increasing capital-intensity and productivity even in these service industries. Labor-intensive industries typically experience slower growth in worker productivity than capital-intensive industries.

Table 6.2 shows output produced (minus materials used) per unit of labor for various industries. Can you identify the capital-intensive and labor-intensive industries in the table? Which industries would you expect to experience higher growth in worker productivity?

For several decades after World War II, worker productivity in the United States increased about 2.5 percent a year. Increases in worker productivity were the result of more and better capital equipment, more efficient use of resources, better management, and a better educated labor force.

Worker productivity growth slowed during the 1970s and continued low through the 1980s. One reason for the decline in worker productivity growth was a change in the composition of the labor force. More females and teenagers joined the labor force in the 1970s

Table 6.2 Value Added Per Dollar of Payroll. Value of output (less materials cost) per dollar of labor input

	1947	*1973*	*1990*
Tobacco	$3.10	$5.20	$14.88
Petroleum	2.70	4.51	6.08
Chemicals	2.75	3.80	5.09
Food	2.35	2.90	4.21
Instruments	1.60	2.55	2.59
Paper	2.25	2.35	3.16
Rubber	1.65	2.30	2.47
Lumber	1.80	2.25	2.12
Nonelectrical machinery	1.60	2.05	2.34
Transportation equipment	1.55	2.01	2.34
Textiles	1.85	1.98	2.29
Furniture	1.70	1.90	2.20
Apparel	1.75	1.90	2.34
Leather	1.75	1.85	5.24

Thinking Seriously About Economic Issues

DECLINING PRODUCTIVITY GROWTH IN THE UNITED STATES

The foremost scholar of productivity in the United States is Edward F. Denison of the Brookings Institution. Denison notes a marked slowdown in productivity growth beginning in 1973, when the growth rate of potential output fell from almost 4 percent to about $2\frac{1}{2}$ percent. Potential output is defined as production if resource unemployment were to be as low as 4 percent. Actual output per worker has fallen even farther than potential output.

According to Denison, the abrupt decline in worker productivity growth in 1973 was followed by another decline in 1979. His research examines factors that contributed to productivity growth both before and after 1973 and then looks more closely at six "Residual Factors" that may have been responsible for the slowdown:

1. Changes in the pace of technological advance probably did not contribute much to the growth slowdown, since spending for R&D continued at almost the same rate after 1973 as before; but R&D efforts may have been subject to diminishing marginal product. Communication of new technological knowledge (both nationally and internationally) has probably improved since the 1970s.
2. One reason for slower productivity growth has been a deterioration in the performance of business managers. Some managers have paid more attention to legal and regulatory aspects of business than to efficiency in production. Wide fluctuations in market prices, stock prices, interest rates, and profits have required managers to focus more on financial decisions and have reduced the influence of persons knowledgeable in the technology of production. The reward system for business managers does not always compensate fully for changes in production technology that will become profitable only after years of costly effort.
3. Denison found no significant evidence of a decline in work effort, although there was some indication of a decrease in job satisfaction.
4. Another reason for slowing produc-

and 1980s, a result of the so-called baby boom that followed World War II. Because some female and many teenage workers had fewer opportunities for education and skill development, their productivity tended to be low. Growth in the productivity of our capital resources also slowed in the 1970s and 1980s. New legislation requiring use of new environmental and safety equipment reduced the measured output of goods per unit of labor employed. Finally, during the 1970s and 1980s the U.S. economy came increasingly to be dominated by service industries. Because service production cannot be significantly increased through the use of modern machinery, service industries offer fewer opportunities for tivity growth may be some misallocation of resources. A misallocation of labor resources may result from restrictions against the use of testing in hiring decisions and from low minimum qualifications for employment. A misallocation of capital resources may be a result of a tax system that distorted capital investment away from the most technically efficient kinds of equipment. Increasing barriers to trade may also have contributed to a misallocation of domestic resources.

5. The years of 1973 and 1979 were years of energy crises, but Denison found "no consistent relationship" between energy costs and productivity growth. In fact, firms' efforts to minimize the use of energy may have contributed to an increase in labor's productivity.
6. Other factors that contributed slightly to the productivity growth slowdown were inflation (by increasing the costs of information, prediction, and transactions), government regulations (by diverting labor and capital resources to comply with regulations), and delays resulting from legal problems and from deterioration of the nation's highway system.

According to Denison, government's response to the productivity growth slowdown has focused too closely on material investment, which is not primarily responsible for the problem. In the meantime, expenditures for growth-promoting activities (such as education) have not been increased and in many cases have been cut back. Moreover, government has not contributed to a stable business environment that would promote high employment and stable prices.

Edward F. Denison, *Trends in American Economic Growth, 1929–1982,* The Brookings Institution, Washington, D.C., 1985.

productivity growth than are found in manufacturing.

During the 1990s many of these conditions will change. Baby-boom workers are reaching their most productive years, and environmental and safety equipment will be fully operational.

Increasing worker productivity growth is an important goal for workers and for the nation as a whole. Slowing productivity growth brings slower growth in material standards of living. Slowing productivity growth pushes up labor costs and increases the prices of finished goods. For these reasons it is important always to seek new methods for increasing worker productivity.

Self-Check

1. A significant force for economic development is:
   a. Specialization.
   b. Division of labor.
   c. Interregional trade.
   d. All of the above.
   e. None of the above.

2. The employment level of a variable resource is based on:
   a. Its price.
   b. The price for which the final product sells.
   c. The availability of fixed resources.
   d. Both (a) and (b).
   e. All answers are correct.

3. Real wages:
   a. are frequently higher than money wages.
   b. generally reflect the level of worker productivity.
   c. are the sum of money wages and inflation.
   d. rise as the value of the dollar falls.
   e. all of the above.

4. Which of the following describes capital-intensive industries?
   a. Examples are finance, real estate, and insurance.
   b. They experience slower productivity growth than labor-intensive industries.
   c. They may have contributed to slowing productivity growth in the U.S.
   d. They provide workers with large amounts of capital.
   e. Both (a) and (d).

5. Which of the following is most clearly associated with slow productivity growth?
   a. Technological advance has slowed.
   b. Managers have focused on technical decisions.
   c. Work effort has declined.
   d. Energy costs have increased.
   e. Resources have been misallocated.

Theory in Practice

CHANGES IN RESOURCE MARKETS

This chapter has focused on labor as the largest class of productive resource. Land and capital resources are subject to the same kinds of demand and supply conditions as those that affect labor. Throughout the economic system, changes are constantly taking place in the availability of all these resources (supply) and in their productivity and the value of their output (demand). Resource buyers and sellers must constantly adjust to changes in the equilibrium price and quantity of land, labor, and capital resources.

Figure 6.3 illustrates an increase in resource supply and a fall in equilibrium price. How does a lower equilibrium price affect quantity employed? In general, we would expect a lower equilibrium price to encourage buyers to employ more of this more plentiful resource. (They move down their demand curves and employ larger quantities.)

Figure 6.4 illustrates a decrease in resource supply and an increase in equilibrium price. The higher equilibrium price discourages buyers from using this relatively scarce resource. (They move up their demand curves and employ smaller quantities.) At the same

Figure 6.3 Increased Supply, Lower Price

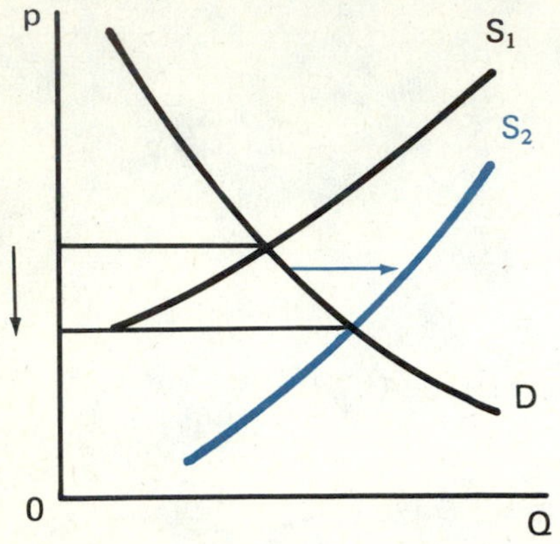

time, the higher price encourages sellers to increase the quantities they supply to this market.

When buyers and sellers adjust to changes in resource prices, the result is improved efficiency in resource employment. Throughout the economy, buyers substitute more plentiful (and cheaper) resources for less plentiful (and more costly) resources. Movement of buyers and sellers into and out of resource markets helps adjust supply to demand at competitive prices.

Figure 6.4 Decreased Supply, Higher Price

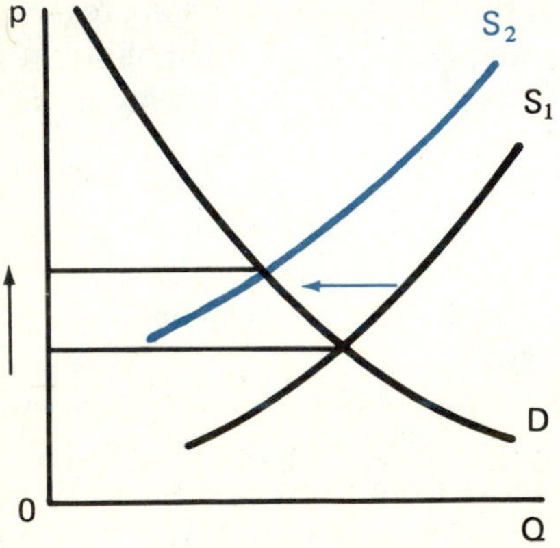

TEST YOURSELF

Trace the effects on resource supply of an increase in demand and a higher equilibrium price. What is the effect on economic efficiency? Now trace the effects on resource supply of a decrease in demand and a lower equilibrium price. What are the effects on the nation's total output?

What productive resources are you developing as a student? Was your decision influenced by supply and demand in a particular resource market? How would changes in supply or demand affect your decision?

Now consider the following examples of changes in supply or demand. Explain the responses of buyers and sellers to each change. Then draw a freehand graph of the affected resource market or markets and show the change in price and quantity employed.

1. The Defense Department reduces its orders for military aircraft. What labor markets are affected first? Are there shifts in demand or supply? What other resource markets may eventually be affected?
2. A change in technology causes a reduction in the price of compact discs. How does a lower product price affect the demand for resources used to produce compact discs?
3. Jamaica, a substantial producer of bauxite used in manufacturing aluminum, reduces its shipments to U.S. manufacturers. How does this change affect the market for aluminum used in the production of automobiles? What substitute or complementary markets may also be affected?
4. World famine raises the export price of American grain. How do higher grain prices affect the market for U.S. farmland and farm implements? Are there also effects in markets for suburban homes?

Viewpoint

LABOR MARKET CHANGES IN GERMANY

Until November 9, 1989, the Berlin Wall limited the ability of East German workers to seek higher paying jobs in West Germany. Since the collapse of the Wall, however, thousands of workers have left East Germany, and thousands more commute daily to jobs in the West.

Before Germany was reunited, East Germany had a command economy, with no free labor market and no unemployment. Workers were simply ordered to work at specific jobs, whether or not those jobs efficiently used the workers' skills. Today, free movement across Germany has brought changes in labor markets in both East and West. In the West, the increased supply of workers has held down wage increases and increased profits and growth prospects for Western firms. In the East, the reduced supply of workers might have been expected to cause wage rates to increase. On the contrary, because East German consumers prefer goods made in the West, many East German manufacturers have gone out of business, thus reducing demand for labor and keeping wage rates low. Unless new businesses are established and workers retrained for new jobs, wage rates in the East will drop further and unemployment will increase.

East German workers have criticized wage disparities and pressed for increased wage rates in the East, but they may face a no-win situation. Unless Eastern wage rates increase, the best workers will leave for the West; but if wage rates increase too much, more businesses will fail, unemployment will increase, and some of the unemployed will move out.

Good education in the East has produced a well-educated work force, even though the lack of modern equipment and technology has kept worker productivity low. Thus, the solution to Germany's labor dilemma may lie in increased incentives for business firms to locate in the East. Moving some government jobs to the East, expanding professional and technical training programs, and increasing unemployment compensation would also help reduce worker unrest until a true market economy can begin operating throughout Germany.

Bernd Hoene, "Labor Market Realities in Eastern Germany," *Challenge*, July–August 1991.

CHANGES IN DEMAND FOR LABOR

Growth in job opportunities has been uneven among industries. More workers have been needed in state and local government, retail trade, transportation and public utilities, and services. The demand curves for these workers have been shifting to the right over the last decade, contributing to a rising equilibrium wage.

Employment opportunities have grown more slowly in the federal government, mining and construction, and certain manufacturing industries. The demand curves for these work-

Table 6.3 Average Hourly Wages.

	Hourly Wage 1971	*Hourly Wage 1991*	*Change in Real Wage (%)*
Mining	$4.00	$14.21	19
Construction	5.56	14.01	−84
Lumber and wood products	3.06	9.28	−33
Furniture and fixtures	2.84	8.77	−27
Stone, clay, and glass products	3.55	11.36	−16
Primary metal products	4.09	13.33	−10
Fabricated metal products	3.67	11.20	−31
Machinery, except electrical	3.90	12.17	−24
Electrical and electronic equipment	3.43	10.73	−23
Transportation equipment	4.44	14.79	−3
Instruments and related products	3.48	11.71	0
Miscellaneous manufacturing	2.94	8.85	−35
Food and kindred products	3.32	9.88	−39
Tobacco products	3.02	16.89	223
Textile mill products	2.54	8.30	−10
Apparel	2.48	6.75	−64
Paper products	3.58	12.70	102
Printing and publishing	4.08	11.50	−54
Chemicals and allied products	3.84	14.07	30
Petroleum and coal products	4.49	17.02	43
Rubber and miscellaneous plastics	3.32	10.10	−32
Leather products	2.58	7.16	−59
Transportation and public utilities	4.08	13.23	−12
Finance and real estate	3.24	10.42	−15
Services	2.95	10.24	11
Wholesale and retail trade	2.83	9.08	−15

ers have either increased very little or declined. In turn, their wage rates have not increased much in real terms or have fallen.

Some examples of average hourly wage rates before taxes for workers for 1971 and 1991 are in Table 6.3. Data are from the *Monthly Labor Review*, published by the U.S. Department of Labor. Column (3) in the table shows the gain in real wages—wages corrected for inflation—over the period.

A BACKWARD-BENDING SUPPLY CURVE OF LABOR

A resource supply curve depends on the willingness of resource owners to offer it in the market. The supply of labor sometimes differs from that of other resources because labor is inseparable from its owner. This may make for a peculiar supply curve.

We have said that the price of a resource reflects its opportunity cost: the value of the resource's alternative employment in another kind of production. But labor's opportunity cost includes also the cost of the leisure a worker sacrifices when working. Deciding to supply labor in production requires a wage that is high enough to offset the sacrifice of the worker's own leisure time.

In general, supplying small quantities of labor involves such a small sacrifice of leisure time that a low wage is sufficient. Supplying larger quantities involves greater sacrifice and requires a higher wage rate. The result is a typical upward-sloping supply curve like the one we saw in Figure 6.1. But if a worker reaches a very high level of income, enjoying leisure may seem more valuable than additional work, even when the work earns a higher wage. When a worker reaches an income level sufficient for his or her desired standard of living, the worker's supply curve becomes very steep and may even bend backward to the left.

Figure 6.5 illustrates a backward-bending supply curve. At a wage rate of w_1 a worker offers h_1 hours of work for total income represented by the rectangle formed by $Ow_1 \times Oh_1$. If the wage rate rises to w_2, workers can enjoy a higher income of $Ow_2 \times Oh_2$ by supplying more hours of work. But working only Oh_3 hours yields the same income as before and leaves more hours for leisure. The higher wage rate could have the effect of reducing quantity supplied.

What is the actual wage rate at which a worker begins to reduce hours worked? Of course, the answer depends on the worker. It depends on a worker's current living standard relative to his or her desired living standard; and it depends on a worker's attitude toward work and leisure. For a "workaholic" the

Figure 6.5 A Backward-Bending Supply Curve of Labor

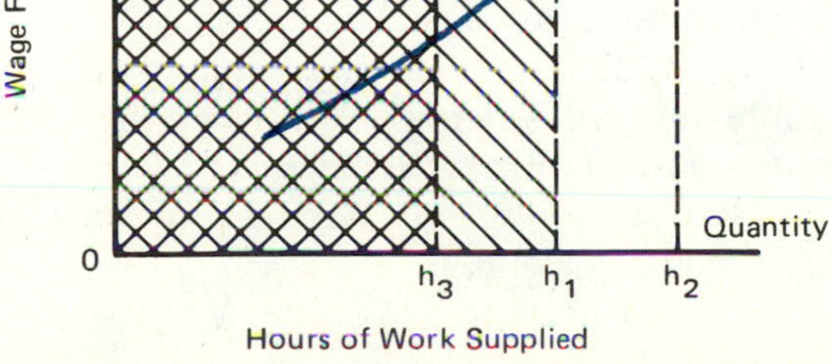

backward bend in the labor supply curve would occur at a very high level of w. Workers in tropical climates probably experience the bend in labor supply at a lower level of w than workers in temperate climates. Can you explain why? Can you identify groups in the U.S. economy for whom the bend in supply might occur at a lower level than others? Might other resources also be subject to backward-bending supply curves? Why? (Hint: Consider crude oil or timber resources.)

LABOR MARKETS AND INCOME

We describe the demand for a resource as a derived demand: firms employ resources because there is a demand for the products the resource can produce. Firms employ the quantity of resources at which the value of the last unit's output is just enough to pay the resource price. In competition all resources are paid a price equal to the value of the product of the last unit hired. In fact, in competition the incomes of all variable resources are determined by the value of the product of the last unit.

After all variable resources have been paid, the remaining revenue from the sale of output goes to the owners of fixed resources. Competition in resource markets ensures that each type of resource is rewarded according to the value of its contribution to output.

Look again at Figure 6.1. Can you show on Figure 6.1 the area that represents the share of total income that is paid to labor? How does the size of the area reflect labor's productivity and market demand for labor's output?*

Of the four types of resources, labor receives the largest share of national income.

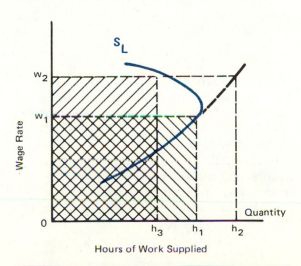

* Labor's share of total income is the rectangle formed beneath the demand curve at the equilibrium wage. The area of the rectangle is determined by multiplying the equilibrium wage rate by the quantity of labor employed.

One reason for labor's large share is the large size and high quality of the labor force. More and better workers have contributed to growth in national output and merited a growing share of income for labor. From only 60 percent of national income in 1929, labor's share grew to 65 percent in 1992.* Rental income declined from 6 percent to less than 1 percent over the period, and interest income rose from 5 to 11 percent. Income of unincorporated businesses, corporate profits, and farm income also declined, from 29 to 14 percent of national income.

In competition, differences in income shares are the result of different supply and demand conditions in resource markets. In markets where an especially productive resource is in limited supply, its share of national income is relatively high. Less productive resources in more plentiful supply may receive smaller shares. Likewise, changes in resource supply and demand cause changes in income shares. Whether income shares increase or decrease with change depends on price elasticities, much as total expenditure in the markets for goods and services depend on price elasticities of demand and supply.

THE LABOR MOVEMENT AND LABOR UNIONS

In the early years of the Industrial Revolution, two classes of resource suppliers struggled to gain larger shares of national income: a large, disorganized class of workers and a small, well-organized class of owners of capital (the capitalists). The capitalists' power over available jobs enabled them to increase their share of income relative to the share paid to workers. According to Karl Marx, a nineteenth-century political and economic theorist, private ownership of capital resources leads inevitably to conflict over income shares, which leads in turn to revolution. Marx argued that the first great revolution in world history moved medieval Europe from feudalism to capitalism. The next would move capitalist nations to socialism. The greatest revolution of all would finally move socialist nations to communism.

When Marx was living, the possibility of class conflict and revolution was a real concern. During the Industrial Revolution in England, large landowners forced tenant farmers off the land in order to use their land to raise sheep for producing wool. Forced into the towns in great droves, the peasants sought jobs in the new factories and coal mines. The increased supply of workers pushed wage rates down, so that workers' income shares fell relative to the income shares of the capitalists. Marx told stories of workers' wives and young children working long hours in sweatshops and dying of disease or malnutrition after a short and miserable life.

During any period of industrial development, a nation needs workers to build the capital resources necessary for increasing the nation's productive capacity. Producing capital goods requires a sacrifice of consumer goods. (Remember the production possibilities curve and the limits to total production.) The early capitalists found it relatively easy to require sacrifices from unorganized and desperate workers, who regarded any employment at all as better than starvation.

According to Marx, workers' hardships would eventually create class consciousness and revolution, which would destroy the capitalist class. Workers would seize the mines and factories and operate capital resources in their interests alone.

* Labor's increasing share of national income is in part the result of a movement away from self-employment, where earnings would be reported as profit, to work for others.

Revolutionary Unions and Business Unions

When the first labor unions were organized in Europe, Marxists thought they were the start of a workers' revolution that would overthrow capitalism and replace it with socialism. Such a revolution did occur in what became the Soviet Union. In the United States, however, the revolutionary unions were soon replaced by **business unions**, concerned more with improving the material conditions of workers than with overthrowing capitalism. U.S. workers did not think of themselves as part of a revolutionary class and were generally willing to cooperate to improve job conditions within the capitalist system.

Indeed, the most successful unions in the United States have emphasized specific problems in the workplace: wage rates, hours, sick leave, retirement, seniority, and fringe benefits. Contrary to Marxian expectations, the U.S. economy has provided higher incomes both for capitalists and workers. It has enabled many workers to become capitalists themselves, something else that Marx did not foresee.

Craft Unions and Industrial Unions

The earliest U.S. labor unions were typically **craft unions**, similar to the guilds of the Middle Ages. Their members specialized in skilled crafts such as shoemaking, carpentry, or printing. Most of the unions were small, and they quickly disbanded if their employers complained. In fact, until 1842 unions were considered illegal and forced to operate in secret.

As the Industrial Revolution spread, craft unions grew in number and size. But a conflict arose over who should be eligible for union membership. Craft unions were exclusive organizations, limiting their membership to workers in the skilled crafts. Some workers wanted more inclusive unions, unions that would invite workers in an entire industry to join. An example of an **industrial union** was the Knights of Labor, which planned a nationwide federation of unions of all workers—skilled and unskilled—in particular industries.

By 1886, the exclusive, craft formula was again dominating the labor movement. Cigarmaker Samuel Gompers organized the American Federation of Labor (AFL), and many local craft unions joined up. At the turn of the century, union membership amounted to 750,000 workers, roughly 3 percent of the labor force. By 1920 membership had grown to five million, 12 percent of the labor force.

The 1920s and 1930s

Union growth slowed during the 1920s because of general prosperity and economic progress. It declined further with the high unemployment of the Depression years. (Can you suggest a reason?*)

By the time of the Great Depression in the mid-1930s the U.S. government was struggling with the problem of growing joblessness. The administration of President Franklin Roosevelt was sympathetic to unions, and in 1935 Congress passed the Wagner National Labor Relations Act. The new law gave workers the right to organize and to bargain collectively with employers.

In that same year, the lingering conflict between the skilled, exclusive craft philosophy and the unskilled, inclusive industrial approach to union membership again divided the labor movement. Craft unions of skilled workers remained with the AFL. Unions of un-

* When jobs are scarce, having a job becomes more important than being a union member.

skilled workers formed the more inclusive Congress of Industrial Organizations (CIO) under mineworker John L. Lewis. The CIO became a national federation of unions of unskilled mass-production workers in modern automated industries.

By the end of World War II, union membership included almost one-fourth of the civilian labor force.

Postwar Labor Problems

Unions generally refrained from strikes and wage demands during World War II. But after the war ended, their members insisted on higher wages to offset rising inflation, and a wave of strikes broke out. Congress responded by passing the Taft-Hartley Act of 1947, which reduced the power of unions. The law guaranteed unions' bargaining rights but placed limits on strikes and certain "unfair labor practices." It gave the President the power to obtain an 80-day injunction to postpone a strike, and it outlawed certain union practices, including *closed shop* and *secondary boycotts*.

A **closed shop** requires employers to hire only union members at union wage rates. Although the Taft-Hartley Act outlawed the closed shop, it allowed the **union shop**, in which workers can be required to join a union after they are hired. A boycott is a refusal to do business with a firm because of certain of its policies; this is generally legal. A **secondary boycott** is a boycott by one union because of a firm's policies toward another union; this is illegal.

Perhaps the most controversial part of the Taft-Hartley Act is Section 14B. Section 14B allows individual states to pass "right-to-work" laws. Right-to-work laws forbid the union shop within the state and reduce a union's power over the work force. Twenty states, mostly in the South and Midwest, have such laws.

In 1955, the AFL and CIO buried their differences and merged into a single organization—the AFL-CIO. The two federations decided that by combining their strengths they would be better able to deal with growing public opposition to unions. Later, the Teamsters broke apart from the AFL-CIO.

Corruption in national unions in the 1950s prompted a Congressional investigation, and Congress passed new laws to regulate the internal affairs of unions. The Landrum-Griffin Act of 1959 required democratic election of union officials and called for detailed reporting of union finances.

UNIONISM TODAY

Union membership in the United States has grown slowly in recent years. In 1950 about 15 million workers belonged to unions. By the beginning of the 1990s, union membership was about 17 million. However, this number represents a shrinking share of the labor force—from one-third in 1950 to less than one-fifth today.

In part, declining union membership is a result of the changing structure of the U.S. economy. We are becoming increasingly a service economy. More than half of consumer expenditures today go for health, education, recreation, housing, and other services. Three-fourths of the nation's workers now work in service industries: transporation and public utilities; trade, finance, and real estate; and government. Many service occupations require skilled white-collar or professional workers. Such workers have traditionally been the most difficult to organize. Other service occupations are relatively unskilled and are difficult to organize because workers change jobs frequently, often leaving the labor force entirely for long stretches of time.

In one sense, labor's weakness today is a result of its past successes. Wage increases won by unions have priced some union members out of the job market. High union wages have forced some firms out of business and disrupted entire industries. For example, the U.S. automobile industry lost much of the U.S. auto market because of high wage costs relative to low wage rates abroad. In other industries, high-cost union workers have been replaced by nonunion workers at lower wage rates. This is particularly true in the building construction industry.

As their power has shrunk, unions have turned their attention to establishing a political climate favorable to labor's goals. They support government policies promoting high employment, federally supported job training, union wage scales for federal contractors, a legal minimum wage law, and national health insurance.

The largest unions today are the Teamsters, the United Auto Workers, and the Steelworkers, each with more than a million members. Other strong unions are the Brotherhood of Electrical Workers, Retail Clerks, and Communication Workers. The fastest growing union today is the Association of State, County, and Municipal Employees, with more than a million workers.

UNION LABOR MARKETS

Unions affect resource markets in much the same way that imperfect competition affects product markets. In both cases, the goal is to control supply and keep price higher than it would be in a freely competitive market.*

* Economist John Kenneth Galbraith believes that the trend toward union organization was actually a reaction to imperfect competition in product markets. He describes unions as ''countervailing power,'' labor power to balance the power of industrial giants.

Practice Determining Union Wage Rates

As we saw earlier in this chapter, a craft union is composed of workers with a particular skill, like the International Brotherhood of Electrical Workers. In effect, members of a craft union represent the entire supply of a particular type of labor.

Historically, craft unions have tried to limit their membership, much as the American Medical Association and the American Bar Association have tried to limit the number of doctors and lawyers. Unions limit supply by requiring long apprenticeship programs and limiting access to the programs.

The result of restrictions on union membership is that there are probably fewer workers in certain crafts than there would be under perfect competition. Thus, there is no competitive supply curve like the one in Figure 6.1. Instead, the supply curve for a particular type of labor is a vertical line drawn at the quantity of labor supplied by the union. Look at Figure 6.6 and note the effect on the equilibrium wage rate for members of a craft union. Whereas the competitive wage rate would be about $7 per hour, the rate for craft union members is about $11 per hour.

In contrast to a craft union, an industrial union represents all workers in an industry, whether skilled or unskilled. Again, control of the supply of labor enables the union to establish a higher wage rate. In this case, the union determines its wage rate through **collective bargaining** with employers, keeping as an ultimate threat the possibility of a strike if a satisfactory wage agreement cannot be reached. Once a contract is signed, no labor will be supplied at a rate lower than the agreed-on wage. Thus, the supply curve becomes horizontal at that level, as shown on Figure 6.7. Firms can hire any quantity of workers shown on the horizontal portion of the supply curve. Firms can hire larger quantities by moving up

Figure 6.6 A Craft Union

A craft union limits supply to raise the wage rate above the equilibrium wage.

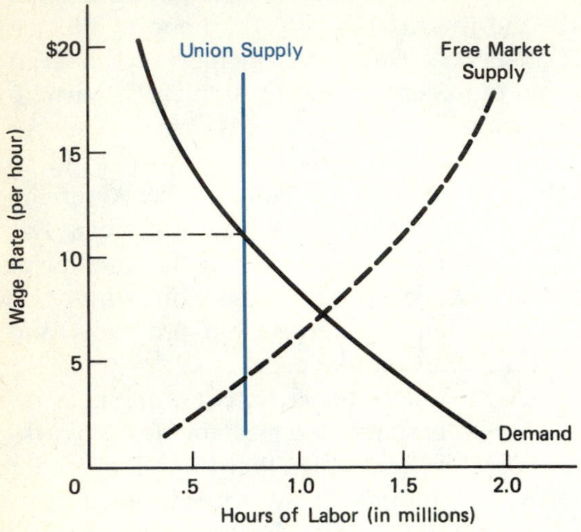

Figure 6.7 An Industrial Union

An industrial union negotiates a wage rate higher than the equilibrium wage.

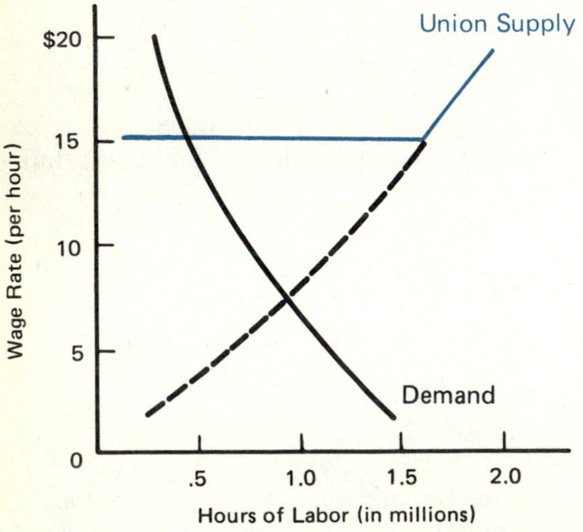

the supply curve and paying a higher wage. Control of supply pushes the wage rate from the competitive wage of $7 to a union wage of $15.

Notice the effect of unions on employment in Figures 6.6 and 6.7. When unions control supply, they can prevent many willing workers from entering certain markets. The result may be lower employment and higher labor costs than without a union. Lack of free competition interferes with the free flow of labor resources and reduces economic efficiency.

TEST YOURSELF

In Figure 6.6 what is the difference in employment at a wage rate of $11 and $7? In Figure 6.7 what is the difference in employment at a wage rate of $15 and $7?

Unions, Wages, and Employment

Our simple example suggests that labor unions reduce unemployment and increase wage rates. In the real world, it is impossible to measure precisely the effect of labor unions on wages and employment. Why? Because it is impossible to separate the economic effects of unionism from the effects of other tendencies in the economic environment. For example, rising wage rates may result not only from union power but also from:

1. A greater willingness of business firms to grant wage increases.
2. Government policies promoting full employment.
3. Oligopolistic pricing, where large oligopolistic firms can pass on their higher wage costs to consumers in the form of higher prices.
4. The end of the nation's rural-to-urban migration, which formerly provided cheap labor and held wages down.

How Things Have Changed

WORK STOPPAGES

Year	Number	Workers Involved ($\times 10^3$)	Days Idle ($\times 10^3$)	Percentage Estimated Work Time
1960	222	896	13,260	0.09
1965	268	999	15,140	0.10
1970	381	2,468	52,761	0.29
1975	235	965	17,563	0.09
1980	187	795	20,844	0.09
1985	54	324	7,079	0.03
1986	69	533	11,861	0.05
1987	46	174	4,468	0.02
1991	40	392	4,584	0.02

Statistical Abstract of the United States, 1992

The combination of unionism with these other factors has probably kept wages higher during recessions than they would otherwise have been. In fact, while most prices tumbled during the Great Depression, wages of union members fell only slightly. When economic activity is on the upswing, however, union contract negotiations may lag behind price inflation, so that unions may actually slow the pace of wage increases. In both these cases, unions may keep income and total spending more stable than they might be otherwise.

During periods of economic growth and rising employment, union wage rates may rise faster than the prices of finished goods, squeezing business profits and discouraging new capital investment. Falling investment could become a problem, leading to low productivity growth and rising labor cost per unit of output.

The most powerful unions are those of skilled craftsmen for whom demand is relatively inelastic. When there are no clear substitutes, firms must continue to employ necessary workers at higher and higher wage rates. This means that skilled craftsmen can insist on higher wages with little fear of losing their jobs. Over the long run, however, substitutes can be developed for high-priced labor, so that labor demand becomes more elastic. Also, consumers can find lower-priced substitutes for goods produced by high-priced union labor. Labor demand will become more elastic, further reducing the quantity demanded at high wages.

A good example of labor substitution is the bituminous coal-mining industry. A strong mine-workers' union drove wage rates up to a point where mine owners and consumers sought substitutes. Mine owners developed

Thinking Seriously About Economic Issues

POLITICAL ECONOMY

"Workers of the world unite. You have nothing to lose but your chains."

That was Karl Marx's message to industrial workers more than a century ago. It was a call for revolution to overthrow the capitalist owners of capital resources. Marx believed that history would move economic society inevitably to communism, when the tools of capitalism would be owned "in common" and operated in the interests of workers.

What has been the actual outcome for capitalism? How correct were Marx's predictions?

The twentieth century has brought tremendous changes in manufacturing. Mass production has permitted greater specialization, with all the benefits of economies of large scale. Workers in industrialized nations have enjoyed more and better goods at lower relative prices than ever before in history.

The news has not all been good, however. Mass production has aggravated some of the problems that Karl Marx predicted. Remember Marx's prediction that large-scale production would lead to the alienation of the working class. As mere cogs in an impersonal capitalist machine, workers would lose the drive to achieve high levels of craftsmanship, and their productivity would fall. They would grow bitter toward the system they felt oppressed them.

Fortunately—and this was not predicted by Marx—capitalist nations have been flexible enough to adjust to the needs of workers. Democratic political institutions have provided the means for workers to express their job dissatisfaction in constructive ways.

Many Japanese and European firms have established innovative ways of dealing with problems at the workplace. In Germany, for instance, coal and steel firms have organized worker councils to

coal-mining machinery to replace high-cost union labor, and consumers and business firms substituted cheap oil and gas for high-priced coal. The result was fewer jobs for coal miners.

When high wages destroy jobs in unionized industries, unemployed workers must move into nonunion jobs, increasing the supply of workers in these industries and causing wages in these markets to fall. The result may be lower wages in the nonunion sector and lower average wages for the nation as a whole.

PRACTICE WITH COLLECTIVE BARGAINING

As a worker in U.S. industry, you may be invited (or required) to join a union. Peri-

4. Rising gasoline prices have been particularly hard on workers in the U.S. automobile industry. This may be a long-range problem that will require major adjustments in labor markets over the coming decades. What adjustments would you predict? Explain your answer in terms of demand, supply, and equilibrium price (wage). Include markets for other types of labor as well as for automobile workers.
5. Some of the blame for declining productivity growth in the United States has been placed on labor. With all the advantages of large-scale technology, managers may be failing to motivate U.S. workers to contribute their maximum effort to production. This is in sharp contrast to management techniques in Japan, which have apparently earned the loyal enthusiasm of workers for their jobs. It has been suggested that business firms should hire industrial engineers to be used as "vice-presidents of human productivity."

   Imagine that you have accepted such a position in a large U.S. firm. How would you approach the problem of motivating workers? What production information would you need and how would you use it? What new programs or policies would you initiate?
6. Can you think of any disadvantages of joining a union? What are the advantages? Compare the advantages and disadvantages of unionism as a whole. What are the effects on society? Does your answer depend on the type of union and the quality of union leadership? Explain.
7. Rising energy prices have caused some policymakers to recommend new "soft" energy sources: sun, wind, biomass (organic waste). Discuss the implications in terms of the derived demand for resources.
8. Only about 30 of the nation's 15,000 banks are unionized. A small Minnesota bank suffered a long strike when eight female employees formed a union to protest discriminatory employment practices. Why do you suppose banks have been slow to unionize, and what do you expect will be the effect on other banks of the strike in Minnesota?
9. What do pecan rolls in Alaska's Westward Hotel have to do with traffic on the New Jersey turnpike? If you were the hotel pastry chef and you were offered double wages to leave the hotel and follow construction crews at work on the Alaskan pipeline to help provide eastern commuters with gasoline, you would be well aware of the connection. At a cost of at least $4.5 billion, the Alaskan pipeline turned out to be the largest construction job ever attempted. Discuss the probable effects of the pipeline project on these other markets:

   Pick-up trucks and hardware
   Crane operators
   Housing and linens
   Movies and radios
   Transportation services
   Illicit activities

10. Trace the effects on resource supply of an increase in demand and a higher equilibrium price. How are the results helpful to the economy? Now trace the effects on resource supply of a decrease in demand and a lower equilibrium price. What are the results for the economy as a whole in terms of the allocation of resources?
11. What productive resources are you developing as a student? Was your decision influenced by supply and demand in a particular resource market? How would changes in supply or demand affect your decision?
12. In what sense is the demand for oil transport a derived demand? Give other examples of derived demand. Illustrate graphically how increasing costs of a resource affect the market for a finished product.
13. Write a good definition for "productivity." Demonstrate mathematically how changes in the composition of the nation's output can affect average productivity of the nation as a whole. Give some reasons for low productivity growth in the service sector of the economy.
14. If specialization and division of labor increase worker productivity, why do you think some employers are retraining workers to perform multiple tasks?

consult with management on all decisions affecting jobs. Employees are represented along with stockholders on the board of directors of every major corporation in the nation.

Is the United States ready for this type of industrial democracy? In the 1970s Louis O. Kelso proposed an important change in labor-management relationships in the United States. Kelso proposed to "make every worker a capitalist"—but not in the way Marx predicted. Kelso's way is to enable workers to invest their own savings at their place of work.

In Kelso's "universal capitalism," a firm establishes an Employee Stock Ownership Plan—ESOP, for short. The ESOP obtains funds through bank loans and through the sale of stock to employees. Then the ESOP buys stock in the firm itself. It uses the dividends from the stock, first to pay interest and principal on the bank loan and, ultimately, to pay dividends to worker-owners. In the meantime, workers and their representatives accumulate greater power to influence the company policies and share its profits.

ESOPs have several advantages for business firms and for the economy as a whole. Firms benefit from a work force that is committed to increasing production; workers realize that their own prosperity depends on the company's prosperity and are less likely to make unreasonable wage demands. The economy benefits from a more equal distribution of income; modern technology can be capital-intensive without depriving workers of adequate income.*

Now the question: Was Marx right? Or wasn't he?

* A disadvantage to workers is that their investment may be concentrated in one firm, with increased risk of loss.

odically, your union leaders will negotiate a contract with management; the negotiating process is known as collective bargaining. A union contract covers wages, hours, fringe benefits, pension and insurance plans, and other conditions of employment. It may also include a no-strike provision for the life of the contract (generally from one to three years).

The wage clause establishes a wage scale for various job classifications. It provides wage differentials for night work, supervisory responsibilities, hazardous or dirty work, and overtime work. It guarantees workers certain paid holidays and paid vacations depending on their length of service. It may allow the firm to collect union dues through automatic deductions from workers' paychecks. This is called a union check-off clause, and it increases the power of the union. Many union contracts have clauses that guarantee cost-of-living increases* when prices rise. An example is a clause providing a ten cent an hour increase in wages for each .5 percent increase in the consumer price index.

A typical union contract provides for workers' pensions and insurance, paid for through regular contributions of employers and employees. Firms in the auto, steel, and aluminum industries (and some others) have established supplemental unemployment benefits financed entirely through employer contributions. With certain limitations, these funds provide cash benefits to workers who are laid off when production is cut.

A union contract also includes provisions for job security. Generally, a unionized firm must give preference in layoffs and rehiring to workers with greater seniority (length of service). Seniority is less important in promotions, however, which are usually made on the basis of merit.

A union contract generally establishes procedures for disciplining or discharging workers for specified "good and proper" reasons. Proper reasons include violation of company rules, excessive absenteeism, incompetence, or substance abuse. If a worker believes he or she was unjustly disciplined or discharged, the dispute may be taken to a grievance committee. Members of the grievance committee attempt to settle the dispute fairly through discussions with employers.

During the process of negotiating a union contract, a mediator may be called in to help resolve differences between the bargaining parties. A mediator is an impartial outsider who helps the parties reach a compromise on particular issues; however, his or her recommendations are not generally binding.

If a conflict arises during the life of a contract, an arbitrator may be called in to settle the dispute. An arbitrator is an expert in the field of industrial relations. He or she is registered with the Federal Mediation and Conciliation Service and is expected to judge the dispute impartially. The judgment of the arbitrator is binding on both sides.

There is no clear evidence to prove whether or not unions have actually raised the level of wages in U.S. industry. (It is impossible to know what wages might have been without unions.) It is probably correct to say that unions have helped stabilize wages and employment. To the extent that union leaders understand that increases in real wages depend on increases in productivity, they may persuade union members to improve their productivity before demanding higher money wages.

* Cost of living adjustments are called COLAs.

SUMMARY

1. People achieve identity and status through their work. Primitive society took a great step forward when specialization and division of labor brought great increases in production.
2. Labor is a variable resource. Firms hire labor to use along with fixed resources to produce goods and services. An economically efficient firm employs labor up to the point where the cost of hiring the last unit of labor is just equal to the value of its product.
3. Supply and demand for resources determines resource prices. A high price discourages the use of a relatively scarce resource and encourages its production. A low price encourages use of a relatively plentiful resource and discourages further production.
4. Labor unions interfere with the smooth adjustment of supply in resource markets. The result may be a wage level that is higher than the free-market equilibrium wage. At the higher union wage, there is likely to be some unemployment of labor resources.
5. Two types of unions sought to organize workers in the United States. Craft unions were exclusive, each one consisting only of workers with a particular skill. Samuel Gompers' American Federation of Labor (AFL) includes unions of this type. An alternative approach was industrial unions, which were inclusive and aimed at organizing all skilled and unskilled workers in an industry. The Knights of Labor was an example.
6. In 1935 the Wagner National Labor Relations Act was passed, guaranteeing labor's right to organize and bargain collectively. Also in the 1930s, unions under the leadership of John L. Lewis broke away from the AFL and organized unskilled, mass-production unions into the Congress of Industrial Organizations.
7. After World War II public sentiment turned against unions. The Taft-Hartley Act was passed in 1947 to limit strikes and compulsory union membership.
8. Through collective bargaining, a union draws up a contract with management. Provisions of the contract may include no strikes for the life of the contract, a guaranteed wage rate, an escalator clause, and pension and insurance plans.
9. Labor is becoming more active in the ownership and control of business.

TERMS TO REMEMBER

task management: a system of production in which a job is divided into small tasks, and workers specialize in a small portion of the total job
worker alienation: the separation of a worker from the product of his or her work
fixed resources: resources (such as land and capital) whose quantities the firm cannot change in the short run
variable resources: resources (such as labor) whose quantities the firm can change, changing the level of output produced with the firm's fixed resources
law of variable proportions or **law of diminishing marginal product:** as more variable resources are added to a fixed quantity of plant and equipment, total product eventually increases by smaller amounts
capital or **labor intensive:** production processes using substantial quantities of capital or labor resources per unit of output
business unions: unions that are concerned with job needs, such as wages, hours, and working conditions, rather than with radical politics
craft unions: unions whose members specialize in a particular craft or skill
industrial unions: unions whose members include all workers in a particular industry, skilled and unskilled alike
closed shop: an agreement made by a firm to hire only workers who are union members; outlawed by the Taft-Hartley Act of 1947
union shop: a rule, permitted in some states, in which workers must join the appropriate union after they are hired
secondary boycott: a boycott by a union against a firm because of its policies toward another union; outlawed by the Taft-Hartley Act of 1947
collective bargaining: the negotiating process between a union and management aimed at reaching an agreement on the union contract
ESOP: employee stock ownership plan

TOPICS FOR DISCUSSION

1. Explain each of the following expressions and tell how it is significant in the use of labor resources:

    Specialization and division of labor
    Alienation
    Opportunity cost
    Countervailing power

2. Distinguish between each of the following pairs of expressions:

    Craft unions and industrial unions
    Fixed and variable resources

3. How did the following pieces of legislation contribute to the growth of the labor movement:

    Wagner National Labor Relations Act
    Taft-Hartley Act

ANSWERS TO TEST YOURSELF

(p. 124) 4

(p. 130) 1. Demand curves for engineers, designers, technicians, steel, and other raw materials shift to the left. Eventually demand curves for homebuilders and producers of consumer goods and services also shift to the left.

2. Resource demand curves shift to the left.

3. The supply curve of aluminum shifts to the left. Demand curves for substitute materials (tin, steel) may then shift to the right.

4. Demand curves for farmland and farm implements will shift to the right. Supply curves of suburban homes will shift to the left.

(p. 138) About .4 million workers; about 1.1 million workers.

FURTHER READING

Baily, Martin N., "Productivity and Competitiveness in American Manufacturing," *Brookings Review,* Winter 1993.

Blinder, Alan S., ed., *Paying for Productivity,* Brookings, Washington, 1990.

Briggs, Vernon M., Jr., "U.S. Immigration Policy Shapes Labor Force," *Challenge,* September/October 1991.

Ferleger, Louis and Jay R. Mandle, "Poor Math Skills, Poor Productivity Growth," *Challenge,* May/June 1992.

Ferleger, Louis and Jay R. Mandle, "Reverse the Drain on Productivity with Mass Education and Retraining," *Challenge,* July/August 1990.

Hutchens, Robert M., "Seniority, Wages and Productivity," *Journal of Economic Perspectives,* Fall 1989.

Mangum, Stephen L., "Impending Skill Shortages: Where Is the Crisis?" *Challenge,* September/October 1990.

Miles, Jack, "Blacks vs. Browns," *The Atlantic,* October 1992.

Nulty, Leslie E., "Looking for Labor in All the Wrong Places," *Challenge,* September/October 1990.

Reder, Melvin W., "The Rise and Fall of Unions," *Journal of Economic Perspectives,* Spring 1988.

Symposium: The Slowdown in Productivity Growth, *Journal of Economic Perspectives,* Fall 1988.

Thurow, Lester C., Chapter 7, *Dangerous Currents,* Random House, New York, 1983.

Chapter 7

Measuring Economic Activity

Tools for Study

LEARNING OBJECTIVES

After reading this chapter you will be able to:

1. Describe the circular flow of spending, production, and income.
2. Explain the relationship among national income, personal income, and disposable income.
3. Define gross domestic product (GDP) and explain how it is measured.
4. Define aggregate demand and aggregate supply.
5. Show how changes in spending affect the circular flow.

CURRENT ISSUES FOR DISCUSSION

How is a price index used to compare real GDP over time?

How do social costs affect economic welfare?

How has the level of government spending changed over the years?

How will current trends in consumer spending affect job opportunities in the future?

We have used the concepts of supply and demand to describe markets for finished goods and services and markets for productive resources. The study of individual markets is called **microeconomics**. In this chapter we begin our study of total production in the economy as a whole. The study of all markets taken together is called **macroeconomics**. To begin our study of macroeconomics we show how to measure the value of all goods and services produced during the year, and we make some judgments about how well our economic system is satisfying the needs of our people.

THE CIRCULAR FLOW OF SPENDING, PRODUCTION, AND INCOME

It is helpful to divide economic activity into two types of flows:

1. Spending flows paid to business firms for the goods and services people want to buy.
2. Income flows paid to households for business firms' use of productive resources—land, labor, capital, and entrepreneurial ability.

Flows of spending and income are shown in Figure 7.1, arranged to form a circle.

Flows of Spending

The upper loop of the circular flow in Figure 7.1 shows total spending in all the nation's

Figure 7.1 The Circular Flow of Spending, Production, and Income

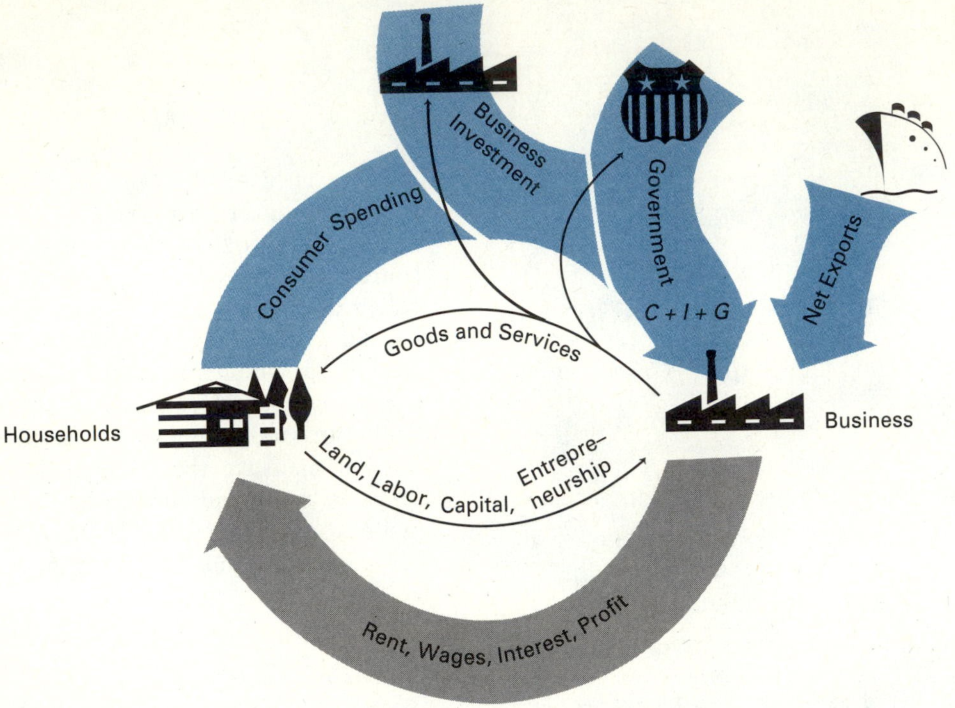

markets for goods and services. These are the markets we described in Chapters 2 through 5. In all these markets, spending flows in one direction, and newly produced goods and services flow in the opposite direction.

Notice that the largest part of spending comes from households. Households purchase consumer goods and services, such as autos, appliances, food, clothing, and recreation and health services.

Business firms also spend. They purchase raw materials, parts, equipment, buildings, and services from other business firms. Business spending for plants, equipment, and inventory is called **investment**.

The third major spender is government. Governments purchase goods and services to be used in the operation of government agencies and for carrying on government programs. Only government purchases of goods and services are included in the spending flow. Not included in government spending are **transfer payments**—government income-support payments such as social security benefits, welfare checks, unemployment compensation, food stamps, and veterans' benefits. Until such payments are spent for new goods and services, they are not part of the circular flow.

Foreigners also purchase goods produced by American business, and Americans buy from foreigners. The difference between foreign purchases of goods produced in the United States and U.S. purchases of goods produced abroad is called **net exports**. Net exports can be negative, if Americans buy more from foreigners than foreigners buy from us.

Foreign purchases and sales are becoming an increasingly important component of total spending in the U.S. economy. Because of the complexity of international trade, we consider foreign purchases in greater detail in Chapter 15.

Total spending by all these groups is a measure of all goods and services produced for sale during the year:

consumer spending
+
business *investment* spending
+
government purchases
+
*n*et exports
$= C + I + G + X_n =$
total spending for new goods and services

Total spending is also a measure of business revenue from sales, which is available for distribution to the owners of resources used in production:

total spending for new goods and services
= business firms' revenue from sales

Flows of Income

Business firms use their revenue from sales to employ productive resources: land, labor, capital, and entrepreneurship. Productive resources are supplied by people in households, who receive income in return for the use of their resources. The lower loop of Figure 7.1 represents all the markets for resources. We discussed resource markets in detail in Chapter 6. We found that demand for a resource depends on the demand for the things it can produce, and that supply depends on the willingness of resource owners to offer various quantities of resources for sale at various prices. In resource markets, land, labor, capital, and entrepreneurial ability flow in one direction; income, in the form of rent, wages, interest, and profit, flows in the opposite direction.

Not all revenue received by business firms is actually paid to households as income. A portion of business revenue from sales must be paid in taxes, and a portion is set aside in the form of business saving, including allowances for depreciation of capital equipment. Only the remaining revenue—after taxes and business saving—is available for paying productive resources.

The sum of wages, rent, interest, and profit is **national income**: national income $= w + r + i + \pi$. Strictly speaking, national income is income earned by productive resources. Thus, government transfer payments are not counted in national income, because they are not earned payments for contributions to production. The income that is actually received by individuals, including transfer payments, is called **personal income**. Personal income minus personal taxes (income tax, property tax, and inheritance tax) is the amount known as **disposable income**.

The derivation of disposable income can be summarized as follows:

total spending for new goods and services	= business revenue
	− business saving
	− business taxes
national income (income earned)	$= w + r + i + \pi$
	+ transfer payments
Personal income	(income received)
	− personal taxes
	disposable income

Most households save part of their disposable income. However, they spend the largest part for new consumer goods and services. Their new spending returns to the circular flow and becomes part of the flow of spending in the next period.

GROSS DOMESTIC PRODUCT

The circular flow represents a concept that is familiar to many of us: gross domestic product, or GDP. **Gross domestic product** is the final value of all goods and services produced in the United States for sale during the year: trucks, stereos, blue jeans, eggs, dental care, mail service, and so forth. Gross domestic product also includes finished goods and parts produced in the current year and held in business inventories to be sold in later years.*

Note that GDP includes only the final value of current production and leaves out intermediate goods and materials such as steel for autos and flour for bread. Including intermediate goods would overstate the current value of GDP. If an auto, for example, sells for $10,000, it may include a chassis worth, say $4000, an engine worth $3000, $500 worth of electrical equipment, and a transmission worth $500. Including all these parts along with the car's final value would be double-counting.

GDP also leaves out sales of goods produced in earlier years. This means that sales of used cars, sales of existing houses, and sales from last year's inventory are not included. Stocks and bonds are not included either because they are not goods or services. The same is true of sales of unimproved land.

Government transfer payments are not included in GDP because they are not payments for producing goods and services. (However, when consumers spend their transfer payments for goods and services, those purchases are counted as consumer expenditures.) Nonmarket exchanges of goods and services are also omitted from GDP: gifts of homegrown vegetables, volunteer work, and the unpaid services of homemakers.

* Until 1992, the most familiar measure of total production in the United States was gross national product, or GNP. GNP differs from GDP in the treatment of production by U.S. citizens abroad and foreigners' production in the United States. GNP includes the former but not the latter. GDP includes the latter but not the former. Because most other nations use GDP to measure total production, in 1992 statisticians in the United States changed our calculations for better comparability with foreign data.

We measure GDP in two ways:

1. *Spending on output*. GDP is the total value of spending for goods and services produced in the nation in the current year. We have seen that purchases are made by consumers, business firms, governments, and foreigners. Thus, GDP is the sum of spending flows in all product markets, as shown in the upper loop of Figure 7.1. It represents total demand in all the nation's product markets, or **aggregate demand**:

$$\text{aggregate demand} = C + I + G + X_n = \text{GDP}$$

2. *Income of resources*. GDP is also total income received from current production of goods and services. Remember that a portion of business revenue from sales must be used to pay taxes and to save for future investment. But the largest part is divided among resources employed in production, in the form of wages, rent, interest, and profit. Thus, GDP is the sum of income flows in all resource markets, as shown in the lower loop of Figure 7.1. Taken together, business revenue from sales measures the value of all resources used in production and is, therefore, the value of total production or **aggregate supply**: GDP $= w + r + i + \pi +$ business taxes and saving $=$ aggregate supply.

We can express these relationships with a simple formula:

$$\text{aggregate demand (spending)} = \text{GDP} = \text{aggregate supply (income)*}$$

* The expression $AD = \text{GDP} = AS$ is actually an identity: that is, the two sides of the expression measure essentially the same thing, approached from different directions.

You may say that total spending (aggregate demand) may not always equal total production (aggregate supply). In fact, a difference between current spending and current production can cause major headaches for business firms. Nevertheless, in a real sense the two values are always equal. The reason is the effect of inventories. Firms that are unable to sell all of their current production, in effect, "purchase" their own output and add it to their inventory stocks. Whenever such "unplanned" inventory investment occurs, "planned" aggregate demand does indeed differ from aggregate supply. In this and the next chapter, we distinguish between planned and unplanned investment expenditures and show how differences in "planned" spending and production may bring on changes in the level of economic activity.

The relationship between spending on output and income from production can be illustrated through the simple diagram shown at the bottom of this page. On the left side of the following equality are listed the components of aggregate demand; on the right are the components of aggregate supply. Note that the sums of the two columns are actually two ways of measuring the same quantity: GDP.

CHANGES IN THE CIRCULAR FLOW

Macroeconomics is concerned with the size of the circular flow. Most of us favor a steadily rising GDP, for the rising standards of living that provides. We want GDP to grow fairly steadily, in line with our fairly steady growth in population and in the productivity of resources. If total spending for new goods and services grows more slowly than our nation's productive capacity, workers will be unemployed, and GDP will be lower than it might have been. The nation will be operating inside our production possibilities curve and failing to make efficient use of our scarce resources. When GDP fails to grow at all for two consecutive quarters, we say the nation is experiencing **recession**.

Too rapid growth of total spending creates other problems. If growth in spending exceeds growth in our nation's productive capacity, we will be trying to produce GDP greater than our production possibilities curve. Too rapid growth could mean shortages of materials and skilled labor, with a tendency for prices and wages to rise. The result of too rapid growth of total spending may be price **inflation**.

What determines the level of GDP and its rate of growth?

The level of total production depends on aggregate demand (*AD*). Aggregate demand is the sum of consumer spending, business investment spending, government purchases, and net exports ($AD = C + I + G + X_n$). If planned spending from any of these sources increases, the entire circular flow tends to expand. Profit-seeking firms will increase pro-

AGGREGATE DEMAND (*AD*)		AGGREGATE SUPPLY (*AS*)
consumer spending		wages and salaries
+		+
government purchases	= GDP =	rent
+		+
business investment spending		interest
+		+
net exports		profit
		+
		business saving
		+
		business taxes

duction in order to satisfy the higher demand for goods and services. On the other hand, if planned spending falls, the circular flow tends to contract. Business firms will cut back production to avoid losses on unsold goods and services.

The next sections describe how our economic system adjusts to changes in the spending plans of consumers, business firms, government, and foreigners.

An Increase in Aggregate Demand

An increase in aggregate demand (*AD*) might begin with an increase in consumer spending (*C*). If many consumers become optimistic about the future, they may cut back on their saving in order to enjoy the "good life" now with little fear of hard times ahead. They may go on a spending spree and purchase a variety of new durable goods: campers, video cameras, and hot tubs.

Another reason for an increase in aggregate demand (*AD*) might be an increase in planned business investment (*I*). Business firms may decide to invest in new products or new technical processes. Or, faster population growth may encourage business firms to build new factories, rail lines, and power plants to satisfy expected growth in consumer demand. Some business firms may increase their inventory investment in expectation of an increase in consumer spending.

A third reason for an increase in aggregate demand (*AD*) might be an increase in government purchases (*G*). The federal government may decide to spend more for national defense or for research and development of new technologies. Or perhaps state and local governments may increase their spending for schools, roads, or parks.

Finally, an increase in aggregate demand might come from increased sales of U.S. goods abroad or from a decrease in U.S. purchases of foreign goods. Such changes might result from changes in the relative costs or quality of U.S. products, with accompanying gains in the competitiveness of U.S. business firms. Either change would involve increased spending for domestic production and an increase in aggregate demand.

Whatever the source of the increased spending, the result is greater incentives to produce goods and services, in order to satisfy the increased demand. More workers are hired, raw materials ordered, and factories built. The increased spending circulates throughout the economy, raising incomes of workers and suppliers. Workers and suppliers spend their higher incomes for consumer goods and services, and their increased spending adds to the incomes of other workers and suppliers. Thus, the initial increase in spending is magnified as higher incomes spread throughout the economy. An increase in spending increases the size of the circular flow, increases the production of goods and services, and increases employment of the nation's productive resources.

A Decrease in Aggregate Demand

Eventually the new spending that began the upward spiral in incomes will slow down. Unsold goods will pile up in inventories. When inventories begin to accumulate, retailers reduce their orders from manufacturers, and factories reduce production. They lay off workers, and economic activity slows. Cutbacks in spending circulate throughout the economy. More workers are laid off and they cut back their own spending for consumer goods and services. The entire circular flow contracts.

A decrease in aggregate demand (*AD*) may begin with any of the four major groups of spenders we have described. Sometimes a decrease in aggregate demand is caused by consumers' decisions to spend less of their incomes. They may be overstocked with consumer goods and pessimistic about the future. Instead of spending all their incomes now, they may decide to put aside more savings for hard times ahead.

More often, a decrease in aggregate demand (*AD*) is caused by business firms' decisions to reduce their spending for new investment. If business firms have completed all desired new projects, they may not need additional productive capacity. They may already be holding too many goods in inventories that are gathering dust in warehouses.

A third reason for a decrease in aggregate demand (*AD*) may be government's decision to reduce spending for public projects. Government spending is tied to the production of community services and defense. Because these needs come along irregularly, government spending tends to fluctuate widely, adding to aggregate demand in some years and reducing it in others.

Finally, a decrease in aggregate demand may result from a decrease in U.S. sales to foreigners or an increase in U.S. purchases abroad. Either change would reduce the sales of U.S. business firms and reduce aggregate demand in the United States.

Whatever the source of the decrease in aggregate demand, the result is a decrease in the production of goods and services. Business firms want to avoid losses on unsold goods; so they cut back on orders for materials and lay off workers. They cancel plans for new buildings and equipment, and incomes of workers and suppliers fall.

As incomes fall, workers are forced to reduce their spending for consumer goods and services. Then even more business firms are forced to cut back production. The initial decrease in spending is magnified as falling incomes circulate throughout the economy.

INFLOWS AND OUTFLOWS

It is helpful to think of changes in the circular flow in terms of flows into and out of the spending stream. Spending by consumers, business firms, governments, and foreigners constitutes inflows into the circular flow. Expenditures included in aggregate demand flow into business firms, as shown in the upper loop of Figure 7.2.

Spending flows received by business firms are paid to households as income. Households use their incomes in any of three ways. Taxes must first be paid (T), a portion of income is saved (S), and the remaining income is spent for consumer goods and services (C). Consumer spending remains in the flow and continues to circulate, but taxes and saving flow out of the circular flow.

Outflows represent the part of consumer income not spent: autos, appliances, and clothing not bought, trips not taken, homes not built. In order for the circular flow to remain stable at the current level of GDP, some other groups must spend an amount equal to what consumers fail to spend. Government or business firms must purchase the new goods and services that are not bought by the household sector. In effect, outflows from the household sector must be balanced by new inflows from business or government.

There are several ways outflows from spending might be replaced by new inflows. Saving outflows (S) may be returned to the circular flow by new investment spending (I) on the part of business firms; tax outflows (T) may be returned by government spending (G). Or the sum of saving and tax outflows may be returned to the circular flow by some combination of new investment and government spending; thus, $S + T = I + G$.

If all outflows from spending are returned as new inflows, the circular flow remains stable. Aggregate supply is equal to aggregate demand at the current income level:

Figure 7.2 Inflows and Outflows in the Circular Flow

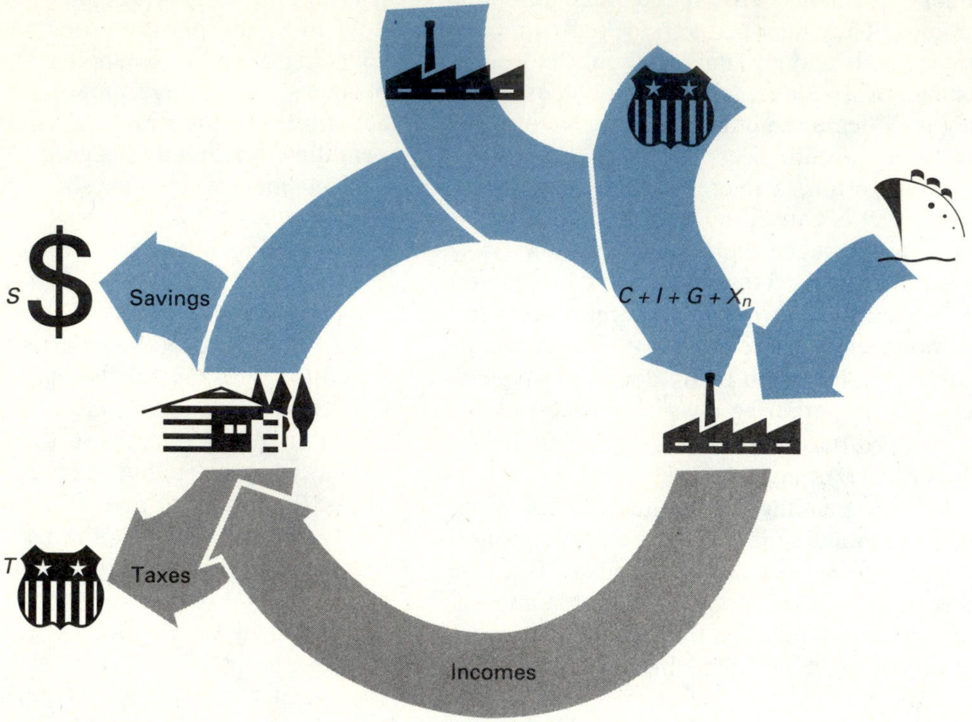

$$S + T = I + G$$
means
$$AS = AD$$

But if outflows are not balanced by new inflows, there will be changes in the entire circular flow.

Consider first an excess of inflows over outflows: $I + G > S + T$. If inflows of new spending are greater than outflows from the spending flow, GDP tends to increase. The higher level of aggregate demand (*AD*) encourages an increase in aggregate supply (*AS*), and the circular flow expands. Now consider an excess of outflows over inflows: $S + T > I + G$. If outflows are greater than inflows, GDP falls. Lower aggregate demand causes a drop in aggregate supply, and the circular flow contracts.

When inflows and outflows are precisely in balance, we say the economy has reached equilibrium. There is no tendency for GDP either to expand or to contract.

In the remainder of this chapter, we look at GDP in more detail. In the next chapter we develop an economic model that explains how aggregate demand determines the equilibrium level of spending, production, and income.

Thinking Seriously About Economic Issues

ROADS TO PROSPERITY

Roads belong to a class of goods and services that is often referred to as "infrastructure." Infrastructure includes assets provided by governments that benefit all citizens: highways, water systems, some electric power plants, public schools, and government-supported research and development (R&D).

David A. Aschauer has studied the relationship between government spending for infrastructure and per capita income, with some interesting results. For example, he found that industry profits in a particular region are directly related to the quality of the region's transportation services. Superior transportation services are associated with higher returns on business investment and increased investment in new productive facilities, he says, all of which bring growth in a region's total output and income.

Aschauer collected data describing highway quality and capacity and per capita income in the contiguous forty-eight states (1960 to 1985). The data show a clear correlation between public spending for surface transportation and growth in per capita income. For example, he found a .009 percentage point decrease in per capita income growth for every one-percentage-point decrease in pavement quality. These results suggest that government spending to improve highway quality can stimulate economic growth.

Research conducted by the Congressional Budget Office reaches similar conclusions and suggests that carefully chosen federal spending yields economic rates of return higher than the average rate of return on private investments. Federal spending for education, job training, and work experience programs, for example, have led to modest gains in the average earnings of program participants. Such programs probably yield noneconomic benefits as well, which are difficult to measure. Finally, federal spending for research and development (R&D) in science and engineering, health and agriculture has brought generally high rates of return. On the other hand, most other federally funded R&D appears to increase productivity less effectively than privately funded R&D.

David A. Aschauer, "Highway Capacity and Economic Growth," *Economic Perspectives*, Federal Reserve Bank of Chicago, September/October 1990; and "How Federal Spending for Infrastructure and Other Public Investments Affects the Economy," Congressional Budget Office, July 1991.

Self-Check

1. **Which of the following is included in GDP?**
   a. An appendicitis operation.
   b. An antique table.
   c. Wood flooring in a new house.
   d. Purchase of a U.S. Treasury bond.
   e. A gift of homemade cookies.

2. **The major groups of spenders are:**
   a. Consumers, savers, and investors.
   b. Consumers, business, and government.
   c. Land, labor, capital, and managers or entrepreneurs.
   d. Savers, investors, and government.
   e. Aggregate demand and aggregate supply.

3. **Productive resources:**
   a. Flow in return for consumer expenditures.
   b. Are outflows from the circular flow.
   c. Flow from households to business firms.
   d. Flow from business to government.
   e. Are rent, wages, interest, and profit.

4. **GDP is likely to grow if:**
   a. Consumers are pessimistic about the future.
   b. Business has completed all desired investment projects.
   c. Consumers are well stocked with goods.
   d. The government cuts back on its defense program.
   e. Population growth causes higher aggregate demand.

5. **The circular flow will stabilize at the level of spending and income at which:**
   a. Aggregate demand is equal to aggregate supply.
   b. $C + I + S = C + T + G$.
   c. New inflows of spending = outflows from income.
   d. All of the above.
   e. Both (a) and (c).

6. **Changes in consumer, business, or government spending:**
   a. Have no effect on production plans.
   b. Are a subject of microeconomics.
   c. May cause recession or inflation.
   d. Constitute aggregate supply.
   e. All of the above.

Theory in Practice

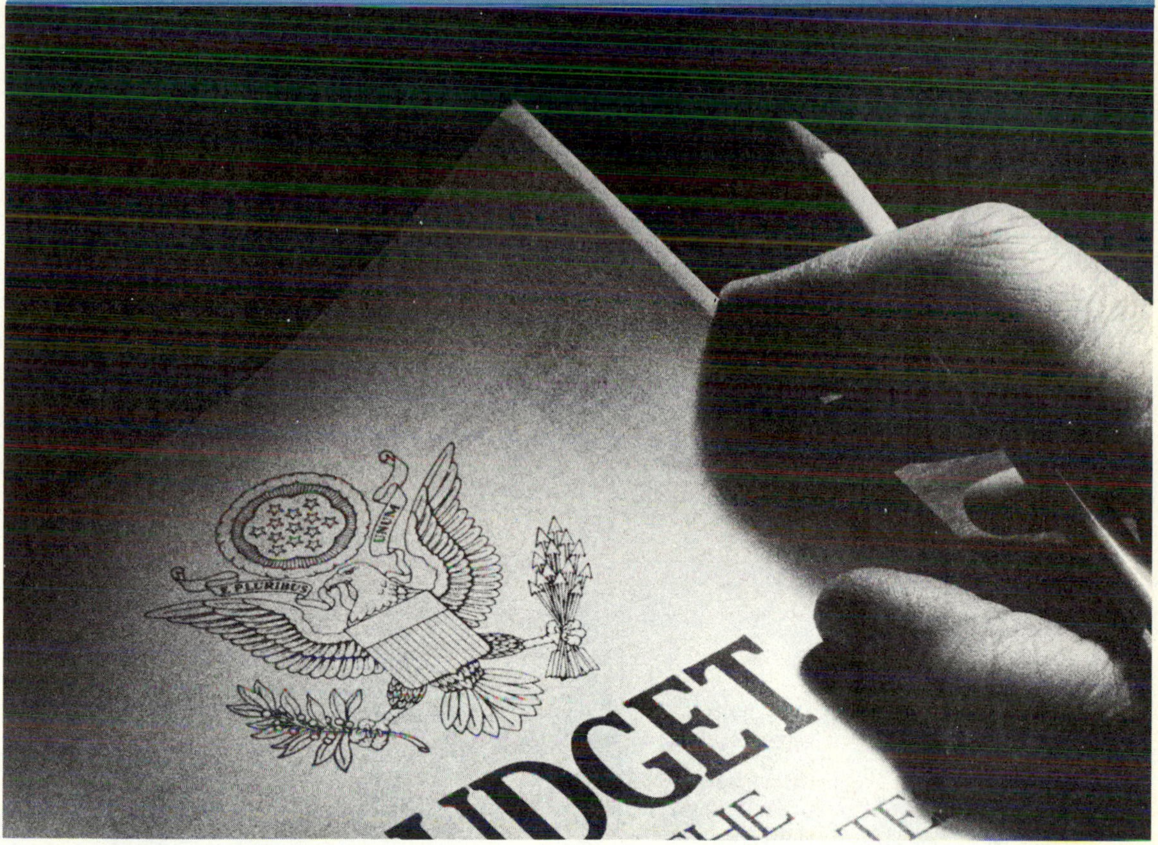

PRACTICE MEASURING GDP

In this section you will use recent data from the U.S. economy to measure actual GDP. (Data are altered slightly for simplicity.) Table 7.1 lists the components of GDP and income for 1991. Pencil the data into the appropriate places in the circular flow shown in Figure 7.3. Then answer the following questions. (Answers can be found at the end of Topics for Discussion.)

1. Calculate aggregate demand by measuring upper-loop spending on output. ______
2. Calculate aggregate supply by measuring lower-loop income from production. (Include business taxes and capital consumption to ensure that aggregate supply is indeed equal to aggregate demand.) ______
3. Now calculate national income, income earned by productive resources. ______
4. In addition to income from production, many households receive transfer payments from government. Transfer payments increase an individual's or family's personal income. Add transfer payments to national income to find personal income. ______

5. Now compute the following percentages:

   Consumer spending as a percent of aggregate demand. _____
   Government purchases as a percent of aggregate demand. _____
   Wages as a percent of income earned in production. _____
   Profit as a percent of income from production. _____

6. What percent of personal income was saved in 1991? _____
7. What was the total value of outflows? _____ What was the value of new inflows? _____ (For this purpose, con-

Table 7.1 Summary Data from National Income Accounts, 1991.
(Billions of Dollars)

Personal consumption expenditures	3887
Gross private domestic investment	725
Government purchases of goods and services	1087
Indirect business taxes (sales and excise taxes)	471
Business saving	659
Rental income	0
Wages and salaries	3388
Interest income	481
Profit income	700
Government transfer payments	759
Business and personal taxes	1737
Personal saving	222

Figure 7.3 Calculating GDP

sider government transfer payments as a kind of "negative tax" and include them along with government purchases as a new inflow.)

These calculations should give you a better idea of how GDP is measured and of the quantities involved. *The Economic Report of the President*, published in January each year, supplies these data for the last 30 years. You may be interested in comparing data for the most recent year with earlier years.

MEASURING ECONOMIC GROWTH

Over the years, GDP has grown in the United States, bringing rising incomes and higher material standards of living. This is true both in terms of total production and on a per capita (per person) basis.

Money GDP and Real GDP

Not all increases in GDP bring these kinds of benefits, however. In fact, the dollar value of GDP can grow without any increase in the quantities of goods and services produced. This happens when inflation raises the prices of most goods and services.

To understand the effect of price changes, it is necessary to distinguish between money GDP and real GDP. Money GDP is GDP measured in dollar prices of the current year. Real GDP is GDP in dollars of constant purchasing power. If prices have risen, money GDP must be "deflated" to determine real GDP. For example, suppose total dollars spent on GDP increase from $100 billion to $110 billion in one year. But suppose also that prices at the end of the year are 10 percent higher than at the beginning. If this is true, the real quantity of GDP has not changed at all. With prices 10 percent higher, the $110 billion in expenditures has bought only $100 billion in real goods and services. Money GDP has increased by $10 billion, but real GDP is the same as before.

Correcting money GDP for price changes requires the use of a price index.

Using a Price Index

A price index is a percentage comparison of current prices with prices in a base year. To illustrate, suppose a dollar's worth of goods in the base year included a loaf of bread, a bus ticket, and a pair of socks. Then suppose five years later the same collection of goods sells for $1.25. The price index for the current year is

$$PI = \frac{\text{current year price}}{\text{base year price}} = \frac{\$1.25}{1.00} = 1.25$$
$$= 125 \text{ percent}$$

With prices 25 percent higher, a worker must now earn 125 percent of what he or she earned in the base year in order to enjoy the same standard of living.

Suppose a worker can live comfortably in the base year on an income of $6000. Five years later the price index has risen to 125. Income of $6000 will be worth

$$\frac{\text{(current income)}}{PI} = \frac{\$6000}{125 \text{ percent}} = \frac{\$6000}{1.25}$$
$$= \$4800$$

In order to live as comfortably as before, the worker must now earn 125 percent of what his or her income was in the base year:

$$1.25 \times \$6000 = \$7500$$

TEST YOURSELF

Suppose the price index falls to 90 percent. This means that a worker needs only $.90 to buy what a dollar bought in the base year. How much is income of $6000 worth now? How much would a worker have to earn to live as comfortably as in the base year?

Economists calculate the consumer price index each year from prices for a "market basket" of goods and services purchased by a typical family. Economists also calculate a producer price index based on industrial commodities purchased by business firms. The GDP deflator is another price index based on all goods, services, and industrial commodities taken together.

Growth in Real GDP

You can use the following formula to calculate real GDP:

$$\text{real GDP} = \frac{\text{money GDP} \times 100}{PI}$$

Using this formula, you can set up equations for measuring the growth of GDP over time. Table 7.2 provides data on GDP and its components in selected years since 1960. Data are expressed both in current dollars of each year and in constant dollars, dollars corrected for inflation.

In the table, 1987 is used as the base year for calculating the price index. Notice that money GDP and real GDP for 1987 are identical at almost $4540 billion. This is understandable, since the price index for 1987 is

$$PI = \frac{\text{current year price}}{\text{base year price}}$$
$$= \frac{\$1.00}{1.00} = 1.00 = 100 \text{ percent}$$

The price index for 1960 is only 26.0. This means that prices in 1960 were about one-fourth of prices in 1987. The price index for 1991 is 117.0, indicating that 1991 prices were on the average about 17 percent higher than the prices of 1987.

Table 7.2 Gross Domestic Product in Current Dollars (1) and in Constant Dollars of 1987 (3–6).

Year	*(1) Money GDP ($ billions)*	*(2) Price Index*	*(3) Real GDP ($ billions)*	*(4) Real Personal Consumption Expenditures ($ billions)*	*(5) Real Gross Private Domestic Investment ($ billions)*	*(6) GDP per capita (in 1987 dollars)*
1960	$ 513.4	26.0	$1973.2	$1210.8	$290.8	$10,903
1965	702.7	28.4	2473.5	1497.0	413.0	12,712
1970	1010.7	35.1	2875.8	1813.5	429.7	14,013
1975	1585.9	49.2	3221.7	2097.5	437.6	14,917
1980	2708.0	71.7	3776.3	2447.1	594.4	16,584
1981	3030.6	78.9	3843.1	2476.9	631.1	16,710
1982	3149.6	83.8	3760.3	2503.7	540.5	16,194
1983	3405.0	87.2	3906.6	2619.4	599.5	16,672
1984	3777.2	91.0	4148.5	2746.1	757.5	17,549
1985	4038.7	94.4	4279.8	2865.8	745.9	17,944
1986	4265.6	96.9	4404.5	2969.1	735.1	18,299
1987	4539.9	100.0	4539.9	3052.2	749.3	18,694
1988	4900.4	103.9	4718.6	3162.4	773.4	19,252
1989	5244.0	108.4	4836.9	3223.1	789.2	19,556
1990	5513.8	112.9	4884.9	3262.6	745.5	19,513
1991	5671.8	117.0	4848.4	3256.7	672.6	19,077

SOURCE: Economic Report of the President, various years.

Table 7.2 shows fairly steady growth of real GDP except for the recession of 1982. There have been eight recessions since World War II. Real GDP grew from an estimated $21.6 billion in 1869 to $4848 billion in 1991 (both expressed in dollars of 1987). In per capita terms this represents a real increase from about $578 in 1869 to $19,270 in 1991.

MEASURING NET ECONOMIC WELFARE

There are some problems with the use of GDP as a measure of a nation's well-being. GDP measures goods and services produced. It doesn't, however, measure the "bads" that might also be produced! In addition to autos, calculators, and soft drinks, our nation's business firms also produce polluted air and water, scars on the landscape, and junk piles.

When a business firm measures the costs of production, it includes the market prices of all resources purchased in resource markets; that is, the prices of land and buildings, raw materials, machinery, labor, and managerial personnel. However, many kinds of production require the use of resources that are not exchanged in resource markets and therefore have no price: air and water for disposing of waste materials, quiet and pleasant surroundings, and even vacant land for eventual disposal of the product itself. Although such costs are real, they are difficult to measure.

Economists refer to the costs of using these kinds of resources as external costs because they are imposed on the community outside the business firm. They are social costs, as opposed to the private costs that appear on a firm's accounting statements. The community as a whole pays for a firm's use of these kinds of resources—in the form of air and water pollution, noise, and damaged landscapes.

Because clean air and pleasant surroundings are not exchanged in resource markets, a business firm is not generally required to pay for them. However, as communities become aware of the scarcity of such valuable resources as pure air and water, some are requiring firms to pay for them. They are levying taxes or fines against polluting firms, actions that have the effect of reducing the firm's current ouput and reducing its measured contribution to GDP.

To adjust GDP by the value of external costs would make GDP a better measure of actual levels of well-being. Some economists have defined a new measure—net economic welfare, or NEW—that takes into account external costs. Computing NEW requires that the "bads" produced in any year be subtracted from the measured value of GDP. Thus, NEW would more correctly measure improvements in the quality of our lives.

Measuring such things as polluted air and water is a difficult task. Still, efforts are now being made to measure social or external costs and shift them back to the firms that produce them. Coal-burning utilities, for example, are being required to install "scrubbers" in their smokestacks so as to remove impurities from their discharge. Firms guilty of water pollution are being required to clean up their discharge. In some cases, daily fines of thousands of dollars have been imposed, with the revenue to be used by government to build and operate purification facilities.

Concern for the environment is certainly healthy, and it is healthy to require business firms to assume responsibility for their external costs to the community. Some problems remain, however. If communities impose rigid anti-pollution laws, some firms will be forced out of business. Others will decide not to locate in communities with such laws. This could mean a loss of jobs and lower incomes. Furthermore, when firms are required to pay for the external resources they use, their costs will rise. They will have to increase their prices to consumers, and their sales will fall. Consumers must be willing to pay the full costs of "clean" production if they are to have the goods and services they want.

MEASURING TRENDS IN GOVERNMENT EXPENDITURES

Over the years, several factors have combined to increase the government spending (*G*) component of aggregate demand:

1. The more threatening nature of international relations and the increasing role of the United States in world affairs.
2. Our growing prosperity, which has made us want a better quality of public services.
3. Social and technical changes in ways of life that require collective action. (Our population has shifted from rural areas to crowded cities; we are living longer and are dependent for more years after retirement; modern industry is more complex and requires a longer period of technical education for the young.)

As a result of all these factors, by 1992 tax receipts and government outlays had grown to more than a third of GDP. This fraction has drifted upward over the last fifty years, showing the greatest increase in years of unstable international conditions or economic crisis. Table 7.3 shows the percentages going to various purposes for selected years.

The percentages in Table 7.3 may overstate the actual shift in resources toward the government sector. Much of government spending goes for services, the costs of which have risen faster than the costs of consumer

Table 7.3 Percentages of GDP Used for Public Purposes.

Year	*(1) Government Purchases of Goods and Services Percentage of GDP*	*(2) Total Taxes State, Local, and Federal as Percentage of GDP*	*(3) Government Transfer Payments as Percentage of GDP*
1929	8.3	11.0	1.0
1933	14.3	16.6	2.7
1939	14.3	16.9	2.7
1945	38.7	25.1	2.7
1950	13.3	23.5	5.0
1955	18.6	25.2	4.0
1960	19.8	27.8	5.3
1965	20.0	27.6	5.4
1970	22.5	31.0	7.6
1975	21.9	31.4	12.4
1980	20.3	31.7	11.2
1981	20.3	32.6	11.0
1982	21.2	31.7	11.6
1983	20.9	31.4	12.2
1984	19.5	31.0	14.2
1985	20.4	31.6	14.6
1986	20.7	32.0	12.1
1987	20.5	32.4	11.8
1988	19.9	32.0	11.7
1989	19.8	32.0	11.7
1990	18.9	30.7	12.2
1991	19.1	30.6	12.3

Source: Economic Report of the President, various years.

goods. Also, in earlier years, resources may have been used for public services without having a price tag attached.*

Column (1) lists federal, state, and local government purchases of goods and services as a percent of GDP. The data show the greatest increase in expenditures between 1939 and 1945, a result of military spending for World War II. Not shown in Column (1) is the distribution of expenditures between federal and state and local governments. In 1992 state and local spending constituted 11 percent of GDP, and federal spending only 8 percent.

Column (2) shows the percentages of GDP governments have collected in business and personal taxes. Taxes at the state, local, and federal level include personal income taxes, corporate profits taxes, indirect business taxes, and contributions to Social Security. Total taxes claimed almost one-third of GDP in 1992. Again, the greatest increase was in 1945.

Column (3) lists transfer payments as percentages of GDP. Transfer payments have grown from only a small part of GDP during the 1930s to more than 13 percent in 1992. The higher percentages in the mid-1980s were partly a result of a severe business recession. When GDP growth slows and workers lose their jobs, government outlays for welfare and unemployment compensation increase.

FORECASTING SPENDING TRENDS

Crystal balls grow cloudy when it comes to predicting consumer behavior in the future. Who in the 1960s could have predicted the popularity of home computers or the disappointing sales of luxury automobiles in the 1980s? Consumers are influenced by such a wide range of circumstances that it is impossible to know for certain what products will sell best in the 1990s, what businesses will be most profitable, and what training will earn you the highest income.

It is possible, however, to note some long-range trends that have been affecting markets since World War II. Increased productivity in agriculture and manufacturing has given Americans more income to spend and more leisure time to enjoy the things we buy. Nowadays we are spending a smaller share of our earnings for the ordinary necessities of life. Whereas nondurable consumer goods like food, clothing, gasoline, home heating oil, and so forth comprised more than half of consumer spending in 1946, by 1992 the typical family spent less than a third of its income on such necessary items. While real spending for all goods grew about 3 percent annually, consumer spending for nondurable goods grew much more slowly. The only exception was spending for gasoline and oil, which grew at the rate of almost 14 percent a year in real terms. These changes have meant decreasing job opportunities for workers producing food, textiles, shoes, and other nondurable goods.

While spending for nondurable goods was growing relatively slowly, consumers were spending a larger share of their incomes for durable consumer goods. Spending for such durable goods as automobiles, furniture, and household appliances rose from 11 percent of consumer purchases in 1940 to 14 percent in 1986. For this reason, workers employed in factories producing dishwashers, stereos, and pleasure boats, for example, enjoyed better job opportunities and higher wages. (In the recession of 1991, spending for durable goods was down to 11 percent of consumer spending.)

The greatest change in consumer spending has been the spectacular increase in spending

* In another way, the percentages understate the shift of resources toward the public sector, because they fail to account for the cost to private firms of complying with government regulations.

for services. In 1992, services absorbed 56 percent of the typical family budget, compared with only 31.5 percent in 1946. The greatest gain occurred in spending for housing and household services, which increased more than 9 percent a year in real terms.

Another reason for the increase in services has been increased spending for health care, in part a result of government programs like Medicare and Medicaid. Because supplies of health care resources are limited, this field offers good job opportunities for workers and even provides some government support for education and training.

Recreation, including travel and entertainment, is also a fast-growing service industry. Hotel and restaurant chains have benefited from rising consumer incomes and increased leisure time. The effects of early retirement and an increasing elderly population have also been favorable for recreation services. The outlook is less favorable for education. Slower population growth has reduced the demand for primary and secondary education, but community colleges and adult education programs are continuing to grow.

The tremendous growth of service industries has important consequences for the nation's economy. Probably most important is the fact that services are relatively labor-intensive. In contrast to manufacturing, many services require a greater use of labor relative to capital resources. When machines cannot be used to supplement human labor, there are fewer opportunities to increase productivity. This means that production costs cannot be reduced very much; increasing demand for services is likely to mean rising prices.

Slow productivity growth in service industries will mean slow growth in real incomes. During the years of rapid growth in manufacturing, U.S. workers became accustomed to regular increases in income. Workers' families used their higher incomes to increase their spending, which, in turn, contributed to further growth in manufacturing. The shift to service industries may mean slower economic growth.

There is a positive side to the growth of service industries. To provide certain services requires a higher level of skills than many manufacturing jobs, so that service jobs may be more challenging. This may help workers develop their creative skills and enjoy increased job satisfaction.

Finally, production of many services is relatively nonpolluting. Services involve few smokestacks, result in little chemical discharge, and are generally free of industrial blight.

SUMMARY

1. An economic system can be described in terms of flows of spending and income: spending flows paid from *households* to purchase consumer goods and services, from *businesses* to purchase capital investments, from *governments* to purchase goods and services, and from *foreigners*, whose purchases of U.S. products contribute to net exports; and flows of income received in the form of wages, rent, interest, and profit.
2. The gross domestic product (GDP) is the final value of all goods and services produced for the market. GDP can be measured as total spending for output or as total income received from resource employment.
3. When consumer, business, government, or foreign spending increases, the flow of production and income expands. When spending decreases, the flow of production and income contracts.
4. An increase in spending can be seen as an increase of new spending inflows into the circular flow; inflows are investment spending and

ANSWERS TO PRACTICE MEASURING GDP

1. 3887 + 725 + 1087 = 5699
2. 3388 + 0 + 481 + 700 + 471 + 659 = 5699
3. 3388 + 0 + 481 + 700 = 4569
4. 4569 + 759 = 5328
5. 3887/5699 = .68
   1087/5699 = .19
   3388/4569 = .74
   700/4569 = .15
6. 222/5328 = .04
7. 222 + 659 + 1737 + 471 = 3089
   725 + 1087 + 759 = 2571

ANSWER TO TEST YOURSELF

(p. 159) $6000/90 percent = $6000/.90 = $6666.67; .90 × $6000 = $5400

FURTHER READING

Aaron, Henry J. and Charles L. Schultze, eds., *Setting Domestic Priorities*, Brookings 1992.

Aschauer, David Alan, "Infrastructure: America's Third Deficit," *Challenge*, March/April 1992.

Blecker, Robert A., "The Consumption Binge Is a Myth," *Challenge*, May/June 1990.

Modigliani, Franco, "The Role of Intergenerational Transfers and Life Cycle Saving in the Accumulation of Wealth," *Journal of Economic Perspectives*, Spring 1988.

Passell, Peter, "What Counts Is Production and Productivity," *New York Times*, December 13, 1992.

"Reinventing America: Meeting the New Challenges of a Global Economy," *Business Week*, Special Bonus Issue, 1992.

Chapter

8

Cycles in Economic Activity

Tools for Study

LEARNING OBJECTIVES

After reading this chapter, you will be able to:

1. Use a consumption function to describe consumer spending.
2. Show graphically how planned spending determines the equilibrium level of GDP.
3. Explain how changes in spending plans can lead to an inflationary or recessionary gap.
4. Show how the multiplier works to bring on cumulative upswings and downswings in economic activity.

CURRENT ISSUES FOR DISCUSSION

How has the U.S. economy performed in recent years?

What are the effects on GDP of government expenditures for public projects?

How do changes in aggregate demand and aggregate supply affect prices?

As we saw in Chapter 7, GDP reaches equilibrium at the level of production at which planned spending for goods and services is just equal to the value of goods and services produced during the year:

$$\begin{aligned} AD &= \text{aggregate demand} = \text{GDP} \\ &= \text{aggregate supply} \;\; = AS \end{aligned}$$

If planned spending increases during the year, business firms are encouraged to increase production; thus, increasing aggregate demand means an increase in aggregate supply and GDP. If planned spending decreases during the year, business firms cut back production to avoid losses on unsold goods; thus, decreasing aggregate demand means a decrease in aggregate supply and GDP. Only if planned spending is just equal to production for the year will GDP remain stable at the current level of production and income.

The business sector learns about changes in aggregate demand through unplanned changes in inventories. An increase in aggregate demand causes inventories to shrink and encourages business firms to increase production and rebuild their stocks. A decrease in aggregate demand causes inventories to accumulate and encourages firms to cut production until inventories return to their desired level. If aggregate demand is equal to aggregate supply, there is no unplanned change in inventories, and GDP remains stable.

A perfectly stable, unchanging GDP is not always desirable. It is better for GDP to grow steadily in line with the nation's growing productive capacity. Unfortunately, things do not generally work out that way. More often, the nation experiences fluctuations in economic activity, with periods of too rapid growth followed by periods of slower growth or even decline.

Irregular growth creates either of two kinds of problems. If aggregate demand and GDP grow too rapidly, the result can be inflation. If aggregate demand and GDP grow too slowly, the result can be layoffs and business failures, with hardships for unemployed workers.

Alternating starts and stops in economic activity are called **business cycles**. Figure 8.1 is a simplified illustration of a busness cycle. The dashed line represents the long-run tendency toward growth in national output and income over the months marked on the horizontal axis. The solid line shows actual output, which grows faster than the long-term trend in the upswing of the cycle and slower in the downswing.

In this chapter we study the Keynesian explanation of business cycles, developed by John M. Keynes (1883–1945). In the next two chapters we learn about economic policies designed to deal with the problems of too fast or too slow growth of GDP.

Figure 8.1 A Business Cycle

In the upswing of a business cycle, output and income grow faster than the long-term trend; in the downswing, slower.

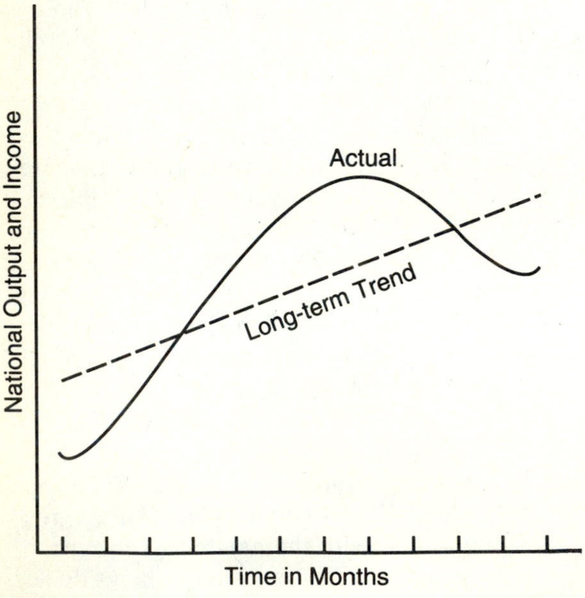

CONSUMER SPENDING (C)

Many economists explain fluctuations in GDP growth in terms of changes in demand, and they explain changes in demand through use of the Keynesian model of income determination. The Keynesian model focuses first on consumer spending, and then on total spending of consumers, business firms, government, and foreigners. Economists refer to consumer spending as Consumption (*C*), business spending as investment (*I*), government spending as government expenditures (*G*), and net foreign spending as net exports (X_n).

The Marginal Propensity to Consume

The largest part of total spending comes from the household sector. Consumers plan their spending in relation to their incomes. In fact, a typical U.S. consumer spends about $.96 of each dollar of his or her take-home pay for consumer goods and services.

Because business cycles are caused by *changes* in spending, economists are particularly concerned with the amount a consumer spends from *changes* in disposable income. The amount a consumer spends from a change in income is called the **marginal propensity to consume** (*MPC*). To illustrate changes in spending, suppose a consumer's income rises from $10,000 to $12,000 a year, and he or she increases spending from \$9500 to \$11,000. Out of the additional \$2000, this consumer would have increased spending by \$1500, or by

$$\frac{\text{change in consumer spending}}{\text{change in income}} = \frac{\$1500}{\$2000} = \frac{3}{4} \text{ of each additional dollar.}$$

Thus, the consumer's marginal propensity to consume is:

$$MPC = \frac{\Delta \text{ consumer spending}}{\Delta \text{ income}} = \frac{\Delta C}{\Delta DI} = \frac{3}{4}$$

where Δ stands for "change in."

Different consumers have different *MPC*s. A high-income consumer probably spends a smaller fraction of each additional dollar of income than a low-income consumer. Thus, a high-income consumer may have an *MPC* of

$$MPC = \frac{\Delta C}{\Delta DI} = \frac{\$10{,}000}{\$20{,}000} = \frac{1}{2}$$

and the low-income person may have an *MPC* of

$$MPC = \frac{\Delta C}{\Delta DI} = \frac{\$100}{\$100} = 1$$

Some consumers have an *MPC* greater than one. An *MPC* greater than one is possible by borrowing or by using accumulated savings.

TEST YOURSELF

Can all consumers have an *MPC* greater than one? Explain.

The Consumption Function

The consumption plans of all households in the economy can be combined to describe the consumption plans of the nation as a whole. Table 8.1 shows what spending might be for the nation as a whole at various levels of GDP. Column (2) shows hypothetical consumption $C >$ GDP if GDP is very low, $C =$ GDP at some middle value of GDP, and $C <$ GDP if GDP is very high. The change in consumer spending with each \$500 billion change in hypothetical GDP is \$375 billion. Thus, the *MPC* for the nation shown in Table 8.1 is

$$MPC = \frac{\Delta C}{\Delta DI} = \frac{375}{500} = \frac{3}{4}$$

Figure 8.2 is a graph of the hypothetical data shown in the table. GDP = Income is measured on the horizontal axis, and con-

Table 8.1 Expenditures and Aggregate Demand (billions of dollars).

(1) Income = GDP	(2) Consumption (C)	(3) Investment (I)	(4) Government Expenditures (G)	(5) Net Exports (X_n)	(6) Aggregate Demand ($C + I + G + X_n$)
0	125	150	300	50	625
500	500	150	300	50	1000
1000	875	150	300	50	1375
1500	1250	150	300	50	1750
2000	1625	150	300	50	2125
2500	2000	150	300	50	2500
3000	2375	150	300	50	2875
3500	2750	150	300	50	3250
4000	3125	150	300	50	3625

Figure 8.2 The Consumption Function

Consumer spending depends on income for the year. This consumption function is drawn on the assumption that all consumers taken together spend three-quarters of each additional dollar in disposable income: $MPC = \frac{3}{4}$

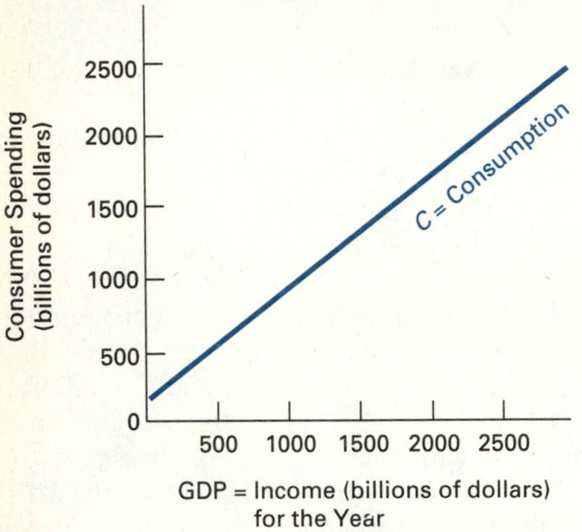

Figure 8.3 The 45-Degree Line

A 45-degree line connects all points where quantities on the vertical axis are equal to quantities on the horizontal.

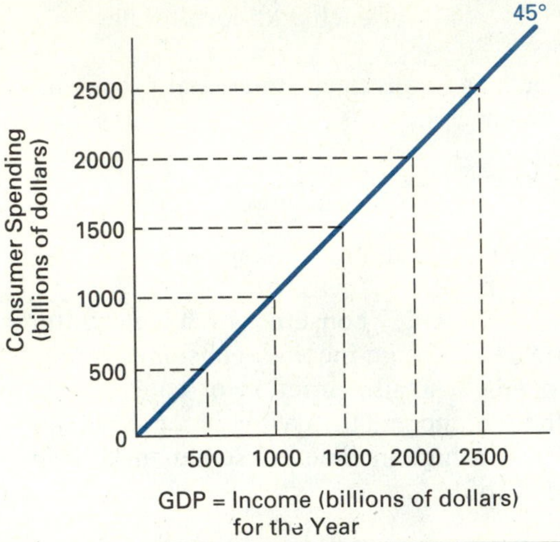

Figure 8.4 C = GDP = $500 billion

Consumption is equal to GDP = income at income of $500 billion for the year.

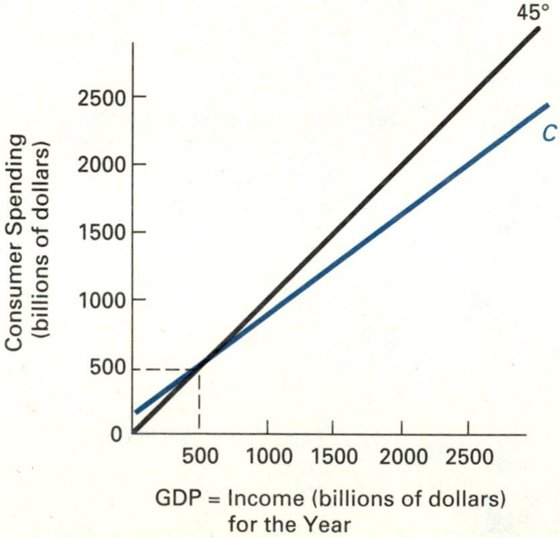

sumption (*C*) on the vertical axis. The line labeled *C* represents consumer spending and is called the **consumption function**. The consumption function in Figure 8.2 is drawn to show that all consumers taken together spend 3/4 of each additional dollar of current income.

Now look at Figure 8.3. The 45° line drawn from the origin on Figure 8.3 connects points with equal values on both axes, so that *C* = GDP = income all along the line. Combining the 45° line with the consumption function allows us to compare consumer spending with GDP (or income) at all levels of income. This has been done on Figure 8.4. On Figure 8.4 we see that $C >$ GDP if GDP is low, and $C <$ GDP if GDP is high. The point where the consumption function crosses the 45° line identifies the level of income at which consumer spending is equal to GDP = income. At that point, consumer spending alone is just equal to the total value of all new goods and services produced. In Figure 8.4 consumer spending is equal to income at GDP of $500 billion. Refer to Table 8.1 and verify that C = GDP at GDP = $500 billion.

TOTAL SPENDING ($C + I + G + X_n$)

Now let us combine our hypothetical consumer spending data with the spending of business firms, government, and foreigners. None of these kinds of spending is strongly related to income in the current period. Business investment spending depends on expectations of profit, which may or may not be affected by the current level of income. Moreover, investment plans take months or even years to complete and do not rise or fall quickly in response to changes in current income. Table 8.1 shows planned investment spending of I = $150 billion at every level of current income.

Government spending is also independent of income in the current period. Government spending is based on our nation's need for public services and defense and does not depend on changes in current income. Thus, government spending is listed in Table 8.1 as G = $300 billion, regardless of the level of income. Net foreign spending depends on incomes abroad and is not strongly affected by current income in the United States. Net exports are shown in Table 8.1 as X_n = $50 billion at every level of income.

Adding business planned investment (I), government spending (G), and net exports (X_n) to the consumption function (C) produces an aggregate demand function (AD). An AD function is shown on Figure 8.5 by drawing a line parallel to the consumption function and $500 billion above it. The AD function shows total spending associated with every level of current income:

$$AD = C + I + G + X_n$$

Figure 8.5 $C + I + G + X_n$

Adding planned investment, government expenditures, and net exports to the consumption function produces an aggregate demand curve for the year.

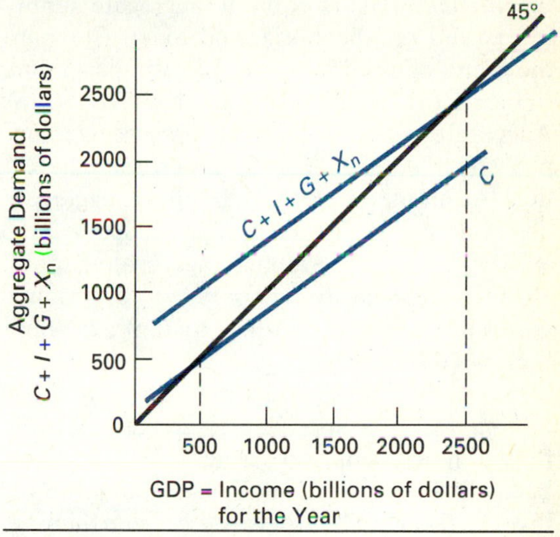

as measured on the vertical axis. The next section shows how the interaction between aggregate demand and aggregate supply determines the equilibrium level of GDP.

EQUILIBRIUM GDP ($AD = AS$)

Figure 8.5 represents the Keynesian model of income determination. The model allows us to measure the components of aggregate demand and illustrate their effects on aggregate supply and GDP. We have said that the actual level of GDP for any year tends toward the level at which aggregate demand equals aggregate supply:

$$AD = AS$$

With aggregate demand equal to aggregate supply, planned spending for new goods and services is just enough to purchase total production for the year. We call the level of GDP at which aggregate demand is equal to aggregate supply equilibrium GDP.

Look again at the 45° line drawn from the origin in Figure 8.5. The 45° line marks all points where aggregate demand (measured on the vertical axis) is equal to aggregate supply (measured on the horizontal axis). Compare the graph of $C + I + G + X_n$ with the 45° line to locate the level of GDP at which $AD = AS$. Aggregate demand is equal to aggregate supply where $C + I + G + X_n$ crosses the 45° line. At an income of $2500 billion, aggregate demand = $C + I + G + X_n$ = $2000 + $150 + $300 + $50 = $2500 = aggregate supply. Business firms are encouraged to produce goods and services worth a total of $2500 billion = GDP.

For all levels of income less than $2500 billion, planned spending is greater than the flow of new goods and services. We know this because $C + I + G + X_n$ lies above the 45° line. With aggregate demand greater than aggregate supply, business firms have to make sales from existing inventories. In order to fill the higher demand and maintain their inventory stocks, business firms increase their orders from manufacturers and expand production, so that GDP expands toward $2500 billion.

For all levels of income greater than $2500 billion, planned spending is less than total production: $C + I + G + X_n$ lies below the 45° line. With aggregate demand less than aggregate supply, unplanned inventories begin to accumulate. In order to avoid losses on unsold inventories, business firms cut back their orders from manufacturers and reduce production. GDP contracts toward $2500 billion.

Only at an income of $2500 billion are the combined spending plans of all buyers equal to the production plans of all business firms. With $AD = AS$, GDP is in equilibrium.

These results are easy to read from Table 8.1. For all levels of income less than $2500 billion, $AD = C + I + G + X_n > AS$, and GDP tends to expand. For incomes greater than $2500 billion, $AD = C + I + G + X_n < AS$, and GDP tends to contract. At income of $2500 billion, $AD = C + I + G + X_n = AS$, and GDP is stable. The economy is in equilibrium.

What can we learn from the Keynesian model of income determination? The model helps us locate the equilibrium level of spending, production, and income. It does not tell us whether the equilibrium level of GDP = income is a technically efficient level of income. To determine whether the equilibrium level of GDP is technically efficient, we must answer two important questions:

1. Is the equilibrium level of GDP too low to employ all available resources? Too low a level of spending, production, and income means that we are failing to use our scarce resources productively, and we are sacrificing the goods and services we might have had. This cannot be considered an efficient equilibrium level of GDP.
2. Is the equilibrium level so high that we are pushing against the limits of our resource capability? Too high a level of spending, production, and income could mean rising prices, as rising demand creates shortages in the markets for goods and resources. This cannot be considered an efficient level of GDP.

Only if equilibrium GDP is neither so low as to cause unemployment nor so high as to cause inflation can we say that the economy is technically efficient.

Changes are constantly taking place in spending, changing the position of the consumption function (C) and increasing or decreasing planned business investment spending (I), government spending (G), and net exports (X_n). All these changes move the economy to new equilibrium levels of GDP. Economic analysis helps project and evaluate future equilibrium levels of GDP. If the projected equilibrium level is not technically efficient, macroeconomic policy may be designed to correct it. Macroeconomic policy to correct tendencies toward business cycles is the subject of Chapters 9 and 10.

CHANGES IN EQUILIBRIUM GDP

What lies behind changes in aggregate demand that move the economy to new equilibrium levels of GDP? Remember that changes in spending plans can come from any of the four groups of spenders: consumers, business firms, government, or foreigners.

Changes in Total Spending

Consumers may decide to spend more for household appliances, recreation equipment, or personal services. They may save less from their current incomes, spend from past savings, or borrow against future earnings. An increase in consumer spending shifts upward the *C* component of aggregate demand. Total spending increases, and business firms expand production and employment.

The same results follow an increase in the investment plans of business firms. The development of new manufacturing processes, for example, requires new investment spending and shifts upward the *I* component of aggregate demand. Figure 8.6 shows new investment spending of $250 billion, causing an increase in equilibrium GDP from $2500 billion to $3500 billion.

Figure 8.7 shows the effect of a decrease in government spending. Suppose government spending (*G*) falls, perhaps in response to the end to the Cold War or to voters' insistence on the elimination of public programs. If government spending falls from $300 billion to $50 billion, equilibrium GDP will fall to $1500 billion, as shown on Figure 8.7.

Figure 8.6 An Increase in Investment Spending

An increase in *I* causes a greater increase in income. Compare the increase in *I* with the increase in GDP for the year.

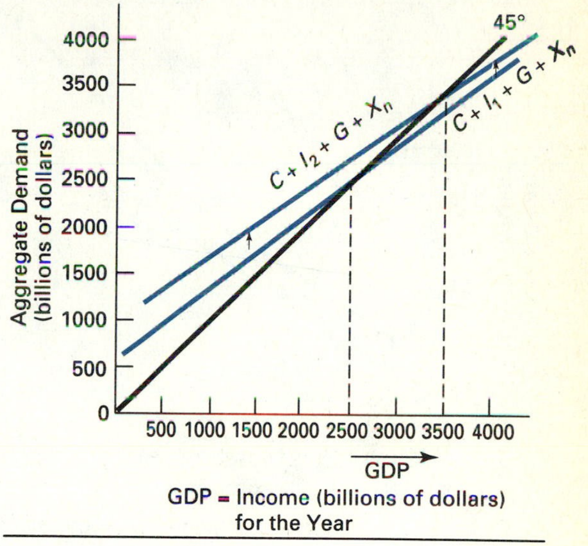

Changes in the attractiveness of U.S. products to foreign buyers could cause similar changes in net exports.

The Multiplier Effect

Have you noticed that the $250 billion in new investment spending in Figure 8.6 caused equilibrium GDP to increase by $1000 billion? And that the $250 billion reduction in government spending in Figure 8.7 caused equilibrium GDP to fall by $1000? In both cases, the change in equilibrium GDP was greater than the initial change in spending. The greater change in equilibrium GDP was a result of what economists call the multiplier effect.

Figure 8.7 A Decrease in Government Spending

A decrease in G causes a greater decrease in income. Compare the decrease in G with the decrease in GDP for the year.

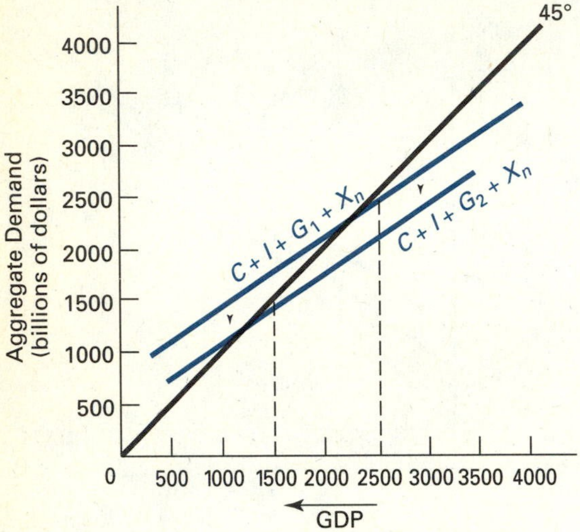

The **multiplier effect** results from the fact that people who receive as income the increase in business investment, for example, tend to respend a portion of their own increase in income. Then people who receive their respending enjoy an increase in income, too, which they also spend. Finally, many people will have received additions to income, such that the total of all new income will be greater than the initial increase in spending.

An illustration may be helpful. Remember that the tendency to spend changes in income is called the marginal propensity to consume and that the MPC in our example is $MPC = \frac{3}{4}$. The $250 billion in new investment spending increased the incomes of income earners around the country by $250 billion. With $MPC = \frac{3}{4}$, these income earners tend to increase their spending by $MPC \times \Delta I = \frac{3}{4}(250) = \$187.50$ billion. The $187.50 billion is paid to other income earners who increase their spending by MPC ($MPC \times \Delta I$) $= \frac{3}{4}(187.50) = \$140.63$. This means that still other income earners receive additional income totaling $140.63 billion and increase their spending by MPC [$MPC(MPC \times \Delta I)$] = $105.47 billion.

The process of spending and respending continues until the total of all increases in income is a multiple of the initial change in spending. The value of the multiplier for measuring the change in income is determined by the following formula*:

$$\text{multiplier} = k = \frac{1}{1 - MPC}$$

or in our example:

$$k = \frac{1}{1 - \frac{3}{4}} = \frac{1}{\frac{1}{4}} = 4$$

The total change in income or GDP is

$$\Delta GDP = k \times \Delta I = \frac{1}{1 - MPC} \times \Delta I$$

Substitute the values from our examples into the formula and verify the results.

The important consequence of the multiplier is that changes in C, I, G, or X_n have substantially greater effects on the equilibrium level of GDP than the initial change in spending. Does this result make our economy more or less efficient?

The answer depends on the current level of resource use. If there are unemployed resources available to be drawn into production, it is technically efficient to use them. The multiple effect of new spending would be welcome. On the other hand, if the economy is already producing at full employment, any fur-

* The formula for the multiplier is the arithmetic formula for the sum of a geometric progression, in which the terms to be added change in a constant proportion. Of course, changes in the real world are never as precise as those in a mathematical formula, so that the value of the multiplier cannot be precisely determined.

ther increase in GDP makes the economy less efficient. This is because increases in *C, I, G,* or X_n will only aggravate the problem of scarce resources and tend to cause inflation.

Inflationary Gap

In this section we use the Keynesian model of income determination to show how increases in equilibrium GDP may make the economy less technically efficient. On Figure 8.8, $C + I + G + X_n$ shifts upward by \$250 billion, as before, and the increase in spending causes equilibrium GDP to increase from \$2500 billion to \$2500 + 4(250) = \$3500 billion. But suppose the nation's productive resources can produce only \$2500 billion worth of goods and services when fully employed; that is, maximum production possibilities are \$2500 billion. The full-employment level of output is shown on Figure 8.8 by a vertical line drawn at GDP = \$2500 billion.

If aggregate demand is \$3500 billion, total spending is greater than the full employment output of the economy. The nation's business firms will produce \$2500 billion worth of goods and services for which \$3500 billion will be spent. Result: inflation!

The difference between total spending and the full employment level of production is a measure of excess spending. The excess is measured by the difference between aggregate demand and the 45° line at full employment. We call the difference between *AD* and the 45° line at full employment the **inflationary gap**. Spending greater than the productive capacity of our economy is not a technically efficient use of our nation's scarce resources.

Figure 8.8 Inflationary Gap

Aggregate demand is greater than aggregate supply at full employment. Follow the dashed line up from the full-employment level of \$2500 billion. The portion of the dashed line above the 45-degree line and below $C + I + G + X_n$ measures the inflationary gap.

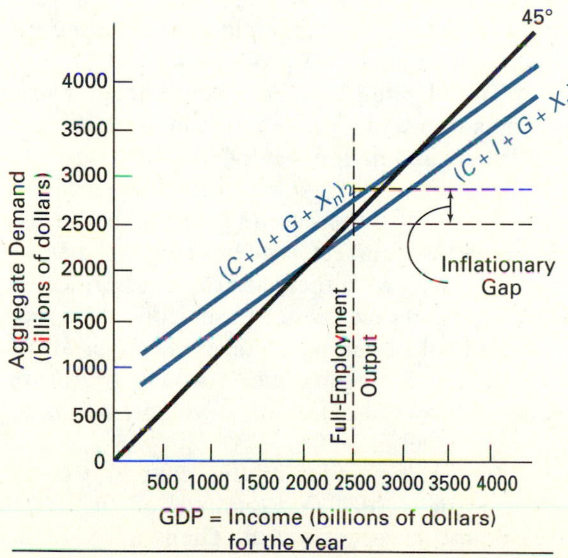

Recessionary Gap

Figure 8.6 illustrated an increase in investment spending that caused a multiple increase in equilibrium GDP. In contrast, Figure 8.7 showed a downward change in government spending and a similar change in the downward direction. In fact, if any of the components of planned spending falls, there will be a multiple contraction in GDP. Spending not received as income is not spent and not respent.

If consumers become worried about the future, for example, and decide to increase their saving, the *C* component of aggregate demand will fall. Unsold inventories will pile up, and manufacturers will reduce production. Likewise, if business firms decide to invest less, the *I* component will fall. Equipment orders will be canceled, and construction workers will be laid off. If public projects are completed or abandoned, the *G* component of aggregate demand will fall. Or finally, if foreigners reduce their purchases of U.S. exports, the X_n component of aggregate demand will fall.

TEST YOURSELF

What kinds of workers are likely to lose their jobs as a result of the end of a public construction project?

Figure 8.9 illustrates a multiple downward shift in income. If planned investment, government spending, or net exports fall from \$300 billion to \$50 billion, the equilibrium level of GDP in our hypothetical economy will fall from \$2500 billion to only \$1500 billion.

Compare the lower equilibrium GDP in Figure 8.9 with the full-employment output of \$2500 billion. Then look at the aggregate demand line at the full-employment level. The difference between aggregate demand and the 45° line at full employment is a measure of the deficiency of spending. The difference between total production and total spending at full employment is called a **recessionary gap**. As long as aggregate demand is less than aggregate supply at the full-employment level of output, resources will be idle and workers unemployed.

Too little spending relative to the productive capacity of the economy is not a technically efficient use of our nation's scarce resources.

Figure 8.9 Recessionary Gap

A decrease in I or G causes a greater decrease in spending, production, and income. Compare the drop in $C + I + G + X_n$ with the drop in GDP. Follow the dashed line up from the full-employment level of \$2500 billion. The portion of the dashed line from $C + I + G + X_n$ to the 45-degree line measures the recessionary gap.

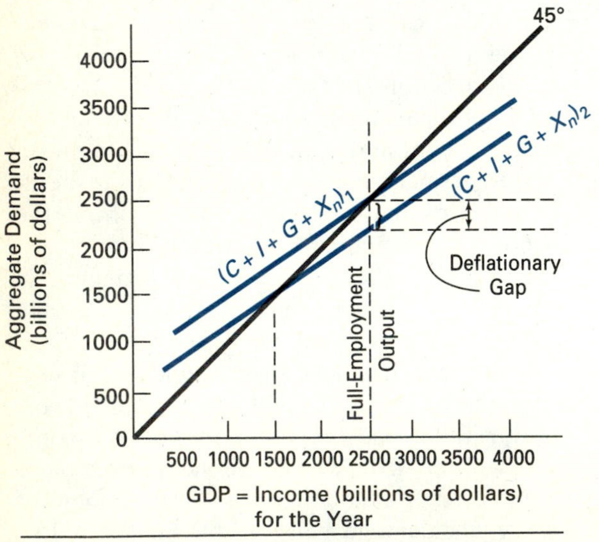

CUMULATIVE UPSWINGS AND DOWNSWINGS

Even small changes in any of the components of aggregate demand can produce much larger changes in equilibrium GDP. A small increase in C, I, G, or X_n can send the economy into a strong upward spiral of employment, production, and income, with increasing tendencies toward price inflation. A small decrease in C, I, G, or X_n can start the economy into a deep slide of increasing unemployment, falling incomes, and declining production.

The United States experienced many swings in production and income over its first 150 years as a nation. Many economists finally came to believe that some form of government involvement in the economy might be necessary to help correct tendencies toward business cycles, with their alternating periods of inflation and recession. These economists recommended offsetting changes in government tax and spending policies to push aggregate demand toward a full-employment, noninflationary level of GDP.

In the remainder of this chapter we describe the actual performance of the U.S. economy in recent years. Then, in the next

Viewpoint

AN EARLY EXPLANATION FOR BUSINESS CYCLES

Some early economists blamed business cycles on sunspots!

According to their theory, sunspot activity produced a favorable climate and good crops, increasing the incomes of farmers and encouraging spending for the products of manufacturing industries. Greater spending then encouraged business firms to increase productive capacity, increasing the number of jobs in industry and generally stimulating expenditures throughout the economy. As sunspot activity slowed, the process would go into reverse. Incomes and spending declined, followed by bankruptcies, general pessimism, and lower rates of economic growth.

Indeed, in years past, there did seem to be some correlation between the highs and lows of economic activity and the eleven-year cycles of sunspots. Circumstances may be different today, however. Today the farming sector is such a small part of the U.S. economy, it can hardly be blamed for wide changes in total spending. (Even today, however, a worldwide recession may be worsened by climatic changes and crop failures in the world's farming regions.)

two chapters, we examine the federal government's two instruments for influencing aggregate demand: fiscal policy and monetary policy. Fiscal policy involves the use of government spending and taxing powers to affect total spending. Monetary policy involves control of the supply of money to affect consumer and business spending.

Self-Check

1. **An individual's marginal propensity to consume may depend on all but which of the following?**
   a. The quantity of goods already owned.
   b. The level of consumer debt outstanding.
   c. Plans for future spending.
   d. The portion of total income spent.
   e. The backlog of saving already accumulated.

2. **Equilibrium GDP:**
   a. Is determined where aggregate demand is equal to aggregate supply.
   b. May leave workers unemployed and factories idle.
   c. May exceed the nation's productive capacity.
   d. May change if $C + I + G + X_n$ changes.
   e. All of the above.

3. **You carry mail for Uncle Sam during the Christmas season and spend your earnings for a skin-diving trip to Florida. This is an example of:**
   a. Noneconomic behavior.
   b. Recession.
   c. The multiplier effect.
   d. A business cycle.
   c. The sunspot theory of economic activity.

4. **Enrollment increases at your college and a hamburger chain enlarges its restaurant nearby. This is an example of:**
   a. Technological advance.
   b. Inflation.
   c. The multiplier effect.
   d. An increase in investment expenditures.
   e. Excess saving.

5. **In 1975 Queen Elizabeth II decided that, "in view of the economic situation," she would postpone redecorating her vacation home. The queen must have believed there was:**
   a. Excess saving in the British economy.
   b. An inflationary gap.
   c. A recessionary gap.
   d. A high level of unemployment.
   e. Excess capacity in industry.

6. **In 1975 Congress voted to send taxpayers a rebate on their 1974 income taxes. Congress must have believed there was:**
   a. Too much business investment spending.
   b. An inflationary gap.
   c. A recessionary gap.
   d. Too much demand in relation to our productive capacity.
   e. A cumulative upswing in GDP and income.

Theory in Practice

PRACTICE EVALUATING THE U.S. ECONOMY

Since World War II ended in 1945, the United States has experienced eight recessions. A recession is a period in which real GDP (GDP corrected for inflation) fails to grow for at least two quarters.

To illustrate business cycles since 1945, we are using data for GNP (rather than GDP) because data for GDP are not currently available for the years prior to 1959. We have constructed a time series graph showing real GNP on Figure 8.10, showing each of the years since 1945. (Money GNP has been corrected for inflation through the use of a price index with base year 1982.) The eight postwar recessions are marked by shaded bars.

The first postwar recession followed World War II by about three years. Civilian industries were unable to employ the large numbers of returning servicemen, and unemployment rose from 3.8 percent in 1948 to 5.9 percent in 1949.

There were two recessions in the 1950s, one immediately following the Korean War in 1954 and one in 1958. A contributing factor was business firms' optimistic production of consumer goods, which could not be sold and were piled up in inventories. Many firms were forced to cut back production and lay off workers.

Figure 8.10 Growth of Real GNP Interrupted by Eight Recessions

The usual definition of recession is two consecutive quarters of negative real growth of GDP (or GNP).

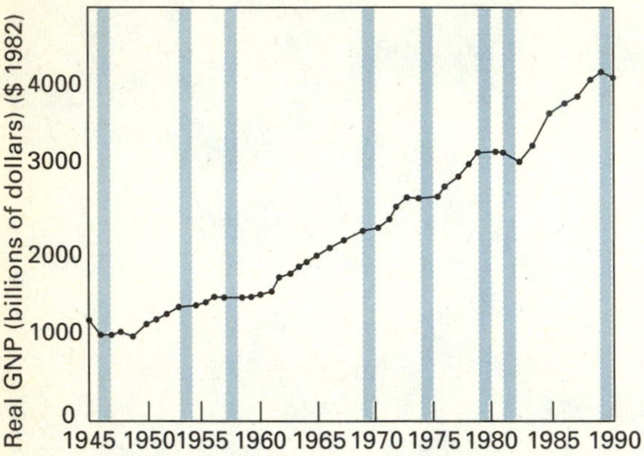

Unemployment remained high until 1961, when increases in government spending began to be effective in stimulating total spending and production. Vietnam War spending and spending for President Johnson's "Great Society" program picked up in the mid-1960s and absorbed much of the slack in the labor force.

Unemployment reached more than 9 percent during the "OPEC" recession of 1974–1975, which followed a sudden, large price increase for oil supplied by the Organization of Petroleum Exporting Countries. The oil embargo and a tripling of oil prices caused GNP to fall by 2 percent in real terms.

Three years of strong growth followed the OPEC recession. The expansion weakened in 1979 when OPEC announced another quadrupling of oil prices. In early 1981, the economy seemed to be floundering again, and by 1982 the economy was suffering the worst of the postwar recessions. Real GNP fell .6 percent during the year, and unemployment climbed to 10 percent. Recovery began early in 1983, and the last half of the year was marked by a substantial expansion of economic activity. Strong growth continued through the mid-1980s, but growth leveled off as the decade ended. Real growth was less than 1 percent in 1990, and recession hit again as the year ended, with negative growth of almost 1 percent and unemployment climbing. Positive growth resumed in the spring of 1991; but growth was still weak and unemployment remained above 7 percent in 1992.

What are the common factors in all these recessions? Each followed a period of heavy new spending: for military equipment, increased inventory investment, or new government programs. Increases in spending raised incomes and encouraged increased consumer spending, which further stimulated factory construction and employment. All good things must come to an end, however, and eventually new spending slackened. Incomes failed to rise further, new factories were not needed, and unemployment spread.

The recession of 1990–1991 was made especially severe by a 5 percent drop in real investment spending in 1990 and a further 10 percent drop in 1991. Wide swings in investment spending put strains on the nation's productive resources. Increases in investment spending create shortages and push up the prices of food and industrial commodities. When costs rise too high, firms are forced to cut back investment spending and lay off workers.

Once a decrease in spending occurs, other changes take place that reduce chances for recovery. In the last half of the 1980s, for example, much consumer spending was financed by borrowing. Mortgage debt grew by almost 10 percent a year and consumer debt by 5 percent. Unemployment (or the fear of unemployment) makes large debt especially burdensome. Consumers cut back on new spending to pay off old loans. This is particularly true in the market for "big ticket" items: durable goods like autos, appliances, and furniture, whose purchase can be postponed until old loans are paid.

PRACTICE USING THE MULTIPLIER

Many large U.S. cities are planning mass-transit systems to reduce the use of private automobiles in urban areas. One Southern city decided on a plan for mass transit with an estimated cost of $2.1 billion. The U.S. Urban Mass Transportation Agency agreed to contribute part of the cost, perhaps as much as 80 percent. The remainder was to come from local tax revenues.

Local economists predicted that as a result of the construction project, personal income across the entire state would increase an average of $475 million a year over the ten years required for construction. An estimated 35,300 new jobs would be created, and tax collections would increase by an average of $16.2 million per year.

Construction projects like this illustrate the multiple effect new spending can have on GDP. Contracts are signed with designers, landowners, earth-moving companies, equipment manufacturers, electricians, and builders. Firms hire new workers, order steel and cement, and install new machinery. Incomes grow throughout the area. Rising incomes allow consumers to increase their spending for homes, furnishings, and recreation. All these expenditures add a further push to incomes and GDP.

Occasionally, things don't turn out so well. For years Britain and France dreamed of a connecting tunnel under the English Channel. The project finally got under way in the 1970s and was nicknamed the "Chunnel." For several years many millions of British pounds and French francs were spent for planning and construction costs. Nevertheless, in 1975 planners decided the project was impractical and too costly, and the Chunnel was abandoned.

Remember that the multiplier works in reverse when spending falls. What were the probable effects for the British and French economies of the reduction in government spending? What were the effects of orders not made, income not spent, workers not hired? Trace through the chain of events and their effects on economic activity in Britain and France.

Fortunately for workers in the construction industry, the Chunnel story did not end in 1975. Work resumed on the project in 1988, and the Chunnel is expected to be completed early in the 1990s.

MORE PRACTICE WITH AGGREGATE DEMAND AND AGGREGATE SUPPLY

Throughout this text we have been concerned with supply and demand. Demand reflects the willingness of people and organizations to spend their dollars for certain goods and services. A demand curve for a particular good is drawn in relation to its price. Typically, quantity demanded is greater at low prices, so that a demand curve slopes downward from left to right. The demand curves in Chapters 2 through 6 were drawn according to this fundamental law of demand.

In this chapter we have been concerned with aggregate demand—the total of spending for all goods and services taken together. We have expressed aggregate demand in relation not to price but to income; that is, we assumed that consumer spending as a whole depends on the nation's income. Thus, the aggregate demand curves in this chapter were drawn in relation to income.

Aggregate demand may also be thought of in relation to price, however. In this case, we would assume that real purchases of goods and services depend on the general price level. An aggregate demand curve drawn in relation to price would look very much like a market demand curve, sloping downward from left to right according to the law of demand.

In Figure 8.11 the horizontal axis measures real output of goods and services. The vertical axis measures prices, in terms of a

Figure 8.11 Aggregate Demand

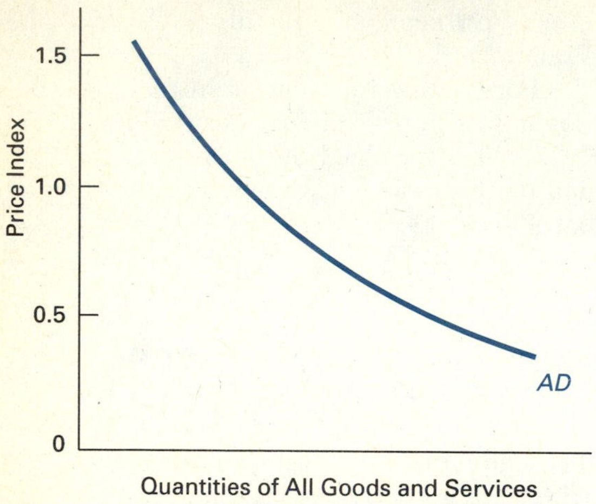

current price index that varies from zero to 150. The line labeled *AD* is drawn by dividing the current equilibrium level of GDP by various price indexes. Thus, the *AD* line represents the real value of current output, whatever the level of prices. At prices higher than a price index of 100, current real output is less than the money value of GDP. At prices lower than a price index of 100, current real output is higher than money GDP.

Aggregate supply can also be drawn in relation to a price index. Aggregate supply represents the sum of all production plans in business firms. Remember that for a single firm, supply obeys the law of supply: that is, larger quantities are supplied only at higher prices. We drew individual firms' supply curves to slope upward from left to right because of increasing marginal costs in the short run.

Aggregate supply may behave differently. When all firms are considered together, larger quantities may be produced with no increase in price. This is because new firms can enter the market, adding their output to that of existing firms, all of which are operating within the range of constant average cost. This means that over a wide range of output, quantities supplied may increase without putting upward pressure on the price index. Aggregate supply may actually be drawn as a horizontal line, as shown in Figure 8.12.

A horizontal aggregate supply curve is an advantage to all of us. It makes it possible for us to purchase larger quantities of goods and services without having to pay higher prices. In fact, as our population grows and as demand for goods and services increases, we would expect the nation's aggregate demand to increase, shown by shifting the aggregate demand curve to the right. With a horizontal aggregate supply curve, aggregate demand can shift to the right without causing prices to rise. (Pencil in a series of aggregate demand curves on Figure 8.12 and show the effect on prices when the aggregate supply curve is horizontal.)

Of course, the picture is not yet complete. We know that real output of goods and services cannot increase indefinitely at constant prices. New firms cannot continue to enter the market producing additional output without eventually experiencing rising costs. Existing firms will enter that range of production where average costs are rising. Morever, as re-

Figure 8.12 Aggregate Supply

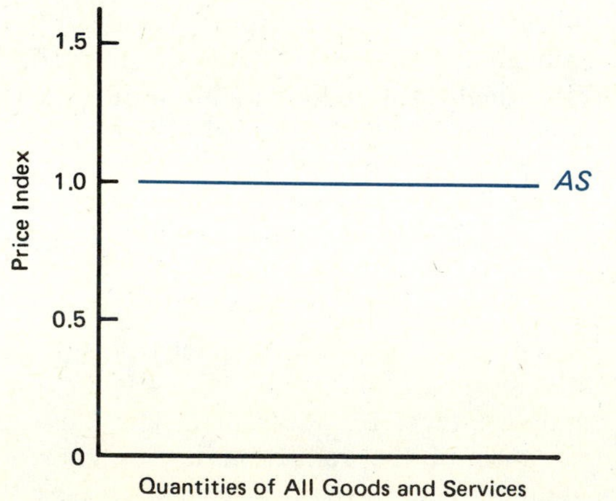

Thinking Seriously About Economic Issues

REGAINING THE COMPETITIVE EDGE

The behavior of aggregate supply depends strongly on the productivity of a nation's resources. Although the United States leads the world in resource productivity, U.S. productivity growth has slowed relative to years past and relative to other nations. In such areas as product quality, service to customers, and speed of product development, U.S. companies are no longer perceived as world leaders. Moreover, the pace of invention and innovation in the United States appears to have slowed relative to the pace abroad. If the trend continues we may experience smaller rightward shifts of aggregate supply and increased tendencies toward inflation.

MIT's Commission on Industrial Productivity has examined the production system in eight sectors of the U.S. economy and has identified these sources of the productivity slowdown:

- The mass-production system that once served the U.S. economy so well is not suited for serving today's small, segmented foreign markets. In fact, our mass-production system may have stifled the search for new technology and worsened adversarial relations with suppliers and subcontractors.
- The high cost of borrowing in the United States discourages long-term investment and development of new products and processes. Instead, it encourages firms to enter less risky and more immediately profitable service industries.
- Outstanding successes in basic research in the United States have yielded fewer successes in new products. Business firms tend to award low status to production-related skills, and they fail to coordinate new product engineering with manufacturing processes.
- The U.S. education system produces poorly educated workers with skills that are narrow and subject to rapid obsolescence. Workers' easy mobility leads firms to focus their on-the-job training too narrowly on the job at hand and give too little attention to retraining and lifetime learning.
- Specialization and compartmentalization of manufacturing mean that decisions that should be made together are instead made separately. The result is unnecessary complexity and a lack of coordination.
- Although the MIT study found the effects of government regulation only slightly more negative in the United States than abroad, relations between industry and government regulators are significantly more adversarial in the United States. The result is less power-sharing, negotiation, and collaboration, along with less attention to improving productivity.

The Commission cited good performance in certain U.S. firms, but generally found superior processes at work in Japan and Germany.

Michael L. Dertouzos, Richard K. Lester, and Robert M. Solow, *Made in America: Regaining the Competitive Edge*, MIT Press, Cambridge, Massachusetts, 1989.

sources become fully employed, their prices will rise, and firms must raise their prices for finished goods. When all these things happen, the aggregate supply curve will begin to slope upward. At the absolute limit of the nation's productive capacity, aggregate supply will become very steep. No additional quantity of real output is possible, but sharply rising prices are indeed possible.

Figure 8.13 combines a shifting *AD* curve with an *AS* curve that becomes steeper as real production approaches the full employment capacity of the nation's resources. Increases in consumer spending, business investment spending, government purchases, and net exports are not inflationary as long as there are unemployed resources ready to be drawn into production at constant prices. As resource markets tighten, however, increases in aggregate demand will cause the price level to rise.

Figure 8.13 Aggregate Demand and Aggregate Supply at Full-Capacity GDP

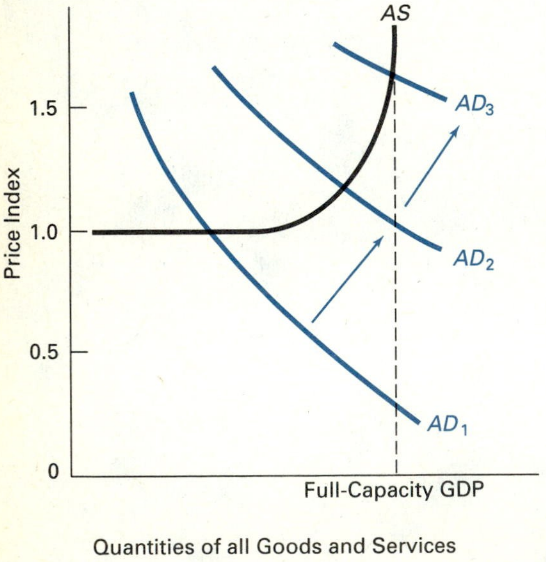

Aggregate demand may continue to increase, but the real quantity of goods and services produced cannot increase. The result of aggregate demand greater than full-employment output is an inflationary gap.

Fortunately, there is still more to this story. Aggregate supply may also change with time. Improvements in the quantity and quality of resources are constantly working to increase our nation's productive capabilities. The full-employment limit to aggregate supply has moved to the right fairly steadily from year to year. We may hope that it continues to do so in the future. (Pencil in a new aggregate supply curve and comment on the implications.)

SUMMARY

1. A rising GDP means more goods and services for the population, but if spending for GDP rises faster than the nation's capacity to produce goods and services, the result may be inflation. A falling GDP, or one that rises too slowly, may mean unemployment and low production. Alternating periods of rising and falling GDP are called business cycles.
2. Consumer spending at various levels of income is shown graphically by the consumption function. Consumer spending depends on the marginal propensity to consume (*MPC*). *MPC* measures the fraction of additional income that consumers will spend.
3. The economy will tend to stabilize at an equilibrium level of GDP at which aggregate demand is equal to aggregate supply. At equilibrium there is no tendency for production to expand or contract.
4. If aggregate demand is greater than aggregate supply at the full-employment level of GDP, there will be an inflationary gap. If aggregate demand is less than aggregate supply at the full-employment level of GDP, there will be a recessionary gap.
5. Small changes in aggregate demand produce cumulative changes in income because of the multiplier effect. Changes in total spending

have been a result in part of irregular changes in business investment spending.

6. Increases in aggregate demand may be satisfied by increases in aggregate supply at constant prices. However, as resources become fully employed, increases in aggregate supply will be associated with rising prices.
7. Improvements in the quantity and quality of resources can increase a nation's full-employment output, so that the aggregate supply curve remains flat over a longer range of output. The hoped-for result is that aggregate demand can increase without price increases.

TERMS TO REMEMBER

business cycles: recurring upswings and downswings in the level of economic activity

marginal propensity to consume (*MPC*): the fraction of each additional dollar of income that consumers will spend

consumption function: the graph showing consumer expenditure at every level of GDP (income)

equilibrium GDP: the level of GDP at which aggregate demand is equal to aggregate supply; total spending is equal to total output

multiplier effect: the multiple change in income that results when an initial change in spending is spent and respent many times

inflationary gap: an excess of aggregate demand over aggregate supply at full employment

recessionary gap: a deficiency of aggregate demand below aggregate supply at full employment

TOPICS FOR DISCUSSION

1. Explain and illustrate each of the following pairs of terms:

   Aggregate demand and aggregate supply
   Inflationary gap and recessionary gap

2. During a recent recession, trash collectors in a large U.S. city were interviewed. They reported a noticeable drop in the appearance of usable items in trash collections, even from wealthy neighborhoods: fewer pairs of shoes, pieces of furniture, and repairable small appliances. Does this suggest anything about the rate of consumer saving in hard times? What does this imply about the chances of recovery from a recession?
3. Producers of most goods suffer declining demand during recessions, but others may enjoy *rising* demand. How would you explain the increasing sales of the following goods during a recent recession?

white bread	sewing machines
beer	movie tickets
home freezers	dehydrated foods

4. During a recession, economists worry about the high level of inventory accumulation in business firms. What signals does a business firm receive from an exceptionally high level of inventory stock relative to monthly sales? Discuss this situation in terms of flows of spending and income. What implications do you foresee for the levels of employment, production, investment, and prices?
5. Droughts in the 1980s reminded many meteorologists of the historical pattern of dry spells that have often damaged U.S. agriculture. The dustbowl days of the 1930s and the long dry spell of the 1940s are examples. There were fears that recent droughts signal a new prolonged period of reduced output from U.S. farms. Some believed the droughts were related to sunspot activity.

   Discuss the implications of prolonged drought for the U.S. economy. How would prolonged drought affect production in other sectors of the economy, real income of workers, the federal government's budget, and technological progress?
6. Explain the origins of inflation and recession as summarized in Chapters 7 and 8. What are the characteristics of each? How is each related to the rate of growth of GDP? What rate of growth of GDP would be most efficient for the nation?
7. Using the multiplier developed in this chapter, compute the effect on GDP of a $20 billion drop in government expenditures. Explain why the marginal propensity to consume is incorporated in the formula for the multiplier.

8. In the recession of 1991 economists were concerned about a decrease in "consumer confidence." The source of the problem seemed to be a high level of consumer debt. What is the basis for concern regarding consumer confidence? Explain the relationship between a high level of debt and (a) economic growth, (b) interest rates, (c) inflation.
9. Many U.S. firms are adopting the Japanese "just-in-time" approach to inventory control. How might improved inventory control affect the nation's tendency toward business cycles?

ANSWERS TO TEST YOURSELF

(p. 171) An *MPC* greater than one for all consumers is possible only if consumers have accumulated savings from previous years when their *MPC* was less than one.

(p. 178) Surveyors, designers, engineers, draftsmen, equipment operators, carpenters, technicians.

FURTHER READING

Brusca, Robert A., "Recession or Recovery," *Challenge*, July/August 1992.

Feldstein, Martin, *The Risk of Economic Crisis*, U. of Chicago Press, Chicago, 1991.

Galbraith, J. K., *The Great Crash*, Houghton Mifflin, Boston, 1961.

Havrilesky, Thomas, "Electoral Cycles," *Challenge*, July/August 1988.

Kindleberger, Charles P., *The World in Depression*, 1929–1939, U. of California Press, Berkeley, 1973.

Kindleberger, Charles P., *Manias, Panics, and Crashes*, Basic Books, New York, 1989.

Mankiw, N. Gregory, "Real Business Cycles," *Journal of Economic Perspectives*, Summer 1989.

Pollin, Robert, "Destabilizing Finance Worsened the Recession," *Challenge*, March/April 1992.

Wolfson, Martin H., *Financial Crises*, M. E. Sharpe, Armonk, N.Y., 1986.

Chapter 9

Government Finance and Fiscal Policy

Tools for Study

LEARNING OBJECTIVES

After reading this chapter, you will be able to:

1. Describe three ways governments finance their expenditures.
2. Define three kinds of taxes.
3. Explain how the federal government's fiscal policy helps stabilize the nation's economic activity.
4. Discuss some advantages and disadvantages of fiscal policy.
5. Explain the origin, advantages, and disadvantages of the national debt.

CURRENT ISSUES FOR DISCUSSION

How well does fiscal policy do its job?

What were the major fiscal policies of the 1980s?

What are the fiscal issues for the 1990s?

Nobody loves the tax collector. The story is told of how Saint Peter stood at the "pearly gates" checking the qualifications of all who wanted to enter Paradise.

First, a politician convinces Saint Peter of his good intentions during his life. Still, he is told he must pass a test before entering Paradise. "Spell 'God'," he is told, and upon answering correctly he is ushered in.

Next a police officer tells of her sufferings in life, carrying out her duties as preserver of the peace while she is ridiculed and spat upon by lawbreakers. Likewise, she must be tested. "Spell, 'God'," she is told, and likewise, she successfully passes through the pearly gates.

Finally, a tax collector tells of his tribulations in a thankless and friendless job. Saint Peter agrees that he is also worthy; but he, too, must pass a test. "Spell 'asafoetida'," he is told.

ALLOCATION OF RESOURCES: PUBLIC OR PRIVATE?

Early in our nation's history, the first U.S. citizens willingly combined their energies and talents to construct public projects: roads, meeting houses, fortresses, and even stockades. Later, as the nation grew, citizens continued to contribute a few days each month to maintain the community's property. In those days, there was a direct and visible relationship between citizen participation, on the one hand, and the growth and security of the community, on the other.

Direct citizen involvement created bonds of satisfaction often lacking today. Today we merely complete tax form "1040" and thus assign a part of our production to the U.S. Treasury. Rather than feeling a part of government, the taxpayer often feels that he or she is its victim, struggling to escape its clutches!

Taxes represent a major form of government involvement in the market system. Through taxes, government takes purchasing power away from spending for private purposes and spends it instead for public purposes—for producing goods and services to be used by the community as a whole. When you pay your dollars for sales and property taxes, income and social security taxes, you have fewer dollars to spend for autos, appliances, clothing, and trips to the shore. Government casts some of your "dollar votes" for you—for schools, highways, and national defense.

Purchase of some goods and services is clearly an individual's responsibility; other goods and services can be provided best by citizens acting together. In the United States, the first category includes consumer goods, like food, clothing, and automobiles. The second category includes defense and international relations, highway systems, and regulation of interstate and foreign commerce. In a gray area, where public and private responsibilities mingle, are education, health and nutrition, housing, and the arts.

As a nation, we try to produce the most efficient combination of goods and services for private enjoyment and goods and services for the use of the entire community. Given our limited productive resources, we try to allocate resources in a way that will best serve the objectives of the community and its citizens.

Our choice of private goods and public goods can be shown on a production possibilities curve like the one in Figure 9.1. The axes represent private goods—for the consumer's own use—and public goods—for the use of the community as a whole. Our willingness to give up part of our income in taxes permits us to use some of our nation's scarce resources for producing goods and services to be enjoyed by the community as a whole.

Figure 9.1 Private Goods and Public Goods

Through our taxes, we channel some of our resources into production of public goods.

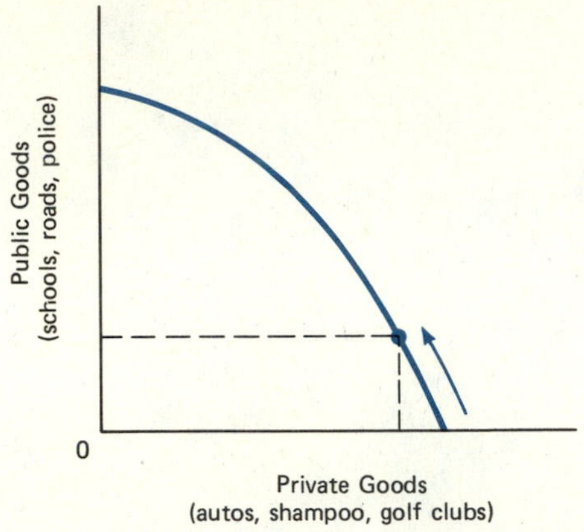

SPENDING FOR PUBLIC GOODS AND SERVICES

In the fiscal year 1992, the federal government's outlays in the United States were almost $1.4 trillion. Shares of the federal budget allocated to specific purposes for the year are shown in Figure 9.2.

National defense and defense-related expenditures comprised the largest part of the federal budget. National defense consumed more than $298 billion, or about 22 percent of the total. Defense-related expenditures—international affairs, space research and technology, interest on the public debt, and veterans' benefits and services—consumed an additional $266 billion (19 percent). Health,

Figure 9.2 Allocative Shares of the Federal Budget for 1992 (dollar figures in billions)

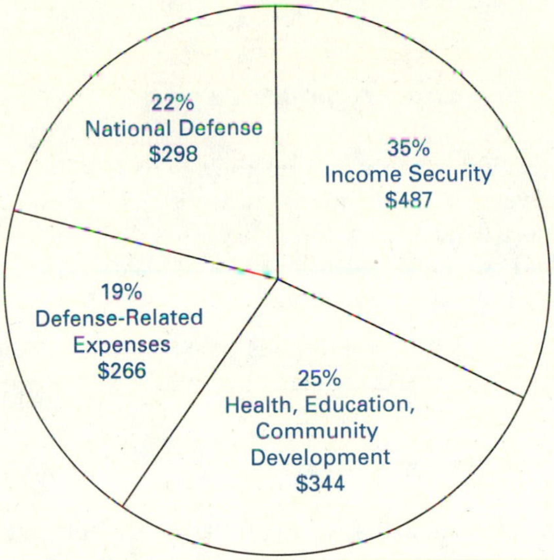

energy, education, housing, commerce and transportation, agriculture, and rural and natural resource development took about $344 billion (25 percent). Transfer payments to individuals (such as social security benefits, welfare, and unemployment compensation) were about $487 billion (35 percent).*

Shares of federal expenditures going for various purposes have remained fairly constant over the years. An exception has been the greater emphasis on military expenditures in wartime. The emphasis on public services such as education and health has varied also, depending on the priorities of the administration in power and on the mood of the public, as expressed in voting trends and in public opinion polls.

* Note that the individual percentages add up to 101 percent, the result of rounding.

State and local government expenditures focus mainly on community services. Education is highest on the list of local government expenditures, with highways an important second. Fire and police protection, water and sewage, and parks and recreation are other local government responsibilities.

GETTING THE MONEY

How does government obtain the money it needs to finance its programs? Government outlays can be financed in three ways:

1. By printing new money.
2. By borrowing from the public.
3. By taxing the public.

Let us look at each of these methods in more detail.

Printing Money

Printing new money sounds like a safe and easy way for the federal government to finance its expenditures.* In fact, it is the least efficient way to obtain funds and is not generally used by the U.S. Treasury. The reason has to do with its effect on the nation's inflation rate. If the government were to print money for its own spending without taking money away from consumers, consumer spending would continue at the same level. Then consumers would be competing with government for the limited supplies of goods and services. Government and consumers would bargain and bid for the things they want, causing prices to rise and making all money worth

* Only the federal government enjoys the option of printing money, not state and local governments.

less. The result of printing new money would be inflation.

After World War I the German government needed money to make its reparation payments to the victorious powers. Many of those debts were paid by printing new money. The German money supply increased by almost 10 billion times in only four years! The result of excessive money growth was inflation so severe that workers had to be given time off during each day to spend their pay before prices could rise again.

Borrowing from the Public

A better way to raise money is to borrow from the public through the sale of securities to consumers and business firms. (When you buy a government security, you are, in effect, lending your savings to government.) If consumers and business firms buy government securities with money they otherwise would have spent, their own spending will fall by the amount government wants to spend. If buyers of securities use money they otherwise would have loaned to banks or other businesses, investment spending will fall by the amount government wants to spend. Thus, the sale of securities to consumers and business firms withdraws enough from private spending to offset the amount government wants to spend.

Taxing the Public

Perhaps the most efficient way to finance government spending is through taxation. Through taxation, other spending can be reduced by the amount government wants to spend.

In 1992 federal tax receipts were more than $1 trillion. Personal and corporate income taxes were the major source of federal tax revenue, making up more than half of the total. The U.S. Treasury ran a deficit of more than $290 billion, which was financed by borrowing.

A CLOSER LOOK AT TAXES

Because taxes make up the major portion of government revenue, here we look at taxes in more detail. The various taxes are often classified by comparing the amount paid in taxes with taxpayers' income base:

$$\frac{\text{total taxes paid}}{\text{taxpayers' income}}$$

Regressive Taxes

A tax that takes a larger fraction of income from low-income earners than from high-income earners is a **regressive tax**. Examples are:

1. Any uniform "head" tax, which takes the same dollar amount from every taxpayer regardless of the taxpayer's income.
2. Social security taxes, which take a fraction of an employed person's earnings up to a certain amount, above which earnings are not taxed.
3. Sales taxes.

The regressivity of items 1 and 2 is easy to see. But why is a sales tax regressive? A sales tax is a fixed percentage of expenditures for goods. However, a sales tax is considered regressive because low-income families generally spend a larger fraction of their income on taxed goods than do higher-income families. High-income families generally spend more of their earnings on untaxed services, and they save more, all of which reduces the fraction of income they pay in sales taxes. (To exclude such necessary purchases as food and medicine from the sales tax would make it less regressive.)

There is some difference of opinion on the proper classification of the property tax. Most agree that low- and middle-income families are likely to spend a larger fraction of their incomes for housing than are high-income families. This would make the effects of the property tax regressive.

Proportional Taxes

A tax that takes an equal fraction of income from all taxpayers is a **proportional** tax. An example is the Illinois personal income tax, which is $2\frac{1}{2}$ percent at all income levels. (However, exemptions for dependents have the effect of altering the proportionality of the tax.)

Progressive Taxes

A tax that takes a larger fraction of income from high-income earners than from low-income earners is a **progressive tax**. The personal income tax is the clearest example. Personal income tax rates increase as the taxpayer moves into higher income brackets. For a typical married couple, the tax rate on the first $35,800 of taxable income is 15 percent: thus, 0.15($35,800) = $5370. The tax rate on income between $35,800 and $86,500 is 28 percent: thus, 0.28($86,500 − 35,800) = $14,196. For a family earning precisely $86,500, therefore, the fraction of income paid in tax is ($5370 + $14,196)/$86,500 = 0.23 = 23 percent. Families earning less than this amount pay a smaller fraction, and families earning more pay a larger fraction. Families earning more than $86,500 pay 31 percent of income above $86,500.

TEST YOURSELF
What are the disadvantages for the economy as a whole of (a) a regressive tax and (b) a progressive tax?

The Tax Structure as a Whole

Federal taxes, dominated by income taxes, are progressive. State and local taxes, dominated by sales and property taxes, tend to be regressive.

The progressivity of the federal tax structure is also affected by the existence of negative taxes. **Negative taxes** are government payments to individuals or groups and are called transfer payments. (Transfer payments were discussed in Chapter 7.) Remember that transfer payments are not payments in exchange for goods or services but are additions to the disposable incomes of particular groups. When negative taxes received from government are subtracted from taxes paid to government, the result is **net taxes**: the net amount government has withdrawn from private income.

The effect of negative taxes is to increase the progressivity of the federal tax structure. This is because low-income families, who pay a lower tax rate, are also more likely to receive government transfer payments of some kind. When you subtract negative taxes received from taxes paid, the net tax rate paid by low-income families falls, perhaps even below zero. High-income families, who pay a higher tax rate, receive fewer transfer payments. This makes their net tax rate relatively high.

In 1986 Congress and President Reagan decided on a new tax law. One objective of the new law was to reduce tax rates while eliminating certain tax advantages high-income earners enjoyed under the old law.

For example, under the old law many high-income taxpayers arranged to receive a

EFFECTIVE RATES OF TOTAL FEDERAL, STATE, AND LOCAL TAXES (percent of income)

Decile	*1966*	*1980*	*1988*
Lowest	16.8	17.1	16.4
Second	18.9	17.1	15.8
Third	21.7	18.9	18.0
Fourth	22.6	20.8	21.5
Fifth	22.8	22.7	23.9
Sixth	22.7	23.4	24.3
Seventh	22.7	24.4	25.2
Eighth	23.1	25.5	25.6
Ninth	23.3	26.5	26.8
Highest	30.1	28.5	27.7
Top 5%	32.7	28.9	27.4
Top 1%	39.6	28.4	26.8
All taxpayers	25.2	25.3	25.4

SOURCE: *Brookings Review,* Spring 1990.

A decile is a tenth of the population, here ranged from the lowest income earners to the highest. Look down each column to see the level of progressivity of the tax structure as a whole. Look across the lines to see how the level of progressivity has changed over the years shown.

portion of their income in the form of capital gains. A capital gain is the difference between the original cost of an asset and the selling price when it is eventually sold by the taxpayer. Before the 1986 tax law, a capital gain was taxed at less than half the rate of the tax on the taxpayer's earned income.* The 1986 law eliminated this tax advantage and called for a tax rate on capital gains equal to the rate on the taxpayer's other income.

*If an asset is sold for less than its purchase price, the seller experiences a capital loss.

The net effect of the 1986 tax law has been lower taxes for individual taxpayers and higher taxes for business firms. There is some disagreement as to whether this has made the tax structure as a whole more or less progressive. The reason for the disagreement has to do with the incidence of the corporate income tax. Corporations pay taxes, but the funds for paying taxes come from charging higher prices for their products, paying lower wages to their workers, or paying lower dividends to their stockholders. Thus, the effect of corporate income taxes is spread across all incomes and may actually be heaviest on low- and middle-income families.

FISCAL POLICY

The U.S. government spends its tax revenue for public goods and services; but government taxing and spending policies also have important consequences for the level of economic activity in the nation as a whole. The use of federal tax and spending programs to affect economic activity is called **fiscal policy**. The word *fiscal* evolved from the Latin word "fisc," a money basket carried by tax collectors in the days of the Roman empire.

The Keynesian Revolution

The Great Depression of the 1930s awakened Congress to the painful effects of wide swings in economic activity, with alternating periods of unemployment and inflation. Voters insisted that Congress adopt policies to reduce the high current level of unemployment and to guard against periods of unemployment and inflation in the future. In the late 1930s the British economist John Maynard Keynes presented his suggestions for government stabilization policies to President Franklin Roosevelt.

Keynes' basic proposition was simple. Any time total spending is too low, such that there is unemployment and recession, government should increase its spending and reduce taxes and in that way increase aggregate demand. If total spending is too high, with worsening shortages and inflation, government should reduce its own spending and raise taxes. In other words, changes in government spending and taxes should offset unwanted changes in private spending, so that the nation can avoid the painful effects of unemployment and inflation.

Keynes denied there is any necessary relationship between government expenditures and tax revenues. This was a rather startling pronouncement, since it meant that government should not be required to balance its budget. According to Keynes, in times of too little private spending, government spending should exceed tax revenues. Higher government spending would funnel more income back into the circular flow than is taken out through taxes. Operating "in the red" would cause a **deficit** in the government budget:

$$\text{government expenditures} - \text{tax collections} = G - T = \text{government deficit}$$

When private spending is too high, the relationship between government spending and tax revenues should be the reverse. In this case, tax collections should exceed government spending, draining out more income from the circular flow through taxes than is put back through spending. Collecting more taxes than it pays out yields a **surplus** in the government budget:

$$\text{tax collections} - \text{government expenditures} = T - G = \text{government surplus}$$

In deficit years, government spending greater than tax receipts would be financed through the sale of securities. Then in surplus years, tax revenues greater than spending would make it possible to redeem securities for cash. If by some (unlikely) coincidence government borrowing during deficit years is precisely offset by loan repayments in surplus years, there is no permanent increase in total federal debt. Keynes probably hoped this would be the case. But if not, he said, small increases in government debt are a small price to pay for ensuring full employment and an efficient economy.

Keynes's ideas were considered revolutionary. For several decades, policymakers hesitated to recommend that government spend more than it collected in taxes. During recessions the budget tended to show a deficit anyway, since incomes (and income-tax collections) tended to fall. It was not until the 1960s that the federal government actually planned a budget deficit. (We discuss the first planned government deficit in more detail in the second part of this chapter.)

Some kinds of fiscal policy are automatic, including built-in tax and spending changes that take effect automatically when private spending changes. Other kinds of fiscal policy are discretionary. They require acts of Congress and the president before they can be put into effect.

Automatic Fiscal Policy

Automatic fiscal policy has two parts: the progressive tax schedule, including tax rates that increase with income; and negative taxes, like farm subsidies, unemployment compensation, welfare benefits, veterans' benefits, and other benefit payments that tend to fall with income. The two parts work automatically to reduce wide swings in spending and help stabilize economic activity.

With a progressive tax schedule, when incomes rise, taxpayers automatically move into higher tax brackets. They pay higher taxes, and they must cut their spending to a smaller fraction of income. On the other hand, when incomes fall, taxpayers move into lower tax brackets and pay lower tax rates, so that their spending need not fall as fast as income.

Negative taxes have a similar effect. When incomes rise, welfare benefits, subsidies, food stamp allotments, unemployment compensation, and other transfer payments tend automatically to fall. Smaller transfer payments tend to slow the increase in personal income and slow the increase in spending. On the other hand, when incomes fall, negative taxes add more to incomes and keep spending from falling so far.

Discretionary Fiscal Policy

We have seen that automatic fiscal policy works to correct changes in spending without the intervention of public officials. (This may be seen as an advantage or a disadvantage, depending on one's confidence in public officials.) Occasionally, however, automatic fiscal policy is not enough to maintain spending at a full-employment, noninflationary level of GDP. In such times it may be necessary to make fundamental changes in the tax schedule and in government outlays. Changes in the entire tax structure and government outlays are called discretionary fiscal policy. Discretionary fiscal policy to increase the level of spending and maintain full employment is called expansionary fiscal policy. Discretionary fiscal policy to contract spending and reduce inflationary pressure is called contractionary fiscal policy. Together, expansionary and contractionary fiscal policy work to increase efficiency in the nation's employment of its scarce resources.

Discretionary Policy to Increase Employment

In times of especially high unemployment, expansionary fiscal policy may be needed to increase aggregate demand. As a part of expansionary fiscal policy, Congress might decide to reduce all tax rates for individuals and corporations. Lower personal tax rates will leave households with more money to spend for consumer goods and services; and lower corporate income taxes will leave business firms with more money for making new investments. Or, Congress might decide to increase funds distributed as transfer payments. Increasing transfer payments reduces net taxes, increases disposable income, and increases the level of private spending.

Finally, Congress might decide to increase government expenditures. Expenditures might be increased for public projects like dams and highways, education and health services, or scientific research and resource development. Increasing government spending increases aggregate demand and causes employment, production, and income to rise.

Discretionary Policy to Reduce Inflation

In times of exceptionally high inflation, contractionary policy may be needed to reduce aggregate demand and hold down the level of resource use. Congress might decide to increase tax rates or impose a temporary surtax on tax bills. (A surtax is an extra tax—a tax on a tax.) Higher tax rates will leave families with less money for consumer spending and leave business firms with less money for investment spending.*

Congress might also decide to reduce government expenditures. However, reducing expenditures may be difficult if essential public projects are under way and must be continued. Reducing transfer payments may be difficult, too, since transfer payments generally go to low-income families who suffer severely from inflation.

The best remedy for unemployment or inflation is probably some combination of discretionary policies that avoids the disadvantages of a single policy. For example, during the recession of 1974–1975, President Ford recommended that Congress:

1. Reduce personal and corporate tax rates.
2. Increase unemployment compensation.
3. Appropriate funds for public-service jobs in highway maintenance, library and hospital services, and other public projects.

During the inflation of 1979, President Carter recommended that Congress:

1. Allow tax collections to increase automatically.
2. Reduce the growth rate of federal spending.
3. Encourage labor-management cooperation in a voluntary program of wage and price restraint.

* If families and business firms cut back on their saving in order to pay their higher taxes, however, they can offset at least part of the higher taxes and continue to spend at roughly the same rate.

Some Disadvantages

One disadvantage of expansionary fiscal policy is the lack of well-planned and needed public projects for which to spend government funds. A major energy research and development program or a space exploration program may come up only once in a generation—make that a century! Moreover, massive government spending programs are difficult to administer without waste and duplication. Occasionally, government programs completely fail to achieve their intended aims.

They are also slow to put in place. Ideally, policymakers would maintain a backlog of desired projects, engineered and ready to go. The plans could be begun quickly when needed and in spending amounts ranging from very small to rather large. Better long-range planning and flexibility in the injection of new spending would improve the efficiency of discretionary fiscal policy.

Another disadvantage of discretionary fiscal policy involves deficiencies in economic information. Economic forecasting and planning is not as exact a science as, perhaps, horticulture. The story is told of a New York apartment dweller who owned a collection of cactus plants and wanted a precise indicator to tell her when they should be watered. She solved her problem by subscribing to an Arizona newspaper. Whenever the paper reported rain, she watered her plants.

Unfortunately, Congress has no equally precise indicator that signals when to inject or hold back new spending, and there are no foolproof ways to accomplish the desired results. Proposals must be debated and compromised, voters must be informed and persuaded, and finally, administrative procedures must be designed and put into effect. All in all, it is a frustratingly difficult and time-consuming process. By the time any decision is put into effect, the problem may be much worse (or it may have disappeared altogether).

The most serious disadvantage of discretionary fiscal policy stems from political considerations. Tax and spending proposals often depend more on election-year politics than on what is best for the nation's long-range economic health. Spending for rural development or for space exploration affects different groups of voters differently. Each legislator tends to support tax and spending proposals that provide the most help for his or her own constituents. It is very difficult to separate economics from politics.

Political considerations give an inflationary bias to discretionary fiscal policy. Congress finds it easy to turn on the faucet and allow more government spending to flow into the spending stream. Spending bills and tax reductions receive little objection from voters and maintain a legislator's popularity in his or her district.

The reverse is not so agreeable. Closing off spending through reductions in government outlays and increases in taxes, doesn't secure a legislator's seat in the next Congress. The result is that expansionary fiscal policy to fight unemployment is generally favored at the expense of contractionary fiscal policy to fight inflation.

TEST YOURSELF

Some tax revenue collected by the federal government is distributed for spending by state and local governments. What are some advantages and disadvantages of this arrangement?

THEN THERE'S THE NATIONAL DEBT . . .

According to **Keynesian economic policy**, it is acceptable for the federal government to spend more than it collects in taxes. If consumer spending and business investment spending fall short of the full-employment level of spending, more government spending and lower taxes should make up the difference. A balanced federal budget is desirable only if a balanced budget plus private spending will achieve full employment.

Spending more than tax collections requires government borrowing. Deficits in the federal budget are financed by the sale of securities to individuals, business firms, financial institutions, and state and local governments. Fortunately, many savers look on government securities as a safe way to store their financial wealth. Government securities generally pay enough interest income to offset the effects of inflation, and they provide financial security for the holder's retirement years.

The first major increase in government borrowing occurred in World War II, when federal debt soared from $45 billion to more than $250 billion. In the year following the war, the government's total debt amounted to 125 percent of GDP. Obviously the increase in debt was not a result of government spending to achieve full employment. In fact, the great increase in the debt was necessary to finance spending for defense.

Between World War II and the 1970s, federal debt grew at an average annual rate of about $5 billion. During the 1980s it grew at an average annual rate of $200 billion. By 1992, total federal debt amounted to $4.0 trillion. This was 67 percent of GDP for the year, up from 34 percent in 1980.

TEST YOURSELF

What do you think happened between World War II and 1980 to reduce the debt from 125 percent of GDP to 34 percent?

Some Advantages

An advantage of the federal debt is that it provides the government a way to stabilize economic activity through variations in taxes and spending. Furthermore, the purchase and sale of government securities is a way to change the quantity of money in circulation, as the Federal Reserve buys and sells securities from its own holdings. (We discuss this subject in detail in Chapter 10.)

Government securities provide financial security to many small investors. Many individuals and institutions regard U.S. government securities as a safe and convenient way to store their savings for their future needs.

Because the U.S. government is a continuing operation, it is never necessary to repay the debt entirely. While retired people are redeeming their government securities for cash, young people are buying securities for their long-range security. Only when foreigners cash in their securities is it necessary to send dollars outside the country.

Some Potential Disadvantages

The disadvantages associated with the federal debt have very little to do with the need to repay it. In fact, to repay the debt entirely would require only that taxes be increased by the amount of the debt in order to pay cash to holders of government securities. The result would be a redistribution of wealth away from taxpayers toward holders of securities. Because holders of government securities would likely be from the higher-income groups, they would probably spend a smaller fraction of their receipts. So another result might be a decrease in total spending and a decline in economic activity. Nevertheless, to repay the debt would not significantly reduce the nation's total wealth.

Similar reasoning applies to the collection of taxes for paying interest on the debt. All income earners are taxed to pay interest charges to holders of government securities—almost $200 billion in 1992. Interest payments amount to about 15 percent of all federal outlays and almost 4 percent of GDP. Holders of debt gain from their interest income, of course, but most of these gainers are also taxpayers, whose tax payments offset part of their interest income. The extent to which some groups gain and others lose from the effects of the federal debt has never been precisely measured.

The chief disadvantage of the debt has to do with the fact that, at any point in time, there is a limited quantity of savings for lending. Thus, government borrowing absorbs savings that might have been used for new investment. Economists call the diversion of savings from investment to government "crowding out." The result of crowding out could be a failure to create enough new capital resources to ensure rising productivity of the nation's labor force. Indeed, a test of the efficiency of the national debt might be whether borrowed funds spent by government help achieve a more productive economy than would have resulted from the private use of the same funds.

Supply-Side Economics

The Keynesian model of income determination dominated economic theory for a quarter of a century. Economic policymakers tended to follow Keynesian recommendations, with increases in government spending to increase aggregate demand and correct tendencies toward recession.

Through the 1970s and into the 1980s, however, a new group of economists began to question the effectiveness of Keynesian policies. Keynesian policies concentrated too much on increasing demand, they said, in the expectation that increases in consumer spending would encourage the investment spending necessary to produce more goods and services. Critics of Keynesian policies argued that high taxes to finance government spending programs had, in fact, reduced taxpayers' ability to save. Lower saving had the effect of pushing borrowing costs up and driving investment spending down. They worried that without investments in new productive capacity, increases in aggregate demand would lead to accelerating inflation.

Thinking Seriously About Economic Issues

THE BUDGET AND NATIONAL SAVING AND INVESTMENT

During the "perpetual Christmas" of the 1980s, the U.S. saving rate dropped to barely a third of the rate in the 1950s and 1960s. The corresponding drop in investment included a large drop in business investment, a small drop in the share of residential housing, and a large drop in U.S. ownership of investments (net) abroad.

Through its effect on productivity growth, real ouput, and real wages, lower investment means lower living standards for U.S. consumers. According to the growth-accounting model of Edward Denison and Nobel laureate Robert Solow, if the nation's saving rate had been 7.5 percent instead of 3.5 percent in the 1980s, GDP at the end of the decade would be 3 percent (or about $150 billion) higher. That translates to an increase of about $1200 in real income for every U.S. family.

Increasing national saving and investment requires, first, reducing consumption and, second, channeling saving into high-priority investment. William Nordhaus believes that "price-affecting" policies (such as higher interest rates, lower tax rates on income, and special incentives for saving) are ineffective for increasing saving. Instead he recommends "income-affecting" policies: higher taxes on personal income or consumption, energy taxes, excise taxes on alcohol and tobacco, and environmental taxes.

According to Nordhaus, investment priorities should include increasing corporate investment and increasing foreign investment. Toward this objective, he suggests a redesigned investment tax credit to reward investors through tax reductions. He recommends increased investment in the public infrastructure as well, including intangible investments in research and development (R&D) and education and environmental investments.

How do you suppose Nordhaus distinguishes "price-affecting" policies from "income-affecting" policies? Why are their effects different?

What are their efficiency and equity consequences?

William D. Nordhaus, "What's Wrong with a Declining National Saving Rate?" *Challenge*, July-August 1989.

This new group of economists rejected what they called demand-side economic policies and, instead, supported supply-side policies. **Supply-side economic** policies included tax cuts to increase saving and investment and stimulate the production of goods and services.

Ronald Reagan campaigned for president in 1980 on a platform that emphasized supply-side solutions to the nation's economic problems. Tax cuts and cuts in civilian spending programs were put in place late in 1981, but the results were not as expected. In fact, in 1982 the economy moved into the most severe recession since World War II, with record unemployment and business failures.

Thinking Seriously About Economic Issues

BUDGETS HAVE CONSEQUENCES

Ordinarily, to talk about "reforming the budget process" is to induce slumber in the most habitual insomniacs. But such talk from Herbert Stein is different. Stein's book *Governing the $5 Trillion Economy* is an exciting and valuable contribution toward the resolution of major macroeconomic policy issues in the United States.

Stein's fundamental thesis is simple: Our national fixation on allocating federal taxes and expenditures has blinded us to the more critical problem of allocating the nation's gross domestic product (GDP). Until we have decided our objectives and priorities for the entire $5 trillion national output (and considered how our budget decisions affect these objectives), we cannot make sensible decisions regarding taxes and spending.

Moves toward budget reform tend to emphasize budget balance. But, according to Stein, it is incorrect to believe that the cost of government programs is the taxes we pay to finance them. In fact, the cost of government programs is the alternative production (both public and private) we sacrifice by using resources to produce government programs. By this reasoning, budget policy serves not an economic but a political function—to remind us of that cost.

Stein recommends, first, that the president set out his view of the nation's priorities relative to defense, public and private investment, health and education, and consumption by the poor and the nonpoor. Second, the President should submit to Congress a four-year plan for the allocation of the GDP that is consistent with these priorities. Finally, he should submit a comprehensive budget plan, along with two-year appropriations bills that make explicit the means to achieve the desired allocation of the nation's output.

"Lip-reading" and television "sound bites" are no way to solve critical budget questions. By forcing ourselves to think in terms of the implications of budget decisions for broad, long-range national goals, we will bring a degree of rationality to the budget process that has been missing in the past.

Herbert Stein, *Governing the $5 Trillion Economy*, Oxford University Press, New York, 1989.

After the recession, the nation experienced a strong expansion, with growth averaging 3.8 percent over the next four years. Saving actually fell as a fraction of income, however, and investment spending grew by less than one-half percent as a fraction of income. Some economists began to worry that slower growth in tax collections and rising government deficits were depriving private investors of the funds they needed for investment.

In the remainder of this chapter, we discuss in detail the record of fiscal policy over the past several decades.

Self-Check

1. The largest single federal outlays go for:
a. Health, education, and welfare.
b. Revenue-sharing to states.
c. National defense and defense-related expenditures.
d. Interest on the national debt.
e. Highway construction.

2. When negative taxes are considered, the federal net tax structure:
a. Is generally regressive.
b. Includes primarily sales and excise taxes.
c. Is considered roughly proportional.
d. Requires low-percentage tax rates on high incomes.
e. Becomes more progressive.

3. Automatic fiscal policy depends on:
a. Changes in net taxes as incomes change.
b. Lower tax payments during inflation.
c. Lower transfer payments during recession.
d. Congressional action to change tax rates.
e. The consent of voters.

4. Discretionary fiscal policy:
a. Will never create a government deficit.
b. Is a foolproof instrument of economic policy.
c. Requires congressional action.
d. Is easiest to accomplish during inflation.
e. Focuses on welfare payments and subsidies.

5. As a result of national debt:
a. The United States is heavily indebted to foreign banks.
b. Many private investors are dependent on risky assets.
c. We must tax heavily to redeem government securities as they mature.
d. There is some redistribution of spending power.
e. We have placed an unfair burden on our grandchildren.

6. The federal government provides funds for industrial development in areas of high unemployment. This is an example of:
a. Automatic fiscal policy.
b. Discretionary fiscal policy.
c. Expansionary fiscal policy.
d. Contractionary fiscal policy.
e. Both (b) and (c).

7. Which of the following would be an appropriate way to deal with inflation?
a. Build a dam.
b. Increase farm subsidies.
c. Reduce social security taxes.
d. Run a deficit in the federal budget.
e. Run a surplus in the federal budget.

Theory in Practice

EVALUATING KEYNESIAN POLICIES

During the Great Depression of the 1930s, Keynesian policy was still a new and untried idea. Expansionary fiscal policy was not used vigorously enough to offset the decrease in private spending. Keynes himself joked that it might be a good idea to bury jars of money around the countryside and encourage people to dig them up. In that way, consumers would obtain spending power that, when spent, would increase someone else's income and spending. Ultimately there would be a multiple increase in spending and income and, finally, increased employment.

Such schemes were not carried out, of course, but the federal government did sponsor public works projects under the Works Progress Administration, Civilian Conservation Corps, and Public Works Administration. Through these agencies, unemployed workers were hired to construct public roads, bridges, parks, and so forth. Still, the level of government spending was rather small. Tax revenues fell, however, so that by 1940 the federal government had incurred automatic deficits averaging almost $4 billion a year for seven years. Fear of increasing debt drove policymakers to cut spending, and in 1940 there were still 10 million people unemployed.

During the recessions of the Eisenhower years (1954–1955 and 1958–1959), the balanced budget philosophy dominated policymaking. It was not until the early 1960s that Keynesian economic policy was actively applied. Walter Heller, chairman of President John F. Kennedy's Council of Economic Advisors, persuaded the president to ask Congress for a tax cut at a time when the federal budget was already in deficit.

Heller argued that the current deficit was caused not so much by tax collections that were too low but by tax rates that were too high. High tax rates kept consumer and business spending low. Low spending kept employment, income, and hence, tax revenues low. Heller recommended reducing tax rates and leaving consumers and business firms with more income for spending. The result would be more job opportunities and higher incomes, with higher tax revenues for the Treasury.

The tax cut was finally implemented in 1964 under President Lyndon Johnson, and Dr. Heller's prediction proved correct. The federal budget went from a $3 billion deficit in 1964 to a $1.2 billion surplus in 1965. Tax revenues for 1965 were nearly $10 billion higher than revenues in 1964 before the tax cut.

The success of expansionary fiscal policy (along with increases in the money supply, a topic that is considered in Chapter 10) enhanced the confidence of economic policymakers and strengthened their commitment to Keynesian economic policies. Toward the end of the 1960s, however, economic conditions changed from recession to inflation. Inflation called for contractionary fiscal policy.

The problem of inflation illustrates the principal weakness of Keynesian fiscal policy, a weakness that results from political realities. When spending for the Vietnam War began to overheat the U.S. economy in the late 1960s, inflationary pressures began to build up. Keynesian fiscal policy called for increased taxes to channel spending away from private purposes and move resources into defense production. However, the unpopular war and the insecure political positions of the president and Congress prevented a tax increase until 1968. By that time inflation had accelerated beyond the point where simple policy tools could correct it.

The end of the Vietnam War and the slowing of government spending in the early 1970s brought rising unemployment, while inflation continued at abnormally high levels. Keynesian remedies for unemployment seemed only to aggravate inflation.

Some economists belive it is impossible to control both unemployment and inflation at the same time. For policymakers in the 1970s it seemed impossible to control either.

PRESIDENT REAGAN'S FISCAL POLICY

President Reagan came to office sharply critical of Keynesian economic policies. High inflation and unemployment, weakening status in world affairs, and faltering economic growth seemed to call for a change in economic policies.

We have referred to President Reagan's economic program as supply-side economics. Supply-side economists argued that demand-side economics focused too much on consumer spending, expecting that a high level of consumer spending would create incentives for investment and growth. Instead, they said, high taxes to pay for government social programs had reduced the nation's saving, so that investment had shrunk. Without new investment, productivity growth had slowed and inflation had accelerated.

Policy Changes

The new administration proposed a set of programs to change the fiscal policies that it believed contributed to the crisis:

1. *A reduction of government's role in the economy.* Throughout the 1970s total federal tax revenues and government outlays (including government spending and transfer payments) had grown significantly as a percent of GDP. Fearing increasing government involvement in the allocation of scarce resources, the administration proposed significant cuts in taxes and government spending.
2. *Personal tax cuts.* Personal income tax rates were to be cut substantially, with the greatest cuts going to high-income families who pay proportionally higher taxes. Tax cuts were expected to increase work incentives, thus raising incomes and ultimately increasing tax revenues. Higher disposable incomes were expected to increase saving, thus increasing funds for investment. Beginning in 1985, tax rates were "indexed," or adjusted downward to offset inflation. Indexing would prevent automatic increases in taxes when money wages rose without any increase in real income.
3. *Business tax cuts.* Business firms were to be allowed larger tax deductions, leaving greater after-tax profits to finance expansion and modernization.
4. *Government spending cuts.* Tax cuts would reduce government revenues and increase the government's deficit, at least at the beginning. To offset reductions in tax revenues, government spending programs that were judged wasteful or not essential would have to be reduced or eliminated.
5. *Increased defense spending.* A perception of military weakness relative to the Soviet Union and a fear of increasing world tensions would require a significant increase in defense spending.
6. *Decreased government regulation.* Environmental health and safety regulations of the 1970s were believed to have increased the risks of investment and stifled innovation. Therefore, regulatory agencies were asked to reduce the level of new regulatory activity and consider carefully the impact of existing regulations.

The Results

The gravity of the economic situation ensured substantial public support for the President's proposals. Unfortunately, the actual results differed sharply from expectations:

1. Although supply-side economic policies were expected to reduce the role of government, the recession of 1981–1982 so reduced the growth of GDP that federal tax revenues and government outlays grew further as a percent of GDP. Gross investment, industrial production, housing construction, and corporate profits fell, and the level of plant utilization fell to less than 70 percent. The business failure rate jumped to the highest rate in 20 years.
2. Personal income tax cuts favored high-income taxpayers, whose work incentives were already high, at the expense of low-income taxpayers, who had to reduce their savings to maintain their former standard of living. Indexing had been expected to reduce future tax revenues, and in fact the federal deficit continued in the three-digit range throughout the 1980s and into the 1990s.

Thinking Seriously About Economic Issues

THE POLITICS OF ECONOMICS

Our democratic political system guarantees a voice for the interests of many citizen groups, no matter how small. There are some disadvantages to this. Decision making in a democracy requires a consensus from many groups before action can be taken. Problem solving cannot proceed smoothly from description to analysis to policy. The interests of affected groups must first be considered, and compromises must be made. The result of consensus politics may be economic policies that are too little or too late—or just plain wrong.

The problem is particularly serious when it involves decisions regarding fiscal policy. Different groups of voters have different opinions about the appropriate types and amounts of government spending programs. In general, voters tend to favor spending programs that increase their own incomes, whether or not those programs promote the nation's economic welfare. This may be particularly true of spending for national defense. Spending for defense raises the incomes of some groups and raises the tax bills of many others. Particular regions or occupations often use their power in Congress to benefit proportionally more from defense spending. (A distinguished senator from Georgia was for many years chairman of the Senate Armed Services Committee. It was sometimes said that if his state received one more defense installation, it would sink into the Atlantic Ocean.)

What is politically desirable for a particular interest group may be undesirable for the economy as a whole. For example, when resources are diverted to defense production instead of to long-range economic development, the result may be slower economic growth. Moreover, when defense spending is eventually cut off, affected areas may suffer severely from the loss of jobs and income. (Citizens of California are learning that the multiplier works in reverse.)

The farming sector is another that is strongly affected by government economic policy. Farmers generally favor free markets, and they oppose price-fixing for the farm equipment they must buy. At the same time, farmers sometimes insist on government price supports for the farm commodities they sell. In the end, farm price supports increase the prices consumers pay for many other goods. Strong farm lobbies in Congress can exert political pressure (and contribute campaign funds) in support of policies that benefit farmers.

Decisions regarding fiscal policy must be made in the light of political realities. What is politically popular may at times outweigh what is economically efficient. It is little wonder, therefore, that the study of economics was originally known as political economy.

3. Business tax reductions were of little use in recession, when firms experienced slowing sales growth and falling income. Moreover, record federal deficits forced the government to compete against private business borrowers for the limited stock of savings, causing interest rates to rise and investment spending to fall, when both values are corrected for inflation.
4. Cuts in government spending reduced the incomes of many families and business firms, who cut their own spending and made the recession worse.
5. Increases in defense spending required the Department of Defense to spend vast sums quickly, and there was evidence of waste and inefficiency. Also, increased defense production put upward pressure on the wages of skilled workers and on the prices of basic commodities essential in non-defense industries.
6. Efforts to reduce government regulation met with mixed success. Deregulation of certain industries did allow competition to increase, but at the cost of a record number of business failures. The public opposed significant cuts in environmental and safety regulations.

In 1982 President Reagan bowed to political pressure and agreed to a tax increase to reduce the federal deficit. Congress began considering new policies to deal with high unemployment, and in 1983 the nation began recovery from recession.

Real economic growth continued throughout the 1980s.* In 1988, President Bush was elected in a climate of prosperity. Although the budget deficit remained high, candidate Bush promised voters "No new taxes." He hoped that continued growth would provide the increased tax revenues eventually to balance the budget without an increase in tax rates. By 1990, increased deficit projections made that hope appear unrealistic. At the end of that year, Congress and the President agreed on a new budget plan to cap spending in each of the three main categories: defense, international affairs, and domestic programs. Increased spending in any category would have to be paid for by a spending reduction in that category or by special new taxes. The top income tax rate was increased slightly.

* The 1986 Tax Reform Act reduced tax brackets from fourteen to three—15 percent, 28 percent, and 31 percent—and eliminated many tax deductions that had formerly reduced the tax liabilities of some high-income taxpayers.

Table 9.1 Federal Budget (in billions of dollars).

Year	*Receipts*	*Outlays*	*Surplus or Deficit*
1929	3.9	3.1	.7
1939	6.3	9.1	−2.8
1943	24.0	78.6	−54.6
1951	51.6	45.5	6.1
1959	79.2	92.1	−12.8
1968	153.0	178.1	−25.2
1975	279.1	332.3	−53.2
1980	517.1	590.9	−73.8
1981	599.3	678.2	−79.0
1982	617.8	745.8	−128.0
1983	600.6	808.4	−207.8
1984	666.5	851.8	−185.4
1985	734.1	946.4	−212.3
1986	769.1	990.3	−221.2
1987	854.1	1003.9	−149.8
1988	909.0	1064.1	−155.2
1989	990.7	1144.2	−153.2
1990	1031.3	1251.8	−220.5
1991	1054.3	1323.0	−268.7
1992[e]	1075.7	1441.0	−365.2
1993[e]	1164.8	1497.5	−332.7

[e]Estimates

SOURCE: *Economic Report of the President,* various years.

Thinking Seriously About Economic Issues

LETTING GOVERNMENT DO IT

If you are ever in Beaver Creek, Minnesota, on Saturday night, don't miss the big dance at the community recreation center just outside town. There, in a giant Quonset hut, a small contribution will buy you an evening of foot-stomping music and a rousing good time. Just about everyone in town will be there, for in many ways this is the center of the town's social, economic, and political life.

It also illustrates an important relationship between citizens and their government. The voters of this small, isolated community agreed to combine their resources for construction of a community recreation center. In effect, they agreed to "tax" themselves a small amount each week, and in return they enjoy the recreation services at the hall. Ticket sales long ago paid off the borrowing to build the center and are now paying to build tennis courts on adjacent land.

That is the way it has always been in the United States. Citizens have perceived needs for community services and have elected representatives to plan programs to fill the needs. In the beginning, most services were provided by local government—usually on a small scale. But since the Great Depression, the federal and state governments have been providing more services for their citizens.

How well does the system work? The answer depends in part on the level of government involved. Some needs can be perceived and filled most effectively at the local level. Public education and local law enforcement are examples. Services like these can be provided on a small scale, and the administrative costs are small. Other needs, like dam construction, agricultural research, and forest conservation, are more complex and extend over larger areas. Plans must be made and carried out at the level of the state or even federal government.

There are advantages and disadvantages in drawing up broader programs to deal with more complex needs. Providing coordinated services for a large area may be cheaper than having each community provide services separately. Large-volume purchasing and large-scale production often cost less and are more efficient than small programs serving individual communities. But large-scale production sometimes means higher administrative costs that may offset these savings.

In terms of overall productivity, the government sector is probably far behind the private sector. One reason is mechanization. Gains in productivity are generally the result of mechanization, but government services are not easily mechanized. The high labor-intensity of government services makes it difficult to cut costs. Moreover, at the local level especially, it is difficult for governments to establish clear goals and to use scientific management to carry out programs.

How can governments be helped to perform better? Critics have offered some suggestions:

1. Local governments might be combined into metropolitan or regional units. Larger units could use professional management techniques for a more systematic approach to broad, area-wide problems. Higher levels of government could provide technical help with budgeting, accounting, and reporting procedures. Links between government workers at various levels would help coordinate programs and avoid waste.
2. Another way to improve government performance might be to hire private firms to produce some public services. Private firms have long experience in cutting costs. Garbage collection, school lunch programs, data processing, fire protection, and even law enforcement are examples of services that might be provided more efficiently by private firms.
3. Finally, if public services are to be produced efficiently, they must be performed at the level of government that can do the job at the lowest cost. This may mean that taxes should be collected by one level of government and revenues spent by another level. On the one hand, the federal government appears to be better at collecting taxes than state and local governments. This is partly a result of the progressive income tax, which yields more revenues as national income grows. On the other hand, spending programs conducted at the federal level have often been inefficient. State or local governments may be better able to tailor spending programs to their particular needs. Actually, the federal government currently distributes some of its tax revenues to the states for use in particular programs. Federal grants to states now comprise one-fifth of total state and local government revenues, amounting to $150 billion in 1991.

In the United States, we ask government to do for us what we cannot do for ourselves. Unfortunately, some jobs may be too complex even for government. When government programs fail to accomplish their objectives, it is unfair to compare the failed results with some ideal standard. A truer test would be to compare results with results at another level of government—or with no government programs at all.

SUMMARY

1. Civilized communities have long depended on the cooperative work of their citizens to provide services to be enjoyed by the community as a whole. Nowadays, we provide public services indirectly through payment of taxes, which governments use to finance the services the community wants.
2. Nearly one-third of total spending in the nation goes to satisfy our collective demand for public services and national defense. About 20 percent of national income and output is used by the federal government and about 10 percent is used by state and local governments. The largest single purpose of federal expenditures is defense and defense-related expenditures. State and local governments provide community services.
3. Taxes are classified as regressive, proportional, or progressive, depending on the fraction of income paid at various income levels.
4. A progressive tax structure provides a degree of automatic stability in the level of economic activity. It helps moderate a tendency toward inflation or recession. Stability is accomplished by withdrawing more net taxes from the spending stream when income rises too fast and withdrawing less net taxes when income falls.
5. When the automatic changes in tax payments are not sufficient to prevent unemployment or inflation, discretionary changes in tax rates or government spending may be necessary. Discretionary fiscal policy is difficult because of the time required to plan, debate, and finally, put new proposals into effect. Furthermore, political pressure may favor types of government projects or tax policies that do not serve the long-range interests of the nation.
6. When government spending exceeds tax revenues, the Treasury borrows by selling securities. U.S. Treasury securities are held by individuals, businesses, financial institutions, and local governments and are considered a safe way to store purchasing power. Because government securities are held largely within the United States, the interest costs are paid by U.S. taxpayers to U.S. holders of government securities. If borrowed funds are used wisely, they can improve quality of life in the nation.
7. Disillusionment with the results of Keynesian economic policy in the 1970s led to the emergence of supply-side economics and the election of President Reagan. Supply-siders recommended cuts in federal taxes and spending and increased incentives to business investment. These programs were implemented late in 1981, but the results differed from the administration's expectations, and taxes were raised in 1982. Recovery from the recession began in 1983 and continued into 1990, when a new recession began.

TERMS TO REMEMBER

regressive tax: a tax that takes a larger fraction of income from low-income earners than from high-income earners

proportional tax: a tax that takes the same fraction of income from all income earners

progressive tax: a tax that takes a larger fraction of income from high-income earners than from low-income earners

negative taxes: government income-support payments to individuals; transfer payments

net tax: the tax paid by income groups after subtracting payments *received* from government

fiscal policy: the use of the federal government's tax and spending powers to promote economic stability

deficit: an excess of spending over revenues

surplus: an excess of revenues over spending

Keynesian economic policy: the use of government tax and spending policies to affect the level of aggregate demand

supply-side economics: policies to stimulate production of goods and services through tax cuts to encourage private investment

TOPICS FOR DISCUSSION

1. Explain the effects of each of the following on national income and expenditures:

negative taxes and net taxes
revenue sharing
federal deficits and surpluses

2. What is meant by the statement that our tax structure is regressive at low income levels, proportional at medium income levels, and progressive at high income levels?
3. Subjects for debate:

   What is the proper allocation of economic responsibility to the public sector and to the private sector?
   What is the proper allocation of economic responsibility to the federal government and to state and local governments?

4. The respected British economist Barbara Ward once called for an "international fiscal policy." What do you think she meant by that? Can you think of any current examples of this process?
5. In contrast with government, private enterprises must attempt to balance their budgets each financial period. Can you envision a time when a large, healthy corporation might spend more than it collects in revenues? How might such a condition come about? Where would the corporation get the extra funds to spend? Would you like to own stock in such a company? Explain your answer.
6. Some analysts view the growth of government debt as less a threat than the growth of consumer installment debt. In what ways is growing consumer debt a threat to economic stability? What policies might be useful for managing the level of consumer debt?
7. The author suggests that lower tax rates may actually *increase* tax revenues collected by the government. Explain this paradox. Is the reverse also possible?
8. British taxpayers took to the streets in 1990 to protest a revolutionary change in taxes. The change was from a property tax levy on dwellings to a "head tax" on each adult living in the dwelling. Explain the economic basis for opposition to this tax. How would such a tax be greeted in the United States?
9. Consult the most recent edition of *The Economic Report of the President* for information regarding the latest government deficit. Calculate the fraction that defines the deficit as a share of GDP. Compare the current deficit share with the share in earlier years. Explain the basis for notable trends in deficit share.
10. The U.S. Office of Management and Budget (OMB) projects the federal budget deficit for 1993 at $194 billion. In the same year the Social Security trust fund is expected to have a surplus of about $100 billion. What are the advantages and disadvantages of using the Social Security surplus to finance the deficit in the general budget? How would this take place? What are the likely consequences with respect to the progressivity of the nation's tax structure, economic growth, interest rates?
11. In 1992 fears of recession made cutting the nation's budget deficit difficult. Explain how fears of recession tend to (a) increase the deficit and (b) make it more difficult to agree on solutions to the deficit problem.

ANSWERS TO TEST YOURSELF

(p. 195) A regressive tax may be considered unfair. Moreover, by reducing the spending power of low-income families a regressive tax may slow economic growth. A progressive tax may stifle the incentive to earn high incomes and thus reduce initiative and entrepreneurship.

(p. 200) An advantage is that state and local governments are more aware of public needs and can employ local workers on needed projects without increasing their primarily regressive taxes. A disadvantage is that funds may be used inefficiently or wasted in their passage through several government bureaucracies.

(p. 200) The debt grew more slowly than GDP, so that by 1980 the ratio of debt to GDP was lower.

FURTHER READING

Aaron, Henry J., "The Capital Gains Tax Cut," *Brookings Review*, Summer 1992.

Barro, Robert, "Are Government Bonds Net

Wealth?" *Journal of Political Economy*, November 1974.

Barro, Robert, "The Ricardian Approach to Budget Deficits," *Journal of Economic Perspectives*, Spring 1989.

Calleo, David P., *The Bankrupting of America*, William P. Morrow, New York, 1992.

Eisner, Robert, "Budget Deficits: Rhetoric and Reality," *Journal of Economic Perspectives*, Spring 1989.

Feldstein, Martin, "Counterrevolution in Progress," *Challenge*, July/August 1988.

Friedman, Benjamin M., *Day of Reckoning*, Random House, New York, 1988.

Friedman, Benjamin M., "Evolution Prevails," *Challenge*, July/August 1988.

Gramlich, Edward M., "Budget Deficits and National Saving," *Journal of Economic Perspectives*, Spring 1989.

Heilbroner, Robert, and Peter Bernstein, *The Debt and the Deficit*, Norton, New York, 1989.

McIntyre, Robert S., "Tax Inequality Caused Budget Deficit," *Challenge*, November/December 1992.

Minarik, Joseph J., *Making America's Budget Policy*, M.E. Sharpe, Armonk, N.Y., 1990.

Niskanen, William A., "The Case for a New Fiscal

Constitution," *Journal of Economic Perspectives*, Spring 1992.

Niskanen, William A., *Reaganomics*, Oxford U. Press, New York, 1988.

Ooms, Van Doorn, "Budget Priorities of the Nation," *Science*, 11 December 1992.

Pechman, Joseph A., *Federal Tax Policy*, 5th edition, Brookings, Washington, 1987.

Rivlin, Alice, *Reviving the American Dream*, Brookings, Washington, 1992.

Sawhill, Isabell, and Steven Sachs, "Distributional Impact of the 1991 Budget and Changing Interest Rates," *Challenge*, January/February 1991.

Schultze, Charles L., "Is There a Bias Toward Excess in U.S. Government Budgets or Deficits?" *Journal of Economic Perspectives*, Spring 1992.

Spinney, Franklin C., "Uncle Sam's Budget Shambles," *Challenge*, May/June 1992.

Stein, Herbert, *Presidential Economics*, Simon and Schuster, New York, 1984.

Swartz, Thomas R., and John E. Peck, eds. *The Changing Face of Fiscal Federalism*, M.E. Sharpe, Armonk, N.Y., 1990.

Tobin, James, *National Economic Policy*, Yale U. Press, New Haven, 1966.

Chapter 10

Financial Institutions and Monetary Policy

Tools for Study

LEARNING OBJECTIVES

After reading this chapter, you will be able to:

1. Explain how the use of money avoids the disadvantages of barter.
2. Describe how banking developed and explain how banks create and destroy money.
3. Explain the role of the Federal Reserve System in controlling the nation's money supply.
4. Describe the financial services provided by nonbank financial institutions.
5. Explain how monetary policy works to stabilize economic activity and discuss some of the problems.

CURRENT ISSUES FOR DISCUSSION

What is the debate over the quantity of money?

How successful has monetary policy been?

How do changes in bank lending affect the nation's money?

How do politics affect monetary policy?

Natives of the North Georgia mountains tell about an illiterate country fellow who is particularly ignorant about money matters. According to the tale, this old gentleman is unable to distinguish between the value of a half-dollar and that of a quarter. When offered his choice between the two coins, he always chooses the quarter. In the fall of the year, when it's ''leaf-looking'' time in the Blue Ridge, tourists line up before his bench on the courthouse lawn for the opportunity to offer him coins. True to legend, he invariably selects the quarter and drops it into his overalls pocket.

We should all be so ''ignorant'' in money matters as this mountain gentleman!

MONEY IS AS MONEY DOES

The first use of money was a kind of watershed in the history of economic development. Before money came into use, exchange was possible only through barter. In **barter**, goods are exchanged for other goods. Thus, barter requires a ''double coincidence of wants.'' Traders have to find someone willing to accept their own goods in exchange for the goods they want. (You have a pig and want cloth; I have cloth and want a pig.)

Barter makes trade difficult, time consuming, and expensive (in terms of search and transactions costs). Payment in the form of tokens or symbols for goods, rather than the goods themselves, helped overcome the disadvantages of barter. The use of tokens promoted specialization and division of labor. With specialization, each worker could devel-

Viewpoint

BARTER: ITS TIME HAS COME

Barter requires a "double coincidence of wants." This requirement makes barter difficult and time consuming—at least it did before the age of computers.

Certain changes in the U.S. economy have had the effect of reviving barter as a means of exchange. In years of high inflation, the value of sellers' receipts has fallen faster than sellers could spend them. Barterers are not bothered by inflation because they receive what they want simultaneously with the sale of what they don't want. High taxes have also discouraged sales for cash and encouraged barter. Barterers are supposed to report their gains from bartering as taxable income, but some don't.

And how do computers fuel the growing "barter fever"? Computers can be used to identify goods and services for trade. They help identify people with a "double coincidence of wants," and they make barter more convenient.

Around the nation, barter clubs, barter newsletters, and barter exchanges have sprung up. With improved information, barterers can trade such things as legal services for recreation equipment, prime beef for dental work, and house plans for stereos. U.S. exporters have even traded Pepsi Cola for Russian vodka and airplanes for Yugoslavian ham.

There is no way to measure precisely the extent of barter in the United States, but one government agency is trying—the Internal Revenue Service!

What do you think about barter? Are there advantages and disadvantages not mentioned here?

op a skill for producing a particular good or service and receive some type of token as payment. Then workers could use their tokens to purchase the products of other workers.

These tokens served as the first money. They provided flexible purchasing power that could be used for whatever a worker wanted to buy.

Functions of Money

The preceding section implied that in order for something to serve as money, it must perform certain functions. There are, in fact, three necessary functions of money.

First and most important, money is a medium of exchange. It is accepted as payment for goods and services and, in turn, can be used to buy other goods and services.

Second, money is a standard of value or a common denominator for measuring the relative value of goods and services. For example, in the United States, the standard of value is measured in dollars. A pound of chicken may be worth half a dollar while a pound of beef may be worth two dollars, or four times as much.

Finally, money serves as a store of value. It can be saved and used to buy goods and services sometime in the future.

Bones, Bullion, and Bank Notes

Money can take many shapes and forms. Whatever is generally accepted as money by the public becomes money. Throughout history the functions of money have been carried out by such diverse things as shells, cattle, and bones.

For many years gold and silver served well as money. Precious metals are scarce and durable, they are easily divided into small pieces, and they have relatively few uses other than as money. In ancient times, chunks or flat pieces of gold and silver served as money for traders in the Near East and Europe.

Occasionally, cheaters would chip away the edges of these early coins to form more pieces. Eventually, it became necessary to make coins round with serrated edges so that any tampering could be detected.

The difficulty of storing and transporting gold and silver led to the development of banking. (Primitive banks may have existed as far back as the seventh century B.C.) The first banks held gold on deposit for their customers and issued certificates or notes promising to pay gold to the bearer on demand. They charged a small fee for the service, and their notes circulated widely as money.

Banks soon discovered they could not earn enough income simply by storing gold for their depositors. By the seventeenth century, they began to make loans for borrowers to invest in new business ventures. Loans took the form of new bank notes, issued to borrowers with the expectation that profits from the business venture would enable the borrower to repay the loan with interest.

Issuing new bank notes meant that the amount of bank paper outstanding would exceed a bank's supply of gold, but this was not considered a problem. Bankers reasoned that not all depositors would want their gold at the same time. On any given day while some depositors might be withdrawing gold, others would be depositing gold. As long as holders of bank paper had faith in the bank and did not all insist on withdrawing their gold at once, lending was reasonably safe.

BANKING IN THE UNITED STATES

Banking developed in the United States during the early 1600s. The first independent banks tended to overissue bank notes. A bank with one million dollars in gold might issue several times that much in notes. At first, the notes would be perfectly good as purchasing power. They would circulate freely until holders began to suspect that the bank would never be able to redeem all its notes in gold. Many holders would rush to exchange their bank notes for gold. With the loss of its gold the bank would vanish and, along with it, the savings of many of the bank's trusting depositors.

Some banks were called wildcat banks because they grew up in the wilderness, "out where the wildcats howl." Wildcat banks accepted gold deposits from trappers and miners and went through a brief orgy of lending. Many wildcat banks collapsed when holders of gold certificates insisted on exchanging them for the real McCoy.

A Move Toward Centralized Banking

After the U.S. Revolution, Secretary of the Treasury Alexander Hamilton helped set up a central bank to regulate bank lending and protect depositors' accounts. Many voters distrusted centralized government control, however, particularly control by powerful moneyed interests of the Northeast. Southern and western opposition to the central bank brought on its collapse in 1836 during the administration of President Andrew Jackson.

The problem of overissue of bank notes and frequent bank failures worsened until 1863, when Congress passed the National Banking Act to regulate banks chartered by the federal government. The National Banking Act set up cash reserve requirements for national banks and limited their lending. This brought some stability to the supply of bank notes. However, the states still had power to charter state banks, and state regulations were much more lenient than the regulations of the National Banking System.

The Federal Reserve System

Around the turn of the century the nation again experienced a series of financial crises, with bank failures and loss of deposits. Following the Panic of 1907, voters finally began to support the idea of a strong national banking system. They hoped that centrally regulated banking would protect the value of their deposits and ensure stability in the supply of bank money.

In 1913, Congress passed a new National Banking Act setting up the Federal Reserve System (commonly called the Fed). Commercial banks throughout the country are now regulated by the Federal Reserve. The Fed is controlled by a seven-member Board of Governors appointed by the president with Senate approval. Governors serve staggered terms of fourteen years. The fact that these governors do not have to run for office reduces their political pressure; and their staggered terms make it difficult for one president to appoint more than two governors during a four-year term. Late in a president's term he names one member of the Board of Governors chairman, and that chairman serves for part of the next president's term.

The Fed and Commercial Banks

Federal Reserve Banks are located in twelve Federal Reserve districts. They do not deal with the U.S. public, but rather with the Treasury and with commercial banks and other bank-like institutions. Their most important function is to hold deposits, or reserves, for these financial institutions. The discussion that follows shows how their holdings of reserves provide a useful tool for regulating the nation's money supply. Finally, Federal Reserve Banks act as bankers for the U.S. Treasury, holding the government's tax revenues and paying its bills.

Most of us are more familiar with commercial banks than with the Fed. Commercial banks deal with individuals and business firms, accepting demand (**checkable**) **deposits** and **time** (savings) **deposits** and making loans. They may be chartered by the federal government or by a state government. In 1980 Congress extended banking regulations to all commercial banks and other bank-like institutions. According to the Depository Institutions Deregulation and Monetary Control Act of 1980, all depository institutions must keep a certain fraction of their deposits in reserve accounts at the Fed, and all must submit to regular supervision and examination.

In return for their compliance with Federal Reserve regulations, all depository institutions receive these benefits:

1. *A central clearinghouse for checks.* Depository institutions receive as deposits checks drawn on other institutions. The checks are then sent to the Federal Reserve for return to the issuing institution. This process is called check clearing. It allows all depository institutions to record their customers' withdrawals promptly.
2. *Deposit insurance through the Federal Deposit Insurance Corporation (FDIC).*

Depository institutions pay a small fraction of their deposits into an insurance fund for compensating depositors of failed institutions.

3. *A source of borrowed reserves.* Depository institutions may borrow from the Fed to keep their reserve accounts at the level required by Fed regulations.
4. *Financial information.*

OTHER FINANCIAL INSTITUTIONS

Commercial banks are important financial "intermediaries." Intermediaries occupy a position in the market between buyers and sellers of a good or service. For financial intermediaries the good or service exchanged is money, and the buyers and sellers are borrowers and lenders.

Most of us are both borrowers and lenders, dealing with many financial intermediaries for our various financial needs. We deal with commercial banks for deposits and day-to-day financial services. In 1992, for example, commercial banks held almost $2 trillion of our demand and time deposits; they held outstanding loans amounting to almost $3 trillion, including real estate loans, loans to business firms and other financial intermediaries, and installment loans to individuals—all of which comprise banks' main sources of current income. Until 1981 commercial banks were prohibited from paying interest on checkable deposits. Because commercial banks must pay out their checkable deposits on demand, most commerical bank loans are short-term.

Thrift Institutions

Other financial intermediaries perform certain other specialized functions. For instance, savings and loan associations and mutual savings banks engage in longer-term borrowing and lending. Fewer of their deposits are subject to immediate withdrawal than is true for commercial banks, and all can earn interest. In 1992 these so-called "thrift" institutions held savings deposits of more than $900 billion, making them second only to commercial banks in size. Until the 1970s, when interest-rate ceilings prompted many savers to withdraw their thrift deposits, thrift institutions enjoyed a more stable source of funds than did commercial banks. This enabled them to make loans for long-term purposes at rather low interest rates. In 1992 almost $700 billion of their funds were invested in home mortgages. You can understand why savings and loan associations and mutual savings banks have been important to the health of the nation's housing industry.

Credit Unions

In recent years, credit unions have been emerging as a third type of financial intermediary. Most credit unions are made up of workers who have a common bond—they work for a particular firm or in the same industry. A credit union collects the savings of members and makes short-term loans and mortgage loans to other members. Because borrowers are well known to the credit union, there is a smaller risk of default than for other depository institutions. As a result, interest charges can be kept relatively low. Also, the administrative costs of running a credit union are low, making it possible to pay relatively high interest to savers.

Money Market Funds

In the 1970s a new type of financial intermediary was created: money market mutual funds. A mutual fund is an organization of savers who pool their funds to purchase a diversified portfolio of investments. A money market mutual fund purchases only short-term securities and pays its shareholders dividends according to current interest rates. By 1992, money market mutual funds held assets of $543 billion.

Money market funds became a competitive threat to other financial intermediaries when market interest rates rose above what commercial banks and thrift institutions were allowed to pay on savings. A shift of funds into money market mutual funds reduced banks' lending ability and reduced profits for many other financial intermediaries. The 1980 Monetary Control Act removed the artificial ceiling on interest rates and allowed the regulated firms to compete for deposits.

A well-developed system of financial intermediaries has helped promote our nation's economic growth. Safe financial intermediaries have encouraged saving and provided funds for business investment. Although the major financial intermediaries tend to specialize in particular kinds of borrowing and lending, there is some overlap in services. When services overlap, there is basis for competition among intermediaries, with the expectation that service will improve and costs fall. The Monetary Control Act of 1980 removed many of the legal restrictions on services performed by financial intermediaries so that now they can compete freely. Savings and loan associations and credit unions are free to offer new kinds of checkable deposits, and commercial banks may pay interest on their checkable deposits as well. In the future, banks or their subsidiaries may be allowed to sell stocks and bonds.

Increasing competition among financial intermediaries should improve efficiency and strengthen our nation's financial system. On the other hand, competition may also force some institutions out of business. Many small financial intermediaries will not be able to compete successfully and may be absorbed into larger ones. Still, the final result should be a more efficient financial sector for the nation.

HOW DEPOSITORY INSTITUTIONS CREATE AND DESTROY MONEY

Financial institutions have a particular function over and above their role as caretaker of the community's savings. Financial institutions that hold checkable deposits and make loans act in ways that create or destroy money.

Economists define money most narrowly as the sum of cash in the hands of the public and checkable deposits in commercial banks, thrift institutions, and credit unions. All are money because all are acceptable in exchange for goods or in settlement of financial obligations. Cash is a very small part of the money supply, involving only about one-fifth of all transactions.

A Bank's Balance Sheet

Financial institutions that accept deposits are required to hold a certain fraction of their checkable deposits in reserve accounts at the Federal Reserve. A depository institution may make loans in the amount by which its actual reserve account exceeds the required amount.

The most familiar depository institution is the commercial bank. Table 10.1 is a simplified model of a commercial bank's balance sheet. A balance sheet shows the bank's financial position on a certain date. It is sometimes called a T-account, since items are arranged under the bar of a T.

The bank's assets are listed on the left side of the balance sheet. Assets are the things the bank owns: its building, cash in the vault, reserve account at the Fed, interest-earning securities, and loans to customers. Loans to customers are assets because they represent

Table 10.1 Balance Sheet for Wall Street Bank, December 31, 1992.

Assets		*Liabilities*	
Cash and Reserves at Fed	$ 250,000	Checkable Deposits	$1,000,000
Loans to Customers	750,000	Other Liabilities	150,000
Securities	200,000		
Building	100,000		1,150,000
		Capital Account	150,000
Total Assets	1,300,000	Total Liabilities and Capital	1,300,000

promises to pay the bank. Loans are normally made to credit-worthy individuals or business firms who are expected to repay their loans with interest when they come due.

The bank's liabilities and capital account are listed on the right side of the balance sheet. Liabilities are the amounts the bank owes. The checking and savings accounts of its depositors and borrowings from businesses and other banks are a bank's chief liabilities.

Notice that the sum of the asset side is equal to the sum on the liabilities side. This is because any excess of the value of assets over liabilities is added to the liabilities side as the capital account. The **capital account** represents the *net* amount owned by the bank:

amounts owned − amounts owed
= capital account

The capital account is the portion of total assets that would remain if the bank used all its assets to pay off all its liabilities. Equality of Total Assets on the left side and Total Liabilities and Capital on the right makes the statement balance; hence the name balance sheet.

Making Loans and Increasing the Money Supply

Suppose the Wall Street Bank shown in Table 10.1 is required to keep 25 percent of its checkable deposits in its reserve account. Notice that the bank is complying with Federal Reserve regulations (25 percent of $1 million in checkable deposits is $250,000 in its reserve account).

Now suppose the bank receives a new cash deposit of $100. This might be cash from under someone's mattress, proceeds from the sale of a government bond, or cash received from the sale of goods to a foreign buyer. Let us watch what happens to the bank's balance sheet as a result of the cash deposit. For simplicity, we will show only changes in assets and liabilities. Notice that every change on either the assets side or the liabilities side requires an equal change on the other side (or an offsetting change on the same side) so that the balance sheet will remain in balance:*

1. The $100 deposit adds $100 to Wall Street Bank's cash assets and $100 to its checking account liabilities.

Assets	*Wall Street Bank*		*Liabilities*
Cash	+ $100	Checkable Deposits	+$100

2. Excessive vault cash is of little use to the bank, so it sends the cash to its reserve account at the Federal Reserve Bank.

* Notice for simplicity that some later calculations are rounded to the nearest dollar.

Wall Street Bank

Assets		*Liabilities*	
Cash	− $100		
Reserves	+ $100		

3. Before the new deposit was made, the Wall Street Bank was maintaining its required reserve account at the Fed; but it is required to hold only 25 percent of its new deposit: 25 percent of $100 = $25. The bank can extend loans in the amount by which its reserve account exceeds required reserves:

actual reserves − required reserves
= excess reserves
$100 − $25 = $75

With $75 in excess reserves, the Wall Street Bank will normally encourage a credit-worthy borrower to take out a loan, possibly at the same time reducing its interest charge to make the loan more attractive. When the bank makes the loan, it issues a check for $75, which the borrower very likely deposits in a checking account in the same bank. On the left side of the balance sheet, the bank adds the $75 loan; the loan is the borrower's promise to pay and therefore is an asset for the bank. On the right side, the bank adds $75 to the borrower's checkable deposit.

Now Wall Street Bank is using its excess reserves as an interest-earning loan. It has complied with Federal Reserve regulations and loaned out only the amount by which its reserves exceed the required percentage of its checkable deposits.

Wall Street Bank

Assets		*Liabilities*	
Reserves	$100	Checkable Deposits	$100
Loans	+ $75		+ 75
			$175

4. Suppose the borrower now decides to spend the $75 by writing a check in that amount. Whoever receives the check deposits it in his or her own checking account in another depository institution, say, the Lombard Bank. The Lombard Bank adds the amount to its customer's account and sends the check to the Federal Reserve to be cleared. The Federal Reserve clears the check by adding $75 to Lombard Bank's reserve account and subtracting $75 from Wall Street Bank's reserve account. Then it returns the canceled check to Wall Street Bank for return to the payer in his or her monthly bank statement. When Wall Street Bank reduces the payer's checking account and its own reserve account by $75, actual reserves are precisely equal to required reserves: 25 percent of $100 = $25. Notice that Wall Street Bank's balance sheet remains in balance.

Lombard Bank

Assets		*Liabilities*	
Reserves	+$75	Checkable Deposits	+$75

Wall Street Bank

Assets		*Liabilities*	
Reserves	$100	Checkable Deposits	$175
	− 75		− 75
	$25		$100
Loans	$75		

5. Now the Lombard Bank has excess reserves. The Lombard Bank is required to keep 25 percent of the new checkable deposit in its reserve account: 25 percent of $75 = $19. It can extend a new loan in the amount by which its reserve account exceeds required reserves:

actual reserves − required reserves
= excess reserves
\$75 − \$19 = \$56

Assets	*Lombard Bank*		*Liabilities*
Reserves	\$75	Checkable Deposits	\$ 75
Loans	+\$56		+ 56
			\$131

6. Just as before, this second borrower will probably decide to write a check for \$56 to make a purchase. The person who receives the check eventually deposits it in a third depository institution, say, the Peachtree Bank. Peachtree Bank sends the check to the Fed to be cleared and deposited in its reserve account. The Federal Reserve adds \$56 to the Peachtree Bank's reserve account and subtracts \$56 from the Lombard Bank's account. When the Lombard Bank reduces the second borrower's account and its own reserve account by \$56, actual reserves are precisely equal to required reserves: 25 percent of \$75 = \$19.

Assets	*Lombard Bank*		*Liabilities*
Reserves	\$75	Checkable Deposits	\$131
	− 56		− 56
	\$19		\$75
Loans	\$56		

Assets	*Peachtree Bank*		*Liabilities*
Reserves	+\$56	Checkable Deposits	+\$56

Let us stop here and calculate the amount added to the nation's money supply as these new loans were created. Thus far, the original \$100 in new deposits has led to the creation of \$75 + \$56 = \$131 in additional new money. Presumably, the Peachtree Bank will also make a loan in the amount of its excess reserves. When it does, another depository institution will receive a new check on deposit and use the excess reserves to extend a new loan. Finally, the money supply will have increased by as much as \$400: the original \$100 deposit plus \$300 in created money.

How do we know this? With a 25 percent reserve requirement, the initial \$100 increase in reserves permits the nation's depository institutions to increase checkable deposits by up to four times the increase in reserves. Because new reserves of \$100 are equal to 25 percent of \$400 in new checkable deposits, depository institutions remain in compliance with the regulations of the Federal Reserve.

The original deposit of \$100 constitutes part of the increase in checkable deposits. *The remaining \$300 is created money*. It is created by extending loans and adding to the checking accounts of borrowers. Depository institutions as a whole can create money equal to excess reserves times the reciprocal of the required reserve ratio:

$$\text{created money} = \text{excess reserves} \times \frac{1}{\text{reserve ratio}}$$

Thus, in our example:

$$\text{created money} = \$75 \times \frac{1}{\frac{1}{4}} = \$75 \times 4 = \$300$$

Collecting Loans and Reducing the Money Supply

Depository institutions can destroy as well as create money. They *must* destroy money when they lose reserves and are failing to maintain the required reserve ratio. The process is the reverse of the process outlined above.

Suppose a commercial bank loses a deposit of $100 in cash. This time it might be a withdrawal of cash to put under someone's mattress, to buy a government security, or to buy goods from a foreign seller. As the $100 check clears at the Federal Reserve, the paying bank loses reserves. In order to maintain its required reserves, the bank will have to reduce its deposits.

How does a bank reduce its deposits?

A bank reduces deposits by reducing its lending. Every day old borrowers repay loans by writing checks to the banks. Every day new borrowers receive new loan checks. If a commercial bank needs to reduce its deposits to comply with reserve requirements, it will accept loan payment checks and not extend new loans in their place. Loan payment checks will reduce borrowers' checking accounts until checkable deposits are the permitted multiple of bank reserves.

In effect, the bank has destroyed money.

TEST YOURSELF

Follow the procedure that we used to describe money creation to describe how money is destroyed.

MONETARY POLICY

The Federal Reserve System is responsible for planning and carrying out the nation's monetary policy. **Monetary policy** involves changes in the supply of money to meet the nation's changing needs. Because about three-fourths of the nation's money supply is held in depository institutions under the regulatory authority of the Federal Reserve, a decision by the Board of Governors can significantly influence the nation's money supply.

The objective of monetary policy is to ensure the appropriate supply of money for achieving an efficient level of economic activity. As our capacity for producing goods and services increases, we may need a larger supply of money. More money would enable consumers and business firms to increase their spending, so that our nation's productive capacity will be fully utilized.

On the other hand, if the supply of money increases too rapidly, total spending may exceed our nation's capacity to produce goods and services and increase inflationary pressures. In such times, the Federal Reserve should reduce money growth and limit consumer and business spending.

How are changes in the money supply accomplished? (It isn't generally practical to fly over cities and towns scattering currency from airplanes.)

The Federal Reserve System has three tools to influence the supply of money. All three tools work primarily by changing the level of checkable deposits in depository institutions. The Fed changes the level of checking accounts by changing a depository institution's ability to make loans.

The Fed changes a depository institution's lending capacity by:

1. Changing the required fraction of deposits to be held as reserves in the Federal Reserve Bank.
2. Changing the discount rate on borrowed reserves from the Federal Reserve.
3. Conducting open-market operations, which involve the purchase and/or sale of U.S. government securities.

We will consider each of these tools in turn.

Changes in Required Reserves

The first tool of monetary policy involves the fraction of a depository institution's checkable deposits that must be held in its reserve account at the Federal Reserve. (The current fraction or **required reserve ratio**, is about 12 percent.) Remember that a depository institution can make loans only up to the amount by which its actual reserve account exceeds its required reserve ratio.

Like any other depository institution, a bank must be careful not to extend too many loans. Otherwise, when its checks are cleared and paid to other banks, the bank will lose too much from its reserve account, so that it is no longer in compliance with reserve requirements. (How do you like the thought of your bank being "overdrawn"?)

Increasing the Money Supply

Consider a situation in which all depository institutions are maintaining their required reserve accounts. For simplicity, we will assume that the required reserve ratio is 25 percent. There are no excess reserves, so no new loans may be made.

Now suppose the Board of Governors wants to increase the nation's money supply, hoping to encourage new spending and increase production and employment. The governors might decide to reduce the required reserve ratio to 20 percent so that all depository institutions have excess reserves available for lending. Then depository institutions might even reduce the interest charges on their loans to encourage consumers and business firms to borrow. The new borrowers would deposit their loan checks in their checking accounts.

Eureka! From nothing there is money!

Before the change in the reserve ratio, checkable deposits in banks, thrifts, and credit unions amounted to four times total reserves. After the change, checkable deposits can increase to five times reserves, with the possibility that spending, production, and employment can increase as well.

A Numerical Example: Expansionary Monetary Policy

Imagine depository institutions as a whole have checkable deposits of $100 billion. If we ignore cash in the hands of the public, we can regard the $100 billion in checkable deposits as the nation's money supply. Under the 25 percent reserve requirement depository institutions must be holding $25 billion as reserves at the Federal Reserve.

Now the Board of Governors decides to pursue an **expansionary monetary policy**: that is, to expand the money supply. It changes the reserve requirement to 20 percent. Depository institutions are now required to hold only $20 billion; immediately they have excess reserves of $5 billion.

Loans will be made and loan checks deposited in the accounts of borrowers. As checkable deposits expand, the nation as a whole experiences an increase in the money supply.

What will finally be the level of deposits in the banking system? With reserves of $25 billion and a 20 percent reserve requirement, depository institutions as a whole can hold checkable deposits of $125 billion: reserves of $25 billion = 20 percent of $125 billion in checkable deposits.

In fact, the money supply may grow by as much as $25 billion:

$$\begin{aligned}\text{created money}\\ &= \text{excess reserves} \times \frac{1}{\text{reserve ratio}}\\ &= \$5 \text{ billion} \times \frac{1}{\frac{1}{5}} = \$25 \text{ billion}\end{aligned}$$

Reducing the Money Supply

Of course, this process works also in reverse. This time suppose the Board of Governors wants to reduce the supply of money to discourage spending and hold down inflationary pressures. The governors might decide to increase reserve requirements, perhaps to 33.33 percent. Now depository institutions must reduce their checkable deposits until total deposits are only three times reserves.

Banks, thrifts, and credit unions will collect old loans and make fewer new loans. They will increase their interest charges on loans to discourage borrowing. Old borrowers will pay off loans by writing checks, and the level of checking accounts in the country will fall.

A Numerical Example: Contractionary Monetary Policy

Again, imagine total checkable deposits of $100 billion and a 25 percent reserve requirement. Depository institutions as a whole are holding reserves of $25 billion. The Board of Governors decides on a **contractionary monetary policy**: that is, to reduce the money supply. It changes the reserve ratio to 33.33 percent. With deposits of $100 billion, depository institutions are required to hold $33.33 billion in reserves. Under the new reserve requirements they have negative excess reserves, or deficit reserves:

$$\text{actual reserves} - \text{required reserves} = \text{excess reserves}$$
$$\$25 - \$33.33 = -\$8.33$$

With negative excess reserves, banks, thrifts, and credit unions must collect old loans, deducting the loan payment checks from borrowers' checking accounts. Throughout the nation, checkable deposits will fall, and the money supply will fall as well.

What will be the final level of checkable deposits in the nation's financial system? With reserves of $25 billion and a 33.33 percent reserve requirement, the nation as a whole may have checkable deposits of $75 billion:

$$\text{reserves of \$25 billion} = 33.33 \text{ percent of \$75 billion}$$

The money supply must decline by at least $25 billion:

$$\text{destroyed money} = \text{excess reserves} \times \frac{1}{\text{reserve ratio}}$$
$$= -\$8.33 \times \frac{1}{\frac{1}{3}} = -\$25 \text{ billion}$$

The Discount Rate

Now we discuss the second way the Federal Reserve can change depository institutions' ability to make loans. This way is through changes in the interest rate charged on Federal Reserve loans to banks, thrifts, and credit unions.

Just as individuals go to their commercial banks for loans, depository institutions can go to their banker, the Federal Reserve Bank, for borrowed reserves. A depository institution may need to borrow reserves to comply with reserve requirements, particularly if reserve requirements have recently been increased. It may borrow from the Fed to meet seasonal needs or to pay depositors and avoid failure.

The interest rate charged on loans to depository institutions is called the **discount rate**. If the Board of Governors wants to encourage lending, it can reduce the discount rate, encouraging banks, thrifts, and credit unions to borrow to maintain their reserve accounts. However, if it wants to discourage new lending, it will increase the discount rate. A higher discount rate will force banks, thrifts, and credit unions to reduce their checkable deposits to avoid the Fed's higher borrowing charges. There will be fewer new loans made and fewer loan checks to deposit in borrowers' checking accounts. The money supply will fall.

Open-Market Operations

The third tool for changing the level of checkable deposits is open-market operations. This tool is used most often because it can be carried out quickly and quietly, without embarrassing headlines to aggravate ulcers on Wall Street!

The Federal Reserve Banks and most financial institutions, as well as many individuals, hold some of their savings in the form of U.S. government securities. U.S. Treasury

How Things Have Changed

CHANGES IN THE DISCOUNT RATE CLOSELY PARALLEL CHANGES IN OTHER INTEREST RATES

		Interest Rates		
Year	***Discount Rate***	***U.S. Treasury 3-month bills***	***High-grade Corporate Bonds***	***New Home Mortgages***
1960	3.53	2.93	4.41	NA
1965	4.04	3.95	4.49	5.81
1970	5.95	6.46	8.04	8.45
1975	6.25	5.84	8.83	9.00
1980	11.77	11.51	11.94	12.66
1985	7.69	7.48	11.37	11.55
1986	6.33	5.98	9.02	10.17
1987	5.66	5.82	9.38	9.31
1988	6.20	6.69	9.71	9.19
1989	6.93	8.12	9.26	10.13
1990	6.98	7.51	9.32	10.05
1991	5.45	5.42	8.77	9.32
1992	3.25	3.45	8.14	9.15

SOURCE: *Economic Report of the President*, various years.

Identify the years in which the Federal Reserve was attempting to slow credit creation. Explain the differences in interest rates among Treasury securities, high-grade corporate bonds, and new home mortgages.

bills, notes, and bonds are considered a safe investment and provide interest income to their owners. **Open-market operations** involve the purchase and sale of these securities.

The Federal Reserve Bank of New York is constantly buying and selling U.S. government securities in financial markets. If the New York Fed buys more securities than it sells, it pays for them with new money, which increases the nation's money supply. To illustrate, suppose the Federal Reserve increases its holdings of Treasury securities by $100 million. Individuals, business firms, and financial institutions throughout the country send their securities to the Federal Reserve and receive checks in return. They deposit their checks in checking accounts in financial institutions. Federal Reserve clearinghouses add a total of $100 million to reserve accounts, and the stage is set for the expansion of loans.

As you might have expected, the process works also in reverse. Consider what would happen if the Federal Reserve sells more securities than it buys. Suppose the Federal Re-

Thinking Seriously About Economic Issues

REFORMING THE FEDERAL RESERVE

Milton Friedman favors free-market solutions to economic problems and worries about potential mistakes when individuals or institutions are given too much power to affect economic policy. His concerns are directed primarily at the power of the Federal Reserve System.

Friedman distinguishes between the tactics used by the Fed to accomplish monetary policy and the strategy and institutions through which monetary policy is carried out. The tactics have to do with the choice of a target variable for policy (the quantity of money or interest rates), the growth path of the target variable, and procedures for achieving the growth target. Friedman believes that the Fed has too much discretion in using these tactics and recommends a change in monetary institutions.

First, Friedman recommends a monetary policy rule to determine the appropriate size of the money base. The money base is the sum of commerical bank reserves plus currency in the hands of the public. Because public holdings of currency shift easily back and forth between bank reserves and cash holdings, they are potentially available to support increases in the money supply. Therefore, according to Friedman, Congress should pass legislation limiting the increase in currency plus bank reserves to between 3 percent and 5 percent per year.

Following passage of a money growth rule, Friedman recommends removing responsibility for bank regulation and supervision from the Fed and limiting the Fed to open-market operations to achieve

serve reduces its holdings of securities by $100 million. Buyers receive securities and send their payment checks to the Federal Reserve banks. Federal Reserve clearinghouses deduct the amounts from reserves, and checking accounts must fall as well. This time the result is to reduce the money supply.

All these changes take place so quietly that one scarcely knows whether the Federal Reserve has been expanding or contracting the money supply.

SOME PROBLEMS

Monetary policy can help achieve economic stability. It is not always completely successful, however, and it can create some problems.

If the Board of Governors correctly forecasts the state of the economy, if it quickly prescribes the proper remedy, and if financial institutions and borrowers respond as expected, the Federal Reserve's purpose will be accomplished. The problem is that all of these conditions are seldom fulfilled in the real world.

During recessions, for example, when spending, production, and employment are low, an increase in investment spending would be most welcome. But at those times, business firms may very sensibly hesitate to take on the risks of borrowing to increase their production. After all, who will buy the newly prothe appropriate growth of the money base. Then the Fed should be converted from an independent agency to a bureau of the Treasury Department. An advantage of this change is that it would make a single, unified agency of government responsible for the conduct and performance of monetary policy. Another advantage is the resulting political influence over the Fed, which Friedman believes would result in more stable money growth.

Friedman would allow the increasing variety of money forms—in the form of price-index futures similar to stock-market futures—to compete with currency issued by the government. Futures markets permit holders of currency to hedge their long-term contracts against the risk of changes in the price level. Allowing financial institutions to borrow and lend on the basis of interest rates tied to the price level would protect borrowers and lenders against inflation.

Finally, Friedman would freeze the supply of Federal Reserve currency and deposits. Eventually, financial institutions might be freed from all restrictions on the creation of claims against the existing money supply. Furthermore, as the nation's total output increases, new financial institutions and instruments would develop to use the fixed supply of money more efficiently. Or, alternatively, prices would fall. According to Friedman, transition to the new financial arrangements could take place over a period of about five years.

Milton Friedman, "The Case for Overhauling the Federal Reserve," *Challenge*, July/August, 1985, 4–12.

duced goods and services if income and employment are low? This means that monetary policy is least effective for increasing business spending in recession.

Alas, it may be just as difficult to put the brakes on inflation. Once business borrowers come to expect inflation, higher interest costs may not discourage borrowing for new investment. Business firms will expect prices on finished goods to rise faster than the cost of borrowing, so that new investment will still be profitable. Moreover, in inflation, business borrowers know they can repay their loans with dollars that are worth less than the dollars originally borrowed.

Another problem with monetary policy is the lag between deciding on a new policy and waiting for it to take effect.* Delays in the effects of policy can cause alternating periods of expanding and contracting the money supply, by turns helping and hurting the situation the policy was designed to correct. An easy money policy may last too long and aggravate a tendency toward too rapid growth and inflation. Then changing to a tight money policy may cause a recession, with worsening unemployment and slowing growth.

Critics of monetary policy worry that certain borrowers are more seriously harmed by high interest rates than others. Small home builders are particularly hurt by a shortage of

* We noted a similar problem of delay in the effectiveness of fiscal policy.

funds for home mortgages. In contrast, large firms with substantial retained earnings may be able to finance major investment projects without having to borrow. State and local governments are also harmed by high interest rates. High borrowing costs may cause them to neglect local services, leading to demands that such services be provided by the federal government.

Other critics worry about the effect of monetary policy on economic growth. When the Federal Reserve is fighting recession, it may want to increase the money supply and push interest rates down. But low interest rates in the United States may cause many wealthy individuals, financial institutions, and business firms to lend their savings to foreign borrowers for higher interest earnings. In this case, dollars will flow abroad where they are unavailable for fighting the domestic recession.

On the other hand, when the Federal Reserve is fighting inflation, it will want to reduce money growth and push interest rates up. High interest rates may be expected to hold down business investment spending. But business investment is the principal means by which we increase the productivity of our economy. Thus, policies to reduce inflation may also reduce the growth of productivity in the nation as a whole.

High interest rates also affect the U.S. Treasury. The Treasury owes a total debt of almost $4 trillion, and annual interest charges are considerable.

All these problems suggest that rapid or radical changes in monetary policy may not be wise. It may be better to combine rather consistent monetary policy with flexible fiscal policy to ensure a healthy level of economic activity.

In the second part of this chapter we consider in detail the debate concerning the effectiveness of monetary policy.

Self-Check

1. Which of the following is not a true description of money?
   a. It permits specialization in production.
   b. It facilitates trade among producing regions.
   c. It provides a standard of value.
   d. It makes barter necessary.
   e. It permits division of labor in production.

2. Which of the following is not a characteristic of monetary gold?
   a. It serves as a medium of exchange, a store of value, and a standard of value.
   b. It is scarce and durable.
   c. It is safely transported and stored.
   d. It has few uses other than as money.
   e. All are characteristic of gold.

3. Which of the following is not a function of the Federal Reserve System?
   a. It provides loans to individuals and businesses.
   b. It holds the accounts of the U.S. Treasury.
   c. It provides a system for clearing checks.
   d. It holds reserve accounts for member banks.
   e. It helps stabilize the nation's money supply.

4. Changes in the money supply:
   a. Aim at influencing the level of total spending.
   b. Are accomplished primarily by purchases and sales of securities.
   c. Are actually changes in the lending capacity of banks.
   d. All of the above.
   e. None of the above.

5. A disadvantage of monetary policy is that:
   a. Low interest rates retard economic growth.
   b. High interest rates cause loanable funds to flow to other countries.
   c. Business firms may not respond properly to changes in interest rates.
   d. It is removed from political influence.
   e. High interest charges benefit home builders.

6. Which of the following policy actions is most appropriate for reducing inflation?
   a. Federal Reserve purchases of U.S. government securities.
   b. An increase in required reserves.
   c. Easy money to hold down interest rates.
   d. Encouragement of banks to borrow from the Fed.
   e. An increase in the growth rate of the money supply.

Theory in Practice

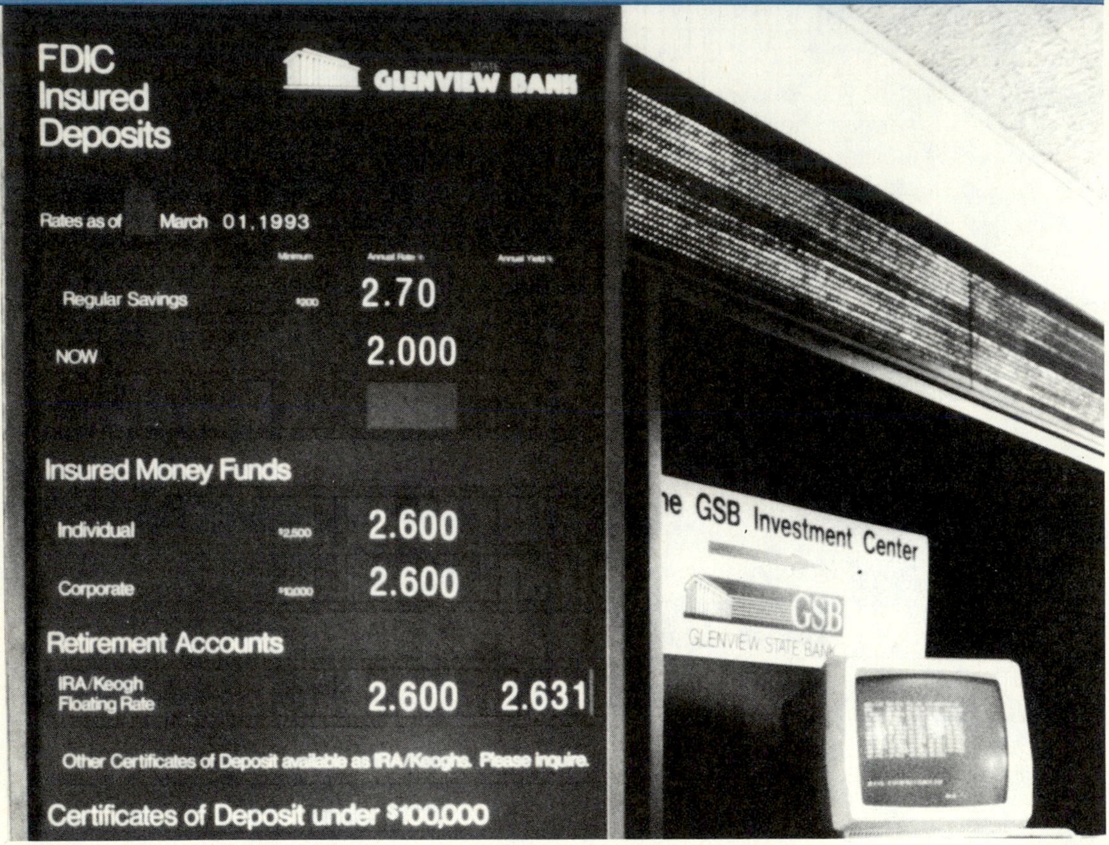

MIND YOUR P'S AND Q'S

Much of monetary theory can be summed up in a simple expression: $MV = PQ$. The left side of the equation measures total spending over a particular period of time: the quantity of money in the system (M) times its velocity (V), or the average number of times each dollar is spent during the period. The right side of the equation measures the value of total production over the same time period: the prices of all goods and services (P) times the quantities sold (Q).

This simple equation describes the quantity theory of money. Because total expenditures (MV) will always equal the value of output (PQ), the equation must always balance.

The expression $MV = PQ$ is the source of much controversy among economists, and the debate concerns the proper conduct of monetary policy. One group of economists believes that the supply of money (M) is the most important factor in determining economic activity. In their view, a steady increase in M in line with our nation's growing productive capacity will keep production (Q) growing at the fastest possible rate without increases in prices (*P*).

Economists who emphasize the central importance of money are called **monetarists**. Their leader is Nobel prizewinning economist Milton Friedman. Friedman favors automatic increases in the money supply of about 4 percent a year. He believes that regular, automatic increases in the money supply will allow spending to increase in line with increases in productive capacity, thereby avoiding either rising prices or falling production. Moreover, automatic increases in the money supply have the advantage that they do not depend on decisions made by the Board of Governors (who sometimes disagree with Professor Friedman).

There is another advantage to regular, automatic money growth. Decisions to change money growth, says Friedman, cannot take effect for a year or more, during which time economic conditions can turn completely around, so that current policy decisions are no longer appropriate. Unless policymakers follow clear, unchanging rules for money growth, they are likely to make mistakes.

Another group of economists counter that steady, automatic increases in *M* will not ensure steady growth in *PQ* if *V* is changing at an unpredictable rate. In fact, during recessions with high unemployment and low consumer confidence, the rate of turnover (*V*) of the available money supply could fall. To allow the growth of *M* to offset the decline in *V* in recessions, policymakers should increase *M* faster than normal. On the other hand, in periods of inflation the rate of spending (*V*) tends to increase; in this case policymakers should cut back the growth of *M* to offset the increase in *V*. Adjusting the growth of *M* to offset changes in *V* could achieve stable growth in *PQ*.

Measuring Money

Before deciding the proper monetary policy, it is necessary first to measure the money supply (*M*). The traditional definition of the money supply includes checkable deposits in depository institutions plus cash in the hands of the public. This most spendable form of money is designated *M1*. In 1992, *M1* amounted to $900 billion.

In addition to cash and checkable deposits, some other financial assets are almost as spendable as *M1*: small savings accounts and time deposits, travelers checks issued by nonbanks, and shares in money market mutual funds. Holders of these assets probably feel wealthier as a result of their holdings and spend more freely than they would otherwise. Including these other financial assets in the money definition produces *M2* money, which amounted to $3500 billion in 1992. Other large time deposits and dollars held by foreigners are added to *M2* to yield the *M3* definition of the money supply, $4200 billion in 1992. (See Table 10.2 for a breakdown of money measures.)

Controlling the growth of such diverse forms of money has become increasingly difficult, and the Federal Reserve has come under increasing criticism. Worsening inflation during the 1970s seemed to call for slower money growth, but attempts to reduce lending were

Table 10.2 Money Forms—December 1992.

M1	Cash and checkable deposits in commercial banks, savings and loan associations, credit unions, and mutual savings banks	$1019 billion
M2	*M1* plus savings and short-term time deposits and money market fund shares	3508 billion
M3	*M2* plus long-term time deposits in all financial institutions	4191 billion

ineffective or—if effective, as they were in 1990—plunged the economy into recession.

HOW SUCCESSFUL HAS MONETARY POLICY BEEN?

How closely does the reality of monetary policy conform to the theory? How successfully has the Federal Reserve managed the money supply to promote stable prices and steady growth of production?

Fluctuations and Frustrations of the 1970s

As the 1970s began, the economy was experiencing a recession. To deal with the recession, the Fed purchased government securities and allowed the supply of currency and checking accounts to grow about 6 percent annually. By 1972, the recession had ended, and the Fed cut back reserves to hold down the growth of the money supply. Still, the money supply continued to grow, by 9 percent that year, and the Fed began to worry about inflation.

Contractionary monetary policy was begun in earnest in 1973, with six increases in discount rates during the year. The interest rate charged by banks to their best customers rose ten times to reach 12 percent in 1974, and rates on short-term business loans rose to almost 14 percent. Reserve requirements were increased also. Still, business firms expected new investment to be profitable; so they continued to borrow, and inflation soared.

Inflation increased to dangerous levels in 1974, and the Federal Reserve cut money growth sharply. Finally, business borrowing fell, the business failure rate jumped, and unemployment spread. By February 1975, the money supply was actually shrinking. Many economists predicted that the drastic reversal in monetary policy would throw the economy into a severe recession, and in fact, the bottom of the fifth postwar recession was recorded in March.

The Fed was not entirely to blame for the slowdown in money growth. Evidence suggests that by early 1975 the Board of Governors was trying to relax the earlier contractionary monetary policy. They were buying U.S. government securities and increasing reserves, but financial institutions were not making new loans. Business firms were just too pessimistic to take on the risks of borrowing.

The situation in 1975 gave economists an opportunity to use one of their old sayings: You can't push on a string. You can pull money out of the economy during inflation. But you can't push money into the economy during recession if banks are unwilling to lend and if credit-worthy borrowers are hard to find.

Recovery from the 1975 recession was slow, in part because of high consumer and business debt built up during the previous expansion. Especially stubborn inflation and job uncertainty also reduced consumer confidence and held spending down. The Fed struggled to achieve the appropriate monetary policy for ending the recession without increasing inflation. For the first time, the Fed announced its target rate of money growth for the year: a growth range of between 5 percent and $7\frac{1}{2}$ percent for currency and checkable deposits. All the tools of monetary policy were put to use to achieve this goal, but the money supply grew by less than 5 percent.

Money growth speeded up to 6 percent in 1976, but high unemployment and inflation continued. Hoping to avoid a new recession, the Board of Governors decided to reduce money growth gradually until inflation subsided. Consumer, business, and government spending continued to grow, however, pushing the economy closer to the limits of productive capacity and pushing money growth higher (8 percent) than the Fed's targets.

Vigorous expansion continued in 1978, and inflation rose further. Higher food and labor costs and declining worker productivity led to a program of voluntary wage and price controls under President Carter. Nevertheless, beat-the-price-rise psychology continued to increase consumer spending, and inflation accelerated.

An Experiment with Monetarism

Paul Volcker was appointed chairman of the Board of Governors in 1979, and the Fed announced a new target for monetary policy. Throughout the 1970s the goal of policy had been to keep interest rates stable. Keeping interest rates stable required frequent increases in money growth: to accommodate abnormally high loan demand without causing interest rates to rise. By the end of the decade the Fed became convinced that varying money growth had worsened inflationary pressures, and the Board of Governors changed its fundamental goal to maintaining steady money growth. The new policy was more in keeping with recommendations of the monetarists.

Slower money growth took took hold in the early 1980s, at the same time fiscal policy was becoming strongly expansionary. With slower money growth, President Reagan's tax cuts and increased defense spending were ineffective against the severe recession. Finally in late 1982 the Fed abandoned its commitment to monetarism and allowed money growth to speed up. A strong expansion began, but budget deficits soared.

Many economists predicted that Federal Reserve Chairman Paul Volcker would be a "tough act to follow." Volcker's contractionary monetary policy was credited with reducing inflation from 9 percent to 3 percent in the 1980s. In 1987, however, President Reagan appointed Alan Greenspan to the job of Fed chairman. Greenspan had formerly served as chairman of President Ford's Council of Economic Advisers.

Alan Greenspan proved to be just as strong an inflation fighter as Paul Volcker. In fact, by 1990 some members of President Bush's administration were complaining that Greenspan's contractionary monetary policy was stalling economic growth and creating a recession.

Some fundamental imbalances remain in the U.S. economy today, largely a result of large government deficits and increasing trade deficits. (We have more to say about trade deficits in Chapter 15.) Financing large government deficits is difficult without cooperation from the Federal Reserve.

Money Growth and Interest Rates

Changes in money growth have their first effect on interest rates. Economic theory predicts that expansionary monetary policy reduces interest rates and encourages investment; likewise, contractionary monetary policy is expected to increase interest rates and retard investment. Indeed, the short-range effects may be as expected; but the long-range effects may be very different.

The long-range relationship between money growth and interest is an example of Gibson's Paradox. A **paradox** is a statement that seems contradictory or absurd, but may actually be true. In the early 1900s, a British statistician named Gibson thought he saw a paradox in the behavior of the money supply, prices, and interest rates.

What happens when the money supply increases? First, banks have more money to lend, and second, people have more money to spend. The first result should cause interest rates to fall, and the second, prices to rise. Thus, falling interest rates would accompany rising prices.

At least this is what we might expect to happen, given our understanding of market supply and demand and the effects of shifts in supply or demand curves on market prices. Gibson's Paradox is that events did not turn out that way at all. In fact, over the years Gibson observed, prices and interest rates tended to move in the same direction, indicating a "contradictory, absurd" result.

The explanation for Gibson's Paradox requires a distinction between nominal interest rates and real interest rates. The **nominal interest rate** is the stated rate paid for borrowing; nominal rates are frequently quoted in the newspaper and always appear on a loan agreement. The **real interest rate** is the real purchasing power paid for the loan and is determined by subtracting the rate of inflation from the nominal interest rate. In cases where the rate of inflation exceeds the nominal rate of interest, the real interest rate is negative. In this case, a lender sacrifices more purchasing power to the borrower than he or she receives in final payment of the loan. In effect, the lender is paying someone else to use his or her money.

Most lenders take steps to avoid this unhappy result. When prices are rising, they build into nominal interest rates a return sufficient to offset inflation. Thus, high prices—and the expectation that prices will continue to rise—prompt an increase in nominal interest rates. On the other hand, stable prices cause nominal interest rates to fall to the real rate of interest that satisfies most lenders. (Historically, the real rate of interest has been about 2 percent.)

Throughout the 1970s, the U.S. economy suffered abnormally high inflation, along with nominal interest rates reaching as high as 20 percent. Expansionary monetary policies, which were intended to keep borrowing costs low and encourage investment spending, instead contributed to inflation and high nominal rates. Maybe Gibson's Paradox was not so "absurd" after all.

BANK LOANS AND MONETARY POLICY

If monetary policy is to be successful, depository institutions must adjust their checkable deposits to the level of reserves supplied by the Federal Reserve. The level of reserves is intended to limit depository institutions' ability to create new deposits. Until the 1970s the system worked rather well; but then changes took place in lending that loosened the link between reserves and money creation.

Remember that a depository institution's assets are primarily its reserves at the Federal Reserve, loans to customers, and securities. Its securities are short-term, interest-earning debt issued by private business firms, the U.S. Treasury, and state and local governments. The permitted level of lending depends on the institution's checking accounts, required reserves, and actual reserves.

In the past, if a depository institution needed more reserves, it could increase its reserve account by shifting its assets. It could sell some of its securities and add the proceeds of the sale to its reserves. The increase in its reserve account would allow the institution to increase its lending.

Selling securities turned out to be an unattractive option for many depository institutions. The reason is the effect of Federal Reserve policy on the market price of securities. In practice, contractionary monetary policy withdraws money from the system and makes it difficult for depository institutions to sell securities; if it wants to make new loans, it has to sell securities for less than their purchase price and suffer a capital loss.* The expectation of a capital loss tends to discourage depository institutions from selling securities and making new loans, all of which reinforces the effects of the Federal Reserve's contractionary monetary policy.

To avoid capital losses on their securities, depository institutions sought a more attractive way to increase reserves. In particular, during the 1970s banks turned to the liabilities side of the balance sheet, offering high interest rates on deposits in savings accounts or certificates of deposit. Then they loaned out these funds, with a comfortable spread between the interest paid to the new depositors and the interest received from business borrowers. Generally, their loans to business firms carried flexible interest rates, to reflect frequent changes in banks' costs of borrowing. Flexible interest charges on loans were expected to maintain the bank's profits, regardless of the interest rate banks had to pay for borrowed funds.

This new process violated a fundamental rule of banking: borrow "long" and lend "short." Make certain you have long-term control over your funds, and avoid the possibility that your depositors will want to withdraw their money before your borrowers are ready to repay their loans.

In years past, most commercial bank loans were short-term, to finance business firms' inventory. As borrowers sold their inventory, they repaid their loans. During the 1970s and 1980s, however, some commercial banks made loans for long-term construction projects, like executive parks and high-rise office and apartment buildings. Such loans depend for repayment on the success of the project, with profitable sales and rental income flowing into borrowers' accounts.

As long as the economy is growing, long-term loans are safe. High rentals and increasing property values enable borrowers to pay interest charges on construction loans. But when growth slows, half-empty office buildings cannot produce enough rental income to pay off the loans. Borrowers default, and banks become the unhappy owners of a great deal of real estate, much of it worth less than the loans the banks had issued. Loan losses in the 1980s made banks reluctant to extend new loans to anyone other than their most dependable borrowers.

The switch to lending based on bank liabilities (rather than assets) made banks less sensitive to Federal Reserve policy than they formerly were. Rising fears of default led to wide swings in banks' willingness to make new loans. Under such conditions, banks would increase their lending during inflationary periods and reduce lending during recessions—contrary to the wishes of the Federal Reserve. (By the beginning of the 1990s, financial institutions and their regulators were shifting their emphasis back to the asset side of the balance sheet.)

POLITICS AND THE FEDERAL RESERVE

From time to time there are conflicts between the interests of the U.S. Congress and the president, on the one hand, and the interests of the Federal Reserve Board, on the other.

The president and Congress may want to use expansionary fiscal policy to stimulate spending and cause production and income to grow. Toward this objective, they may favor increased government spending and lower taxes. Such programs are popular with voters,

* Whenever an existing security is sold before maturity, its price must be competitive with new securities being issued currently. If new securities are paying higher interest rates than that of the existing security, the selling price of the existing security will be lower. In general, contractionary monetary policy causes current interest rates to rise and the prices of existing securities to fall.

Viewpoint

THE THEORY OF RATIONAL EXPECTATIONS

In this text we have been concerned with the Keynesian model of income determination. Remember that a model is a simplified view of reality. It summarizes economic behavior and projects the results of policy according to certain assumptions about behavior. Whether the model's projections are correct or not depends on the correctness of its fundamental assumptions.

Certain changes have been taking place in the U.S. economy that have led economists to doubt some of their fundamental assumptions and, therefore, to question some of the policy recommendations that depend on them. Ironically, this new skepticism is the result of more intelligent understanding of economic conditions among the public at large.

Improved communications have made families and business firms more sensitive to trends in production, employment, prices, and interest rates. Even more important, widespread availability of information about Keynesian economic policy has caused people to anticipate government policy moves before they actually take place. All these factors have worked to change behavior, so that many families and business firms now act according to their expectations of future economic policies.

The theory that explains this new type of behavior is called the theory of rational expectations. Rational expectations may have changed the results of Keynesian economic policies, reducing their effectiveness and possibly causing more harm than the problems they were designed to correct.

To understand the theory of rational expectations, suppose the growth of spending slows and the economy enters a recession. Unemployment increases, and the automatic stabilizers go into effect to push the federal budget toward an automatic deficit. What would a rational person expect to happen next?

Having studied economics, a rational person would probably expect the use of expansionary fiscal and monetary policy to speed recovery from recession. As expan-

but they can cause a deficit in the federal budget that must be financed by borrowing. The Treasury will have to sell government securities to finance the deficit, and it would prefer to pay low interest rates on its debt.

At the same time the government is running a deficit, the Federal Reserve may believe spending is increasing too fast. It may worry about increasing inflationary pressures and favor a slowdown in the growth of production and income. The Board of Governors may decide on a contractionary monetary policy to hold down the level of spending. As a result, there will be less money available for lending, and the Treasury will have to pay higher interest rates on its new securities.

Conflicts between Congress and the Federal Reserve have generally been settled by compromise. When the Treasury desperately needs funds, as it did during World War II, for sionary policies take effect, all the current measures of economic activity would reverse themselves. Unemployment would fall, and inflation would begin to accelerate.

Now suppose that inflation accelerates to the point that contractionary fiscal and monetary policy are put into place to slow the rate of growth. As higher taxes, reduced government spending, and slower money growth take hold, the expansion slows, and the economy moves toward recession. But rational people understand government's reluctance to let unemployment increase, and they will expect expansionary policies to be resumed fairly quickly. Expecting inflation to resume as well, they fail to adjust their wage demands downward, and the eventual inflation is worse than it might otherwise be.

A general belief that recessions will be short and that expansion will be the normal economic condition affects behavior significantly. There is less fear of unemployment and easier acceptance of inflation. In fact, workers and business firms tend to behave as if inflation is inevitable and to protect themselves against it: Workers insist on cost-of-living wage increases, and business firms insist on price increases that guarantee profits even when costs rise. Through these kinds of behavior, workers and business firms bring on the very inflation they expect.

Rational expectations probably reduce the effectiveness of traditional economic policies and aggravate tendencies toward inflation. For government to change worker and business behavior, it must adopt policies so different from expected policies as to startle people into totally new patterns of behavior.

The theory of rational expectations poses new problems for economic policymakers. The extreme version of the theory implies that no policy can affect behavior for long in the intended direction.

How might the theory of rational expectations be used to support or oppose government intervention in the economy? Discuss.

instance, the Fed has been willing to supply money at a faster rate. However, it is important that the Board of Governors have the power to restrict all spending—including government spending—when inflation threatens. Likewise, during recession the Board of Governors should provide the additional money for greater government spending. Otherwise, fiscal and monetary policy might be pushing the economy in opposite directions.

Some legislators have recommended legislation to bring the Federal Reserve more completely under the control of Congress. The aim would be to guarantee a steady increase in money and to ensure that available funds are allocated toward programs to deal with the nation's most pressing needs: housing and productive enterprises, rather than speculative buying and inventory accumulation. Many economists are strongly opposed to

Viewpoint

THE COST OF THE S&L BAILOUT

The federal budget is a way of reducing private spending so that resources can be shifted into spending for the nation as a whole. When borrowing from one group to lend to another accomplishes the shift directly, the transaction should not be considered part of the budget or an addition to the budget deficit. This is the opinion of economist Robert Eisner.

Eisner's point is relevant when considering the bailout of the S&Ls. Compensating depositors of failed S&Ls will cost federal deposit insurance funds more than $200 billion. Some members of Congress are worried that paying the $200 billion will require either additional taxes or additional borrowing to finance a larger budget deficit.

According to Eisner, money loaned by S&Ls continues to circulate in the economy as a result of borrowers' spending for new office buildings, homes, and so forth. When loans are not repaid and S&Ls, are unable to pay their depositors, the government's insurance guarantee is activated to compensate them. Compensating depositors will require the sale of government securities, which will reduce the deposit accounts of buyers of securities. Then, the proceeds of government securities will be paid to S&Ls in the form of Federal Reserve accounts. When S&Ls lend out their Federal Reserve balances, they will create new deposits to take the place of the deposits paid out by buyers of government securities. Thus, there is no need to reduce the nation's money supply or increase taxes in the amount of the bailout. The only effect is to change public debt holdings from an implicit guarantee of deposits by the deposit insurance fund to an explicit debt in the form of government securities.

The cost of the S&L crisis is not the dollars paid to depositors. Rather the cost of the S&L crisis is the use of resources for buildings that many not have economic value, instead of for more valued properties. If more valued properties would not have been built without S&L lending, then the cost is essentially zero.

Summarize the main point of this article in terms of opportunity costs. Do you agree that it is not necessary to reduce the nation's money supply or raise taxes by the amount of the bailout?

Robert Eisner, "No New Taxes for the S&L Bailout," *Challenge*, March-April 1991.

Congressional control of the Fed. They see the Federal Reserve as the only way to balance the occasionally excessive spending plans of the president and Congress.

THE CRISIS IN THE SAVINGS AND LOANS

In the 1990s the U.S. financial sector faces a savings-and-loan crisis. The crisis arises from the kinds of loans and investments S&Ls were allowed to make in the 1980s.

Pre-1980s regulation required S&Ls to limit their lending to long-term mortgages. With a decline in interest received on mortgages and controls on interest paid to S&L depositors, regulation reduced S&Ls' profit potential. Specifically, rising inflation caused depositors to insist on higher interest payments; otherwise they would (and did) withdraw their deposits to take advantage of higher-paying opportunities elsewhere. At the same time, many S&L mortgages, negotiated years earlier when inflation was not a problem, were paying lower interest rates.

Declining profits prompted many S&Ls to demand freedom from regulation, and in 1980 the rules governing S&L loans and investments were relaxed. Up to 20 percent of their assets could be in nonmortgage loans. Many S&Ls took advantage of relaxed regulation and made loans to more risky borrowers in agriculture, energy, and even foreign countries. Because of their higher risk, such loans paid higher interest rates than home mortgages. But because of their higher risk, they were also subject to a higher rate of default. And many borrowers did just that.

When S&L assets turned into worthless paper, S&Ls were unable to pay their depositors. Most deposits were insured by the federal government, however, through the Federal Savings and Loan Insurance Corporation (FSLIC). The regulatory authorities were obliged to step in and protect depositors' funds. They did this in either of two ways: by selling the S&Ls' good assets at a bargain price to investors, who would assume the responsibility of collecting loans and paying off depositors; or by closing the S&L and paying off depositors from FSLIC's insurance fund.* In either case, the federal government was left holding rather shaky loans on questionable properties; it would try to collect the loans and/or sell the properties to cover the cost of paying off depositors.

More than 400 S&Ls have been taken over in the S&L crisis, and the problem is expected to cost the government at least $200 billion during the 1990s.

How did the failing S&Ls violate the basic financial rule to borrow long and lend short?

SUMMARY

1. The first use of money was a milestone in the process of economic development. Money promoted trade, with specialization and division of labor.
2. The development of banking eased the process of exchange and provided credit for expanding investment. Early unregulated banks often caused alternating periods of overexpansion of money, followed by business bankruptcies and bank failures.
3. In 1913 the Federal Reserve System was established. Through centrally regulated banking, the Fed attempts to influence economic activity by expanding the money supply when there are unemployed resources to be brought into production and contracting money growth when spending exceeds the full employment capacity of the nation's resources.

* Because FSLIC's resources were insufficient to do the job, a new agency, the Reconciliation Trust Corporation, was set up to handle it and was awarded billions of dollars for the work.

4. Other financial intermediaries now offer a variety of services, including long-term mortgages, loans to state and local governments, and short-term consumer loans. The growth of lending institutions has helped promote economic growth but may have complicated the Fed's money management role.
5. Monetary policy aims at providing stable increases in purchasing power in line with increases in our nation's productive capacity. Monetary policy is carried out through changes in the required reserve ratio of depository institutions, changes in the discount rate, and Federal Reserve purchase and sale of U.S. Treasury securities (open-market operations).
6. Changes in the level of reserves affect depository institutions' willingness to lend and affect interest rates. Changes in interest rates in turn affect the costs of new business projects, encouraging or discouraging business investment spending.
7. Monetary policy is not always fully effective. If there is a recession, business firms may be too pessimistic to risk borrowing for new investment, even if interest rates are low. If there is inflation, business firms may be willing to pay high interest rates to avoid even higher costs in the future.
8. Contractionary monetary policy may be particularly hard on small business firms, which depend on credit for their investment funds. Contractionary monetary policy also increases the cost of borrowing for state and local governments and for the U.S. Treasury.
9. The quantity theory of money ($MV = PQ$) has been a source of controversy among economists. Part of the controversy stems from the difficulty of defining M. The traditional definition of money, $M1$, is currency and checkable deposits in all depository institutions.
10. The results of monetary policy have not been completely satisfactory. Money growth has had paradoxical effects on interest rates; banks have become less sensitive to Federal Reserve policy; and politics continue to affect Fed decisions.

TERMS TO REMEMBER

barter: trade in which goods are exchanged for other goods

checkable deposits: deposits in checking accounts that are available on demand

time deposits: deposits in savings accounts, often available only after a stated time period

capital account: the difference between the value of a bank's assets and the value of its liabilities; a bank's net worth

monetary policy: deliberate exercise of the Federal Reserve's power to expand or contract the money supply in order to promote economic stability

required reserve ratio: the percentage of its checkable deposits a bank must keep in its reserve account at the Federal Reserve

expansionary monetary policy: policies to increase money growth

contractionary monetary policy: policies to slow money growth

discount rate: the rate of interest a depository institution pays on funds borrowed from the Federal Reserve

open-market operations: Federal Reserve purchases and sales of government securities

monetarists: economists who emphasize money supply as central to all economic policy

nominal interest rate: the stated charge for borrowing

real interest rate: the charge for borrowing, corrected for inflation

TOPICS FOR DISCUSSION

1. From your reading of the text determine the meaning of the following expressions:

   Clearinghouse for checks
   Automatic monetary policy

2. What is meant by the following statement? "Monetary and fiscal policy may at times be pushing the economy in opposite directions."

3. Distinguish clearly among the Federal Reserve's three instruments for affecting the nation's supply of money.
4. Some critics of monetary policy point out that restricting the supply of money and reducing the growth of production may, over time, *increase* prices. Can you suggest reasons for this result?
5. In late 1974 the Federal Reserve announced a reduction in the reserve requirement on certain large certificates of deposit (CDs). CDs are sold by banks to savers, and the money is loaned to business. The CDs affected by the ruling were those sold for over $100,000, with maturities of more than four months. In 1974 the banks were handling almost $90 billion of these large CDs with a reserve requirement of 8 percent. The new ruling reduced the reserve requirement to 5 percent. Calculate the amount of excess reserves this new ruling released for new loans. What results would you expect?
6. The problem of balance between growth in spending and production of new goods and services is complicated by the fact that the existing supply of money is spent several times. An economy that produces $100 billion in GDP annually may need only $20 billion in money, if each dollar is spent five times during the year. Economists refer to the number of times money is spent as its **velocity**. Thus, the quantity of money times its velocity is equal to the value of GDP: MV = GDP. Below are GDP and money supply data for selected years in the United States. Calculate the velocity for each year. What do you notice about velocity in recent years? What factors may influence the speed with which money is spent?

YEAR	*GDP**	*MONEY SUPPLY: CURRENCY + CHECKABLE DEPOSITS**
1960	$ 513	$ 141
1965	703	168
1970	1011	215
1975	1586	288
1980	2708	409
1985	4039	620
1990	5514	825
1991	5672	897
1992	5980	1019

*In billions

7. Explain why headlines describing Federal Reserve intentions might "aggravate ulcers on Wall Street!"
8. Consult the *Economic Report of the President* for data on money growth, prices, and interest rates over recent years. Comment on your findings.
9. Explain how following Milton Friedman's prescription for steady money growth is expected to reduce inflation. Might it also help relieve unemployment?
10. When the former Soviet Union changed from a command to a market economic system, one result was rampant price inflation. To protect themselves against inflation, many consumers resorted to barter. Discuss the disadvantages associated with barter, particularly in a period when a nation is attempting to establish a market system.
11. In 1992 short-term securities in the United States were yielding an interest return of about 3.9 percent, compared with 10.0 percent in Great Britain. How are differences in interest rates worldwide likely to affect the Federal Reserve's use of monetary policy? Give examples of the effects on U.S. employment and prices.
12. Review the provisions of the 1980 Depository Institutions Deregulation and Monetary Control Act. How might the act have contributed to the increase in S&L and bank failures in the 1980s?

ANSWERS TO TEST YOURSELF

(p. 226) When a bank's reserves fall below the required fraction of deposits, it must collect old loans and refuse to issue new loans. Borrowers will pay off their loans by drawing funds from their accounts in other banks. Other banks will lose reserves and be forced to reduce their lending. This process continues until deposit accounts in all banks fall to the permitted multiple of reserves.

FURTHER READING

Barth, James R., R. Dan Brumbaugh, Jr., and Robert E. Litan, *The Future of American Banking*, M.E. Sharpe, Armonk, N.Y., 1992.

Blinder, Alan S., *Hard Heads and Soft Hearts*, Addison-Wesley, Reading, Mass., 1987.

Eisner, Robert, "S&Ls, Deficits and Taxes," *Challenge*, March/April 1991.

Friedman, Benjamin M., "Lessons on Monetary Policy from the 1980s," *Journal of Economic Perspectives*, Summer 1988.

Friedman, Milton and Walter Heller, *Monetary vs. Fiscal Policy*, Norton, New York, 1969.

Hart, Albert Gailord, "How to Reform Banks," *Challenge*, March/April 1991.

Kaufman, Henry, *Interest Rates, The Markets and the New Financial World*, Times Books, New York, 1986.

Kydland, Finn and Edward Prescott, "Rules Rather Than Discretion," *Journal of Political Economy*, v. 85, no. 3, 1977.

Sargent, Thomas and Neil Wallace, "Rational Expectations, the Optimal Monetary Instrument, and the Optimal Money Supply Rule, *Journal of Political Economy*, April 1975.

Volcker, Paul and Toyoo Gyohten, *Changing Fortunes*, Times Books, New York, 1992.

Chapter 11

Inflation

Tools for Study

LEARNING OBJECTIVES

After reading this chapter, you will be able to:

1. Define inflation, identify its causes, and explain its effects.
2. Suggest some policy remedies for aggregate-demand and aggregate-supply inflation.
3. Discuss the consequences of inflationary expectations.
4. Discuss the inflationary effects of economic and social regulation.

CURRENT ISSUES FOR DISCUSSION

Who are the gainers and losers in inflation?

How effective is a wage-price freeze?

How well does price indexing work and what are its disadvantages?

It has been said that if you ask five economists for their opinions on a subject, you will get six opinions—one of the economists won't be able to make up his or her mind.

This is particularly true of the subject of inflation. Because the sources of inflation are difficult to identify, it is difficult to choose a cure. Before the proper cure can be decided, the problem must be carefully analyzed and the process by which it travels through the economic system clearly understood. If the problem is approached haphazardly, the results of policy may be worse than the problem itself.

Economists define **inflation** as a continuing rise in the prices of most goods and services. Some prices are rising and others falling all the time, but if the average price level remains the same, there is no inflation. When the average price level rises, we have inflation.

A LOOK AT HISTORY

Primitive economic societies do not have to worry about inflation. Inflation is mainly a problem of growing, industrialized economies.

From Self-Sufficiency to Specialization

People in primitive societies had to struggle just to stay alive. Because primitive tribes were isolated, they had to be self-sufficient. Each tribe had to produce its entire reserve of game, grain, shelter, and cloth or skins. Later, some tribes began to specialize and trade with neighboring tribes. Specialization made possible greater production so that both tribes could live better. Material gains were accomplished at the expense of self-sufficiency, but that was a small price to pay.

Specialization and trade required the use of money. Primitive tribes used as money whatever tokens they found at hand—special beads and stones and rare shells. As long as the supply of tokens remained in balance with the supply of goods, there was no problem of rising prices. There was just enough money to purchase the available goods at their customary prices.

Money and Prices

As technical knowledge spread, production grew. More money was needed to symbolize the greater quantities of goods and services offered in trade. The need for money created a dilemma: money had to be scarce enough to retain its value, but it also had to be plentiful enough to exchange for a growing quantity of goods. Gold and silver fulfilled both these requirements for many centuries. But eventually, fewer new sources of precious metals (as well as the difficulty of carrying metal around in one's pockets) made it necessary to find a substitute. Paper money "tied" to gold or silver was the result.*

As economic life became more complex, balancing the supply of money with the available supply of goods became more difficult. When the supply of money increased faster than the supply of goods, more buyers would bid for the limited supplies of goods. Prices would tend to rise, and the economy would experience inflation. When the supply of money increased more slowly than the supply of goods, sellers would compete for buyers' money. Prices would tend to fall, and the economy experience deflation.

* Our paper money is no longer tied to gold or silver. Currency is issued by the Federal Reserve Banks, and the supply is not limited by the nation's holdings of precious metals.

Automatic Balance Through Trade

Eighteenth-century economists believed that imbalances between money and goods would be temporary and localized. Imbalances would correct themselves automatically through free trade. More money than goods in one nation would bring on inflation, and buyers would look elsewhere for cheaper goods. They would spend their money in nations with lower prices and, therefore, less money than goods. Money would flow from high-priced nations to low-priced nations until the supply of money and goods would be in balance in all nations. Then prices would stabilize.

This happy result might have come to pass if there had been no barriers to the free flow of money and goods among nations. In fact, in addition to the barriers of distance there were political and economic boundaries, each nation having its own national currency, import quotas and tariffs, and other limits to free trade. (International trade is discussed in detail in Chapter 15.)

Another problem arose with the growth of democracy. When democratic governments face problems of unemployment, poverty, illiteracy, and homelessness, voters insist on new government programs to correct them. (Less frequently do they insist on new taxes to pay for the new programs.) Increases in government spending (without increases in taxes) call for the creation of new money and increase spending for the available quantities of goods and services. Unless government programs succeed in increasing production as fast as the growth of money, there will be inflation.

WHY ALL THE FUSS ABOUT INFLATION?

Why should inflation concern us? A one-dollar bill and a ten look pretty much the same. Why should it matter whether a day's welding, a truckload of soybeans, a college course, or a suit of clothes is counted as ten dollars or one dollar?

It matters if a day's welding today at $100 is to be exchanged in five years for a suit of clothes. By that time the value of the $100 may have shrunk and a suit might cost as much as two or three days' welding. Inflation is especially hard on people who save their money as a store of value for use in the future: savers, the elderly, pensioners. (We'll all be there one day!)

If matters, too, if the price of a college course, for example, rises more slowly than the price of a truckload of soybeans. Workers who depend on income from the sale of college courses may be unfairly penalized by uneven price changes. Inflation brings a lower standard of living to people whose incomes are relatively fixed, including teachers, government workers, and families who receive government transfer payments.

The most unpleasant effects of inflation pertain only to unexpected inflation, however. If inflation is predicted correctly, welders, retired persons, and college teachers may be able to build into their wage agreements and retirement funds a cost-of-living adjustment to compensate for inflation. (Cost-of-living adjustments create other problems, which we also discuss.)

Unexpected inflation interferes especially with our ability to plan for the future. Most of us were taught to save part of our income to provide financial security for our retirement years. Our savings might earn interest of up to, say, 7 percent a year. But suppose inflation is reducing the value of our money at the rate of 10 percent a year. The unsuspecting saver will actually lose 3 percent in real wealth every year. The saver may seem to be worse off than the soundrel who squanders his or her earnings on riotous living.

What is even more disturbing is the fact that the saver's interest earnings of 7 percent are taxed as part of his or her personal income. In effect, savers are taxed twice for being virtuous—once through inflation and again by the Internal Revenue Service.

Those who lend money (creditors) or borrow money (debtors) are affected differently by unexpected inflation. In fact, borrowers are helped by unexpected inflation, because they pay back less in real wealth than they originally borrowed. Unless interest rates compensate fully for inflation, unexpected inflation hurts lenders, who may become reluctant to lock themselves into long-term loans.

TEST YOURSELF

Calculate the real return on a loan with interest at 10 percent, inflation of 8 percent, and an income tax rate of 25 percent.

Rampant inflation is often followed by recession or depression.* During inflation, there is feverish spending for new capital resources, increasing production in line with the increased demand for goods and services. When all firms are fully stocked with equipment and inventories, the level of investment and production falls. With the reduction in economic activity come unemployment and economic distress.

Regrettably, even the expectation of inflation worsens the tendency toward inflation. If producers expect prices to rise, they will hold goods or raw materials off the market to sell later at higher prices. When producers hold goods and raw materials off the market, the imbalance between spending and goods widens. Prices rise even faster. More damaging

* Recession or depression may in fact be caused by contractionary fiscal and monetary policy, put in place to correct inflation.

still, when gains can be made from hoarding goods and raw materials, there is less incentive to invest in factories, machines, and vocational training for new workers. These are the capital resources that enable our nation to produce more goods and services in the future. With fewer resources for increasing production, our economic system is less able to avoid inflation in the years to come.

Some economists worry that continuing inflation brings on social and political problems. Strikes, shortages of goods and services, and loss of confidence in government have been linked to inflation in the past. Uncontrolled inflation may even prompt a radical change in a nation's political philosophy. In times of inflation in the past, nations have turned to demagogues or dictators who promised "painless" solutions to the problem of inflation.

Other economists suggest that creeping inflation of about 2 percent a year may be good for the economy. Slowly rising prices mean higher profits for business firms. Higher profits stimulate increased production, which in turn encourages investment in new manufacturing capacity and creates more jobs. The problem with this theory is the difficulty of making sure inflation continues only to "creep." If business and labor unions, for example, use 2 percent inflation as a base on which to add further price increases and wage demands, the creep may accelerate into a headlong lurch.

ANALYZING AND CORRECTING INFLATION

If we agree that inflation is a serious problem, the next step is analysis. What are the forces producing inflationary pressures in a modern nation? How is inflation transmitted through the economic system? Finally, what policies may be effective for controlling inflation?

The causes of inflation can be divided into two categories: causes related to aggregate demand and causes related to aggregate supply.

When aggregate demand increases faster than aggregate supply, prices tend to rise. Figure 11.1 repeats Figure 8.13 of Chapter 8, which shows aggregate demand (*AD*) and aggregate supply (*AS*). In Figure 11.1 quantities of all goods and services are shown in relation to a price index. According to the figure, until production of goods and services nears the full productive capacity of the economy, increases in aggregate demand can be satisfied without increases in the nation's price index. However, as the nation's resources are more fully employed, further quantities of goods and services can be produced only for higher prices. As aggregate demand (*AD*) shifts to the right, from AD_1 to AD_2 and AD_3, the price index rises from 1.00, and the nation experiences inflation.

Figure 11.1 Aggregate Demand Inflation

Shifts in aggregate demand push production toward the full capacity of the economy and bring on inflation.

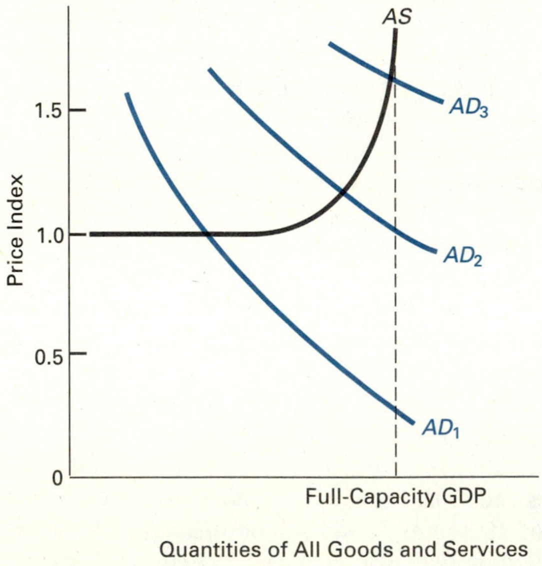

Figure 11.2 Aggregate Supply Inflation

Rising costs of production shift aggregate supply up and bring on inflation.

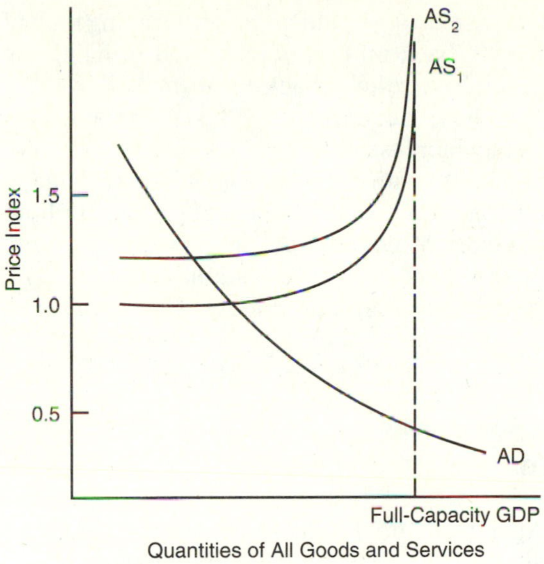

Figure 11.2 illustrates inflation whose causes are related to aggregate supply. In Figure 11.2 *AD* remains stable, but certain factors combine to increase costs of production. In this case, *AS* shifts up (to the left) to reflect higher selling prices for all goods and services, regardless of quantity of output. The equilibrium level of output is determined where *AD* is equal to *AS*, with a higher price index and a smaller quantity of output (and employment) than before the shift.

In the next sections we describe demand-side and supply-side inflation in detail.

Aggregate-Demand Inflation (or Demand-Pull Inflation)

When aggregate demand increases faster than aggregate supply, the frequent result is inflation. Economists say that "too much money is chasing too few goods."

If buyers want more goods and services than a nation can produce, total spending rises beyond the nation's production possibilities curve. With no unemployed resources to be drawn into production, output cannot increase. Excess spending starts an upward spiral of bidding for the limited supply of goods, raising the prices of finished goods and the costs of the labor and raw materials needed to produce them. We say there is aggregate-demand or **demand-pull inflation**.

Aggregate-demand inflation is most common during wars or during periods of heavy social spending or rapid economic development. What policies may be effective for controlling aggregate-demand or demand-pull inflation?

1. Raising Taxes and Cutting Total Spending

When excessive demand heats up inflation, Keynesian economists recommend raising taxes and cutting government spending. The intended effect is to shift the *AD* curve in Figure 11.1 back to the left, or to slow its move to the right. Needless to say, this is very unpopular medicine. Few policymakers campaign on a platform promising to raise voters' taxes and cut their favorite spending programs.

Political considerations were a factor in the inflation of the 1960s and 1970s. The federal government was spending heavily to conduct the war in Vietnam and to pay for costly social programs. But tax increases and cuts in government programs would have been political suicide for many legislators. Consequently, aggregate demand continued to increase. Increased government spending for defense and social programs, along with increased consumer spending for civilian goods, quickly became translated into ever-rising price levels.

2. Stabilizing Money Growth.

Another policy for controlling aggregate-demand inflation is favored by the monetarists, led by Milton Friedman. The monetarists' proposal would avoid the political problems associated with increasing taxes and reducing government spending.

Monetarists argue that if we are to control aggregate-demand inflation, we must keep the quantity of money in balance with the nation's growing capacity to produce goods and services. Our nation's productive capacity has grown an average of about 4 percent each year through increases in the quantity and quality of resources and through improvements in technology. Therefore, according to the monetarists, the Federal Reserve should allow the money supply to increase each year only as much as the average expected growth in productive capacity: about 4 percent.*

Monetarists reason this way: If aggregate demand increases faster than 4 percent, some prices will begin to rise. However, if the Federal Reserve continues to supply new money at the rate of only 4 percent, the general price level cannot rise. Some prices will have to fall, holding growth in aggregate demand down to the rate of money growth and holding down the general price level. Furthermore, the smaller than desired quantity of money will push interest rates up and discourage borrowing for new spending. Without any need for government intervention, aggregate demand will grow only at the rate of growth of our capacity to produce goods and services.

Monetarists believe that constant money growth would also help correct too slow growth of aggregate demand. If aggregate demand grows more slowly than our capacity to produce goods and services, some resources will be unemployed, and some prices will fall. If the Federal Reserve continues to supply new money at the rate of 4 percent, however, the constant addition of new money will be greater than needed for current prices. Too much money will encourage consumer spending and push prices back up. Furthermore, a surplus of money for lending will push interest rates down and encourage borrowing for additional spending. This time, the result will be an increase in aggregate demand, bringing annual growth back up to 4 percent and bringing the general price level back to normal.

Thus, according to the monetarists, a steady increase in the money supply will serve as an automatic regulator of aggregate demand and an automatic stabilizer of prices. Without any sort of government intervention, growth in aggregate demand will stabilize at roughly 4 percent per year, and prices will remain stable as well.

*The 4 percent rate of money growth could be altered if growth in productive capacity were to speed up or slow down.

Aggregate-Supply Inflation (or Cost-Push Inflation)

Aggregate-supply inflation results from upward shifts in aggregate supply (*AS*) that result from higher costs of production. Thus, supply-side inflation is often called cost-push inflation. **Cost-push inflation** may be caused by rising labor costs, "administered prices," government regulation, or expectations of inflation.

Wage-Cost Inflation

The first type of aggregate-supply inflation places the blame for inflation on the increasing cost of labor. When workers insist on larger shares of income from production, business costs of production rise, and prices rise for finished goods and services. Rising prices for goods and services, in turn, create even higher wage demands (or activate cost-of-living clauses in wage contracts).

Rising wages do not necessarily cause inflation. Wages can increase every year without price increases as long as wages increase precisely in step with the increase in worker productivity. If worker productivity increases

Thinking Seriously About Economic Issues

HOW TO FINANCE A WAR

Aggregate-demand inflation is often associated with wars.* To fight a war requires a nation to shift resources out of production of consumer goods and services and into production of the things needed to fight the war. There are three ways to do this, ways that are difficult and desirable in the same order:

1. The most difficult and the most desirable way is through taxation. If citizens are prevented from spending the amount government wants to spend, resources can be moved from production of consumer goods to production of goods for fighting the war. Aggregate demand cannot increase, and there will be no aggregate-demand inflation.
2. The second most difficult and most desirable way is through selling government securities to the public. If consumers can be persuaded to lend their money to government, they will not spend it on consumer goods. Again, aggregate demand cannot increase, and resources can be moved from production of consumer goods to production of goods for fighting the war.
3. The least difficult and least desirable (and most often resorted to) way is through creating new money. A government can avoid prevention and persuasion to reduce consumer spending and simply create new money to pay for the things government needs to fight the war. In the previous chapter we learned how the Federal Reserve banks can enable banks, thrifts, and credit unions to create new money for financing government spending.

The disadvantage of creating new money is that, unlike taxation and government borrowing, it does not reduce consumer spending. Creating new money gives government the dollars it needs without taking money away from consumers. The likely result is an increase in aggregate demand, with aggregate-demand inflation.

We have suggested that fighting a war requires a nation to shift resources out of production of consumer goods and into production of goods to fight the war. Inflation can accomplish this result. When inflation reduces the real value of consumers' incomes, their spending power falls. They cannot buy as many consumer goods as before, so that the nation's resources can be used to produce the goods and services the government needs to fight the war.

With inflation, consumers get fewer goods for their money. Indeed, inflation amounts to a kind of tax; but the tax is hidden and, therefore, less easily measured and probably less equitable than a tax that has been agreed to by the voters. For these reasons, economists generally recommend taxation or government borrowing to finance a war.

* This might be a war on poverty, a war on drugs, or a war on AIDS, as well as a conventional war.

by 3 percent a year, for example, wages can increase by an average of 3 percent without causing cost-push inflation. On the other hand, if wages increase faster than productivity, labor costs per unit of output increase, and we have aggregate-supply or cost-push inflation.

The problem of increasing labor costs is made more complicated because wage costs bear more heavily in certain industries. Labor costs are a small part of production costs in modern, automated manufacturing plants. But the service industries are less easily automated, generally requiring more labor per unit of output than goods manufacture. Unfortunately, services are precisely the things we affluent Americans want most after our basic material needs are satisfied—health and beauty services, educational and environmental services, recreational and travel services, ready-to-eat foods and custom designs. Rising wage costs are especially inflationary when consumers spend more of their incomes for services.

Administered Prices

A second kind of aggregate-supply inflation has been blamed on "administered prices." **Administered prices** are prices set above the competitive price by the largest, most powerful firms in a concentrated industry. Smaller firms in the industry tend to go along with the large firms, worsening the tendency toward aggregate-supply or cost-push inflation.

In certain industries, administered prices may seem necessary because of the industry's large capital requirements. Costly plants and equipment must be operated fairly continuously and the output sold at acceptable prices. Large-scale manufacturers cannot afford price wars. Therefore, they set prices high enough to maintain a target rate of return: a certain percentage return on their invested capital.

Target pricing may cause inflation even when sales are falling. When plant operation must be cut back, each unit of the smaller output must bear a larger share of the target return. Thus, falling sales may force firms to increase price in order to maintain the desired rate of return on invested capital.

Often highly concentrated industries are associated with powerful labor unions. Unions can insist on higher wages, knowing that large firms can pass on their higher wage costs to consumers. Thus, the combination of administered prices and high labor costs leads to significant aggregate-supply inflation.

Regulation

Government sometimes gets the blame for aggregate-supply inflation, when government regulations increase firms' costs of production. In general, government regulation has one of two objectives: economic or social. The economic objective is primarily to protect competition in particular industries. The social objective is to protect workers and consumers. In both cases the result of regulation can be higher costs of production and higher prices.

Regulation for economic objectives is generally directed toward a particular industry or sector of the economy: agriculture, transportation, communication, banking, or energy. These industries tend to be highly capital-intensive, and industrial concentration is fairly high. (In fact, we have referred to some of these industries as natural monopolies). The goal of government regulation is to retain a degree of competition so as to avoid the harmful effects of monopoly. Even when large firms might have lower average costs than small firms, government can set prices high enough to enable small firms to compete.

Regulation for social objectives is a more recent kind of regulation. The objective of social regulation is to require firms to include external costs in their costs of production. External costs are costs generally borne by others outside the business firm that creates them. Some examples of external costs are environmental pollution and the costs of employee health and safety on the job.

Free markets cannot handle external costs well. This is because the benefits of costly environmental, health, and safety programs don't necessarily come back to the firm that pays for them but are distributed over the entire community. Social regulation is needed to force firms to "internalize" their external costs. Ultimately, the "internalized" costs are paid by consumers of products that create environmental, health, or safety problems, in the form of higher prices for finished goods. Thus, aggregate-supply or cost-push inflation.

Regulation of any kind has another inflationary effect. To administer rules requires a staff of lawyers, inspectors, accountants, and specialists of all types. Government employees must be paid salaries comparable to the salaries they could earn in private industry, but they produce no marketable good or service. Again, the result is to raise prices.

Expectations

A final explanation for aggregate-supply inflation focuses on people's expectations regarding future prices. After a period of inflation, workers and business firms tend to expect continuing inflation and put in place programs to protect themselves against it. Workers insist on higher wages to compensate for expected inflation. Business firms insist on higher prices to compensate for expected cost increases. The effect of both is to create the inflation workers and businesses expect.

Expectations inflation can occur when there is unemployment and unused productive capacity. It can even intensify these problems, when higher wages discourage hiring and higher prices discourage consumer spending.

Controlling Aggregate-Supply Inflation

What policies may be effective for controlling aggregate-supply inflation? In general, such policies must reduce costs of production and push *AS* down to the right.

1. Stabilizing Income Shares

If aggregate-supply inflation results from rising wage costs, policies might be put in place to balance the income demands of workers, along with the income demands of suppliers of other resources: land, capital, and entrepreneurship. One such effort was the Wage Guideposts of the Kennedy administration. The Kennedy guideposts were intended to hold down wage demands and preserve the existing relationships among income shares. Wages were allowed to rise only as much as average gains in productivity (3.2 percent). Price increases were allowed only in industries where productivity had grown more slowly than the national average. In industries where productivity had grown faster than the national average, it was expected that prices would fall.

Policymakers experimented with wage and price controls again during President Nixon's administration in the early 1970s. Aggregate-supply inflation moderated somewhat during the Nixon wage-price controls, but there was a "bulge" in prices after controls were lifted. Then in 1973, Arab oil-producing nations decided to raise the price of oil exports, causing the worst aggregate-supply inflation our nation has experienced in recent decades. Presidents Ford and Carter introduced voluntary wage-price controls in an attempt to deal with the inflation that followed the oil price increases.

2. Increasing Productivity

Increasing the growth of resource productivity is another way to reduce aggregate-supply inflation. During the Kennedy administration, programs were begun to encourage business firms to invest in productivity-enhancing equipment. Firms were allowed a tax credit to help pay for new equipment, and they were allowed to deduct larger amounts from taxable income for depreciation of old equipment. Government loans, public works projects, and technical assistance programs encouraged the use of modern equipment and new technologies in depressed regions of the country.

Efforts were also made to increase productivity by increasing the quality of labor. The Manpower Development and Training Act, Job Corps, Neighborhood Youth Corps, and Adult Work programs provided funds for programs to increase labor skills. Many disadvantaged and unskilled workers were retrained. Such programs are costly however. In more recent government programs, on-the-job training in private business firms has received greater emphasis.

3. Limiting Market Power

If aggregate-supply inflation results from administered prices, controlling it might call for breaking up the large firms that practice it. Large manufacturing firms whose price-setting policies add to inflation would have to be separated into smaller enterprises, or their pricing policies would have to be regulated by a public commission. Neither approach is very satisfactory.

Breaking up large firms could sacrifice the benefits of large-scale, low-cost production. Also, large firms may be better equipped than small firms to conduct research and apply new technologies. Regulatory commissions are costly and often poorly prepared for making policy decisions in a complex manufacturing environment.

Nevertheless, the Antitrust Division of the Justice Department, the Federal Trade Commission, and the federal courts in various states continue to monitor the price-setting policies of some highly concentrated industries.

4. Deregulating Industry

Today, economic regulation is fading away and is no longer a major source of cost-push inflation. Once it seemed necessary to protect small firms so that a monopoly could not achive total control over an industry and raise prices. Lately, technological changes and economic growth have increased competition in many industries, so that economic regulation may no longer be necessary.

Social regulation continues to be blamed for aggregate-supply inflation. Some economists worry that social regulation has not only increased firms' costs of production but has also increased business risks, discouraged new capital investment, and slowed productivity growth. Aside from these harmful effects, however, social regulation also yields benefits that our society values and for which citizens are willing to pay; some obvious examples are healthier working conditions and cleaner air and water. Still, it is important to weigh these and other benefits against their costs and to impose social regulations only to the point that the benefits gained clearly justify the costs paid.

In order to do this, Congress has mandated a new benefit-cost approach to social regulation. Social regulatory agencies are now required to estimate the benefits of every proposed regulation and compare the benefits with all the costs: the enforcement costs paid by government, the compliance costs paid by business, and the long-term economic costs that the society pays in the form of reduced investment and lower productivity growth. Making such calculations is difficult and imprecise, but considering benefits along with costs should increase the efficiency of social regulation and reduce its inflationary effects.

5. Changing Expectations

To correct expectations inflation, it is necessary to change expectations, but this is not an easy—or painless—task.

Changing expectations of inflation requires a firm commitment, first, to hold down money growth and government spending and, second, to maintain tax rates at a level that discourages consumer spending. Several years of such policies may be required to convince workers and business firms that prices will not be permitted to rise. In the meantime, unemployment may remain high, and economic activity may slow to recessionary levels.

Contemporary Thinking About Economic Issues

CURING INFLATION

Martin Spechler believes there are two ways to cure big inflations—neither of them very pleasant.

In Latin America and Eastern Europe, big inflations have been cured by authoritarian governments, with a strengthened police force to suppress unions and compel workers to accept painful cuts in living standards. In Western Europe and the United States, curing inflation has required similar pain, but individual liberties have generally not been threatened.

The most dramatic inflations of Western Europe have been associated with war. War destroys production and transportation facilities, depletes the labor force, and breaks apart traditional social and economic ties. Thus, war leads to shortages, hoarding, and loss of confidence in national currencies. Prices rise so fast that people resort to barter, with all the inconveniences barter brings.

After World War I, inflation in Germany reduced the value of the German mark to 4.2 trillion marks to the dollar; in Austria the crown fell to 71,060 crowns per dollar; in France the franc fell to 200 per dollar. In all these countries, curing inflation required high interest rates and tight controls on credit, tax increases and decreases in government subsidies, high unemployment and business failures. After World War II, curing inflation in Germany and Italy was helped by foreign loans, which enabled these countries to import needed materials for rebuilding their war-torn industries. In both these countries, fears of a Communist takeover contributed to strong citizen support for policies to cut spending. What are the lessons from these experiences?

Big inflations cannot be stopped by half-hearted means. In fact, programs to slow spending *gradually* may make inflation worse, since failure to accomplish their objectives reduces their credibility and forfeits public support. Strong measures are needed, even though the effect of strong measures is to hold living standards down. Moreover, the necessary result of strong measures is to increase the share of profits at the expense of wages. The transfer of wealth to the capitalists makes possible new investment, which will ultimately increase productive capacity and restore economic growth.

Our democratic society depends on citizen involvement and cooperation to achieve results that benefit the nation as a whole. Citizen support of painful policies to reduce inflation has helped us avoid the authoritarian measures that have been necessary in other nations.

Martin C. Spechler, "Big Inflations Need Potent Cures," *Challenge*, November/December 1986.

Self-Check

1. **Trade will adjust the balance between money and goods:**
   a. If nations restrict the flow of money over their borders.
   b. As money flows into nations experiencing inflation.
   c. If democratic governments carry on large spending programs.
   d. Helping to achieve price stability.
   e. If consumers buy from high-price producers.

2. **Inflation is hardest on:**
   a. Persons who borrow money to be repaid in future years.
   b. Persons who hoard basic commodities.
   c. Fixed-income recipients and retired persons.
   d. Workers with cost-of-living clauses in wage contracts.
   e. The federal government, whose tax revenues tend to decline.

3. **The main cause of aggregate-demand inflation is:**
   a. Excessive production of goods and services.
   b. Heavy sales of government securities to the public.
   c. Excessive saving by consumers.
   d. A high level of total spending relative to available goods and services.
   e. A substantial increase in the productivity of resources.

4. **According to the monetarists, a steady increase in the supply of money should:**
   a. Give politicians more control over monetary policy.
   b. Be in line with the average growth in productive capacity.
   c. Increase spending during inflation.
   d. Reduce spending during recession.
   e. All of the above.

5. **In order to avoid aggregate-supply inflation, wages must:**
   a. Rise only as much as productivity.
   b. Be distributed equally among wage earners.
   c. Rise faster than the return to owners of capital.
   d. Be taxed at lower rates.
   e. Be controlled by the government.

6. **Concentration in industry:**
   a. Allows monopolistic industries and labor unions to maintain high prices.
   b. May cause high prices even when spending falls.
   c. Permits firms to establish a target rate of return.
   d. Has no simple policy remedy.
   e. All of the above.

Theory in Practice

WINNERS AND LOSERS IN INFLATION—MOSTLY LOSERS!

Inflation shrinks your income and erodes the value of your savings. A 7 percent annual rate of inflation will halve the value of your dollars in about ten years. A 10 percent annual rate will halve the value in only about 7 years. (Divide the rate of inflation into 72. The answer is the number of years before the value of money is cut in half if inflation continues at the same rate. Thus, for a 2 percent annual rate of inflation: $\frac{72}{2}$ = 36 years. This is known as the *rule of 72*.)

TEST YOURSELF

If your income *increases* in value at the rate of 5 percent a year, estimate the number of years before it will *double* in value.

In 1982, per capita income in the United States was $9990 after taxes; in 1992 it was $16,850, an impressive increase. When the 1992 figure is corrected for inflation and translated into 1982 dollars, however, it is worth only $11,490. About one-third of the apparent income gain reflected only higher prices.

Inflation is especially hard on production workers. Weekly earnings of production workers averaged $300 in 1978. By 1992 weekly earnings had risen to $335, but in real terms weekly earnings had actually fallen by more than $40. Without cost-of-living clauses in wage contracts, workers are relatively helpless against inflation.

Savers don't fare much better in inflation. Savers who bought the safest government securities earned about 7 percent annually during the inflationary 1970s. How much were their savings worth? During the decade, inflation reduced the value of the dollar by more than 10 percent per year. This means that many savers saw their wealth eroded by inflation. To make matters worse, savers had to pay income taxes on their interest earnings in addition to their losses to inflation.

Who does gain from inflation? Borrowers gain from inflation, and the biggest borrower is government. With inflation, government can redeem its securities with dollars that are worth less than the dollars it initially borrowed. Thus, inflation channels more of the nation's resources away from production for private purposes and into government programs: social programs, public works, and defense.

Is this what we want? Whatever we decide, we may discover that controlling inflation requires some political decisions as well as economic ones.

Look at Figure 11.3 for a record of inflation over recent decades.

Figure 11.3 Annual Inflation

The most recent period of low and stable inflation occurred in the early 1960s. The Vietnam War of the late 1960s and early 1970s brought aggregate demand inflation, and the oil price increases of 1973 and 1979 brought aggregate supply inflation. Recessions have often brought declining rates of inflation: 1975, 1981-1982, and 1991. Paul Volcker's tenure as chairman of the Federal Reserve Board (1979-1987) brought the greatest drop in inflation in the period shown.

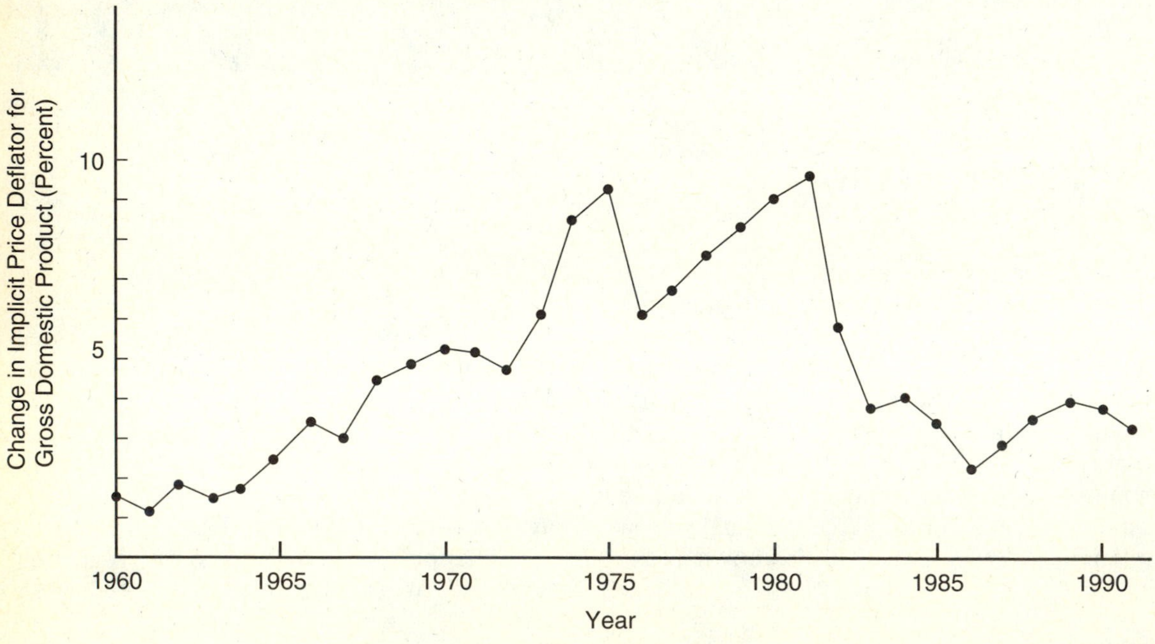

WAGE-PRICE CONTROLS

A politically acceptable and widely debated anti-inflationary tactic has been wage-price controls. (The popular expectation is that your wages are controlled but not necessarily mine; prices I pay are controlled but not necessarily the prices I receive.) Most economists oppose price controls except occasionally as a means of ending inflationary expectations. Recent experience with wage-price controls illustrates some of their advantages and disadvantages.

The Vietnam War required increased government spending for goods and services to fight the war. Without tax increases to reduce civilian spending, aggregate demand shifted far to the right. The Federal Reserve was obliged to use strongly contractionary monetary policy to slow inflation.

By 1971, the shortage of money had pushed the economy into recession. Unemployment was more than 5 percent, and real GDP was declining. Expansionary fiscal policy might have boosted economic activity, but fears of again setting off inflation stood in the way. Finally, President Nixon and the Federal Reserve agreed on a package of policies that included expansionary fiscal and monetary policies, along with a temporary wage-price "freeze."

Except for farm prices, which were not controlled by the freeze, wage and price inflation did slow considerably; the consumer price index rose only 1.9 percent and wages 3.1 percent. After controls were lifted, there was a slight "bulge" in prices, but then the rate of wage and price increase settled down to a rate that was lower than before the freeze.

In the late summer of 1973 inflation heated up again. New price controls were put into effect for sixty days, and for the next decade annual price increases averaged 8 percent.

How successful were wage-price controls? Probably the greatest success of controls came at the very beginning when there was idle productive capacity in the economy. With idle productive capacity, expansionary monetary and fiscal policy could cause spending to increase without causing inflation. Furthermore, at the beginning of controls, public expectations of lower inflation probably reduced workers' demands for higher wages and business firms' for higher prices.

Unfortunately, wage-price controls also create shortages, which lead ultimately to price increases. Farmers who are unable to cover their costs of production at controlled prices may slaughter baby chicks, rather than raise them to maturity and suffer a loss. Business firms that are unable to earn an acceptable profit at controlled prices may eliminate entire product lines. When price controls cause shortages, black markets often develop, charging much higher prices and distributing scarce goods in ways that may be thought inequitable.

The main problem with wage-price controls comes when they are lifted. After controls, business firms worry about another price freeze and rush to increase their prices. Likewise, labor unions insist on catch-up wage increases.

Wage-price controls can have other effects in the long run. Remember that free markets depend on flexible prices to act as signals of changes in resource supplies and consumer demand. Price signals guide buyers and sellers to adjust to changing market conditions. For example, high prices for beef should guide farmers to increase beef production, which should help to bring beef prices down. High wages for auto mechanics should guide more workers to learn these skills, which should help to bring wages down. Price controls interfere with these kinds of adjustments, they prolong shortages of goods and resources, and they make the ultimate price increases even greater. Under a free market system, improved resource availability and new advances in technology may be expected to reduce costs of production in many industries; but when firms are afraid of price controls, they will hesitate to pass such cost savings on to consumers.

Price controls may reduce inflation in highly concentrated industries, but there may also be undesirable side effects. In steel production, for example, President Kennedy used the pressure of his office to hold down price increases in the 1960s. He believed that low steel prices would hold down production costs in the many industries using steel, thus moderating price increases for automobiles, appliances, and building materials. He did not realize that low steel prices would also reduce profits in the steel industry and discourage new investment. One result of low profits in the steel industry was a failure to advance technologically and, ultimately, even higher prices for steel.

INDEXING

We have attributed many of the harmful effects of inflation to expectations of future inflation. Workers and business firms insist on wage and price increases high enough to compensate for expected inflation; lenders insist on interest rates high enough to compensate for expected inflation. Their expectations help bring about the inflation they expect.

Economist Milton Friedman has proposed to correct the problem of inflationary expectations through a process called indexing. **Indexing** would establish a cost-of-living correction, to be added to all incomes. With indexing, all wages, rent, and interest payments would be adjusted upward in line with changes in the general price level. Thus, indexing would keep real incomes from falling with inflation. Milton Friedman believes that ensuring all groups against a loss of purchasing power through inflation would help hold down their wage and price demands.

With indexing, cost-of-living (or "escalator") clauses would be written into all labor contracts, guaranteeing wage earners a fair increase in incomes. Interest rates on loans would vary with the rate of inflation, too. Lenders would be more willing to make loans to home builders and other businesses if they were assured a return high enough to offset inflation. The hope is that indexing would correct the distortions that inflation sometimes creates in the distribution of income.

There are disadvantages, of course. Perhaps the most serious disadvantage of indexing is its effect on the government budget. Indexing adjusts tax brackets, tax credits, and tax rates so that income tax revenues do not increase automatically with inflation. At the same time, indexing adjusts government's transfer payments upward, worsening a tendency toward government deficits.

By maintaining stable income shares, indexing also reduces the ability of the price system to allocate resources efficiently and to reward increased productivity. And finally, protecting all income earners against inflation probably reduces their will to fight against inflation. The result could be wildly accelerating prices, with severe national and international consequences.

SUMMARY

1. Inflation is a continuing increase in the general price level. The difficulty of keeping spending in balance with total output of goods and services may lead to changing prices, usually in the upward direction.
2. An excess of money in one region will tend to cause the price level to rise. If there is free trade, consumers will spend in other, lower-priced regions, causing money to flow out and eventually bringing the supply of money into balance with the supply of goods. However, modern nations have erected international barriers and established domestic economic pro-

grams that interfere with automatic adjustment processes.

3. Aggregate-demand or demand-pull inflation results from an excess of spending by consumers, business firms, and/or government. Spending over and above the nation's productive capacity may be prevented by increasing taxes on consumers and business firms, reducing government spending, or restricting the supply of money for loans.
4. Aggregate-supply or cost-push inflation results from increases in the costs of production. Higher costs of production are passed on to consumers in the form of higher prices for finished goods. To avoid inflation, wages must not rise faster than labor's productivity.
5. Administered pricing may occur in highly concentrated industries in which firms agree among themselves not to reduce prices. The problem of administered pricing may worsen in the coming years because of the large capital requirements of modern manufacturing and the difficulty of maintaining price competition among large firms.
6. Government regulatory policies may add to costs of production and keep prices higher than free-market prices; however, there are some benefits associated with regulation.
7. Inflation imposes particular burdens on savers, the aged, and people on fixed incomes. It creates distortions that may be damaging to our entire society. Some recent programs to deal with inflation are wage-price controls and indexing.

TERMS TO REMEMBER

inflation: an increase in the general price level

aggregate-demand or demand-pull inflation: inflation that results from excess spending, over and above the capacity to produce goods and services

aggregate-supply or cost-push inflation: inflation that results from increasing costs of production

administered prices: prices established by tacit agreement among large firms in concentrated industries

expectations inflation: inflation that results from workers' and businesses' efforts to protect themselves from expected inflation

indexing: automatic changes in incomes and tax rates to compensate for changes in the general price level

TOPICS FOR DISCUSSION

1. Explain the following expressions and discuss the implications of each for price stability:

   Hoarding
   Cost-of-living clauses
   Administered prices
   Indexing

2. Is it correct to say that inflation is the cruelest tax? Explain.
3. Some people say that there is a "chicken-and-egg" relationship between the aggregate-demand and aggregate-supply explanations of inflation. What do you think they mean?
4. A successful U.S. businessperson once said, "The best way to prevent higher prices is high prices." Explain.
5. The 1978–1979 inflation was worsened by lagging productivity growth throughout the U.S. economy. Over the two years the United States experienced a 0.6 percent decrease in output per labor hour. Over the same period, wages rose 18.3 percent. Price increases of 16.2 percent eroded the value of the higher wages and complicated the fight against inflation. Workers claimed their pay was worth less, and employers complained about falling labor productivity. What are the political implications of this kind of problem for policymakers? Do you see any ways to resolve the impasse? What ultimate results would you predict?
6. Federal Reserve Chairperson Alan Greenspan was once quoted as saying that inflation is primarily a political, not an economic, problem. According to Greenspan, a policymaker's dilemma results from an emphasis on short-term gains at the expense of long-term costs. Comment on Greenspan's assessment of the problem of inflation. Do you agree with his

conclusion? What sugggestions would you make to correct the problem?

7. A letter to the editor of a local newspaper stated: ''Let's put all congressional salaries on a 'reverse' cost-of-living basis. Whenever the cost-of-living index goes up, our senators and representatives would have to take a cut in pay.'' What does the writer believe about the causes of inflation? Evaluate his or her policy prescription.
8. Discuss the major advantages and disadvantages of government regulation.
9. It has been suggested that the United States is more prone to inflation than other industrialized nations because of our many diverse interest groups. How would you explain the relationship?

ANSWERS TO TEST YOURSELF

(p. 251) $(1 - 0.25)(0.10) - 0.08 = -0.005$
$= -\frac{1}{2}$ percent

(p. 261) $72 \div 5 =$ about 14 yrs. before your income doubles.

FURTHER READING

Cardosa, Eliano A., ''Hyperinflation,'' *Challenge*, January/February 1989.

Meeropol, Michael, ''Zero Inflation: Prescription for Recession,'' *Challenge*, January/February 1990.

Poole, William, ''Monetary Policy Lessons of Recent Inflation and Disinflation,'' *Journal of Economic Perspectives*, Summer 1988.

Chapter 12

Unemployment

Tools for Study

LEARNING OBJECTIVES

After reading this chapter, you will be able to:

1. Explain the GDP gap.
2. Define frictional, cyclical, and structural unemployment and discuss some remedies.
3. Discuss the relationship between unemployment and inflation.
4. List the various programs that have been adopted to deal with unemployment.

CURRENT ISSUES FOR DISCUSSION

How can a minimum wage actually harm the workers it is intended to help?

What groups in the population are most subject to unemployment?

What are the most favorable employment opportunities for the 1990s?

The Classical economists believed that free markets would make unemployment only a minor, short-term problem. In a free market system, they said, resource markets would operate smoothly and competitively just like product markets. Business firms would enter the market to demand labor resources, and workers would offer to supply labor to business firms. The result would be an equilibrium price, or wage, and a quantity of employment that would clear the market.

The Classical theory of labor markets is shown graphically on Figure 12.1. With the demand for labor shown by D_1, the equilibrium wage rate is \$6 per hour, and employment is 200,000 workers.

Now suppose total spending in the economy falls and the demand for workers falls. The labor demand curve shifts to the left, shown as D_2 on the figure. At the old wage of \$6 per hour, the quantity of workers demanded is now only about 125,000, while the quantity supplied is still 200,000. With a surplus in the labor market, some workers would be unemployed. But in a free market, surplus workers would compete for the available jobs, causing the wage rate to fall to a new lower equilibrium wage of \$5. Once again, the market is cleared. At \$5 per hour, 150,000 workers supply labor and 150,000 workers are demanded by business firms. All workers who want to work for the going wage are employed. Thus, free markets ensure the necessary wage adjustments that eliminate unemployment.

The Classical economists went a step further. They concluded that the lower wage rate

Figure 12.1 Wage and Employment Adjustments in a Free Labor Market

In a free market a decrease in demand for labor would cause the equilibrium wage to fall.

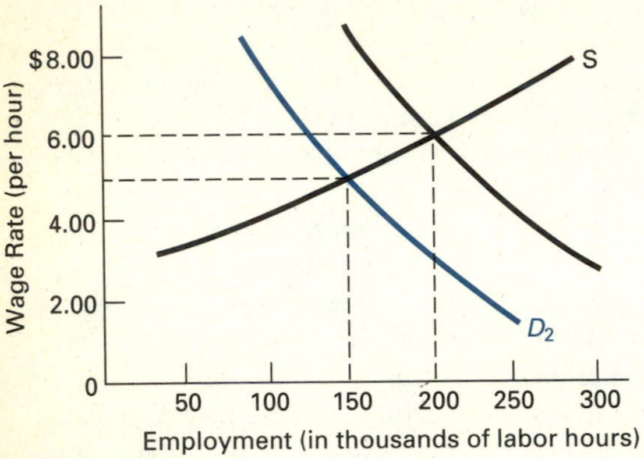

would not necessarily mean a lower standard of living for workers. Because goods and services would be produced at lower labor costs, they would sell for lower prices. Thus, worker's real wages would not fall as much as their money wages.

Classical labor market theory depended on competition for these smooth adjustments to take place. Wages would have to be flexible enough to rise or fall in response to changes in the demand for labor. In periods of slack demand, for example, competition would force surplus workers to work for lower wages. In periods of excess demand, competition would force employers to offer higher wages. Unemployment would be only temporary. Wages and prices would rise and fall together, and real wages would depend on the productivity of the economic system.

Classical theory may have more correctly described economic conditions of the past than those of a modern economy. Modern economic development has brought changes that interfere with the smooth adjustments of free markets. Today, employers and workers organize into groups to fix wages and prices, thus weakening competition. Without wage and price flexibility, a drop in demand for labor creates unemployment.

Prolonged unemployment can bring hardships to particular regions of the country.* Regions with substantial unemployment often suffer social unrest, high crime rates, and environmental decay. For individuals, unemployment often means lower material standards of living, emotional distress, and—even more damaging—the loss of skills and motivation that comes with idleness.

MEASURING UNEMPLOYMENT

Failing to employ resources productively has long-range and short-range effects—economic, social, and perhaps even political. It is impossible to measure all the harmful effects of unemployment, but some of the material costs can be estimated.

The GDP Gap and the "Natural" Rate of Unemployment

Do you remember our discussion of the economic problem? The economic problem describes the scarcity of productive resources and the vastness of wants. Thus, the economic problem requires us to use our available resources efficiently; otherwise, fewer of our unlimited wants will be satisfied. Fewer homes will be built, dental services performed, or consumer goods produced.

When resources are unemployed, we say there is a GDP gap. The **GDP gap** is the difference between potential GDP and actual GDP. It represents the sacrifice of goods and services we might have had if all resources had been fully employed. During the recession of

* Examples are Appalachia in the 1960s, Detroit in the 1980s, and south central Los Angeles in the 1990s.

1990–1991, the estimated GDP gap was more than $200 billion worth of goods and services not produced. The saddest aspect of unemployment is that the loss of labor resources can never be recovered. Coal not produced this year can be mined in the next. Trees not cut remain for cutting some time in the future. But hours of work not used today are gone forever.

The GDP gap is shown on Figure 12.2 as the difference between actual GDP and potential GDP. Actual GDP is defined where aggregate demand (*AD*) is equal to aggregate supply (*AS*). That is the quantity of output that precisely satisfies the spending plans of consumers, business firms, governments, and foreign buyers (net). Potential GDP is defined in terms of aggregate supply, at the quantity of output where the AS curve turns upward. The upward slope begins when shortages of resources begin to push resource prices up.

We might describe the unemployment that occurs at potential GDP as the **natural rate of unemployment**. It is the level of unemployment at which resources are available for producing output without adding inflationary pressures.

Figure 12.2 The GDP Gap

The GDP gap is the difference between actual GDP and potential GDP. The level of unemployment at potential GDP may be called the "natural rate" of unemployment.

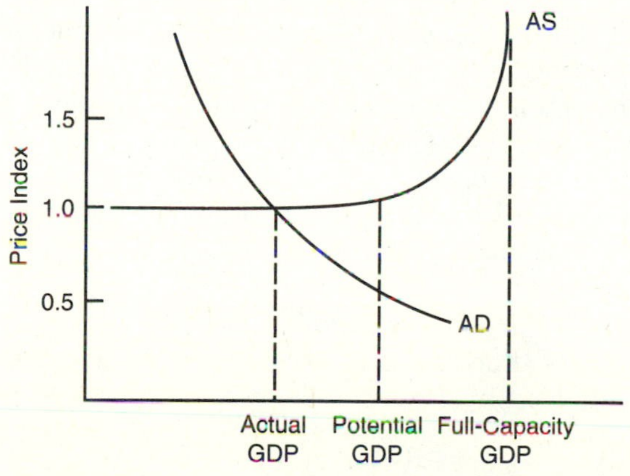

Notice that the natural rate of unemployment does not coincide with the economy's full productive capacity. Full capacity occurs where the *AS* curve finally becomes vertical. At this quantity of output no further production is possible, and the potential for inflation is great. Avoiding such severe inflation requires some level of unemployment.

What level of unemployment is "natural" and desirable? To answer that question we must first define unemployment and describe the groups that are affected by it.

The Unemployment Rate

The most direct measure of unemployment is the unemployment rate. The unemployment rate is estimated by the Department of Labor and expressed as the percentage of the labor force not currently employed.

The **labor force** includes all people sixteen years of age or older, not in school or other institutions, who are employed or who are unemployed but actively seeking work. Persons are counted as employed if they did any work for pay or profit during a given week, regardless of the amount. Persons who worked in a family business for fifteen hours or more during the week are also counted as employed, whether or not they received pay. Persons are counted as unemployed if they were laid off from their latest job or actively sought work within the past thirty days. (Actively seeking work means filling out applications and answering want ads, going to job interviews, or registering with an employment agency.)

The estimated unemployment rate tends to be understated, particularly during periods of high unemployment. A person who would like a full-time job but can find a job working only ten hours per week is counted as employed, as is a person who is working at a job that is beneath his or her full capacity. These workers are considered to be employed, but more correctly they should be considered "underemployed" and included in the unemployment rate. Finally, workers who have stopped looking for work out of discouragement or failure to find a job are not included among the unemployed.*

How can these factors affect the unemployment rate? Between June and July of 1991 the unemployment rate dropped from 6.9 to 6.8 percent. Over the same period, however, total employment also dropped by 180,000 workers. Apparently, large numbers of workers left the labor force and were not counted as unemployed, so that what seemed to be a decrease in unemployment was really a decrease in the labor force.

POLICIES TO REDUCE UNEMPLOYMENT

The Employment Act of 1946 gave the U.S. government responsibility for establishing policies to achieve the maximum practical level of employment in the nation.

Before deciding on policies for employment, it is necessary to identify the causes of unemployment. Then policymakers can design programs to remedy each type. Economists classify unemployment into three categories, depending on the cause: frictional, cyclical, and structural.

Frictional Unemployment

Some portion of total unemployment is workers unemployed because of "frictions" in the movement of workers from job to job or among workers entering the labor force for the first time.

Frictional unemployment is common in a growing economy and reflects the healthy expansion and decline of different sectors of the economy. Markets and production techniques are constantly changing to reflect changes in consumer demand. Workers must move out of declining industries and into expanding industries. If there were no frictional unemployment, expanding industries would have to bid up the wages of employed workers, aggravating tendencies toward inflation.

Frictional unemployment is, by definition, temporary. Its effects may be relieved by policies to provide job information and aids to worker mobility. For example, workers can be provided job counseling, or they can be paid grants to finance a move to a new industrial location where jobs are plentiful.

Frictional unemployment is, by definition, temporary. Its effects may be relieved by policies to provide job information and aids to worker mobility. For example, workers can be provided job counseling, or they can be paid grants to finance a move to a new industrial location where jobs are plentiful.

Cyclical Unemployment

A more serious problem than frictional unemployment is **cyclical unemployment**—unemployment associated with cycles of economic activity. The Great Depression provides the best example of cyclical unemployment. During the Great Depression, the unemployment rate reached as high as 25 percent of the labor force.

Typically, economic activity grows in spurts. Periods of growth and prosperity are followed by slower growth or decline. Once

* Discouraged workers constitute what is sometimes called "hidden unemployment."

homes are equipped with all the latest consumer gadgets, demand for consumer goods diminishes. Retailers cut back on inventories and cancel orders to wholesalers. The whole economic system seems to pause before a new round of innovations creates new gadgets, and the cycle begins again.

Cyclical swings in employment are most severe in industries producing durable goods. Purchase of a VCR, microwave oven, or personal computer can be postponed if consumers are worried about their jobs. Cyclical swings are less severe in industries producing nondurable goods and services. Purchases of food, clothing, and health services, for instance, cannot generally be postponed.

In the past, blue-collar production workers were more likely to suffer cyclical unemployment than were white-collar professional or supervisory workers. Professional and supervisory workers have specialized functions and, often, employment contracts that formerly made dismissal difficult. These same workers suffered severely in the recession of 1990–1991, however.

Expansionary fiscal and monetary policy make prolonged cyclical unemployment less a threat to our economic system today than in former years.

Structural Unemployment

The kind of unemployment that is most damaging to our prosperity and social health is the growing problem of structural unemployment. **Structural unemployment** is caused by an imbalance between the structure of the labor force, on the one hand, and the requirements of modern industry, on the other. Unless available labor skills correspond to the needs of business firms, there will be unemployment. In fact, there may be severe unemployment at the same time there are job vacancies. Structural unemployment is worsened by the entry of untrained workers (such as teenagers) into the labor force.

The greatest needs in business today are for skilled workers and for workers in the growing service sector. For example, there are extreme shortages of workers in machine trades, some types of engineering, nursing, and transportation.

Policies to remedy structural unemployment include federal and state programs to train workers in new skills, better job information and counseling, and private on-the-job training.

The "Natural" Rate Again

Having described the categories of unemployed workers, we now can draw some conclusions regarding the level of unemployment that is "natural" and an appropriate goal of economic policy.

Measuring the natural rate of unemployment is impossible, of course. It is impossible to know precisely the maximum quantity of goods and services the nation can produce before shortages of resources begin to push prices up. Moreover, the rate of unemployment that is natural at one point in time may not be natural in another. Changes in the quality of resources and in technologies of production can affect the noninflationary quantity of output and change the natural rate of unemployment.

In general, however, economists estimate the natural rate of unemployment at about 5 percent to 7 percent. Unemployment less than about 5 percent is likely to create inflationary pressures. Unemployment of 5 percent would include some frictional unemployment and perhaps some temporary structural unemployment as well. Unemployment greater than

Figure 12.3 Unemployment

Recessions generally brought increases in cyclical unemployment: 1954, 1958, 1970, 1975, 1980, 1981–1982, and 1990–1991. Successive recessions have often left unemployment higher than before, which suggests an increase in the natural rate of unemployment. The rising peaks of unemployment suggest an increase in structural unemployment.

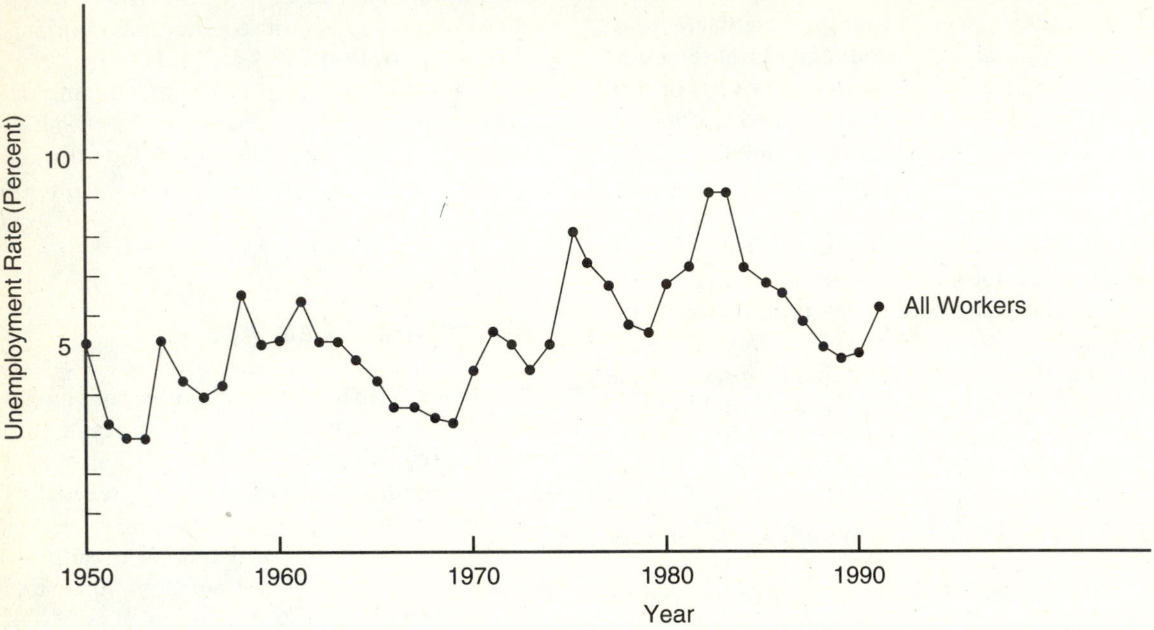

about 7 percent is likely to include cyclical unemployment. This suggests that policies should be designed to maintain unemployment at between 5 percent and 7 percent.

Look at Figure 12.3 for a record of unemployment over recent decades.

HELP FOR UNEMPLOYED WORKERS

The U.S. government has established a number of programs to help unemployed workers. One such program is the national unemployment insurance system, a part of the Social Security Act of 1935. The states administer this program, within federal guidelines. Private nonfarm workers and certain state employees are covered. (Separate programs cover most workers not covered under this plan.)

Unemployment insurance is financed by a tax on employers and is available to persons who have lost their jobs and are actively seeking work. These unemployed persons are normally paid benefits up to a maximum of twenty-six weeks. During periods of high unemployment, emergency legislation may provide additional benefits for up to sixty-five weeks in some states. Funds for additional benefits come from general revenues of the federal government.

Benefits under the unemployment insurance program range from about one-third to two-thirds of a worker's average weekly wage. Some states also provide allowances for children or for a nonworking spouse. Weekly benefits in 1992 averaged about $170.

Some union contracts provide additional private unemployment compensation. United Auto Workers' contracts provide for Supplemental Unemployment Benefits (SUBs) financed by employers. Under combined state and private programs, total compensation for unemployed auto workers amounts to approximately 95 percent of regular earnings. Because unemployment benefits are not taxed, their contribution to workers' purchasing power is greater than the numbers suggest.

In addition to income-maintenance programs, public-service employment programs provide many jobs for the unemployed. The first major program of this kind was the Works Progress Administration (WPA) of the 1930s. During the 1960s, the Neighborhood Youth Corps and Operation Mainstream provided jobs for youths and the elderly, respectively. In the 1970s, the Comprehensive Employment and Training Act (CETA) established training programs, public-service jobs, summer youth programs, and on-the-job training in areas where unemployment was greater than 6.5 percent. In the 1980s the Reagan administration established the Job Training Partnership program, but funds to run the program were cut drastically. In the 1990s President Clinton has proposed still more programs to train workers and provide public-service jobs.

Public-service jobs help workers maintain or improve their skills and help produce useful goods and services. A disadvantage is that public-service jobs sometimes compete for workers with private-sector employers, pushing wages up and aggravating inflation.

UNEMPLOYMENT AND INFLATION

In years past, the levels of unemployment and inflation have tended to move in opposite directions. Increases in aggregate demand have brought increasing price inflation and decreasing unemployment; decreases in aggregate demand have brought decreasing price inflation and increasing unemployment.

The explanation for the behavior of inflation and unemployment has to do with the availability of labor resources. As the economy approaches full productive capacity, fewer workers are available for taking new jobs. If unemployment should fall to zero, employers would have to bid employed workers away from their current employment by offering higher pay. Then higher labor costs would be built into the prices of finished goods, increasing inflation. On the other hand, if unemployment should increase, surplus labor would compete for jobs and their wage rates would tend to fall. Accordingly, the prices of finished goods would fall (or at least fail to increase).

The Phillips Curve

When unemployment and inflation move in opposite directions, we say there is an inverse relationship between the two variables. We illustrate the inverse relationship with a **Phillips curve**, developed by a British economist, A. W. Phillips. A Phillips curve slopes downward, in keeping with the typical inverse relationship between the variables. The Phillips curve in Figure 12.4 includes points that combine rates of unemployment and inflation in the United States for the years 1950–1991. For the years 1950–1969, the relationship between unemployment and inflation was inverse, as expected.

When unemployment and inflation move in opposite directions, an economy may lie within the following ranges on the curve:

1. High inflation with low unemployment (e.g., 1951).
2. High unemployment with virtual price stability, that is, almost zero inflation (e.g., 1961).
3. Moderate inflation with moderate unemployment (e.g., 1957).

Our democratic society has tended to favor the third alternative, which imposes fewer hardships on the population as a whole. As a result, most of the points on Figure 12.4 cluster around the center of the Phillips curve. Whenever economic conditions began to move toward either of the extremes, (1) or (2), monetary and fiscal policy have been used to push the economy back toward the center.

Figure 12.4 A Phillips Curve

The Phillips curve shows the historical relationship between inflation and unemployment. In the past, as unemployment increased, price inflation tended to fall. In the 1970s and early 1980s, high levels of unemployment were associated with high levels of inflation.

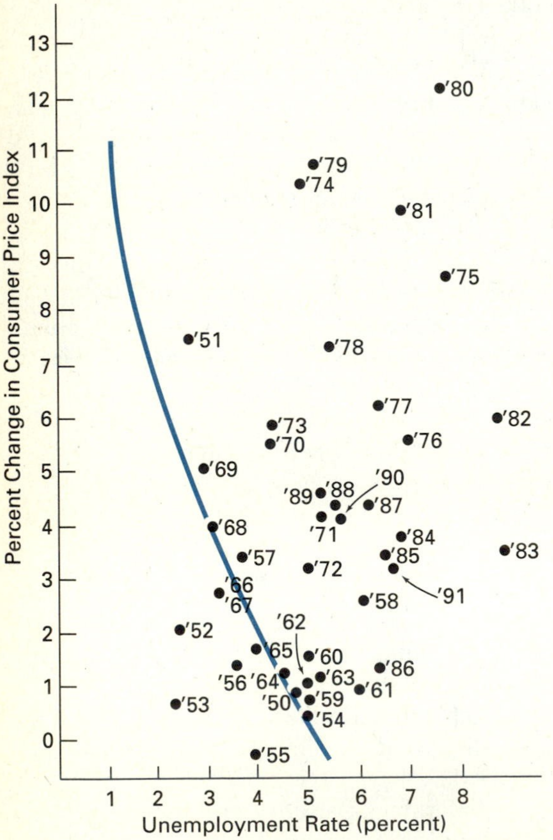

TEST YOURSELF
In what range of the curve is it appropriate to use expansionary policies? In what range are contractionary policies appropriate?

Stagflation

For the years 1970 through 1983, the U.S. economy experienced a fourth alternative position on the Phillips curve:

4. Excessive inflation and excessive unemployment.

The combination of high inflation and high unemployment is represented by points drawn far to the right of the historic Phillips curve.

Some economists coined a new word to describe the combination of stagnant employment with high inflation: stagflation. Stagflation is difficult to correct through monetary and fiscal policies. Expansionary policies to reduce unemployment would increase the already severe inflation, and contractionary policies to correct inflation would increase the already severe unemployment.

Three explanations were offered for the stagflation of the 1970s and early 1980s.

Expectations

Some economists blamed the combination of inflation and unemployment on expectations. When employed workers come to expect inflation, they insist on excessive wage increases; higher wage costs, in turn, are reflected in price increases, even when there is no accompanying increase in employment. Likewise, when manufacturers come to expect increases in their costs of production, they mark up the prices of finished goods. Either way, inflation can occur even when there is substantial unemployment.

The theory of rational expectations pro-

Thinking Seriously About Economic Issues

A CURE FOR STAGFLATION

Martin Weitzman believes he has a cure for the combination of unemployment and inflation that economists call stagflation. According to Weitzman, stagflation is a result of the common practice of tying wages to conditions outside the firm: conditions such as the general level of wages or changes in wages and prices. A better plan would be to tie wages to conditions inside the firm: specifically, the firm's own revenues or profits. Tying wages to revenues or profits inside the firm would provide the appropriate incentives to resist unemployment and inflation, and it would do so automatically.

To illustrate his proposal, Weitzman poses an example of General Motors, which hires, say, 500,000 workers at an hourly wage of \$24. The \$24 wage is the wage rate at which the value of the output of the last worker hired is equal to the wage. Total wages are 500,000 × \$24 = \$12,000,000, which represents two-thirds of GM's total revenue of \$18,000,000. Under these conditions, GM's remaining revenue after paying all labor costs is \$6,000,000. Under these conditions also, there is no incentive to hire additional labor, because additional workers would add less to total revenue than the wage rate and reduce GM's profit.

Suppose instead of paying a flat hourly wage GM paid workers two-thirds of the revenue contributed by workers to GM's total revenue: thus, [$\frac{2}{3}$ × \$18,000,000]/500,000 = \$12,000,000/500,000 = \$24. The wage is the same as before; but under these conditions, GM has incentives to increase employment. To understand this, assume GM hires one additional worker and that total revenue rises to \$18,000,024. Paying workers two-thirds of total revenue yields an average wage of [$\frac{2}{3}$(\$18,000,024]/500,001 = \$23.999984. The total wage bill increases to \$12,000,016, and GM's profit increases to \$18,000,024 − 12,000,016 = \$6,000,008.

Under these conditions, GM would be encouraged to add workers until all qualified workers have jobs. Adding workers would also have the effect of increasing output at constant prices. In fact, GM would have no incentive to increase prices, because only one-third of any price increase would be added to profit. (Two-thirds would go to labor.)

Weitzman proposes a more practical arrangement in which workers would be paid a base wage plus a percentage of the firm's total revenue. He concludes that paying workers according to production would enable the nation to overcome its persistent unemployment problem and hold down inflation, too.

Martin L. Weitzman, *The Share Economy: Conquering Stagflation*, Harvard University Press, Cambridge, Mass., 1984.

vides a more detailed explanation of simultaneous inflation and unemployment. Remember that the rational expectations of workers and employers can cause them to expect expansionary fiscal and monetary policies that stimulate employment and increase inflationary pressures. With these kinds of expectations, wages and prices tend to rise even when employment and production are falling.

Structural Changes

Another explanation for stagflation focused on structural changes in the U.S. economy. Advancing technology has changed the type of labor needed in production, but our labor force has been slow to adapt its skills to these changing needs. The result has been rising unemployment at the same time that many jobs remain unfilled.

Some economists believe that the "natural" rate of unemployment will prevail regardless of government's monetary and fiscal policies. The natural rate of unemployment includes workers whose skills are inappropriate for filling the available jobs, as well as workers who are classified as "frictionally unemployed." If the natural rate of unemployment is between 5 percent and 7 percent, the Phillips curve should become vertical at this level of unemployment. (Notice that many of the recent points on Figure 12.4 do lie in a roughly vertical line at between 5 percent and 7 percent.) The result of a vertical Phillips curve is that expansionary monetary and fiscal policies increase inflation without reducing unemployment.

Other Factors

Financial conditions may also have caused the stagflation shown on Figure 12.4: the availability of unemployment insurance and other income-support programs; the increased wealth of the labor force; and the availability of consumer credit. All these factors allow workers to maintain their standards of living even while unemployed. Their job search may not be as vigorous as in years past; thus periods of unemployment may tend to last longer. Also, because these financial factors allow consumer spending to remain fairly stable, demand for goods and services remains strong in recession and adds to inflationary pressures.

Self-Check

1. **The Classical economists believed that:**
   a. Wages would fall when the demand for labor falls.
   b. At lower wages, labor would be fully employed.
   c. Competition would make wages and prices flexible.
   d. Lower wage rates would not necessarily mean lower living standards.
   e. All of the above.

2. **Which of the following is not generally a result of unemployment?**
   a. Development of new skills during leisure hours.
   b. High crime rates and social unrest.
   c. Loss of material production.
   d. Lower standards of living.
   e. Emotional distress.

3. **Which of the following types of unemployment seems most difficult to correct?**
   a. Frictional unemployment.
   b. Cyclical unemployment.
   c. Structural unemployment.
   d. Phillips unemployment.
   e. All can be corrected with expansionary fiscal and monetary policy.

4. **Public-service employment has all but which of the following advantages?**
   a. Producing generally useful output.
   b. Helping maintain worker skills.
   c. Not competing with the private demand for workers.
   d. Providing on-the-job training for youths.
   e. Providing spending power for workers who would otherwise be unemployed.

5. **Expectations can affect unemployment by:**
   a. Increasing hiring when wages are expected to rise.
   b. Increasing wage demands when prices are expected to rise.
   c. Increasing prices when wages are expected to rise.
   d. Reducing hiring when wages are expected to rise.
   e. (b), (c), and (d).

6. **A Phillips curve shows the relationship between:**
   a. Employment and prices.
   b. Labor force and unemployment.
   c. Labor force and prices.
   d. Unemployment and prices.
   e. Economic growth and prices.

Theory in Practice

THE MINIMUM WAGE DILEMMA

The purpose of a minimum wage law is to increase the incomes of low-income workers. A legally enforced minimum wage acts like a price floor to keep wages from falling below the legal minimum.

The first legal minimum wage was established in 1938, with a minimum of 25 cents per hour for certain employees. In 1989, Congress increased the minimum wage from the 1981 level of $3.35 to $3.80, with a further increase to $4.25 in 1991. Small businesses are exempt from the minimum wage law.

The result of the increase in the minimum wage was expected to be:

1. Pay raises totaling several billion dollars to workers receiving less than the minimum, and additional pay increases to higher-paid workers (so as to preserve customary wage differentials).
2. Higher prices, particularly in labor-intensive retail and service industries.
3. Higher property taxes, a result of the rising cost of hiring workers for jobs in local government.

Although the goal of the minimum wage is to increase incomes, the frequent result is to increase unemployment. Remember that firms hire workers only up to the point at which the value of the output of the last worker is equal to the cost of hiring him or her. When wages are set higher than the equilibrium wage, employers move up their labor demand curves and hire fewer workers.

Figure 12.5 shows the market for a certain type of unskilled labor. In a free market, the equilibrium wage is $2.00 per hour, at which 750 million hours of labor are demanded and supplied. How many hours are demanded and supplied at a government-imposed minimum of $4.25?

The employment effects of the minimum wage are probably hardest on workers who are least able to find other jobs. Consider the market for unskilled workers and teenagers. Because employers can generally find substitutes for such workers, demand for these workers is relatively elastic. When wages rise, employment falls sharply for unskilled workers and teenagers.

Figure 12.5 Effects of a Minimum Wage

A minimum wage has the effect of a price floor. With quantity supplied greater than quantity demanded, there is a surplus of labor at the minimum wage rate. A minimum wage may work against those it is intended to help by reducing the level of employment.

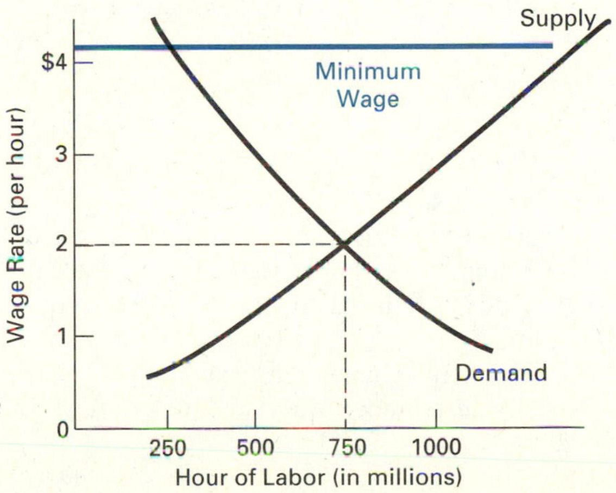

Policymakers face a difficult dilemma. Should there be a minimum wage law if the results include fewer job opportunities for low-skilled workers, higher production costs for labor-intensive industries, and price inflation for many consumer goods? Or should wages be allowed to fall to the free-market level, even though the result might be low earnings for some workers?

WHO ARE THE UNEMPLOYED?

Levels of unemployment differ widely among different groups in the labor force. Unemployment is higher among teenagers than other age groups and higher among blacks than whites. Until the 1980s, unemployment was higher among women than men. Table 12.1 shows unemployment rates broken down into these three categories.

Some groups enter and leave the labor force frequently. Their high job turnover gives them a higher unemployment rate than the national average.* Many teenagers and some

Table 12.1 Unemployment Rates by Age, Race, Sex (1991).

	Unemployment Rate
Whites	6.5
Men, 20 years and over	6.3
Women, 20 years and over	5.4
Teenagers (male)	18.4
Teenagers (female)	15.7
Blacks and other minorities	14.1
Men, 20 years and over	13.4
Women, 20 years and over	11.7
Teenagers (male)	42.0
Teenagers (female)	37.2
Total unemployment rate	7.4

SOURCE: *Economic Report of the President,* 1993.

* High turnover rates for teenagers may reflect the fact that they are changing jobs to achieve work experience and job advancement. If teenagers go directly from one job to another, high turnover may not be a problem.

women, for example, are counted as unemployed if they are seeking a job while working as a student or homemaker. Experienced women, for whom employment is necessary and permanent, have about the same unemployment rate as men. Similarly, teenagers who expect employment to be permanent have lower unemployment rates than students. White-collar workers in clerical or supervisory jobs are less subject to cyclical fluctuations in employment than blue-collar workers.

Unemployment among blacks has been about twice that of whites for many years. However, when only experienced adult workers are considered, unemployment rates are almost the same for both races. Some of the difference that remains may be explained by job discrimination, although fair-employment laws in the states and the Civil Rights Act of 1964 have helped reduce differences resulting from overt discrimination.

A SURPLUS OF LABOR? . . . OR A SHORTAGE OF CAPITAL?

A careful reader of this chapter might think that once and for all we have solved the "economic problem." Remember we began this text by pointing out that every nation faces the problem of scarce resources and unlimited wants. If there is substantial unemployment, might we conclude that we have too many resources?

A more correct conclusion would be that our supply of labor doesn't always match up with other available resources. Labor resources must be used along with capital resources: improved land, buildings, equipment, and inventories. In fact, the average production worker in manufacturing works with invested capital worth more than $50,000. In some manufacturing industries, average invested capital per production worker is much higher: petroleum, $345,000; chemicals, $150,000; tobacco, $115,000. Nonmanufacturing industries like transportation, utilities, finance, real estate, insurance, and mining require still higher levels of capital investment per worker.

The United States has been fortunate in the richness of our resource base. Production and incomes have been high, permitting high levels of saving for investing in capital resources. In the past half-century, real wealth has grown about 2.5 percent a year. Growth in capital resources has been slightly greater than growth in the labor force, providing more capital for each worker every year.

Nevertheless, our need for capital is increasing. New health, safety, and environmental regulations call for more costly capital equipment. Technological change has made some existing plant and equipment obsolete. If we are to employ our expanding work force in productive jobs, new investments must provide the necessary tools and equipment.

Over the years, annual capital investment in the United States has been fairly stable at 16 to 17 percent of GDP. (In the recession of 1991 the percentage dropped to less than 13 percent.) The level of investment spending each year depends on business firms' expectations of profit. When businesses become pessimistic about future profits, investment spending is likely to fall. For example:

1. Recessions and slow growth leave firms with unsold goods and increase the rate of business failures.
2. Rising costs of materials and labor and the persistent threat of price controls reduce business firms' profit expectations.
3. Frequent changes in tax laws increase business uncertainty and discourage investment.

4. New environmental and health regulations threaten to make new equipment obsolete.

In addition to profit expectations, investment spending depends on business costs of borrowing. Borrowing costs rise when interest rates include compensation for expected inflation and when government competes with business borrowers for a limited quantity of funds. Moreover, when savers use their funds to purchase safe, secure assets like raw land, jewels, works of art, and gold, fewer funds are available to finance investment spending. The result is higher borrowing costs and lower investment.

There is no single solution to the problem of insufficient growth of capital resources. A healthy economic climate would probably increase business profit expectations. Greater confidence in government tax and regulatory policies would help, too. Without a substantial revival of private investment spending, the problem of unemployment becomes increasingly a government problem. And government may not have the answer.

EMPLOYMENT OPPORTUNITIES FOR THE FUTURE

Where are the greatest employment opportunities for young people entering the labor force in the 1990s? The demand for workers with particular skills or aptitudes will be high: professionals, technicians, and clerical workers. Openings will grow more slowly in blue-collar fields.

Some service fields such as state and local government, trade, and professional services will also be expanding. Shortages will appear for health personnel, general salespeople, and accountants.

Listed in Table 12.2 are some job categories with expected annual job openings in the

Table 12.2 Projected Annual Job Openings 1986–2000.

Job	*Number of Openings*
Retail, trade, salespeople	85,786
Waiters, waitresses	53,714
Registered nurses	43,714
Building custodians	43,143
General managers and top executives	41,571
Cashiers	41,071
Truck drivers	37,500
General office clerks	33,071
Nurses' aides, orderlies	31,000
Stenographers, secretaries	30,286
Guards	27,357
Accountants	26,929
Computer programmers	23,857
Food preparation workers	23,143
Financial managers	21,560
Elementary-school teachers	21,357
Receptionists	20,143
Computer systems analysts	17,929
Cooks, chefs	17,071
Practical nurses	17,000
Maintenance repairers	16,500
First-line supervisors and managers	14,643
Electrical and electronic engineers	13,643
Lawyers	13,643
Carpenters	13,000
Secondary-school teachers	10,857
Computer operators	8,857
Social workers	8,571
Medical assistants	8,500
Radiologic technologists and technicians	5,357
Welders	−1,000
Private household workers	−2,714
Sewing machine operators	−6,571
Typists	−10,000
Farm workers	−13,571

SOURCE: *Statistical Abstract*, 1989.

Viewpoint

A FOUR-DAY WORKWEEK?

We have characterized our most severe unemployment problems as cyclical and structural. In practice, it may be difficult to separate precisely these types of unemployed persons. On the down side of the business cycle when production starts to fall, the first workers to lose their jobs are often blacks, teenagers, and women. Whereas this kind of unemployment would be described as cyclical, these workers are the ones who are also most subject to structural unemployment.

What is the best way to help cyclically/structurally unemployed workers?

Some labor unions believe they have the answer. A new proposal being tested in some firms is a four-day workweek. A shorter workweek spreads the available work over more workers and reduces layoffs. In general, the proposed shorter workweek involves no cut in wages.

A five-day, 40-hour workweek has been the standard in manufacturing since the Fair Labor Standards Act was passed in the 1930s. In recent years, some firms have been experimenting with four 10-hour days as a means of reducing employee transportation costs. Other firms have cut hours to 32, with the hope that improved employee morale would bring on increased productivity. In many cases, this has not happened. In fact, labor costs have risen and forced up the prices of finished goods. Higher labor costs are the most serious disadvantage of a shorter workweek.

The United Auto Workers union was the first to sign a contract that comes close to a four-day workweek. Because spending for autos drops sharply in a business recession, auto workers are often the victims of cyclical/structural unemployment. In 1977 the United Auto Workers' contract provided for more than forty paid vacation days a year, a major step toward the four-day week.

In general, business firms resist such a change. To establish the four-day standard throughout the economy would require a new labor law, not likely in the near future.

1990s. The projections are taken from a survey by the U.S. Department of Labor.

SUMMARY

1. According to the Classical economists, in a competitive market system unemployment would be only temporary. Wages would rise and fall with changes in the demand for and supply of labor, and all those willing to work at the equilibrium wage would be hired. Prices would fluctuate, too, so that real wages would not change as much as money wages.
2. Organized groups of employers and workers can interfere with the smooth adjustments under the market system. The result has been periods of unemployment with the sacrifice of goods and services that might have been pro-

duced. The loss of production from unemployment is called the GDP gap.

3. Frictional unemployment is a normal result of temporary idleness while changing jobs. Frictional unemployment may be relieved by policies to provide job information and to ease mobility into new types of employment.
4. Cyclical unemployment is associated with a decline in total spending. It is especially severe in industries producing durable goods, whose purchase can be postponed. Cyclical unemployment is treated by expansionary monetary and fiscal policies to stimulate total spending.
5. Structural unemployment results from an imbalance between the skills of the labor force and the jobs available in modern industry. Structural unemployment may be relieved by job counseling and training.
6. In recent years the problem of unemployment has worsened and has often been accompanied by inflation. The usual inverse relationship between unemployment and inflation is shown by the Phillips curve. Changing conditions within the economic system may have increased the levels of unemployment associated with every level of inflation.
7. Unemployment rates differ among different groups of workers. In general, however, experienced workers in their peak years of productivity have about the same rate of unemployment. Women and teenagers may enter and leave the labor force more often and thus experience higher rates of unemployment. Blacks may suffer higher unemployment as a result of past discrimination.
8. Unemployment insurance helps workers maintain a moderate standard of living even while unemployed. Public-service employment provides jobs for the unemployed through the federal government. If we are to provide jobs for an expanding labor force, the nation's capital stock must grow.

TERMS TO REMEMBER

GDP gap: the difference between actual production of goods and services and those that would have been produced at full employment

natural rate of unemployment: the rate of unemployment at which resources are available for producing output without adding to inflationary pressures

labor force: all people aged 16 and over who are currently employed or who are unemployed but actively seeking employment

frictional unemployment: unemployment caused by the movement of workers from job to job or the movement of new workers into the labor force; frictional unemployment is considered normal and desirable

cyclical unemployment: unemployment caused by a decline in economic activity with a drop in total spending; it is treated with expansionary fiscal and monetary policy

structural unemployment: unemployment caused by an imbalance between the structure of the labor force and the requirements of modern industry; it is treated with job training and counseling

Phillips curve: a graph showing the inverse relationship between price inflation and unemployment in years past

TOPICS FOR DISCUSSION

1. Define the following terms and discuss how each is involved in the problem of unemployment:

   GDP gap
   Phillips curve
   "natural" rate of unemployment

2. Distinguish clearly among the three categories of unemployment and describe the types of policies designed to remedy each.
3. Under the Comprehensive Employment and Training Act of 1974, the federal government pumped millions of dollars into state and local programs for public-service employment. Thousands of new jobs were created for unemployed workers, veterans, and welfare recipients. Jobs were in public schools, libraries, parks, hospitals, and fire and police departments. Workers were given on-the-job training in skills that would help them eventu-

ally move into employment in the private sector.

What are the advantages and disadvantages associated with programs of this kind?

4. Recessions typically create a conflict within the labor force over seniority rules. Labor union contracts protect the jobs of experienced members by a "last hired, first fired" rule. In many firms the last workers hired are the minorities who have recently won job opportunities under the Equal Employment Opportunity Act. The result is that women and blacks are more subject to layoffs and are less able to weather a long period of unemployment. This dilemma has sharply divided the labor movement, producing problems for labor leaders. How would you resolve the problem?
5. In the 1970s and 1980s, large numbers of workers were added to the labor force as a result of the post–World War II "baby boom." A substantial number of new jobs were created to absorb these workers and the many women and minority workers who were competing for employment opportunities. Today, many more college-trained workers are competing for the limited number of job openings requiring higher education. What are the social aspects of these changes in the labor force? How might the new conditions change all our outlooks about what constitutes a successful life?
6. The Classical economists believed that wage reductions would increase hiring. However, unions generally resist wage reductions. As a result, much of the government's employment policy in recent decades has brought on higher *prices* rather than more jobs. How has this policy affected *real* wages? How has it affected profits? How might it stimulate employment? If unions refuse to allow wage gains to lag behind price increases, what will be the result?
7. Use the data below to calculate the real value of the minimum wage in the years shown.

YEAR	*MINIMUM WAGE*	*PRICE INDEX ($1987)*	*REAL VALUE*
1974	$2.00	44.9	______
1977	$2.30	55.9	______
1981	$3.35	78.9	______
1989	$3.40	108.4	______
1991	$4.25	117.0	______

8. Congress has been debating a day-care law that would provide low-cost, dependable child care for working mothers. How would you expect such a law to affect:

   the labor force
   the unemployment rate
   the GDP gap.

9. Explain how the unemployment rate can fall at the same time that employment is falling.
10. By the early 1990s, growth in the civilian labor force was slowing, with fewer teenagers and women entering the labor force. What effect will these changes have on the Phillips curve? What effect will an increase in "discouraged workers" have on the curve?

ANSWERS TO TEST YOURSELF

(p. 273) Expansionary policies are appropriate in range 2, where unemployment is high and inflation low. Contractionary policies are appropriate in range 1, where inflation is high and unemployment low.

FURTHER READING

Akerlof, George, "Labor Contracts As Partial Gift Exchange," *Quarterly Journal of Economics*, November 1982.

Burtless, Gary, "The Tattered Safety Net," *Brookings Review*, Spring 1991.

Chase, Elmer P., III, "Wasteland Economics of High Unemployment," *Challenge*, January/February 1992.

Eichner, Alfred S., "Full Employment and the Human Element," *Challenge*, May/June 1988.

Levitan, Sar A. and Frank Gallo, "Wanted: Federal Public Service Program," *Challenge*, May/June 1991.

Mishel, Lawrence and Jared Bernstein, "Job Destruction: Worse Than We Thought," *Challenge*, September/October 1992.

Chapter 13

Poverty and Income Distribution

Tools for Study

LEARNING OBJECTIVES

After reading this chapter, you will be able to:

1. Discuss the origins of our attitudes toward poverty.
2. Describe the extent and characteristics of poverty.
3. Define three kinds of poverty and discuss some remedies for each.
4. Discuss the advantages and disadvantages of direct financial assistance to poor people.

CURRENT ISSUES FOR DISCUSSION

Can the scientific method of analysis be applied to economic problems like poverty?

How successful have antipoverty programs been?

What's ahead for Social Security?

What are the causes and consequences of urban poverty?

There's a story told of a little Spanish town whose only distinction was its annual poetry contest. Eager contestants came from miles around to compete for recognition. For the winners, three prizes were awarded: third prize was an artfully crafted silver rose; second prize, a dazzling golden rose; and first prize (can you guess it?) was a real rose.

Aside from its pleasing quaintness, the story allows us to compare value structures in different societies. To begin, a poetry contest would probably not receive much attention in our materialistic society. Secondly, most of us would demand a different arrangement of awards!

We may conclude that standards of performance and reward differ sharply among people. The incidence of poverty depends to a large extent on these standards. Whatever the performance/reward structure that emerges in a particular society, it virtually ensures a poor status for people at the bottom. (High social status has at various times and places been based on quality of penmanship, length of earlobes, skill in directing a javelin, and even the ability to detect a pea through a stack of mattresses.)

THE SIZE AND SHAPE OF THE PROBLEM

In addition to cultural differences among nations, there are differences in the way poverty is defined. A family with a yearly income of $10,000 may be quite wealthy in a nation such as India but below the poverty line in the

United States. In primitive societies, one's wealth may be based on the number of pigs or cattle one owns.

In the United States, a definition of poverty is established by the federal government, based on the estimated cost of a nutritionally sound diet. By the government's definition, a family is poor if its annual income is less than three times the amount necessary to purchase such a diet. The poverty level is adjusted each year for price changes, and it differs according to family size, sex of family head, and type of residence (farm or nonfarm). In 1992, the poverty threshold for a nonfarm family of four was about $14,000.

Table 13.1 gives a breakdown of persons below the government's poverty threshold in selected years. As the table shows, only 12.6 percent of all persons in the nation were classified as poor in 1970. This represents a significant improvement over 1960, when more than 22 percent of the nation's people fell below the poverty level. Some of these gains were lost by 1991, however, when the poverty rate increased to more than 14 percent. Government benefits paid in cash to poor people are counted as income for measuring poverty, but "in-kind" benefits such as food stamps, public housing, and health care are not.

The period of overall decline in poverty in the United States was largely a result of economic growth. Improved labor skills and productivity and greater participation of women in the labor force increased earnings for many families. The greatest gains were for nonwhite families with a male head. Regrettably, a growing percentage of female-headed families is now classified as poor, particularly among nonwhite families.

When all low-income families are considered together, female-headed families now constitute about half of poor families, even though the percentage of female-headed families in the population as a whole is only about 30 percent. Their higher poverty rate is probably because female heads of families often are not properly trained for employment or are prevented from seeking employment by the responsibility of caring for young children.

More than one-fourth of heads of poor families work, but their wages are not enough to move them above the poverty level.* Lack of education and job skills limits their employment opportunities to the shrinking number of unskilled jobs. Most of the poor are children, old people, or women—only a small percentage of the poor are able-bodied men.

CLASSIFICATIONS OF POVERTY

Poor families may be classified according to the reasons for their poverty. Then, appropriate remedies can be suggested to aid families in the various classifications.

*Working full time at the minimum wage in 1992 would yield annual income of about $8500, well below the poverty line for a nonfarm family of four.

Table 13.1 Families Below the Poverty Level.

	1970	*1975*	*1980*	*1985*	*1991*
Percentage of all white families	8.0	7.7	8.0	9.1	8.8
Percentage of all nonwhite families	29.5	27.1	28.9	28.7	30.4
Percentage of all families with female head	32.5	32.5	32.7	34.0	35.6
Total number of persons (in millions)	25.4	25.9	29.3	33.1	35.7
Percentage of all persons in the nation	12.6	12.3	13.0	14.0	14.2

SOURCE: *Economic Report of the President,* February 1990 and 1993.

Business Cycle Poverty

Some families are temporarily poor because of cycles in the nation's economy. **Business cycle poverty** is the result of a low level of total spending relative to the nation's capacity to produce goods and services. When aggregate demand falls below aggregate supply at potential GDP, the demand for labor falls, or at least fails to rise along with labor supply. The result is to throw many unskilled and semiskilled workers out of work. The Great Depression of the 1930s and the recessions of 1981–1983 and 1991 pushed many families over the poverty line when the principal family wage-earner was laid off.

Expansionary fiscal and monetary policy can keep spending high and help relieve business cycle poverty. Thus, whenever aggregate demand falls short of aggregate supply at potential GDP, government might reduce personal and corporate tax rates, increase spending for public works projects, or expand the money supply to encourage business investment and increase employment.

Locational Poverty

Some families are trapped in poverty when a particular industry or craft collapses and leaves workers with no other source of income. The most familiar examples of **locational poverty** have resulted from the decline of the coal-mining industry in Appalachia and the cutbacks in the auto industry in Detroit.

Locational poverty results from human immobilities—the difficulty of leaving familiar surroundings or abandoning a familiar trade to begin a new way of life. (For many families, five people to a room in a rural shack among family and friends is preferable to five people to a room in an urban slum, even if employment opportunities may be greater in the city.)

Correcting locational poverty presents a particularly difficult question: that is, whether to move new factories into poverty areas or to move unemployed labor out to other industrialized areas. The first solution may be economically inefficient. The second may be socially unacceptable.

One solution for workers in declining industries is retraining for jobs in growing sectors of the economy. The cost of retraining may be looked upon as an investment in worker productivity. (However, this solution may also run into human barriers, when workers are reluctant to move into unfamiliar jobs.)

The Economic Development Act of 1965 and the Appalachian Regional Development Act of 1966 aimed to create jobs through development of entire geographical regions. In 1974, the Comprehensive Employment and Training Act (CETA) began providing on-the-job training and work experience to Native Americans, migrants, and Job Corps participants. Efforts like these aim to correct locational poverty, but real gains have been slow. Many job training programs have been cut in recent years in an attempt to reduce federal expenditures and the budget deficit.

Categorical Poverty

Some people are locked into poverty because of personal inadequacies that prevent them from functioning within our economic system. These poor people are classified according to certain categories: the physically and mentally handicapped, the emotionally unstable, the chronically ill or aged, and children.

Victims of **categorical poverty** require regular, dependable public assistance. Social workers must be trained to locate people in the various categories, inform them of the available aid, and administer special-purpose programs.

The categorical approach to public assistance originated with the Social Security Act of 1935. The Social Security program has two parts, an insurance part and a welfare part.

Viewpoint

DIFFERENT VIEWS OF POVERTY

In 1859, Charles Darwin published *On The Origin of Species*, a revolutionary book on evolution. The book explained Darwin's theory of "natural selection," sometimes called survival of the fittest. According to the theory, nature "selects" the plants and animals that are best suited for carrying on the stream of life. Plants and animals that are weak and unable to adapt to the environment die out, so that only the strongest survive and reproduce.

Eventually some philosophers applied Darwin's theories about plants and lower animals to humans, creating a kind of "social Darwinism." Social Darwinism may have encouraged its followers to oppose government aid to weak or incompetent persons. For government to sustain persons who cannot care for themselves, they said, is to interfere with the laws of nature.

Religious and political principles may have provided support for social Darwinism. The Puritan ethic supported the idea of self-sufficiency, independence, and individualism. Religious sects like the Calvinists felt little responsibility for the well-being of others, and they rejected the idea of a paternalistic government. Personal wealth came to be seen as a sign that the wealthy person was leading a life pleasing to God.

Democratic political theory also supported the idea of each individual's responsibility for his or her own life. A perfectly free and democratic society places no restrictions on economic or social gain. Thus, a democratic society provides everyone equal opportunity to succeed (or to fail) according to his or her own abilities and effort.

With scientific and religious support, revolutions have been fought in the name of freedom and equality. Yet a disturbing contradiction has appeared: Equality of opportunity has often meant inequality of results. In fact, with individual freedom, equality of opportunity virtually guarantees inequality of results.

If a nation guarantees absolute freedom to pursue individual gain, it will ensure misery for the people who are least able to succeed. On the other hand, if the nation guarantees all people equal standards of living, it may destroy incentives to succeed and undermine the drive for achievement.

The Eastern European countries that are struggling to reform their economies are facing this contradiction. Their former Communist governments ensured them equal (but low) standards of living. Today the people are demanding the freedom to achieve a better life. But this very freedom will mean job losses and lower standards of living for people who are least able to succeed. The fear of poverty is causing some workers to oppose reform.

Citizens of Eastern European nations must ask themselves the following questions: Is it better to be equal and poor? Or is it better to be unequal and free?

The insurance part of the Social Security Act is the Old Age, Survivors, Disability, and Hospital Insurance (OASDHI) program. Workers and employers make regular contributions that are used to pay benefits to insured workers. In 1992 employers and employees each contributed 7.65 percent of earnings up to $55,500.* For workers who have contributed to the program, benefits are based on past contributions rather than need.

The noninsurance or welfare part of Social Security makes payments to poor people, whether or not they have paid in contributions to the Social Security program. One noninsurance program that is shared with state and local governments is Aid to Families with Dependent Children (AFDC). Other noninsurance aid is provided to the elderly, blind, and disabled under the Supplemental Security Income program (SSI).

In 1961, the federal food stamp program was put in place to provide further aid to poor families. Under the food stamp program, a family of four with no income receives about $200 in food stamps each month. Other poor families receive various amounts of food stamps, depending on their income during the month. About 20 million people use food stamps annually at a cost to the government of more than $10 billion.

Total outlay of all public assistance programs in 1992 was more than $700 billion, more than half of which represented insured benefits under OASDHI.

A disadvantage of the categorical approach to poverty is the bureaucracy required to administer the various programs. Furthermore, there may be undesirable side effects for families receiving aid. The most serious side effect is the breakup of families, since AFDC aid is generally provided only to families without a father. Moreover, many poor people may not fit into any of the established categories. About half the nation's poor receive no public assistance of any kind. On the other hand, many nonpoor people may qualify for several categories and receive more than their fair share.

* Self-employed workers pay both the employer's and employee's contribution.

PROPOSALS FOR CHANGE

Objections to categorical aid programs for poor people have come from business leaders, sociologists, and economists from both extremes of the ideological spectrum. For example, Milton Friedman generally opposes government intervention in free markets. He recommends eliminating all aid categories and paying direct grants to all poor people solely on the basis of need.

Direct Grants

To raise the incomes of all poor families above the low-income threshold in 1992 would have required **direct grants** of less than $100 billion. This is less than two percent of GDP and less than the normal annual growth of GDP. (The $280 billion actually spent on public-assistance programs in 1991 could have been divided among the nation's 7.7 million poor families for a direct income grant of more than $30,000 for each family.)

Direct grants could be administered without establishing a new bureaucracy, perhaps through the existing Internal Revenue Service. Grants would be made in cash so that poor people could pay for food, housing, and health and social services in free markets. Their spending would provide economic incentives to business firms to provide the services they want. Direct grants would also strengthen an individual's sense of responsibility to budget family income wisely. On the other hand, some people object to direct grants because of the social stigma often attached to public assistance.

With the exception of the United States and Japan, every industrialized nation pays direct grants to all families, regardless of income. Under a progressive income tax structure, some fraction of a family's total income is returned to the government in taxes. Thus, at very low levels of income, a family keeps the entire grant; at some level of income the grant is just offset by taxes; and at higher incomes, taxes paid exceed the grant.

The Negative Income Tax

Another proposal for reducing poverty is the **negative income tax**.* This proposal is based on the fact that families with low incomes from work are unable to use certain tax advantages that are available to upper-income families.

Our tax schedule allows tax advantages in the form of exemptions amounting to $2150 per person and a standard deduction from taxable income of roughly $4550 per family. However, families whose income from work is too low to pay taxes are unable to use these tax advantages. Under the negative income tax proposal, families earning less than the established level of tax exemptions and deductions would pay no tax. Instead, they would receive a negative tax or grant amounting to some percentage of the difference between their earned income and total exemptions and deductions.

For instance, a family of four would be entitled to total tax deductions and exemptions of roughly $13,150: (4 × $2150) + $4550 = $13,150. Families with incomes of less than $13,150 would receive some fraction of the difference between their earned income and the $13,150 income floor. A family earning $4000, for instance, would pay no tax but receive a payment of, say, 50 percent of the family's unused tax deductions and exemptions: .5($13,150 − $4000) = .5($9150) = $4575. Total family income would be $4000 + $4575 = $8575. The family's income from work could rise as high as $13,150 before its negative tax benefit would be cut off.

Both direct grants and a negative income tax would eliminate the need for the welfare bureaucracies that administer categorical aid.* Experiments with direct income grants have been conducted in communities in New Jersey, Iowa, and North Carolina. Policymakers hope that the results will help them predict the possible effects nationwide.

The Problem of Economic Incentives

The major disadvantage of public assistance programs is that they can destroy all incentives to make one's own way in life. Because we depend on human labor for a large portion of production, particularly in the growing service sector of our economy, the loss of work incentives can be a real problem.

The disincentive effect of public assistance may be greatest under plans providing either direct grants or a negative income tax. The reason is that if government makes up the entire difference between earned income and some income floor, there is little incentive for people to strive to increase their earnings.

The disincentive effect of the negative income tax is probably less than for direct grants, particularly when workers are allowed to keep a large fraction of their earned income. Keeping a larger fraction is equivalent to paying a lower tax on earnings. A low tax rate on earnings would increase the cost of the negative income tax; but it might also strengthen economic incentives and help relieve critical shortages of low-skilled workers.

*The current Earned Income Tax Credit for the working poor is a kind of negative income tax.

* It has been suggested that this is one of the reasons bureaucrats often oppose these programs.

Viewpoint

DISCRIMINATION

A major cause of poverty is discrimination: discrimination in employment and discrimination in access to education and housing. Discrimination arises when people are treated differently on some basis other than their individual merit. Discrimination frequently affects blacks and women. One result of discrimination is low-status jobs of low productivity with low earnings and few opportunities for advancement.

Sometimes discrimination is the result of prejudice on the part of an employer, landlord, or school administrator. Although laws prohibit these forms of discrimination, the laws are not fully enforced. Sometimes what appears to be discrimination in employment is really only the result of discrimination in educational opportunities, which makes some workers more productive than others. Sometimes discrimination is actually self-imposed, when blacks or women unconsciously place limits on their own aspirations.

During the 1960s federal laws were passed forbidding discrimination on the basis of race, color, religion, sex, national origin, or age. In response to the new laws, many schools and business firms established "affirmative action" programs, seeking members of groups formerly subject to discrimination. In many cases, institutions reevaluated their admission or hiring standards and eliminated requirements that do not directly affect a potential employee's qualifications for a job.

Discrimination harms us all, whether or not we are ourselves targets of discrimination. When workers are unable to compete freely in the labor market, labor costs are kept artificially high. Then higher labor costs raise the prices of many things we buy. When workers are deprived of educational or job opportunities, our nation's productive capacity is lower than it might be. Total output cannot grow in line with the nation's growing population. When workers' incomes are held artificially low, they cannot buy the goods and services our business firms could produce. Profits and business investment are lower as a result.

Can you cite specific examples of the harmful effects of discrimination?

Another, less substantial, objection to direct financial assistance is that simply making payments to poor families does nothing to correct the basic causes of poverty. This criticism implies that we can identify and deal directly with the specific characteristics that make people poor. It is not clear that this is true. Furthermore, it was our attempt to deal with the specific characteristics of poor people that led to the costly welfare bureaucracy we now employ.

The Problem of Inflation

Direct financial assistance may lead to a problem more difficult to handle than poverty—the problem of inflation. Unless taxes are in-

Thinking Seriously About Economic Issues

CHANGES IN THE FAMILY INCOME

From average annual growth of nearly 4 percent in the three decades following World War II, since 1973 median family income in the United States has experienced about a $\frac{1}{2}$ percent a year decline. (Median family income is the income of the middle family in the income scale and is distinguished from average family income, which may be distorted upward by the high incomes of a small fraction of families.) In real terms, the loss of income per family has been more than $150 per year and has been most severe for families with children. The loss occurred in spite of the fact that many women entered the work force during the period and the number of two-earner families with children increased.

Working for the Joint Economic Committee of the Congress, economists Sheldon Danziger and Peter Gottschalk conducted research into the incidence of poverty in the United States and changes in the poverty population over recent decades. They attributed the decrease in median family income to the poor performance of the economy as a whole. From an average annual growth of 3.4 percent between World War II and 1972, after 1972 GNP growth slowed to less than 3 percent. Real wages and salaries per worker have fallen by almost 1 percent a year. Moreover, many second wage earners work less than full time at less than the median wage. Even after the economy's strong recovery from the 1981–1982 recession, average family income in 1984 was still below the 1973 level, making unlikely any tendencies toward redistribution to families at the lower end of the income scale. Both poverty and unemployment rates remain well above those of 1979.

The authors are concerned about the economic and social implications of slumping family income. The problem may call for an increase in the allocation of resources for the care and support of the nation's children. It may mean a dramatic change in the ability of families to achieve a middle-class life-style. It may also affect decisions to have children and to purchase homes.

Sheldon Danziger and Peter Gottschalk, "How Have Families with Children Been Faring?" Institute for Research on Poverty, The University of Wisconsin, January 1986. Paper prepared for the Joint Economic Committee of the Congress.

creased to pay for financial assistance to poor people, the nation's disposable income will increase. An increase in disposable income means increased spending for goods and services. Unless total production also increases, there will be inflation, as increased consumer spending competes for the same quantity of goods and services.

The threat of inflation requires that incentives be built into financial assistance programs. Work incentives can help increase worker productivity. Research and training

How Things Have Changed

SHARES OF INCOME (%) GOING TO THE WEALTHIEST TAX UNITS

Year	Top 1%	Top 5%	Top 10%	Top 15%
1948	9.8	20.2	27.9	34.3
1952	8.7	18.7	26.7	33.4
1963	8.8	19.4	28.2	35.5
1967	8.8	19.6	28.3	35.5
1972	8.0	18.7	27.8	35.4
1977	7.8	18.9	28.3	36.1
1981	8.1	19.0	28.6	36.5
1986	14.7	26.6	36.8	45.1

Look down the columns to understand changes in the distribution of before-tax income in recent years.

SOURCE: *Brookings Review*, Spring 1990.

programs and investment tax credits may also be a way to encourage increased productivity.

WHAT CAN WE CONCLUDE?

The fact is that we really don't know enough about poverty and its causes simply to solve the problem. Without a simple solution, we must fall back on a variety of partial solutions: programs to improve health and nutrition for children and expectant mothers, educational and vocational training for displaced workers, income-support payments and child-care programs for working parents, and emergency relief for temporarily unemployed workers. To be successful, these programs must be carried on within a climate of increasing production and equality of opportunity.

A chief disadvantage of any program is its initial cost. Also, it is unlikely that there will be measurable results in any short period of time. One of the characteristics of the American approach to problems is excessive optimism at the start of a new program. Often, highly publicized expectations fail to come true immediately, and disillusionment sets in. As a result, many programs are abandoned prematurely, before a legitimate trial period has elapsed.

Self-Check

1. Poor people in the United States:
a. Constitute about 25 percent of the population.
b. Consist mainly of able-bodied men.
c. Include only unemployed people.
d. Are concentrated in industrial areas.
e. None of the above.

2. Which of the following is treated primarily by categorical aid programs?
a. Cyclical poverty.
b. Locational poverty.
c. The aged poor.
d. All of the above.
e. None of the above.

3. Which of the following is a disadvantage of a program of direct grants?
a. Direct grants reduce the need for a large bureaucracy.
b. Direct grants give the poor money to spend as they see fit.
c. Taxes take the entire grant away as earned income rises.
d. Direct grants do not deal with the real causes of poverty.
e. Direct grants abolish categorical types of aid.

4. Which of the following is not a danger of direct grants or the negative income tax?
a. There is a possibility of reducing incentives.
b. Increased incomes may contribute to inflation.
c. Some poor people would not receive aid.
d. There may be a social stigma attached to aid.
e. Many social workers may become unemployed.

5. Which of the following terms is paired incorrectly?
a. Locational poverty—Appalachian Redevelopment Act.
b. Cyclical poverty—expansionary fiscal policy.
c. Categorical poverty—Aid to Families with Dependent Children.
d. Cyclical poverty—contractionary monetary policy.
e. Categorical poverty—Social Security Act.

Theory in Practice

PROBLEMS IN APPLYING THE SCIENTIFIC METHOD

The scientific method of analysis requires that any problem be examined in systematic steps:

1. First define the problem. One of the most difficult problems in economics is the problem of poverty.
2. Second, gather data describing and measuring the problem.
3. Organize the data and pose an hypothesis, a theory that explains the behavior of the data.
4. Test the hypothesis by changing certain data within the problem (while holding the other factors constant) and noting whether the results of the change support the hypothesis.
5. Continue to alter the hypothesis until the results of changing certain data do in fact support the hypothesis. The hypothesis is finally accepted if it can be used to predict the actual results of a change in the data. Finally, the hypothesis can be stated as a scientific law or principle that explains the problem under investigation.

In economic analysis, we might add another step to the scientific method. The practical goal of economic analysis is to suggest policy to correct the problem under investigation.

Problems of Designing Policy

Economic analysis suffers from a disadvantage not encountered in scientific analysis. It is much more difficult to test hypotheses in an economic system than in a scientific laboratory. To test an economic hypothesis, for instance, may require changes in government tax and spending policies (all the while holding other things in the economic environment constant). Needless to say, such changes are more difficult to accomplish than merely changing the temperature in a chemistry laboratory. For this reason, many economic theories (or hypotheses) cannot be tested to produce definite results and clear policy remedies.

This is especially true of the problem of poverty. There is no scientific law or principle to explain the problem. Consequently, there is no single policy that is clearly acceptable as a cure.

Over the past half century a variety of government programs have been begun to deal with poverty. Their objectives have been humanitarian as well as economic. Evaluating the results of these programs may be considered a form of hypothesis testing. Thus, a successful program may be assumed to have been based on a correct explanation of the causes of poverty. Lack of success would suggest an incorrect explanation of the roots of the problem.

Unfortunately, it is difficult to evaluate the results of a government program even when it appears successful. Many other forces may be operating on the problem, so that a decrease in poverty may be the result not of a new government program but of economic growth or improved education and health care. Thus, even if a program appears successful in relieving poverty, it is impossible to prove whether success is the result of the program alone or of some other outside influence.

An Example

Aid to Families with Dependent Children (AFDC) illustrates the difficulty of designing a program without the benefit of scientific analysis and control. The original purpose of AFDC was to assist families when the father was unable to support the family because of death or disability. In the beginning, about 75 percent of the families involved fit this classification. The remainder had fathers who were absent through divorce, separation, or desertion.

The availability of benefits under AFDC may have had the unintended effect of encouraging unemployed fathers to desert their families. As a result, the number of families receiving AFDC is now five times the number receiving aid in 1950. The more than 3 million families now receiving aid under AFDC constitute almost 6 percent of the nation's population.

How can we deal with the problem of desertion and nonsupport by the fathers of these families? Extending benefits to families with an unemployed father is the approach used by about half the states; but this approach increases the cost of the program considerably.

Another problem with AFDC involves the work status of the mother. Originally, the program's intent was to enable mothers to care for their children without having to work outside the home. Because benefits were reduced dollar for dollar with outside income, the result was to reduce the mother's incentive to find outside employment. Work incentives were added to the program in 1967. Today a working mother loses less than a dollar in AFDC benefits for each dollar earned. She is also eligible for job training and counseling and publicly supported child care under the Work Incentive Program. Still, only about one-sixth of the mothers receiving AFDC are employed.

Without controlled experiments to test the results of various aid programs, it is not possible to predict all the effects. When results are unfavorable, new approaches must be tried. However, new programs are costly and frequently require new or expanded bureaucracies. All of this suggests that the problem of poverty may remain with us despite our sincere efforts to correct it.

WHAT HAS BEEN ACCOMPLISHED?

Average levels of living in the Western world have improved regularly since the Industrial Revolution. For the past several centuries, real income per capita has doubled about every 40 years. We describe the poverty that remains in two ways.

Absolute and Relative Poverty

Absolute poverty is a condition below a certain income level described as the poverty level. In the United States, the percentage of families subject to absolute poverty has fallen about half since World War II.

While absolute poverty has fallen, there has been little change in relative poverty. Relative poverty refers to the proportional shares of income going to various income groups. Relative income shares have remained roughly stable, suggesting that there has been no significant trend toward equality of incomes over at least the past 40 years.

In fact, when all U.S. families are ranked according to income and divided into fifths, we discover that the shares of total income going to each fifth have remained roughly the same in recent decades. Table 13.2 shows the shares of income before taxes and after transfer payments for families in selected years since 1947.

The lowest fifth of families still receive about 5 percent of total income, and the highest fifth, more than 40 percent. Translated into dollar amounts, in 1990 this meant that the lowest fifth were those families with average incomes before taxes and transfer payments of $2096; the second fifth had incomes averaging $14,664; the third fifth, $28,836; the fourth fifth, $45,836; and the top fifth, $93,966.*

The Lorenz Curve

A useful tool for measuring relative poverty is the **Lorenz curve**. The Lorenz curve is drawn

*The disparity of income is aggravated by the fact that the distribution of wealth is also sharply unequal.

Table 13.2 Shares of Aggregate Income (%) Before Taxes Received by Each Fifth of Families, Ranked by Income.

	1947	*1950*	*1960*	*1966*	*1972*	*1981*	*1984*	*1987*
Lowest fifth	5.1	4.5	4.8	5.6	5.4	5.0	4.7	4.6
Second fifth	11.8	11.9	12.2	12.4	11.9	11.3	11.0	10.8
Third fifth	16.7	17.4	17.8	17.8	17.5	17.4	17.0	16.9
Fourth fifth	23.2	23.6	24.0	23.8	23.9	24.4	24.4	24.1
Highest fifth	43.3	42.7	41.3	40.5	41.4	41.9	42.9	43.7
Top 5%	17.5	17.3	15.9	15.6	15.9	15.4	16.0	16.9

SOURCES: *Economic Report of the President*, 1974 and 1992, *A Guide to Consumer Markets, 1977/78*, and *Statistical Abstract of the U.S.*, 1979, 1980, 1985, 1986, and 1989.

in a square as in Figure 13.1. The horizontal axis measures percentage of families, ranked according to income. The vertical axis measures percentage of total income before taxes. As you move from 0 to 100 percent along either axis, percentages are cumulative. That is, values are associated with the lowest 20 percent, the lowest 40 percent, the lowest 60 percent, and so forth.

The diagonal line across the square is a reference line. It associates equal percentages of the values along each axis and represents perfect equality of income distribution. For example, point *A* on the diagonal represents the condition where the lowest 20 percent of families receives 20 percent of income; point *B* represents the condition where the lowest 80 percent of families receives 80 percent; and so forth.

If the actual graph of income shares corresponds to the diagonal, then income is distributed precisely equally. To the extent that the actual graph deviates from the diagonal, there is inequality in the distribution of income.

The Lorenz curve in Figure 13.1 tells us that the lowest fifth of families received about 5 percent of income. The lowest 80 percent of families received about 55 percent. This means that the top fifth of families received more than 40 percent of total income. Put another way, the top fifth of families received more than eight times as much income as the bottom fifth.

Figure 13.1 A Lorenz Curve Showing Distribution of Income (1947)

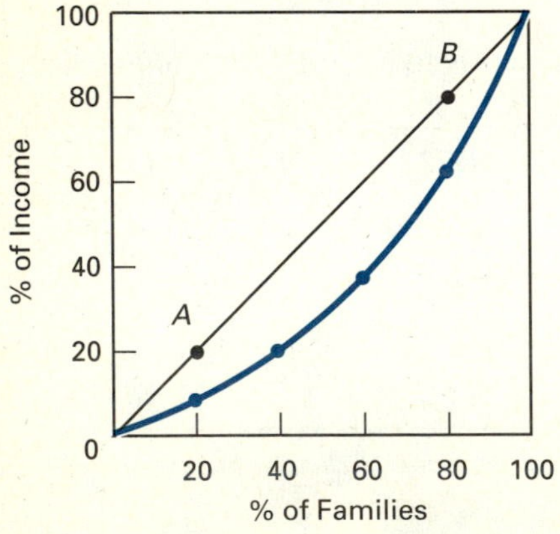

Figure 13.1 illustrates actual income distribution in the United States in 1947. Lorenz curves for the years 1950, 1960, 1970, and 1990 are shown in Figure 13.2. As you can see, the curves became somewhat flatter in 1960 and 1970, but the 1990 curve is nearly the same as that of 1950.

Some Conclusions

We may conclude that absolute poverty has decreased in the United States, along with advancing technology and increased worker productivity. Still, there has been no significant decrease in relative poverty in recent years.

The greatest reductions in relative poverty probably took place in the early decades of this century. Antitrust laws, the growth of the labor movement, and greater opportunities for education and training in new expanding industries had the effect of reducing the relative advantages of the upper fifth of families. The trend toward equality has slowed in recent decades, although antidiscrimination laws are now helping to resume the trend.

WHAT'S AHEAD FOR SOCIAL SECURITY?

Since 1935 social security has been the main public assistance program in the United States. Social security trust funds receive tax payments from workers and employers, and each month the Social Security Administration sends checks to more than 36 million retired persons, orphans, widows, and disabled persons.

Figure 13.2 Relative Income Shares in the United States

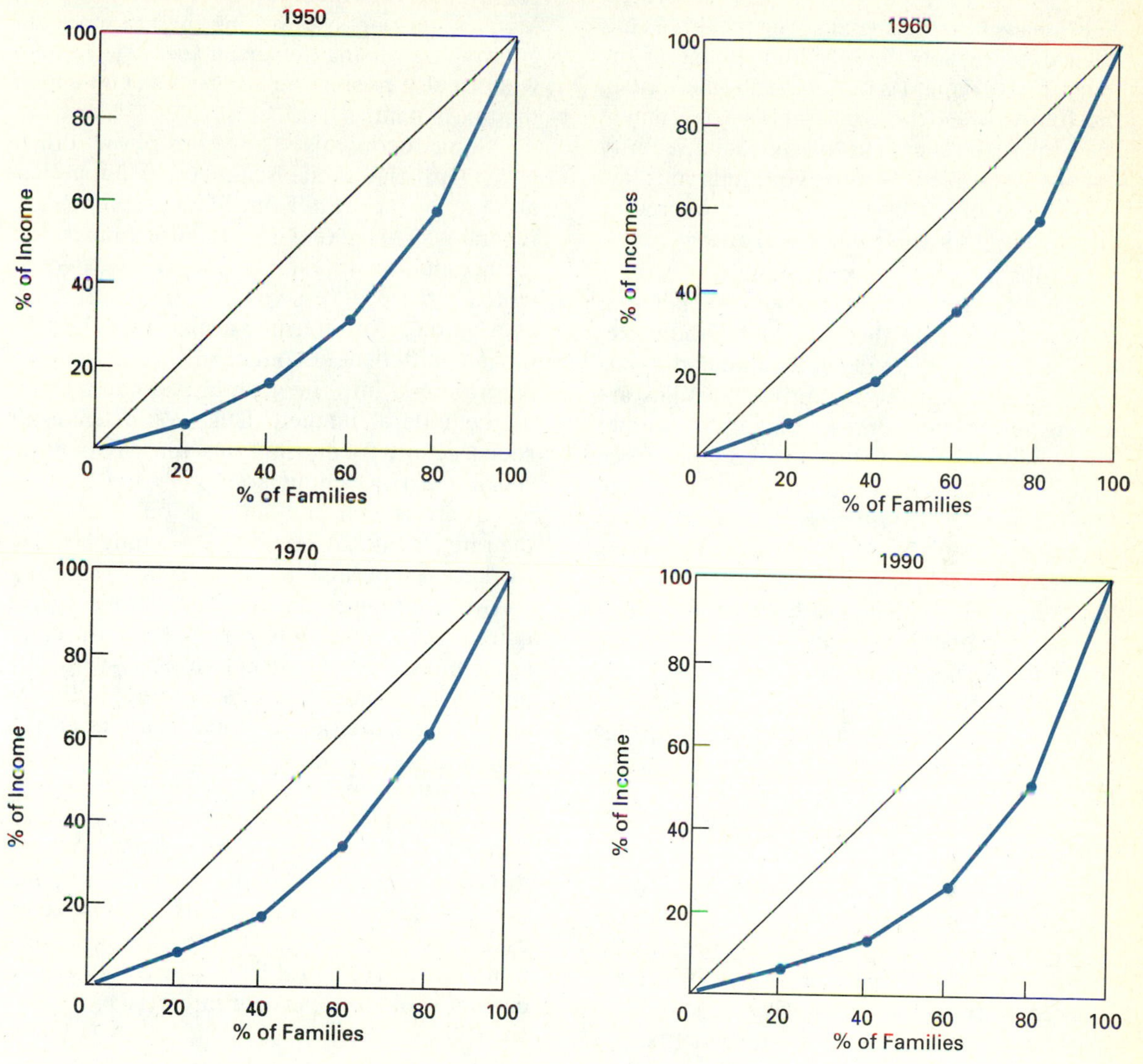

In the early 1980's contributions to social security fell below benefits paid, and the Social Security Administration had to dip into its emergency trust fund. To correct the shortfall in social security contributions, Congress legislated an increase in the social security tax rate and an increase in the income base to which the tax is applied. The result was to increase social security contributions substantially above annual benefits paid. Thus, in 1991 the surplus added to the social security trust fund amounted to more than $50 billion.

By law, the social security trust fund must be invested in U.S. government securities. This means that the social security surplus has been used to help finance the deficit of the federal government as a whole. Some time in the future when the trust fund's government securities are redeemed to pay social security beneficiaries, the federal government must acquire funds either by increasing taxes, reducing spending, or increasing borrowing.

Probably the major reason for serious concern about social security is a change in the composition of the U.S. population. Retired persons are living longer and drawing more benefits. In the meantime, families are having fewer children, so that in the future fewer new workers will enter the labor force each year relative to the numbers of dependent persons who will begin receiving benefits. The current ratio is about 3 taxpaying workers for every social security beneficiary, but the ratio is expected to fall to about 2 to 1 by the year 2030.

If the Social Security Administration has difficulty meeting its obligations to beneficiaries, some changes may be necessary. One possibility would be to reduce the benefits paid. The trend, however, has been to increase benefits in order to offset the effects of inflation, to add new beneficiaries, and to include health benefits in the program. Many recipients of social security are totally dependent on their monthly check. At present the average monthly benefit is about $600 for a worker retiring at age sixty-five. It is difficult to imagine cutting these meager benefits.

Another way would be to increase the tax rate paid by employed workers. The current rate is 7.65 percent of earnings up to an income of $55,500 (as of 1992), for a maximum tax per worker of $4245.75 each year. (An equal amount is collected from each worker's employer.)

One objection to raising the tax rate is that social security taxes are regressive. Remember that a regressive tax takes a higher percentage of low incomes than high incomes. Many voters oppose making the tax more regressive by raising the social security tax rate without also raising the income level on which the tax is paid.

Some economists have proposed doing away with the social security tax altogether and paying benefits from federal income tax revenues. This plan would require an increase in income tax rates, but the change would increase the progressivity of the tax structure as a whole. An alternative plan would be to move health benefits out of the social security program and into the general revenue portion of the federal budget. This would leave all social security contributions for payment to social security beneficiaries.

There is still another possibility. Raising the retirement age would enable many healthy workers to continue to pay into the trust fund and might reduce the benefits ultimately required. An objection to raising the retirement age comes from younger workers, who frequently urge older workers to retire and open up job opportunities to young workers on the way up.

More changes in the social security program will undoubtedly come soon. Social security touches almost every one of us: either through taxes paid, benefits received, or benefits provided to our dependents. This makes it especially important to develop the best solution to its funding problems, preferably before current problems escalate into crisis.

LIVING POOR IN THE CITY

It used to be that poverty was mostly a rural problem. Tarpaper shacks dotted the rural landscape on farms hardly productive enough to supply minimum family needs. Today poverty is increasingly an urban problem. The evidence is aging and overcrowded tenement

Viewpoint

URBAN ENTERPRISE ZONES

Urban poverty is a growing concern for the nation's policymakers. One proposal for remedying urban poverty is to establish urban "enterprise zones," with tax reductions and regulatory relief to encourage job-creating new businesses.

Critics of "enterprise zones" point out that a skilled labor force, accessible transportation and markets, and physical security are more critical to new businesses than are tax reductions. Few new businesses need tax reductions anyway, since their taxable profits are not likely to be significant. Furthermore, tax reductions distort market decisions and include no guarantee that business revenue will be reinvested locally or used to hire local workers.

Attempting to divide enterprise zone benefits equally among many urban areas will spread resources too thinly to do much good. If benefits are provided only for areas with the greatest potential for development, however, the poorest areas are likely to be neglected. If benefits are provided only for the poorest areas, the programs will have little chance of success.

Surveys of businesses currently operating in state enterprise zones found that because of the poor job skills of local workers, businesses could not meet the state's requirements to hire 25 percent of their work force from zone residents. Most of the businesses would have started without government incentives or would have started outside the zone; therefore, zones' gains were other areas' losses.

A better solution to urban poverty would involve direct expenditures to increase basic job skills and enable urban workers to compete effectively in the labor market. Expenditures for infrastructure, public services, and improved physical appearances would help revive blighted urban areas.

What are the costs and benefits of programs to revitalize urban areas?

Sar A. Levitan and Elizabeth I. Miller, "Enterprise Zones Are No Solution For Our Blighted Areas," *Challenge*, May–June 1992.

buildings, idle and bitter urban youths, crime and decay in urban neighborhoods.

The trend began half a century ago. New technology and scientific farming forced small, inefficient farmers off the land and replaced them with modern machinery. A steady flow of displaced farm workers moved into the cities, often poorly educated and ill prepared for work in industry. Unable to find jobs, they were unable to provide their children the attitudes and skills needed for success in a modern economic system. New generations of urban poor have continued to develop in a worsening spiral.

Other factors aggravated the problem of urban poverty. In the past, factories processed goods through the "gravity-flow" method: raw materials were first processed on the top floor of a tall building and then dropped through a chute for successive stages of processing on lower floors. In contrast, modern production methods use the assembly line, which requires that factories be spread out over large continuous spaces. Whereas the older factories could be built in cities, urban land is too scarce and costly for assembly-line factories. Therefore, manufacturing plants have moved to the outskirts of the cities, far from the homes of urban workers. Many of the urban poor lack the transportation facilities for traveling to jobs far from the central city.

The increasing poor population has imposed a severe financial burden on city governments. Poor people need more police and fire protection, more emergency medical care, and more specialized educational facilities—all costly to city governments. To make matters worse, the inflow of poor people has been accompanied by an outflow of middle-income taxpayers in search of more pleasant and less costly living in the suburbs. The outflow of their middle-income tax base has worsened the financial problems of many cities.

Some policies of the federal government have aggravated the problem of urban poverty. Since the 1930s, the federal government has subsidized mortgage loans for middle-income home buyers. It has subsidized the building of highways for low-cost commuting into the city. It has neglected some projects like mass transportation that would benefit the urban poor. Finally, a large part of federal grant funds is paid to state governments. Central city residents tend to be underrepresented in state governments, which tend to be more strongly influenced by voters in affluent towns and suburbs. The result is a tendency to use federal grants for projects that do not directly help the urban poor.

The problem is complex. Current poverty programs tend to focus on particular poor people but do little to correct the problem as a whole. Some new ideas have been proposed to deal with the problem of urban poverty: examples are subsidized housing for the poor in suburban neighborhoods; compensatory education and skill development programs for urban youths; increased federal aid to city governments; and rigorous enforcement of antidiscrimination laws in hiring.

The late sociologist Michael Harrington concluded that American society is becoming two separate societies: poor people are increasingly set apart from the mainstream of American life. Such a division is destructive to the principles on which our nation was founded. It is also wasteful of the potential output the poor could be producing as full participants in our economic system.

SUMMARY

1. A society's standards of performance and values will determine priorities of rewards in which some groups will have low status. The value structure of any society virtually ensures that those at the bottom will be poor.
2. Poverty is classified as business cycle poverty, locational poverty, or categorical poverty. Business cycle poverty is best remedied by policies to stabilize total spending. Locational poverty is associated with isolated, depressed industries or regions. It may be treated by job training and relocation of workers. Categorical poverty requires public assistance to persons who are unable to function in our economic system.
3. The Social Security Act of 1935 provides insurance payments to the aged, dependent, disabled, and unemployed and welfare payments to the needy. A large portion of public welfare goes to Aid to Families with Dependent Children (AFDC).
4. Administration of public assistance is costly, involves undesirable side effects, and may fail to achieve its intended objectives. Some proposed alternatives to current public assistance programs include direct grants to all families and the negative income tax. The problem of

reduced incentives among recipients plagues all public assistance programs.

5. It is difficult to apply the scientific method to economic problems. This means we have no precise explanation for poverty and no clear policy remedies. Also, because many factors affect the economic environment, it is difficult to evaluate a program's success in relieving poverty.
6. Although absolute levels of living have advanced fairly regularly since the Industrial Revolution, there is still marked inequality of income in the United States. Relative shares of income have remained roughly the same since 1947.
7. Social security legislation must be amended soon to deal with the problem of an increasing dependent population. Proposed changes include cutting benefits and raising taxes.
8. The increase in urban poverty has strained the resources of local governments and calls for new policy approaches.

TERMS TO REMEMBER

business cycle poverty: poverty that results from the lack of jobs during a business recession or depression

locational poverty: poverty associated with regions of depressed economic activity following the collapse of a particular craft or industry

categorical poverty: poverty among particular groups who are unable to function in our economic system

direct grants: cash payments to increase the incomes of families

negative income tax: a payment to families whose earned income is less than the level of allowed income tax exemptions and deductions

Lorenz curve: a graph showing a nation's income distribution

TOPICS FOR DISCUSSION

1. Distinguish clearly between each of the following pairs of terms:

   Equality of opportunity and equality of results
   Categorical aid and direct grants
   Absolute poverty and relative poverty

2. Explain the basis of the three major classifications of poverty. What policy recommendations would you propose for dealing with each? Give specific instances of each kind of poverty and specific programs that have been used to remedy them.
3. What are the similarities and differences between scientific analysis and economic analysis?
4. Minimum-wage legislation is usually defended as a means of relieving the plight of the poor. However, it may actually work against the poor. Explain.
5. Consider the dilemma of a low-skilled worker. If the legal minimum wage is kept low, he or she may find it more beneficial not to work and to draw welfare payments. If the legal minimum wage is raised, the worker may be unemployable because his or her skills do not justify paying the higher wage. Keeping welfare benefits low increases the misery of the poor, but raising them reduces economic incentives and raises the burden to the taxpayer. Do you see any hope for resolving this problem in the future? Can you design a statistical study for evaluating the effects on incentives of various changes in welfare payments and the minimum wage?

FURTHER READING

Berlin, Gordon and William McAllister, "Homelessness: Why Nothing Has Worked—and What Will," *Brookings Review*, Fall 1992.

Burtless, Gary, "The Economist's Lament: Public Assistance in America," *Journal of Economic Perspectives*, Winter 1990.

Burtless, Gary, "When Work Doesn't Work," *Brookings*, Spring 1992.

Cutler, David M. and Lawrence F. Katz, "Untouched by the Rising Tide," *Brookings Review*, Winter 1992.

Dreier, Peter and Richard Appelbaum, "America's Nightmare: Homelessness," *Challenge*, March/April 1991.

Fuchs, Victor R., "Women's Quest for Economic Equality," *Journal of Economic Perspectives*, Winter 1989.

Gueron, Judith M., "Work and Welfare: Lessons on Employment Programs," *Journal of Economic Perspectives*, Winter 1990.

Harrington, Michael, *The Other America*, Penguin, Baltimore, 1968.

Haveman, Robert, "Who Are the Nation's 'Truly Poor'?" *Brookings Review*, Winter 1993.

Howe, Neil and Phillip Longman, "The Next New Deal," *The Atlantic*, April 1992.

Levitan, Sar A. and Elizabeth I. Miller, "Enterprise Zones Are No Solution for Blighted Areas," *Challenge*, May/June 1993.

Maital, Shlomo and Kim I. Morgan, "Hungry Children Are a Bad Business," *Challenge*, July/August 1992.

Meadows, Donella H., et al, *Limits to Growth*, Universe Books, New York, 1972.

Phillips, Kevin, *The Politics of Rich and Poor*, Random House, New York, 1990.

Sawhill, Isabel V., "What About America's Underclass?" *Challenge*, May/June 1988.

Smeeding, Timothy M., "Why U.S. Antipoverty System Doesn't Work," *Challenge*, January/February 1992.

Thurow, Lester C., *The Zero-Sum Society*, Basic Books, New York, 1980.

Chapter 14

Economic Growth

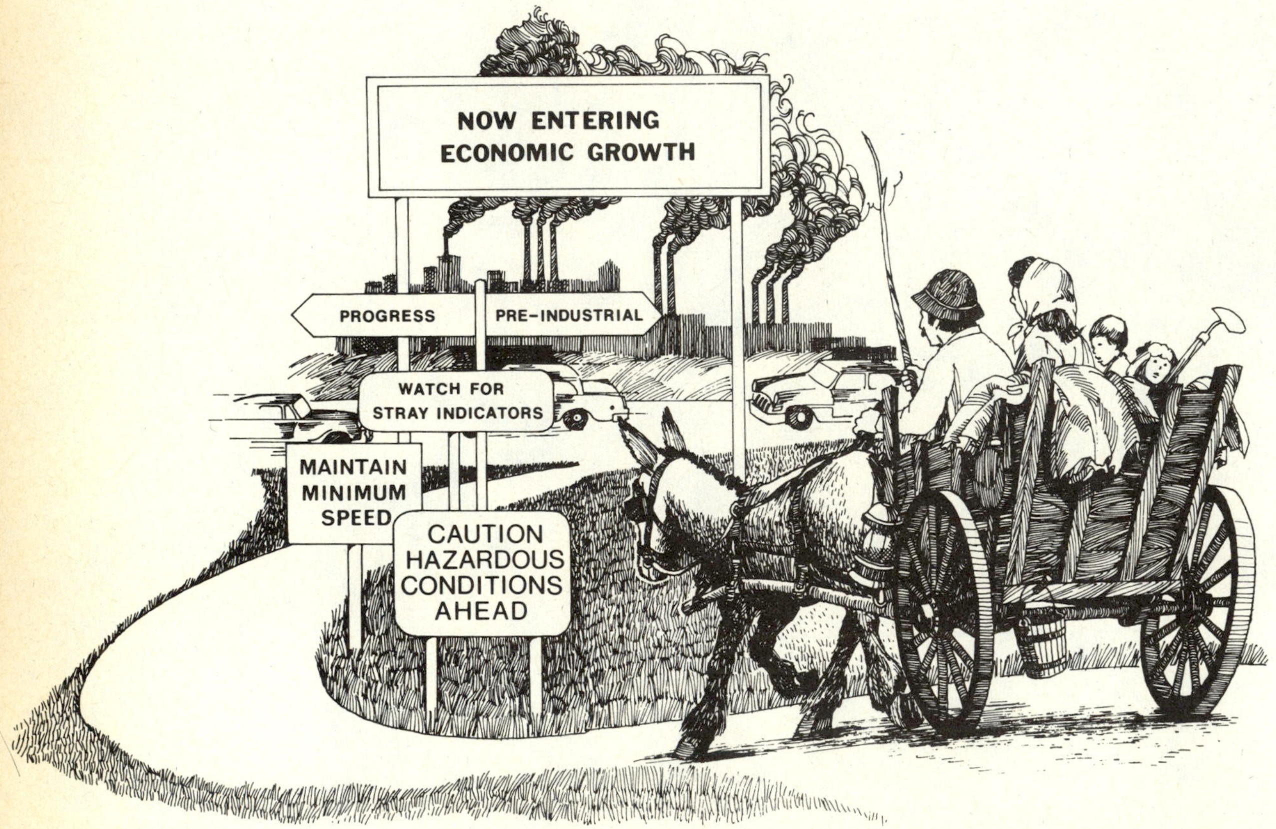

Tools for Study

LEARNING OBJECTIVES

After reading this chapter, you will be able to:

1. Discuss the origins of our attitudes toward economic growth.
2. Describe growth trends in GDP and explain how growth takes place.
3. Discuss the problems that face a mature economy and some possible problems resulting from growth.
4. Explain the sectoral and export-base theories of growth and describe how they affect the choice of growth policy.

CURRENT ISSUES FOR DISCUSSION

What are we doing to promote growth of potential GDP?

How can we make sure the advantages of growth outweigh the disadvantages?

What can be done to ward off a world food shortage?

John Stuart Mill, a leading economist of the nineteenth century, is said to have read Greek literature by the age of eight. I blush to admit that one of the most memorable literary experiences of my own childhood was a little book called *Pigs Is Pigs*.

The story concerned a controversy between a clerk at the post office and the recipient of a package through the mail. The package contained a pair of guinea pigs, and the controversy centered on the amount of postage due—which the recipient refused to pay. During the course of the dispute, the family of guinea pigs grew and grew—and GREW and GREW. And the postal clerk became the guardian of a flock ballooning out of control.

The story suggests the conflicting feelings with which we might view economic growth. Are we sure we want economic growth? Do the benefits of growth outweigh the potential costs? What are the sources of growth and what are the consequences? Finally, can we manage growth so as to enjoy the benefits and reduce the costs?

GROWTH AND GDP

GDP provides a relatively simple way to measure growth trends. Over the period for which comparable data are available, both total and per capita GDP have risen fairly steadily in the United States. Since 1929, GDP growth has averaged about 4 percent a year.

GDP will tend naturally to grow as more and more production is carried on for exchange in the market. GDP grows as Grandpa's vegetable garden, the neighborhood sewing circle, and the live-in maiden aunt (whose value cannot be determined and, therefore, is not included in GDP) are replaced by the commercial farm, the clothing factory, and the nursery school.

In recent years, the decline of the traditional male-headed household has pushed many females into jobs outside the home, which has also had the effect of raising the level of GDP.

Some Limitations on the Use of GDP

In spite of its fairly regular growth, it is not clear that GDP reflects how much better we live than in earlier times. GDP measures the quantity, but not always the quality, of our production. A popular journalist once complained that the strawberries available at the supermarket (included in GDP) are not nearly as tasty as those his grandmother used to raise in her garden (not included in GDP). However, that same journalist showed no inclination to plow up his own yard and spend hours bent over a strawberry patch. Apparently he was willing to give up a little home-grown flavor so that he could work in his chosen profession by day and enjoy professional sports in the evening (included in GDP, by the way).

Measures of GDP leave out some wanted goods—and some unwanted "bads"—that our economic system produces. The "bads" include the changes in the environment (such as water pollution) that are not deducted from the value of goods produced but that certainly reduce the quality of our lives. Adding all the goods and subtracting the bads would provide a more correct measure of growth in the quality of our nation's life. (The discussion of net economic welfare in Chapter 7 treats this topic in more detail.)

HOW DOES GROWTH TAKE PLACE?

What determines the growth rate of GDP? Any economic system, whether primitive or advanced, has potential GDP limited by:

1. The quantity and quality of its human and material resources.
2. Its level of technology.
3. The system through which it organizes its resources for production.

To understand the relationship between growth and resources, consider a simple parable. Imagine a South Pacific island whose workers can produce a certain quantity of fish to feed their families. Total output on the island will grow as the number of workers grows, but per capita output may not grow at all.

At some point, assume that some of the island's workers agree to give up fishing for the day in order to build a boat for trips to richer fishing grounds. In effect, these workers have decided to save a day's labor in order to invest in a capital resource. They have **saved** by not consuming the day's production, and they have **invested** by building a capital resource that will enable them to be more productive in the future.

This parable illustrates the simple truth that creating new capital resources requires sacrifice. Sacrifice is possible, however, only if the necessary food for sustaining life is easily obtained. Sacrifice is possible only if the community is living beyond the bare subsistence level.

With capital equipment, our island community can expand its output more rapidly. Then fewer workers will be needed to catch fish, and more workers will be free to produce still more capital resources. The community will experience even greater economic growth. Ultimately, surplus workers may be diverted to less essential work—such as the production of leisure goods and recreation.

Viewpoint

WHY GROWTH?

Why has the drive toward growth been so strong in the United States?

Some say our drive for material wealth originated with the inferior status of our ancestors in the Old World. Persons who were denied social status because they were born into the lower classes often looked for other routes to advancement: first commerce, then industry and finance. The New World promised social status to hearty settlers and offered plentiful resources for their exploitation.

Historian Arnold Toynbee believed that the drive to growth depends on challenges and rewards. According to Toynbee, an insurmountable challenge frustrates the drive to growth, which is also weakened by an excessive reward. However, the appropriate balance between challenge and reward will encourage work and effort. Fortunately, in the United States surmountable challenges and moderate rewards have provided incentives to achieve rising levels of living.

Other philosophers have attributed our drive toward growth to the Protestant religion. The Catholic Church of the Middle Ages regarded greed as sinful, but the Protestant Church thought idleness was a worse sin than greed. Protestantism encouraged its members to work hard and save their money. The result was fairly steady growth in the production of material goods. In Protestantism, personal wealth became associated with righteousness.

Perhaps the strongest reason that the United States has stressed growth has been our rapidly increasing population. Unless citizens are satisfied with smaller shares of food, clothing, and the comforts of life, production must grow at least as fast as population.

THE "STAGES" OF GROWTH

In his *Stages of Economic Growth*, economist Walt Whitman Rostow described how a primitive economy grows. First the community must develop the necessary *preconditions* for growth: basic health and education and a general sense of purpose among workers to achieve a better life. With these preconditions the economy may experience a takeoff into industrial development. Saving and investment in transportation facilities and electric power will make possible the growth of manufacturing industries. New manufacturing industries will call for the development of supplying industries, and higher incomes earned in manufacturing will provide the means for development of consumer goods industries. Healthy growth will continue until finally the economic system reaches *maturity*.

Having successfully reached maturity, it would seem that an economic system would be "home free." Regrettably, more perplexing problems remain for the mature economy—in particular, the problem of ensuring the fullest possible employment of available

Thinking Seriously About Economic Issues

HAS THE UNITED STATES BECOME A ZERO-SUM SOCIETY?

Lester Thurow of Massachusetts Institute of Technology (MIT) is worried that the United States may have become a *zero-sum society.* A zero-sum society is one in which a gain for one person or group is possible only if another person or group suffers a loss: The sum of a positive gain and an equal negative loss is zero.

In a democratic society like ours, gains and losses are difficult to share. This is because groups whose living standards are threatened with losses will fight vigorously to avoid them. Whereas once upon a time powerful groups in society may have been able to enforce losses on weak groups, a democratic society allows even the weakest minority groups a strong voice in avoiding losses.

Another problem is that as our economic system has grown more complex, we have become more interdependent. In an interdependent society, decisions made to affect one group may affect others indirectly, imposing gains or losses on groups that may not deserve them. Our interdependence has made each of us more concerned about our own security and more determined to hold onto it.

Still, economic growth requires change, and change necessarily brings losses to some of us. Unless we are willing to face up to the possibility of losses, Professor Thurow worries that economic growth may grind to a halt. We will reach a kind of paralysis, in which each of us works steadfastly to keep what he or she already has, and no one can hope for anything better.

According to Professor Thurow, an example of our paralysis is our response to the energy crisis. From plentiful energy at low prices in the 1950s, we moved to scarce energy and the threat of severe shortages in the 1970s. To allow prices to rise high enough to compensate for new energy exploration and development

human resources. Full employment depends on sufficient demand for the goods and services a fully employed labor force can produce.

In Rostow's mature economy, each family will already own all the durable goods necessary for ensuring a comfortable life. When their desire for new goods and services stops growing, the growth of new jobs will slow as well. Rostow warned that a fully mature economic system might have to choose one of three courses if it is to employ its human and material resources:

1. The nation may use idle human resources to produce public goods (instead of more private goods): things like universities, public parks, hospitals, cultural centers, and urban services.
2. The nation may encourage population growth so that it will need more baby carriages, schools, houses, and so forth.
3. The nation may engage in aggression so that it will need military vehicles, food and supplies for military personnel, and explosives for destroying buildings and equipment (which will then require re-

would have reduced the living standards of large groups of people. So we refused to do it. We imposed ceilings on energy prices, and we placed *windfall profits taxes* on energy producers. Recessions in the 1980s kept energy prices from rising and postponed the time when we would have to accept the costs of developing new energy sources. Eventually we will have to pay prices that truly reflect the long-term cost of producing energy. Price increases will be welcomed by groups that expect to gain and resisted by groups that expect to lose.

Another example of the nation's paralysis involves our slowing economic growth and the slowing growth of worker productivity. As citizens of the wealthiest nation on earth, we have become accustomed to enjoying living standards that rise with each generation. Our nation's rapid economic growth has yielded a surplus of income for making investments. Investments, in turn, have created the capacity for still more growth. If growth slows, investment will be possible only through a cut in current living standards. Frequent recessions to curb inflation act further to slow growth by creating excess capacity and stifling incentives to invest.

Solving all these problems will require political decisions regarding the equity of the allocation of gains and losses. Voters have different ideas as to what is equitable, making allocative decisions difficult. To make these decisions, Thurow recommends that leaders acknowledge the necessary costs of growth, inform voters of the costs, and propose ways to share the costs fairly.

Lester C. Thurow, *The Zero-Sum Society*, Basic Books, New York, 1980, and *The Zero-Sum Solution*, Simon & Schuster, New York, 1985.

placement, relieving the nation's unemployment problems far into the future).

AN END TO GROWTH?

An eighteenth-century economist had an even more pessimistic view of growth. Thomas Malthus earned for economics its nickname as the "dismal science," a nickname teachers of economics have been trying to live down ever since.

Malthus reasoned that if the world's total output were to grow faster than necessary for human life, material standards of living would improve. Growing prosperity would encourage higher rates of population growth. The larger population would then absorb the entire world output until all the people would be living barely above starvation. On the other hand, if world output were to become insufficient even for survival, population growth would be halted through disease, famine, and war. The people's misery would increase until the population was living again at the level of starvation.

Pretty dismal, that Malthus!

The Limits to Growth

A report published in the 1970s revived interest in Malthus's predictions about the consequences of growth. The report, published by the Club of Rome, was entitled *The Limits to Growth*. Club of Rome researchers used computer models to project the cause-and-effect results of growth for the world environment. Briefly, this is what they concluded:

1. High birth rates and falling death rates increase population growth.
2. Population growth increases food requirements and presses against limited supplies of farmland.
3. Dwindling food supplies require increased agricultural and industrial production which, in turn, pollutes air and streams.
4. Environmental decay and depletion of productive resources eventually restrict population growth through disease and famine.

The Club of Rome researchers studied feedbacks within and among all these relationships and made projections of the effects of unrestrained growth. All of their tests predicted catastrophic population and resource problems within the lifetimes of many people alive today. The Club of Rome later modified their conclusions and predictions, but the issues they raised should not be ignored.

Exponential Changes

The frightening point made by the *Limits to Growth* was that environmental changes (such as levels of air and water pollution) take place exponentially (like the guinea pigs) rather than linearly.

Linear growth involves changes of the same amount every time period so that a graph describing the change rises (or falls) in a straight line: 1, 2, 3, 4, 5. **Exponential growth** involves a percentage change so that the amount of the change increases (or decreases) every time period: 1, 2, 4, 8, 16. The graph describing an exponential change curves upward or downward. (An example of exponential growth is world fuel consumption. A graph describing annual fuel consumption is rising, not only because larger numbers of people consume energy but also because each person's energy consumption is increasing.)

Environmental Ceilings and Floors

The problem with exponential growth is that the graphs describing environmental changes will reach their limits, whether ceilings or floors, very abruptly. We may bump into the global limits of air, water, and other resources only shortly after we notice the limits are there. When we reach the limits, our entire economic system could collapse. Linear and exponential growth and decline are shown graphically on Figure 14.1.

Critics of *The Limits to Growth* question the validity of its conclusions. In fact, the principles of economics may be instrumental in avoiding its catastrophic predictions. As resource supplies become scarcer, their prices will rise. Higher prices will discourage wasteful use of resources and allocate the scarcest resources to their most urgent uses. Improved efficiency should postpone the appearance of environmental ceilings or floors.

Limitations on growth are particularly worrisome to citizens of poor nations and to some of our own citizens who live in poverty. Modern communications and transportation have exposed the wide gap between the living standards of the world's haves and have-nots. The result has been a "revolution of rising expectations" among the have-nots, both in our nation and abroad. The have-nots are beginning to demand a better life for themselves. Therefore, it may be that the only acceptable course is not to stop growth entirely but to regulate growth and distribute its benefits more equally.

Thinking Seriously About Economic Issues

ESCAPING THE MALTHUSIAN TRAP

The biologists are being attacked by the economists, and victory is still up for grabs.

The basis for the debate is population growth and whether or not population growth is a good thing. The biologists, in the person of author Paul Ehrlich, say that population growth is outstripping the resources of the planet. The economists, in the person of Professor Julian Simon, say that every gloomy prediction of the biologists has turned out to be wrong and that, in fact, population growth has brought technical progress and better lives for more people.

Human ingenuity has led to the creation of new resources and the invention of ways to use them more efficiently. While Simon sees the tremendous increases in the earth's productivity, Ehrlich warns that increased productivity has come at the expense of fertile land and clean groundwater, and thus threatens future productivity.

Can you illustrate each of these positions through the model of production possibilities?

David Berreby, "The Numbers Game," *Discover*, April 1990.

Figure 14.1 Environmental Ceilings and Floors

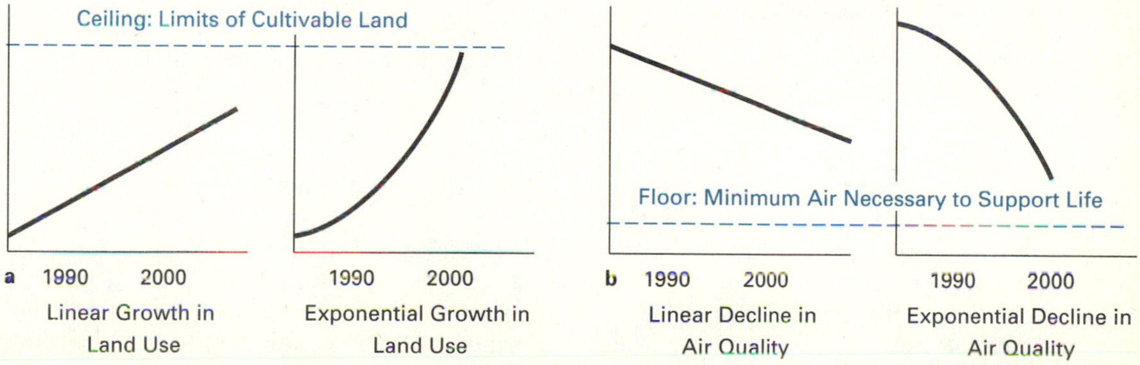

THEORIES OF GROWTH

How can we explain the strong growth trends of some nations and the prolonged stagnation of others? Even more puzzling, how can we explain differences in growth trends among regions within a single nation?

There are two major theories to explain how and why economic growth takes place. One theory focuses on productive sectors within the nation or region and is known as the *sectoral theory* of growth. Another theory focuses on trade relationships between the nation or region and the rest of the world and is known as the *export-base theory* of growth.

The Sectoral Theory of Growth

The **sectoral theory of growth** is based on historical studies showing similar patterns of growth among the various sectors of a growing economy.

Typically, the first sector to experience growth has been the agricultural sector. This is because agriculture provides the basic necessities of life: food, clothing, medicine. Specialization in agriculture encourages a young economy to develop farm equipment and technology for increasing farm productivity. When farm productivity increases faster than the community's need for basic necessities, resources can be released from farming for work in other sectors.

The second sector to experience growth is typically the manufacturing sector. After people's basic needs are satisfied, they begin to want other material goods. Manufacture of consumer goods develops, and support industries spring up to supply raw materials and component parts. An important support industry is transportation. Transportation facilities unite small communities into larger, interdependent markets. Larger markets permit greater specialization and division of labor and provide opportunities for large-scale, low-cost production. As many different kinds of manufacturing mature and prosper, the effects of increased production and rising incomes spread throughout the economic system.

The third sector to experience growth is the service sector. Once basic necessities and other material goods are plentiful, consumers want services that will improve the quality of their lives. Business firms are established to produce personal and household services and business services. In the first group are health and education, recreation and the arts, home decorating, and fashion. In the second are financial and consulting services, communications, marketing, and economic forecasting.

The Export-Base Theory of Growth

The **export-base theory of growth** focuses on trade between the nation or region and the rest of the world. Under the export-base theory a region must produce exportable commodities that are in demand elsewhere. Sales of the export commodity bring income into the region, income that is invested in facilities for producing the export commodity itself and in industries that supply or support the export-base industry.

As rising incomes spread throughout the export and support industries, workers become more prosperous. They use their increased earnings to buy consumer goods and services, stimulating growth in these industries.

POLICIES FOR GROWTH

Understanding the sources of growth should lead to effective policies for managing growth. Designing proper policies is particularly important for poor nations, as well as for poor regions within developed nations. Ideally, we should be able to design programs to achieve the greatest benefits from growth without its more costly side effects.

If we accept the sectoral theory of growth, we might recommend programs to aid the agricultural sector. Such programs might include research and development in agricultural techniques and investment in agricultural education for increasing productivity. There might also be government-guaranteed loans to farmers for investments in agricultural equipment. According to the sectoral theory, greater productivity in agriculture allows resources to move into other sectors of the economy. Development will then follow automatically in the manufacturing sector and, finally, in the service sector.

On the other hand, if we accept the export-base theory of growth, we might recommend programs to promote production of commodities for sale abroad. Gold, diamonds, petroleum, and tin, for example, have been important export commodities for some nations. Or the export base for development might be an agricultural commodity such as cotton, coffee, rubber, sugar, cheese, or wine. In a more highly industrialized economic system, the export base might be manufactured goods, such as precision instruments, electronic equipment, or computers. According to the export-base theory, increasing prosperity in the export-base industry will cause growth to spread to other industries. Then rising incomes in the export-related industries will lead automatically to growth in the production of consumer goods and services.

Note that these two growth theories produce opposite policy recommendations. The sectoral approach calls for increasing agricultural investment. Would this approach be practical in, say, the depressed regions of Appalachia in the United States or in the new nations of Africa? Why or why not?

In contrast, the export-base approach calls for investment in the production of export commodities. Would it be practical to invest in cotton production in the southern United States or in rubber plantations in Southeast Asia? Why or why not?

A single approach to development has certain disadvantages. If the favored sector or industry suffers a decline in demand, the entire nation or region may suffer stagnation. If world food production outstrips demand, for example, the agricultural sector may collapse. Too great a dependence on one crop might also be disastrous. A bumper crop one year could mean falling prices and falling incomes for the exporting nation. Even worse, a technological change may make an export commodity worthless in world markets.

In the past, substantial investment in agriculture or in a particular export industry has not always led to development in other sectors. Sometimes incomes earned in the favored sector are not invested in the less-developed sectors, but instead are sent to other regions or other nations that promise a greater return on investment. If this happens, profits from the first stages of development cannot be used to stimulate further stages of growth, and the region or nation may continue to stagnate at low levels of production and low material living standards.

Self-Check

1. **Which of the following illustrates the most likely sequence of growth?**
   a. Saving, plentiful resources, capital equipment, investment.
   b. Plentiful resources, saving, investment, capital equipment.
   c. Investment, capital equipment, saving, plentiful resources.
   d. Plentiful resources, investment, capital equipment, saving.
   e. Saving, investment, capital equipment, plentiful resources.

2. **When total resources reach high levels of productivity:**
   a. There is danger of unemployment.
   b. They may produce nonmaterial services to enrich the quality of life.
   c. Production may focus on military equipment.
   d. There may be emphasis on wasteful production.
   e. All of the above.

3. **Which of the following is not a limit to growth?**
   a. Pollution caused by increasing agricultural and industrial production.
   b. Rising birthrates relative to death rates.
   c. Limited supplies of farmland.
   d. Exponential trends in resource use.
   e. All are limits to growth.

4. **The sectoral theory of growth:**
   a. Is based on growing productivity in export industries.
   b. Depends on inflows of spending from other nations.
   c. Emphasizes the development of agriculture, manufacturing, and then services.
   d. Would call for policy to increase agricultural investment in order to encourage growth.
   e. Both (c) and (d).

5. **Under the export-base theory of growth:**
   a. A region must produce commodities that are in demand elsewhere.
   b. Sales of an export good will cause outflows of spending from the producing region.
   c. Growth would be encouraged by investment in the production of export commodities.
   d. All of the above.
   e. Both (a) and (c).

Theory in Practice

GRAPHING GROWTH IN PRODUCTION POSSIBILITIES

Economic growth requires increases in the quality and quantity of resources and improvements in technology. In the United States, labor resources have increased substantially over the years. Our population has grown from 5.3 million in 1800 to more than 250 million in 1992. The quality of labor has improved, too, through better health and education and longer years of productive life. Improvements in technology have come about through scientific and engineering advances and through better organizational and managerial techniques.

Growth in the stock of capital has also added to our productive capacity. Investments in transportation and communication facilities, power plants, and manufacturing plants and equipment have made possible even greater growth.

Remember that investment in capital resources is possible only if people refrain from consuming a portion of their incomes. Then savers must make their funds available to business firms for investment in productive facilities. Since 1929, Americans have saved an average of about 6 percent of their disposable income (personal income after taxes).

To be able to save, a nation must first be able to produce more goods and services than the minimum necessary for life. Surplus production makes it possible to shift resources from the production of life's necessities into the production of new capital resources. Fortunately, our plentiful resources have enabled us to increase production and to save and invest significant amounts. In 1992, for example, total investment expenditures in the United States amounted to more than $780 billion. One-third of this amount represented net additions to capital stock; that is, additions over and above replacement of depreciated buildings and equipment.

Increases in a nation's productive capacity can be illustrated as a steady shift to the right of its production possibilities curve. The production possibilities curves in Figure 14.2 illustrate the production capabilities of two countries, one rich in resources and technology and the other poor. Suppose a minimum production of 10 units of goods and services is necessary to sustain the population in each nation. The rich nation can produce the necessary goods and services and also 20 units of capital resources. The poor nation can produce the necessary goods and services and only 5 units of capital.

TEST YOURSELF

How will the ability to invest in capital affect future production possibilities for the rich nation? Pencil in the appropriate changes in production possibilities on the figure. What nations are currently experiencing limitations on growth because of the lack of sufficient resources and technology?

THE EXTERNALITIES OF GROWTH

We humans are the only animals on earth who significantly change the environment. We have used our superior intelligence to produce a growing variety and quantity of goods and services. In the process of production, however, we have produced some unwanted materials that have changed our environment in unintended ways.

Economists call the side effects of production **externalities.** Many externalities are use-

Figure 14.2 Production Possibilities Curve for Two Nations

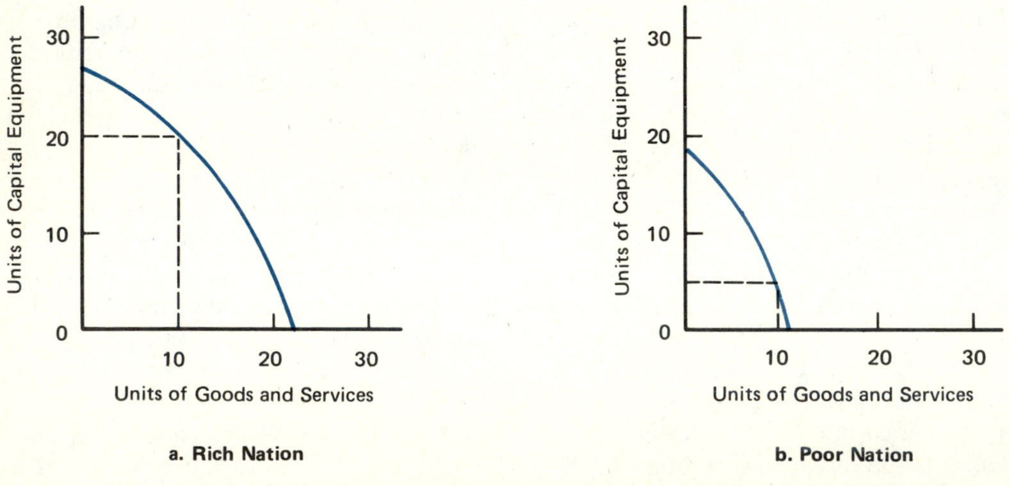

ful and desirable, as when growth in manufacturing increases the skills of workers and enables them to produce a wider range of goods and services. We call externalities that improve the quality of life *positive externalities*. Some other examples of positive externalities are: improved technology of agriculture, which enables more people to live healthy, productive lives and frees labor for other types of work; better housing, which improves our landscape and helps make our neighborhoods more stable; immunization against diseases, which halts their spread and limits exposure even for people who have not been immunized.

The less favorable side effects of production are called *negative externalities*. Negative externalities also extend throughout the society, imposing costs on members of the community as a whole. Most of us are familiar with negative externalities: air pollution, which worsens our health and dirties our homes and clothing; water pollution, which destroys recreation areas and increases the cost of pure water; noise pollution, which damages our hearing and rattles our nerves; discarded junk, which breeds vermin and disease. No doubt, you can add more examples from your personal experience.

The significant fact about externalities is that they are received by people who did not request them. Positive externalities are enjoyed by everyone within reach of the benefits; negative externalities become a burden to everyone in reach of the social costs . . . whether we want them or not!

This fact makes externalities different from goods and services traded in free markets. Free markets are careful to award the benefits of production only to those people who want them and are willing to pay the cost. We say free markets are efficient because participants in markets evaluate the benefits they expect to receive from a good or service and refuse to purchase it unless the benefits are at least as great as the costs. Stated algebraically,

$$\frac{\text{benefits}}{\text{costs}} \geq 1$$

means an efficient market decision. In market transactions there is little danger that goods will be produced whose benefits are less than the costs:

$$\frac{\text{benefits}}{\text{costs}} < 1$$

means an inefficient market decision. Efficiency in many individual markets means efficiency for the economic system as a whole. Thus, a free market system uses scarce resources only to the extent that the benefits received are at least as great as the costs paid.

This efficient result is not necessarily true when there are externalities. When there are externalities, the costs of production are paid for by two groups: those who receive the benefits and pay for them, and those who receive no benefits but suffer the social costs (or negative externalities) nevertheless.

There is another problem associated with externalities. The problem involves a principle called equity, a word that is difficult to define precisely but involves fairness.*

By most definitions, a free market system is fair. That is, it gives people what they pay for. People who want the benefits pay the cost. Those who don't, don't. The presence of externalities changes the distribution of benefits and costs, however, and the result is often not fair.

How can understanding externalities help our nation plan for growth? First, we must recognize that a free market system does not account for externalities. Therefore, some decisions about production must be made outside the market, by the nation as a whole

* What is "fair" may mean different things to different people.

Thinking Seroiusly About Economic Issues

PRESERVING THE ENVIRONMENT

Accounting for externalities and making efficient decisions is not easy. Rules prohibiting production of negative externalities tend to increase costs of production without yielding measurable benefits. Many economists recommend replacing hard-and-fast rules with economic incentives to reduce negative externalities while continuing to increase production.

In each of the following examples, replacing rules with economic incentives would make resource allocation more efficient.

1. When too many fishing boats are depleting fishing grounds, a rule that limits every boat's catch would mean higher average fixed costs and higher average total costs for all fishers. A better solution to the problem of overfishing would be annual fishing fees and transferable quotas for fishing. Revenue from the fees would be used to buy out fishers who would agree to get out of the business. Those fishers who remained would look on the annual fee as an investment in increased fish production.

   In both of these cases, higher costs of fishing would be built into the prices consumers pay for fish. (Explain how.) In the second case, however, excess resources would leave the fishing industry for more efficient employment elsewhere.
2. When an area suffers from environmental pollution, a rule that prohibits the entry of new firms may actually keep out firms with more effective pollution-control systems than existing firms. A better solution to the pollution problem would be to award emission reduction credits to any existing firms that voluntarily reduce their emissions below prevailing regulations. Emission reduction credits could then be sold to new firms at prices that reflect the emissions added by their entry to the

through our democratically elected representatives. Making decisions democratically enables us to measure the "social benefits" of production; that is, the benefits received by persons who purchase the good or service plus the positive externalities its production brings to the community as a whole. Our democratic processes also help us evaluate production's "social costs": the costs paid by purchasers of the good or service plus the negative externalities its production imposes on the community as a whole. Stated algebraically;

$$\frac{\text{total benefits}}{\text{total costs}} = \frac{\text{private benefits} + \text{positive externalities}}{\text{private costs} + \text{negative externalities}} = \frac{\text{social benefits}}{\text{social costs}} \geq 1$$

area. Under this plan, firms that can control their emissions cheaply could benefit from the sale of credits to firms whose emission-control costs are prohibitive. Thus, emissions reductions credits can help reduce pollution at lowest cost.

3. The world as a whole is threatened by the greenhouse effect, which occurs when gases are trapped in the earth's atmosphere so that the sun's radiant heat cannot escape. Instead of rules shutting down emitters of greenhouse gases, a more efficient solution to the problem would be to require new sources of greenhouse gases to offset their emissions by other actions, such as conserving or recycling natural resources, planting trees, or closing their oldest, heavily polluting plants. By increasing the costs of pollution, such a requirement would encourage emitters of greenhouse gases to search for ways to reduce their emissions.

The expected effect of programs like these is to place the cost of negative externalities on the firms that cause them. Profit-seeking firms would then look for efficient ways to reduce environmental costs. Firms that are unable to reduce their negative externalities will then pass their higher costs on to consumers, who may be expected to demand smaller quantities of the offending product at the higher price.

Explain how each of the programs described would work to protect the environment more efficiently than rigid rules and regulations. How does pollution affect GDP? How does pollution control affect GDP?

T.H. Tietenberg, "Using Economic Incentives to Maintain Our Environment," *Challenge*, March/April 1990.

Needless to say, positive and negative externalities are difficult to identify and impossible to measure precisely. However, some effort must at least be made to make sure that resources are used only for production that provides social benefits at least as great as its social costs.

Once production is judged to be efficient in the economic sense, it should be evaluated in terms of equity. Are the benefits and costs distributed fairly? Do those who enjoy the benefits also pay the costs? How much equity are we willing to sacrifice for production that is efficient but whose benefits and costs are distributed inequitably?

TEST YOURSELF

The economics of the environment can be summarized in three E's: efficiency, externalities, and equity. Make sure you

Contemporary Thinking About Economic Issues

THE COSTS OF GLOBAL WARMING

William D. Nordhaus (Council of Economic Advisors, 1977–1979) has attempted to clarify the scientific, economic, and policy issues that underlie decision making regarding the problem of global warming.

Norhaus has created an economic model that describes the costs to society of a changing climate and the costs the economy pays to reduce greenhouse gases. Using familiar microeconomic theory, the model identifies the optimal level of emissions reduction at the point where the marginal cost of reducing emissions equals the marginal damage to the world economy from higher concentrations of greenhouse gases.

Nordhaus estimates that a 3-degree Centigrade increase in global temperature is likely to arrive in the second half of the next century. The accompanying climate changes will cause the loss of between .25 and 2 percent of global output, which amounts to between $7.30 and $66 per ton of CO_2-equivalent emissions. The optimal emissions reduction associated with the loss of .25 percent of global output is 11 percent, for total annual cost of $3 billion. For the loss of 2 percent of global output, the optimal level of emissions reduction is about one-third, for an annual cost of more than $40 billion. The important question becomes: How much are we willing to pay now to reduce greenhouse gases in order to avoid loss of global output in the next century? What other questions must be answered before policymakers can decide policy on emissions reductions? What equity issues will accompany policy decisions? What policies can accomplish the desired results most efficiently?

William D. Nordhaus, "A Sketch of the Economics of the Greenhouse Effect," *American Economic Review Papers and Proceedings*, May 1991.

understand these terms and how they contribute to an understanding of economic choice. Then evaluate each of the following projects in terms of the three E's.

1. A proposed highway would transport commuters quickly from the suburbs to their jobs in the city. But it would also disrupt an established inner-city neighborhood, cut off local business firms from their regular customers, and remove much urban property from the city's tax base. Ninety percent of the cost of construction would be paid by the federal government, and 10 percent by the state.
2. A proposed dam would provide electric power, flood control, and recreational facilities over a large area. It would stimulate industrial and commercial development and raise incomes for poor rural families. However, it would forever change the landscape, destroying valuable farm- and timberland, eliminating white-water canoeing streams, and destroying the habitat of a unique species of fish.

Thinking Seriously About Economic Issues

THE COST OF ENVIRONMENTAL PROTECTION

Programs to improve the environment impose a cost today for the sake of benefits to be enjoyed far in the future. When planning such programs, it is important to ensure that the ratio of future benefits to current costs is at least as great as it is for other uses of the nation's resources.

Consider a $1 investment today that yields a real return of 5 percent, which is reinvested in the project itself. By the year 2050 the original dollar will have grown to $18.68 in real purchasing power. Under these conditions, it makes no sense to use a dollar for environmental protection unless the dollar yields at least $18.68 in improved environmental conditions.

3. A chemical process restructures the molecules of petroleum to produce a fiber for weaving into cloth. The cloth never wrinkles or needs ironing, enabling many homemakers to spend their time in other more creative ways. Although the miracle fiber increases the variety and durability of our clothing, production requires vast quantities of imported oil and natural gas and expels heat, chemicals, and nondegradable materials into the air and water.
4. Fast-food restaurants package their food in containers that keep hot food hot and cold food cold. Busy people come to depend on quick and nutritious meals stored in such containers. Producing the containers expels a gas that destroys ozone in the earth's atmosphere and increases the risk of skin cancer. Because discarded containers do not quickly biodegrade, they occupy space in landfills for years to come.

POPULATION AND THE WORLD FOOD CRISIS

Advances in technology have helped more of the world's people live better and longer—and that's part of the problem!

Better health standards have kept more people alive, such that the world's population is now over five billion and expected to double in only twenty-five years. Growing population and slowly rising living standards have increased our need for food at the same time that the world's stockpile of food is declining.

The Rise and Fall of the Green Revolution

From the early 1950s until 1972, world food production increased dramatically. The "green revolution" extended scientific techniques to agriculture in the form of hybrid seed and livestock, chemical fertilizers and pesticides, and improved irrigation systems. Strains of corn, grain sorghum, soybeans, wheat, and rice were developed to thrive in particular climate and soil conditions around the world.

The green revolution was especially successful in the United States. Corn production per acre quadrupled during the early 1900s. Milk production rose to 10,000 pounds per cow per year, compared to only 600 pounds per cow in India. Chickens were bred to eat less, to grow to maturity in a shorter time, and

Viewpoint

THE TRAGEDY OF THE COMMONS

Does the profit motive drive firms to despoil the environment? And, more critically, does a clean environment require substantial government involvement in business practices?

As far back as 1912, the British economist A. C. Pigou identified the divergence between "social costs" and "private costs" as the chief cause of environmental degradation and the basis for government regulation "in the public interest." More recently, noted environmentalist Barry Commoner has said that social ownership and control of production is the only route to environmental protection.

The logical conclusion of this kind of thinking is that the former command economies of the Soviet Union and Eastern Europe would have a cleaner environment than the market economies of Western nations. Not so, reports Soviet scholar Marshall Goldman. In fact, the Soviet five-year plans encouraged indiscriminate exploitation of natural and environmental resources. Because there was no private property, no long-range asset value was attached to such resources, with the result that the command economies experienced massive air and water pollution, deteriorating wildlife populations, devastating erosion, and acid rain. Estimates are that a third of the people of Poland live in areas of ecological disaster, where they suffer more circulatory disease, cancerous tumors, and respiratory disease than other Poles. Life expectancy for men is lower than it was 20 years ago, and the number of retarded children has increased. Farmland in some parts of Czechoslovakia is toxic from the excessive use of fertilizer to more than one foot in depth. In what was East Germany, nearly 40 percent of the population suffers ill effects from pollutants in the air.

Until the mid-1800s strong protection of property rights in the United States acted to reduce environmental degradation. But the drive to economic growth eventually whittled away at polluting firms' legal liability and created conditions similar to those in command economies. Lately, government has contributed to environmental problems in the United States. Our public institutions are responsible for a large part of hazardous waste, and our agricultural policy probably encourages overuse of land subject to erosion.

Correcting environmental problems (in the United States as well as in the former command economies) requires, first, increased productivity to create the wealth for producing innovative pollution-control technology. An important part of the solution is also sound liability laws and strong private property rights.

Thomas DiLorenzo, "Does Free Enterprise Cause Pollution?" *Across the Board*, January/February 1991.

to produce more eggs. As a result of such scientific advances, our twelve midwestern states alone now feed one-fourth of the world's people.

Worldwide crop disasters in the mid-1970s brought a halt to the dramatic growth in agricultural production. Much of the increased yields had come from the use of chemical fertilizers, primarily petroleum-based and increasingly in short supply. Rising costs of fertilizer present a particularly difficult problem for the newly developing nations that often lack the necessary foreign exchange for importing fertilizer. The problem is so serious that Philip Handler, former president of the National Academy of Sciences, has predicted one million child deaths per month in the world's poorest nations by the year 2025.

Proposals and Problems

What can be done? At present the world's farmers are cultivating only about half of the world's arable land. The most favorable lands are already in use, however, and the additional costs of clearing, transportation, and irrigation associated with developing new farmland would run in the billions of dollars. Adding only 10 percent to the world's cultivated acreage could cost as much as $1 trillion.

Land reform might increase productivity in some nations. New foods from the sea are also a possibility, but the potential gain is limited by pollution and by too intensive fishing in past years. New varieties of seeds are still being developed, but the process is slow and costly. Fertilizer production may also be expanded, particularly in the less-developed countries.

Reduction of waste would also help relieve the food shortage. Decreased consumption in the world's richest nations could increase the quantities available for poor nations. The United States, for example, uses the equivalent of 7 pounds of grain in the production of each 1 pound of meat. Reducing U.S. meat consumption would free this grain for shipment abroad. It is estimated that the average person in poor countries consumes only about 400 pounds of grain per year, compared to the average citizen of North America who consumes a ton (about 100 pounds of which is in the form of beer or whiskey).

Lifeboat Ethics?

Policy involving food distribution must eventually deal with the problem of population growth. Some analysts are beginning to recommend what is called *lifeboat ethics*: In the ocean of life we are all adrift, as if in a boat. We would like to bring all others into our boat, but that would exceed its capacity and we would sink. We must choose to help only those nations that are able and willing to make a tremendous effort to help themselves.

The decision to distribute food only to selected nations is similar to the principle of *triage* in classifying battlefield casualties. Victims of battle are divided into three groups: those who will probably survive without aid, those who will probably survive with moderate aid, and those who will not survive without substantial aid. Limited medical resources are then concentrated on the second group. By implication, the third is left to perish, an ethically difficult decision to make. We may not like it but, in the words of ecologist-biologist Garrett Hardin, it is a little like the law of gravity: "Once you know it's true, you don't sit down and cry about it. That's the way the world is."

In human terms, this conclusion may apply to the one-third of the world's people who live in the poorest nations—nations unable to feed themselves or to produce sufficient goods for export to pay for food imports. These nations are centered in Asia and Africa below the Sahara: Bangladesh and Somalia are tragic examples.

We continue to hope for a more acceptable alternative than slow starvation for these people. Policy to relieve the crisis in food production will require the best efforts of scientists, sociologists, economists, and humanitarians for many years to come.

AN INTERNATIONAL PLAN FOR GROWTH

By now you are probably convinced that economic growth is:

(a) Desirable.
(b) Undesirable.
(c) Possible.
(d) Impossible.
(e) All of the above!

Of course, the problem of growth is much too complex to summarize in a single answer. Even so, it is an important question, and in the 1970s the United Nations established the United Nations Environment Program to study and plan for an International Development Strategy. Guiding the study was Wassily Leontief, a Russian-born economist who is now a professor of economics at New York University.

Professor Leontief is well qualified to conduct such a study. In the 1940s he was responsible for developing a revolutionary new economic model. Leontief's economic model measures the necessary growth in inputs for producing larger outputs from many U.S. industries. The result of his early work was an **input-output table** for the United States, showing all the various inputs required for producing all the outputs demanded by American consumers and business firms.

Measuring inputs and outputs is complicated because many of the inputs to one industry are actually outputs of another. Without the table it would be difficult to measure the necessary growth in inputs (which are also outputs) needed to produce more of any single good.

An example may be helpful. Consider the industry that produces motor vehicles—automobiles, trucks, and moving equipment. On the average, to produce one dollar's worth of motor vehicles requires the following inputs:

textile products	1 cent
paint	½ cent
rubber and plastics	2 cents
glass	1 cent
metals	10 cents
metal products	7 cents
machinery and equipment	2 cents
electrical products	1½ cents
motor vehicle parts	33 cents
retail trade and services	3 cents

To increase production of motor vehicles requires that output in all these other industries increase first. To increase production of any one of these inputs, however, requires additional production in still other industries—and those other industries include motor vehicles. *Motor vehicles are themselves necessary inputs in the industries producing inputs used in the motor vehicle industry.*

Interrelationships among industries create a kind of chain reaction, such that the necessary total change in output is greater than the change required for a single increase in one industry. Making such complicated computations was not possible before Leontief developed his input-output table.

Leontief saw that his input-output model could be expanded to include all the nations in the world. A global input-output table would enable planners to measure the necessary production of, say, chemical fertilizers in Venezuela for increasing rice production in Southeast Asia. Leontief's global input-output table is summarized in 2625 equations, each one describing the interrelationships between production and consumption of a particular good in a particular part of the world. Happily, computers are available for solving the equations.

Using his equations, Leontief was able to predict the necessary growth in all inputs for increasing living standards in any part of the world economy and for promoting more balanced growth worldwide. Where input supplies are scarce, Leontief's model can identify bottlenecks. Where new technology is applied, the model can predict the resulting increase in productivity. A flow of loans or grants from developed to less-developed nations shows up as increased investment for increasing global production possibilities. Even pollution is included in Leontief's model as the net result of new industrial emissions minus the effects of pollution-abatement equipment.

After comparing the expected growth in worldwide demand with potential growth in supply, Leontief came to these conclusions:

1. Under present growth projections, the gap in per capita income between rich and poor nations will remain about 12 to 1 at least until the year 2000.
2. However, technological and institutional changes in poor countries could double their food production.
3. A general scarcity of mineral resources is not yet a serious problem, but gains in mineral production will become more and more costly in the future.
4. Poor nations must increase their investment to as much as 40 percent of their GDP. Increased investment will require cutbacks in personal consumption, increased taxes and government development programs, and more investment funds from rich nations.

If Leontief's model is to become a basis for a global growth strategy, there must first be a new willingness to cooperate toward shared goals. Nations must agree to set aside purely national goals and fit their own growth plans into a world context. The prospects for such cooperation become better as more nations come to see the potential gains of cooperation relative to the costs of going it alone.

SUMMARY

1. Economic growth has long been an accepted national goal. Abundant resources in the United States have helped us achieve rising standards of living.
2. GDP is a way of measuring production and growth. Growth in GDP requires saving so that investment can be made in capital equipment. However, an increasing GDP depends also on increasing demand for goods and services.
3. The potential size of GDP depends on the quantity and quality of resources, the level of technology, and the system of organizing resources.
4. A fully mature society may suffer from unemployment as a result of declining demand for goods and services. To offset declining demand, a society may choose to use its resources to provide for a rising population, for military operations, or for public goods.
5. Some researchers predict that continued economic growth will eventually bring on environmental crises. They recommend planning for environmentally sound growth.
6. Growth may proceed through sectors of the economy, or it may depend on the development of an export commodity. A correct analysis of growth should lead to a correct policy to stimulate and manage growth.
7. The production possibilities curve is a useful tool for illustrating growth. A nation or region with large production possibilities is better able to save and invest for future growth.
8. Attempts are being made to improve agricultural techniques and increase productivity in order to deal with the world food crisis. However, dealing with severe shortages in poor nations may require difficult choices on the part of rich nations.

TERMS TO REMEMBER

saving: refraining from consumption
investing: using resources to construct capital resources
linear growth: growth of the same amount each time period
exponential growth: growth at a constant percentage rate, which adds greater amounts each time period
sectoral theory of growth: the theory that growth takes place systematically, first in agriculture, then in manufacturing, and finally in services
export-base theory of growth: the theory that growth takes place through the development of a major export industry
input-output table: a chart showing all resource inputs needed for producing various types of output

TOPICS FOR DISCUSSION

1. Most of us have heard the old saying, "Necessity is the mother of invention." A commentator on the American scene once observed that today it would be more appropriate to say, "Invention is the mother of necessity." What do you think he meant by that? How is the statement related to our discussion of economic growth? Discuss the advantages and disadvantages of this philosophy.
2. Nations differ with respect to the quantity of personal savings. The *Wall Street Journal* once reported that Swiss citizens were saving annually the equivalent of $5000 per capita, the highest in the world. The British were second with $4000, and Americans were third with $3300. Last on the list of 29 countries was Ethiopia, with annual per capita savings of $4.36. What factors influence the different rates of savings? How do you think savings might be put to use in each of the countries mentioned?
3. Each year in the United States, labor resources increase at the rate of about 2 percent. Productivity per worker also increases. Thus, the potential growth in output is more than 3 percent per year. If new labor is to be employed and higher production to take place, there must be rising demand. Demand must be backed up by spending power. Someone must be willing and able to buy! What problems, if any, can you see in the rising productive potential of the world's richest nation? What solutions would you propose? Are there other long-range problems that might affect your answer?
4. Walt Rostow has suggested that a mature society may have trouble employing all its labor resources unless it encourages population growth, engages in military aggression, or invests in public goods and services. Is this result consistent with the problem of scarce resources, described in Chapter 1? Is it possible to have unlimited wants and unemployed resources at the same time? Why?
5. How do most Americans save and invest? Are you now saving and investing? Explain how your experience in school is an example of the process of saving and investment.
6. Many state legislatures are considering the following proposals to regulate disposble diapers: disposable-diaper taxes or all-out bans on disposable diapers. How would economists regard these proposals? How would economists define the efficient solution to the environmental problems associated with disposable diapers?

ANSWERS TO TEST YOURSELF

(p. 320) Cause it to shift to the right and make possible even greater production of capital goods. Somalia, the Sudan, Russia

(p. 323) 1. The highway may provide commuters more efficient employment and higher incomes, but displaced city dwellers and taxpayers across the country will pay the cost.

(p. 324) 2. Some families will enjoy the benefits of irrigation, electric power, jobs, and recreation. Future generations would pay the cost of fewer woodlands and diminished wild life.

(p. 325) 3. Many people enjoy more carefree clothing, but we may damage the atmosphere and the world's climate.

(p. 325) 4. People who eat fast food enjoy the convenience, but others suffer skin cancer.

FURTHER READING

Abramovitz, Moses, Thinking About Growth, Cambridge, 1989.

"America's New Growth Regions," *Business Week*, October 19, 1992, p. 89.

Bosworth, Barry, *Tax Incentives and Economic Growth*, Brookings, Washington, 1984.

Coase, Ronald, "The Problem of Social Cost," *Journal of Law and Economics*, 2 October 1960.

Commoner, Barry, *The Closing Circle*, Knopf, New York, 1972.

Crandall, Robert W., *Controlling Industrial Pollution*, Brookings, Washington, 1983.

"The Envirnoment," *The Economist*, September 2, 1989.

Friedman, Benjamin M., "Financial Roadblocks on the Route to Economic Prosperity," *Challenge*, March/April 1992.

Frost, Raymond M., "Losing Economic Hegemony," *Challenge*, July/August 1992.

Kneese, Allen V. and Charles L. Schultze, *Pollution, Prices, and Public Policy*, Brookings, 1975.

Litan, Robert E., et al, *American Living Standards*, Brookings, Washington, 1988.

Malthus, Thomas Robert, *Population: The First Essay*, U. of Michigan Press, Ann Arbor, 1964.

Mishel, Lawrence R., "The Late Great Debate on Deindustrialization," *Challenge*, January/February 1989.

Mowery, David C. and Nathan Rosenberg, *Technology and the Pursuit of Economic Growth*, Cambridge U. Press, Cambridge, 1989.

Peterson, Wallace C., "The Silent Depression," *Challenge*, July/August 1991.

Repetto, Robert, "Environmental Production and Why It Is So Important," *Challenge*, September/October 1990.

Scheeeraga, Joel D., "Combatting Global Warming," *Challenge*, July/August 1990.

Teitelbaum, Michael S., "The Population Threat," *Foreign Affairs*, Winter 1992/1993.

Chapter 15

Global Trade and Finance

Tools for Study

LEARNING OBJECTIVES

After reading this chapter, you will be able to:

1. Explain how free trade works.
2. Distinguish between absolute advantage and comparative advantage.
3. Explain how, through comparative advantage, every nation can benefit from international trade.
4. Explain how foreign exchange markets work.
5. Explain the balance-of-payments statement and identify inflows and outflows in international accounts.
6. Name the familiar barriers to trade and discuss their consequences.

CURRENT ISSUES FOR DISCUSSION

What are the relative benefits and costs of tariffs?

How can a nation export its own inflation or unemployment?

What are multinationals and how might they help or hurt the domestic economy?

One historian has identified the beginning of trade as a significant turning point in human progress. Trade began to flourish about 2000 B.C., when the Egyptians discovered how to make bronze by combining tin and copper. Bronze was a stronger and more useful metal than either tin or copper used alone. However, sufficient quantities of the two metals were found only in distant regions: tin in England and copper in India and parts of the Middle East. Trade was necessary to bring the metals together.

Trade opened many other opportunities for production within trading nations and opportunities for other forms of communication as well. It helped bring together the cultural, intellectual, and technical accomplishments of many scattered peoples.

FREE TRADE

Throughout this text, we have associated economic progress with specialization and exchange. We have suggested that groups can increase their productivity if they specialize in producing a particular good or service to exchange for goods or services produced by other groups.

Why Specialization?

There are many reasons why specialization is desirable. Some regions are better suited geographically for certain types of production. Agriculture provides the most obvious examples. Coffee beans grow well in tropical climates; wheat and corn do best in dry, sunny climates; livestock require grassy plains for grazing.

Other geographic features are favorable for other types of production. A sheltered harbor provides protection for shipbuilding; rushing mountain streams provide power for operating machinery; mountainous terrain exposes layers of minerals for use in manufacturing.

Such geographical features are not easily moved and can be used to best advantage by local workers. Among local workers, special skills will develop, and new processes and techniques will be designed to improve productivity and make larger quantities available at lower costs.

With specialization, it is likely that the region will produce more of a particular good or service than it needs. Its surplus production can then be exchanged for the specialties of other regions. Throughout the world, nations will benefit from the large-scale, low-cost production of their trading partners.

Interdependence

There is one small (very small) fly in the ointment, however. Remember that specialization replaces self-sufficiency. Regions that specialize become dependent on other regions for certain goods and services that may be essential for a good life. Interdependent regions must be assured a free flow of goods and services. Otherwise, they will be reluctant to give up their self-sufficiency for specialization in production.

The United States enjoys the benefits of a large trading area. We have many different regions with varied climates, resources, and geographical features. Also, we have one single national government, with laws prohibiting restrictions on the flow of goods and services. The ability to trade freely has enabled regions of the United States to specialize and enjoy the benefits of specialization without the concerns that might otherwise accompany the loss of self-sufficiency.

In recent decades, twelve European nations have entered into agreements that encourage free trade. The nations of the European Economic Community (the EC) have agreed to allow goods, services, and productive resources to flow more freely across their national borders than was the case when each nation acted independently. The result has been increasing productivity and lower costs, with rising standards of living for European populations. In future years, members of the EC hope to combine their economies even more closely, with the further possibility that they may one day adopt a common currency. Fulfilling this hope will require each nation to sacrifice some of its own sovereignty for the sake of more centralized decision making—a sacrifice that is not easily made.

ABSOLUTE AND COMPARATIVE ADVANTAGE

To see how specialization and exchange can increase total output, let us look at two imaginary nations, Kant and Troy. Both nations produce food and machinery for its home market. If they decide to specialize and trade, how will each nation determine its specialty?

Absolute Advantage

Each nation's production possibilities are shown in Table 15.1. The table gives the number of units that can be produced in each nation per labor day.* Thus, Kant can produce either 5 units of food or 2 units of machinery

*A labor day is a unit of labor resources. It is the use of 1 laborer for 1 day. One hundred labor days may be the use of 100 laborers for 1 day, 1 laborer for 100 days, 10 laborers for 10 days, and so forth.

Table 15.1 Production Possibilities in Kant and Troy.

	Number of Units That Can Be Produced per Labor Day		
	Food		*Machinery*
Kant	5	or	2
Troy	3	or	4

per labor day. Troy can produce either 3 units of food or 4 units of machinery per labor day.

Apparently, Kant's resources are better suited for food production and Troy's for machinery. Because Kant can produce more food per labor day than Troy, we say that Kant has **absolute advantage** in the production of food. Because Troy can produce more machinery per labor day than Kant, Troy has absolute advantage in the production of machinery. If each nation specializes in the production for which it has absolute advantage, both will be better off.

Can we prove this?

Self-Sufficient Production

Suppose both nations have 100 labor days to use in production, and no trade is taking place between them. Both nations decide to use 50 labor days to produce food and 50 labor days to produce machinery. What is the total combined output of food and machinery?

Kant can produce 5 units of food per labor day, for a total of 250 units. Troy can produce 3 units per labor day, for a total of 150 units. Total combined food production is 400 units:

		FOOD
Kant	5 × 50	= 250
Troy	3 × 50	= 150
		400

Kant can produce 2 units of machinery per labor day, or a total of 100 units. Troy can produce 4 units per labor day, or 200 units. Total combined machinery production is 300 units:

		MACHINERY
Kant	2 × 50	= 100
Troy	4 × 50	= 200
		300

Production with Specialization and Trade

What happens if both countries decide to specialize and trade. If Kant devotes all 100 labor days to food production, total output is (5 × 100) = 500 units. If Troy uses all 100 labor days to produce machinery, total production is (4 × 100) = 400 units:

	FOOD	*MACHINERY*
Kant	5 × 100	
Troy		4 × 100
	500	400

Specialization and trade have increased total production to 500 units of food and 400 units of machinery, for gains of 100 units of both kinds of output.

Comparative Advantage

When nations enjoy absolute advantage, the benefits of trade are easy to see. Most trade is not based on absolute advantage, however, but on **comparative advantage**. To understand comparative advantage, remember that Troy has absolute advantage for producing machinery. Then suppose Troy discovers a new process that enables it to produce more food than before with each unit of labor resources. Its new production possibilities are shown in Table 15.2.

Troy still has absolute advantage in the production of machinery, but now its resources are equally as productive as Kant's in food. Will specialization and trade still increase total production?

In order to determine this, we must compare the costs of production in the two nations

Table 15.2 Production Possibilities with Technological Advance.

	Number of Units That Can Be Produced per Labor Day		
	Food		*Machinery*
Kant	5	or	2
Troy	5	or	4

Table 15.3 Cost of Production.

	Opportunity Cost of Producing	
	1 Unit of Food	*1 Unit of Machinery*
Kant	$\frac{2}{5}$ units of machinery	$2\frac{1}{2}$ units of food
Troy	$\frac{4}{5}$ units of machinery	$1\frac{1}{4}$ units of food

in terms of goods not produced. (Because this measures trade-offs between goods within a nation, it is another example of our familiar opportunity costs.) Note that Kant can produce either 5 units of food or 2 units of machinery per labor day. If Kant decides to produce food, it must give up 2 units of machinery for every 5 units of food it produces; if Kant decides to produce machinery, it must give up 5 units of food for every 2 units of machinery.

To determine the opportunity cost of 1 unit of food in Kant, we divide units of machinery by units of food. (Can you explain why?*) Units of machinery/units of food = $\frac{2}{5}$. This ratio tells us that for every unit of food produced, Kant must give up $\frac{2}{5}$ units of machinery. To find the opportunity cost of 1 unit of machinery in Kant, we divide units of food by units of machinery: $\frac{5}{2}$, or $2\frac{1}{2}$. Kant must give up $2\frac{1}{2}$ units of food for every unit of machinery it produces.

Now look at production possibilities for Troy. Troy must give up $\frac{4}{5}$ units of machinery for 1 unit of food, and $\frac{5}{4}$ or $1\frac{1}{4}$ units of food for 1 unit of machinery. Opportunity costs for both countries are shown in Table 15.3.

*The formula for computing opportunity costs is a simple algebraic equation. To illustrate, in Kant equivalent production possibilities may be shown by: $2m = 5f$. To find the cost of $1f$ (food), we divide both sides of the equation by 5. To find the cost of $1m$ (machinery), we divide both sides of the equation by 2.

Compare opportunity costs in the two nations, using Table 15.3 as a guide. One unit of machinery costs Troy $1\frac{1}{4}$ units of food and costs Kant $2\frac{1}{2}$ units of food. In other words, Kant must give up more food than Troy if it decides to produce machinery. Since Troy's opportunity costs are lower, it would certainly make sense for Troy to produce machinery. We can say that Troy has comparative advantage in the production of machinery: in terms of food not produced, the cost of producing 1 unit of machinery is lower in Troy than in Kant.

What about the production of food? As we saw, neither country has absolute advantage in food production. Does this mean that specialization should not occur?

Look again at Table 15.3. Producing one unit of food costs Troy $\frac{4}{5}$ units of machinery. However, producing a unit of food costs Kant only $\frac{2}{5}$ units of machinery. In other words, in the production of food Kant gives up less than Troy. Thus, Kant has comparative advantage in the production of food. Because Kant's opportunity costs are lower, it would make sense for Kant to produce food.

If each nation produces the good for which it has comparative advantage, the result is greater total production.

Can we prove this?

Self-Sufficient Production

Again, suppose both countries have 100 labor days to use in production and that no trade is taking place. Both decide to use 50 labor days to produce food and 50 labor days to produce machinery. What is the total combined output of food and machinery? (Use Table 15.2 to calculate total output.)

Without trade, Kant can produce 5 units of food per labor day, or a total of 250 units. Troy can also produce 5 units per labor day, or 250 units in 50 labor days. Total combined food output is 500 units. Kant can produce a total of 100 units of machinery and Troy can produce 200 units. Total combined machinery output is 300 units:

	FOOD	*MACHINERY*
Kant	5 × 50 = 250	2 × 50 = 100
Troy	5 × 50 = 250	4 × 50 = 200
	500	300

Production with Specialization and Trade

What happens if both nations decide to specialize and trade? If Kant devotes all 100 labor days to food production, total output is 500 units. If Troy uses all 100 labor days to produce machinery, total production is 400 units:

	FOOD	*MACHINERY*
Kant	5 × 100 = 500	
Troy		4 × 100 = 400

Again specialization and trade have increased total production. Output of machinery has increased by 100 units without sacrificing any quantity of food.

The benefits of trade may be illustrated on a production possibilities curve like the one shown on Figure 15.1. The production possibilities curves in this example have been

Figure 15.1 Production Possibilities Without Trade (with 100 labor days)

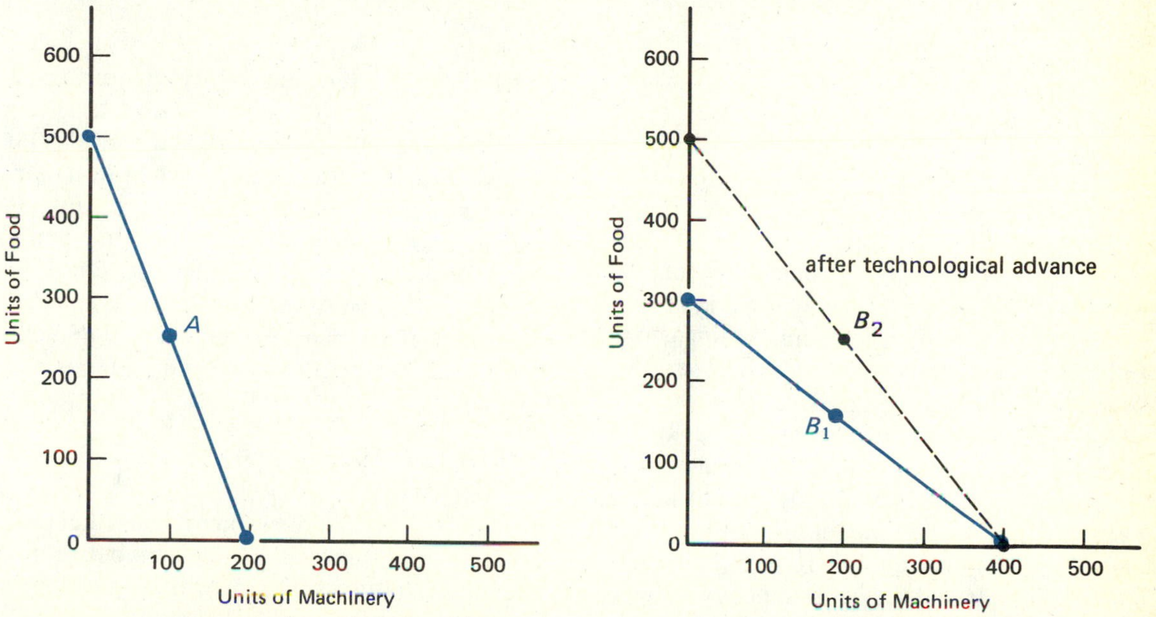

a. Kant's Production Possibilities

b. Troy's Production Possibilities

drawn as straight lines because, for simplicity, we have assumed constant production costs. This means that each nation must give up constant (rather than increasing) amounts of one good in order to obtain additional units of the other good.

TEST YOURSELF
Calculate the opportunity cost of producing 50 additional units of machinery in Kant at point *A*. Must Kant give up $2\frac{1}{2}$ units of food for each unit of machinery?

Without trade, each nation can produce at some point on its own production possibilities curve: Kant may decide to produce at point *A*; Troy may have produced at B_1 before its technological advance and may decide to produce at B_2 after its technological advance.

If Kant and Troy combine their economies into a large, free-trade area, their combined production possibilities can be shown by Figure 15.2. Total production possibilities are greater with specialization and trade.

TEST YOURSELF
Compare total production at *A* and B_2 with total production at *C*.

Figure 15.2 Combined Production Possibilities with Specialization and Trade

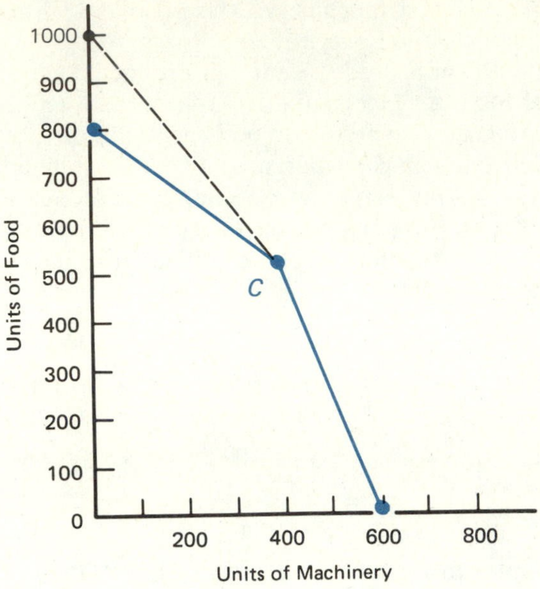

The Basis for Trade

Nations engage in international trade on the basis of comparative advantage. Nations benefit from trade by producing and selling goods and services in which they have comparative advantage and buying goods and services in which other nations have comparative advantage. Because total production is greater with specialization than it would be if each nation were self-sufficient, the entire trading area benefits. Each nation is producing and exchanging goods and services at the lowest possible cost. Of course, the benefits of trade occur only if nations are engaged in free trade: that is, if there are no barriers or restrictions to trade. As we see later in this chapter, trade is not always free.

Who engages in international trade? You engage in international trade when you purchase a Japanese car or German beer, just as the U.S. government engages in trade when it sells surplus military equipment to Israel or grain to India. Business firms engage in international trade when they purchase Jamaican bauxite and sell American-made aluminum.

THE BALANCE OF PAYMENTS

A nation, just like a business, must keep an account of all purchases and sales between it and other nations. The record of a nation's international transactions is known as its **balance of payments**. On the balance of payments, all sales to foreigners are added together to

Thinking Seriously About Economic Issues

THE BENEFITS OF BEING A "TRADING STATE"

Richard Rosecrance of Cornell University has developed an interesting way of thinking about national goals and the relationship between national goals and economic prosperity.

Rosecrance divided nations into two groups according to their national goals: territorial nations and trading nations. Because territory provides resources and resources bring wealth, territorial nations are concerned with maintaining their territory. A nation with vast territory can impose taxes to support a strong army and capture even more territory from other nations. Trading nations follow a different route to prosperity. Trading nations cooperate with other nations and, through trade, produce more wealth than they could have gained through military conquest.

The significant thing about trade is that profitable trade depends on markets, and markets exist only where people are prosperous. Thus, to emphasize trade as a national goal brings together the interests of all nations in a mutual drive to achieve prosperity.

Professor Rosecrance believes that territorial goals dominated international politics until the middle of the twentieth century. Until this century, nations tended to want to get bigger and more self-sufficient. Then after World War II, there began to be a division of the world between the territorial nations and the nations that concentrate instead on trade. The United States and the former Soviet Union, he says, placed more emphasis on territory and the resources and internal markets that keep them self-sufficient. Japan and European nations, on the other hand, emphasized international trade to acquire the resources they once acquired through military force.

World War II persuaded the world that the benefits of war are not sufficient to offset the costs. Instead, gaining power through trade yields more enduring and more widespread benefits, without imposing the costs of war. Because trading nations achieve power through specialization, they value diversity and interdependence. Industrial and population growth strengthen interdependence, says Professor Rosecrance, and make it harder to achieve national goals independently. Moreover, a trading system sets free the productive and trading energies of people, who look for markets and create wealth without any guidance from government at all.

Trading nations can improve national welfare and the allocation of resources through internal development and trade, without preventing other nations from achieving the same goals.

Richard Rosecrance, *The Rise of the Trading State*, Basic Books, New York, 1985.

determine the flow of spending into a nation; sales to foreigners are called *exports*. All purchases from foreigners are added together to determine the flow of spending from that nation to other nations; purchases from foreigners are called *imports*. The difference between exports and imports is the *net* flow of spending.

A positive difference between exports and imports represents a net inflow of spending. We say the nation has a balance of payments *surplus*. A balance of payments surplus leaves a nation holding unspent claims against the wealth of foreigners. A negative difference represents a net outflow of spending. We say the nation has a balance of payments *deficit*. A deficit means that foreigners are holding unspent claims against the wealth of that nation.

Spending Flows

There are three kinds of transactions among nations, listed under three accounts in the balance of payments:

1. The *current account* records flows of spending for goods and services.
2. The *long-term capital account* records flows of spending for long-term investments and for U.S. government spending abroad.
3. The *short-term capital account* records flows of funds for short-term lending.

Table 15.4 lists various types of transactions falling under each heading and indicates whether the transactions normally result in

Table 15.4 Inflows and Outflows in the U.S. Balance-of-Payments Account.

	Inflow or Outflow
Current account (trade)	
1. Exports	
a. Goods sold abroad (e,g,. computers, aircraft, soybeans)	+
b. Services sold abroad (e.g., financial services, insurance, tourism)	+
2. Imports	
a. Goods bought abroad (e.g., petroleum, bauxite, autos, bananas, perfume)	–
b. Services bought abroad (e.g., shipping services, tourism)	–
3. Income	
a. From U.S. investments abroad	+
b. To foreigners from their investments in the United States	–
4. U.S. government military expenditures	–
Capital account (investments or long-term loans)	
1. Long-term capital investments	
a. U.S. investment abroad (e.g., long-term bonds or stocks, factories, hotels, banks, mines)	–
b. Foreign investment in the United States (e.g., long-term bonds or stocks, factories, mines)	+
2. U.S. government grants and aid to foreign governments	–
Short-term capital account (short-term loans)	
1. U.S. lending abroad (e.g., short-term notes, bank accounts)	–
2. Foreign lending in the United States (e.g., short-term notes, bank accounts)	+

inflows (+) of spending into the United States or outflows (−).

Net Flows for the United States

The net flow of spending for goods and services is represented by the balance on current account. Until the mid-1970s, the United States sold more goods abroad than we bought, and this balance was positive; that is, inflows (+'s) exceeded outflows (−'s). Since the mid-1970s, the balance has generally been negative, chiefly the result of the rising cost of petroleum imports into the United States, the increase of consumer goods production in other nations, and certain barriers to U.S. exports in some nations.

The net flow of long-term investment and government spending is represented by the balance on capital account. Until the mid-1980s the balance on capital account was generally negative. An outflow of investment funds represents U.S. purchases of productive facilities in other countries, with a potential inflow of income from operating the investments.

In the mid-1980s the U.S. balance on capital account turned positive, indicating a net flow of long-term capital into the United States. Today, foreigners who have earned dollars from sales to U.S. consumers are using their dollars to purchase investments in the United States. In fact, foreign holdings of U.S. investments (net of U.S. holdings of investments abroad) increased from zero in 1986 to $400 billion in 1990.

Similar changes have been occurring in the short-term capital account. In most of the years since World War II, savers in the United States loaned more short-term funds abroad than foreigners loaned in the United States. The result was a negative balance on short-term capital. In the 1980s this trend reversed, and the United States is now borrowing more from foreigners than we are leading abroad. The chief reason for our short-term borrowing has been to pay for the increase in U.S. imports relative to exports and to finance the massive increase in U.S. government borrowing. For all our borrowing, the United States must pay substantial interest charges to foreign lenders.

When the balances on current, long-term capital, and short-term capital accounts are added together, the result is the net flow of funds between the United States and other nations. Values of each account and the net flow of funds for selected recent years are shown in Table 15.5.

As the table shows, the net flow of dollars has been negative for most of the period. A negative flow means that we are experiencing a deficit in our balance of payments. We are spending more dollars abroad than foreigners want to spend in this country. A negative balance of payments means that there remain unspent claims against the wealth of the United States in the hands of foreigners.

Foreigners with claims against the United States may settle their claims in any of the following ways.

Short-Term Capital Account

Foreigners can lend their dollars on short term to U.S. individuals, banks, and other businesses or to the U.S. Treasury. They can do this by buying bank certificates of deposit or other securities, or by simply depositing their dollars in U.S. banks. Foreigners use their dollars for short-term lending if the interest earnings on short-term loans in the United States are at least as great as the interest earnings on loans made elsewhere.

Long-Term Capital Account

Foreigners may use their dollars to make long-term investments in U.S. business firms. They

Table 15.5 U.S. Balance of Payments (in millions of dollars).[a]

	1960	*1964*	*1969*	*1974*	*1977*	*1982*	*1985*	*1988*	*1991*
Current account									
Merchandise Exports	+20,282	+26,589	+38,448	+98,533	+122,932	+216,946	+214,424	+319,251	+415,962
Merchandise Imports	−14,758	−18,700	−35,807	−100,379	−151,713	−247,606	−338,863	−446,466	−489,398
Services and Transfers (net)	− 964	− 1,149	− 1,763	− 2,355	− 2,008	− 2,621	− 4,311	+ 13,423	+ 34,363
Investment Income (net)									
Difference between income from U.S. investments abroad and foreign investments in the United States	+ 2,287	+ 3,935	+ 3,811	+ 9,516	+ 11,935	+ 27,304	+ 25,187	+ 61,974	+ 16,429
U.S government transactions	− 2,753	− 2,133	− 3,344	− 2,150	− 1,355	− 5,234	− 14,113	− 14,983	+ 18,963
Capital account									
Long term									
Government	− 884	− 1,353	− 1,933	− 2,571	+ 31,237	− 1,793	− 8,006	+ 38,316	+ 27,567
Private	− 2,100	− 4,511	− 70	− 3,287	− 6,384	+ 22,428	+ 62,487	+ 40,902	+ 24,402
Short term									
Net short-term capital flows	− 1,405	− 1,643	− 640	− 14,751	− 4,564	− 45,083	+ 38,524	+ 57,971	− 47,206
Net flow of funds	− 3,677	− 2,696	− 6,081	− 15,655	+ 80	− 35,659	− 24,671	+ 70,388	+ 1078

[a]Values may not total because of minor omissions.

SOURCE: *Economic Report of the President*, and *Federal Reserve Bulletins*.

do this by buying stocks or bonds or by investing directly in productive facilities in the United States. Foreigners will use their dollars for long-term investments if the expected earnings on U.S. investments are at least as great as the expected earnings on investments elsewhere.

Some Problems

Before we look at the third way foreigners can settle their dollar claims against the United States, let us look at some of the problems associated with short-term and long-term capital inflows.

The problem with short-term capital is that it gives the Federal Reserve less freedom to use expansionary monetary policy. Moreover, if the Fed does undertake expansionary monetary policy, it may have little effect.

Why is this so?

Remember that the goal of expansionary monetary policy is to reduce interest rates in the United States in order to stimulate business and consumer spending and speed recovery from a recession. But lower interest rates will cause short-term capital to leave the United States for nations where interest rates are higher on short-term loans. If these dollars flow abroad, they will not be available for spending here and cannot stimulate domestic investment.

TEST YOURSELF
The preceding example describes problems associated with the use of expansionary monetary policy. Can you describe how the possibility of short-term capital inflows interferes with the Federal Reserve's use of contractionary monetary policy?

Long-term capital investments have additional disadvantages in that they imply a degree of foreign control of U.S. businesses. Foreigners already own more than 1 percent of the nation's total of almost $15 trillion in assets, including an increasing share of U.S. government securities. Foreign investment has been growing at the rate of almost 10 percent per year, with the result that investment income paid to foreigners has soared. Moreover, there is always the lurking fear that foreign owners of U.S. capital resources might someday use their economic power to influence U.S. policies.

Having explored the disadvantages of the first two uses foreigners might make of their U.S. dollars, now let us look at the way that is generally preferred by the United States.

Current Account

From the U.S. point of view, the best use of dollars by foreigners would be to purchase U.S.-made goods and services. Foreign purchases of U.S. exports would add enough spending inflows to the current account to offset spending outflows in the other accounts. It would also stimulate production in U.S. factories and provide jobs for U.S. workers. Finally, it would increase incomes in the United States and permit U.S. consumers to buy more goods and services from other nations.

If foreigners are to be persuaded to spend their dollars for U.S. exports, they must be convinced of their high quality and low price. A goal of U.S. industries must be to make our exports attractive to foreign buyers, so that more of the dollars spent abroad flow back into U.S. markets.

THE FOREIGN EXCHANGE MARKET

Some foreign holders of dollars may decide not to spend their dollars for U.S. exports, for long-term investment, or for short-term lending. Instead, they may want to exchange their dollars for other currencies for spending in other nations. For this purpose, they must use the foreign exchange market.

How Things Have Changed

CHANGES IN THE WAY WE FINANCE INVESTMENTS (% of GDP)

	1950–1979	1980–1991
Gross private domestic investment	16.0	16.0
National savings	16.3	14.1
Private:		
Household	5.0	4.3
Business	11.8	12.4
Government:		
Federal	−.6	−3.4
State and local	.2	.9
Net foreign capital investment	−.3	1.6

When national saving falls below gross private domestic investment, the difference may be financed by an inflow of net foreign capital investment. Over the years 1980–1991 net foreign investment in the United States amounted to 1.6 percent of U.S. GDP. This is in contrast with the period 1950–1979, when the United States invested .3 percent of GDP abroad.

SOURCE: *Economic Report of the President*, 1992.

International trade requires the use of many national currencies: francs, marks, dollars, yen, and many others. Foreign exchange markets provide a means for exchanging national currencies and, like other markets, operate according to the laws of demand and supply. The demand for a currency reflects the quantities people around the world would want to buy at various prices (when the price is stated in terms of their own currency). In general, people want to buy a currency because they want to spend it in the nation that issued it. Thus, demand for a currency arises from people's desire to purchase a nation's exports, long-term investments, or short-term investments.

The supply of a currency reflects the quantities people around the world want to sell at various prices (in terms of their own currency). In general, people want to sell currency they have acquired through sales of imports to the nation that issued it or through sales of long-term or short-term investments. We might say that demand for a nation's currency arises out of the "plus" (+) transactions in its balance of payments, and supply from the "minuses" (−).

Figure 15.3 is a model of a foreign ex-

Figure 15.3 The Foreign Exchange Market for German Marks

A fixed exchange rate is agreed to by a nation's government.

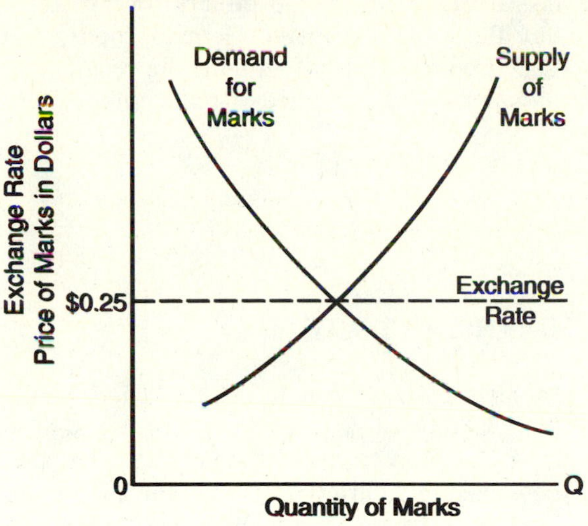

change market showing the demand and supply of German marks, when the price of marks is stated in dollars. The equilibrium price of marks is called its **exchange rate**; in this case, the equilibrium price of marks is $.25.

Fixed and Floating Exchange Rates

In most markets, changes in demand and supply cause changes in the equilibrium price. This is not always true in markets for foreign exchange. In fact, for most of the years since World War II, currency prices were **fixed**: The **fixed exchange rate** of a German mark was about $.25, as shown in the figure; the fixed exchange rate of a British pound was about $2.80. Currency values were agreed to by the financial ministers of major trading nations and were maintained by their Central Banks. A currency's price was maintained by Central Bank purchases or sales of currencies, adding to the demand or supply of particular currencies to push the equilibrium price up or down to the agreed value.

In 1973, Western nations agreed to stop fixing their exchange rates and allow their currencies to **float**. When exchange rates are allowed to float, prices of currencies rise and fall according to demand and supply. An increase in demand for marks, for example, causes the demand curve to shift to the right and the price of marks to rise. An increase in the supply of a currency, on the other hand, causes its supply curve to shift to the right and its price to fall. The expected advantage of **floating exchange rates** is that allowing a currency's value to rise or fall helps correct balance-of-payments deficits.

Floating Exchange Rates and Balance-of-Payments Deficits

When balance-of-payments deficits cause dollars to pile up in foreign exchange markets, the supply of dollars increases and its price tends to fall. A fall in the price of a currency as a result of changes in market demand and supply is called **depreciation**.*

We have said that the value of the dollar depreciates as its supply increases. How will the depreciation of the dollar correct a U.S. balance-of-payments deficit? To answer this question, we must look at the foreign exchange market for dollars, shown in Figure 15.4. With demand at D and supply S, dollars exchange for marks at an exchange rate of 1 mark = $0.25, or $1.00 = 4 marks. If the

*Depreciation is distinguished from **devaluation**, which occurs only when governments have fixed their exchange rates. A government devalues its currency when it gives it a lower value in terms of other currencies.

Figure 15.4 The Foreign Exchange Market for U.S. Dollars

A floating exchange rate rises or falls with changes in demand or supply.

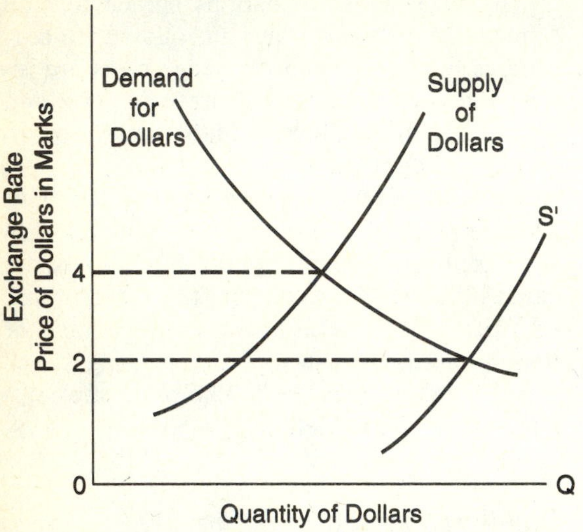

supply of dollars increases to S′, however, the dollar's exchange rate will tend to fall relative to the mark. Under floating exchange rates, the new exchange rate may be 1 mark = \$0.50 or, stated differently, \$1.00 = 2 marks. Refer to Figure 15.4 to verify the decrease in the dollar's exchange rate.

At the lower dollar exchange rate, a German citizen can buy a dollar for only 2 (rather than 4) marks; he or she can buy the same quantity of U.S. exports for half as many marks as before. Thus, depreciation of the dollar makes U.S. exports cheaper to foreign buyers. The German consumer is likely to want to acquire more dollars for spending in the United States, and U.S. exports will increase. The result is to increase the "pluses" in our balance of payments and to reduce the U.S. balance-of-payments deficit.

At the same time, a U.S. citizen will receive only 2 (rather than 4) marks for each dollar supplied to foreign exchange markets; purchasing German goods will require twice as many dollars as before. The U.S. citizen is less likely to exchange dollars for marks to buy the more expensive German goods, and U.S. imports will fall. Again, the result is to reduce the U.S. balance-of-payments deficit.

TEST YOURSELF
Can you think of any disadvantages of depreciation of the dollar?

BARRIERS TO TRADE

In years past, nations have often tried to correct balance-of-payments deficits by setting up barriers to trade. Although these barriers now exist in a variety of forms, the most common trade barrier is a **tariff**, a tax on imports that makes foreign goods more expensive than similar goods produced at home.

Tariffs

A tariff discourages imports and thus reduces the "minuses" in a nation's balance of payments. With a tariff, nations cannot specialize and trade on the basis of comparative advantage. Consumers cannot buy from the lowest-cost producers, and their standards of living are lower than they might be. Moreover, when one nation imposes a tariff to reduce its imports, other nations often impose tariffs, too, in retaliation. International trade declines as a result.

During the years preceding the Great Depression, many nations sought to reduce their balance-of-payments deficits by imposing high tariffs on imports. In the United States, the Hawley-Smoot Tariff of 1930 imposed tariffs as high as 60 percent of the value of many imports. Tariffs reduced international sales of goods and services, causing production and incomes to fall around the world. Lower incomes meant still fewer sales and aggravated the problem of falling production and rising unemployment during the Great Depression.

In 1934, President Franklin Roosevelt embarked on a program of Reciprocal Trade Agreements with other nations to reduce tariff barriers. Cooperating nations agreed to reduce certain tariffs together so that trade could flow more freely. After World War II, the General Agreement on Tariffs and Trade (GATT) continued to liberalize trading relations. The United States and other members of GATT meet regularly in negotiations to reduce tariffs and other barriers to trade.

Trade agreements in recent years have often granted "most favored nation" status to particular nations. This means that any tariff reduction given to a favored nation will immediately be extended to all other nations who are parties to the agreement.

Nontariff Barriers to Trade

Other negotiations have aimed at reducing nontariff barriers to free trade:

1. *Import quotas* that limit quantities of particular imports.
2. *Product standards* that restrict certain imports.
3. *Export subsidies* that enable producers to sell abroad at lower prices than at home.

An import quota limits the quantity of a foreign good or service allowed in domestic markets. Quotas are generally illegal under the rules of GATT. The United States, however, has negotiated Voluntary Restraint Agreements (VRAs) with foreign producers of steel and other manufactured goods.

A quota is similar to a tariff in that it raises the price of the good in domestic markets. The reason is that it limits additions to domestic supply from foreign sources. A quota has another disadvantage relative to a tariff. Because a quota places an absolute limit on imports, it reduces the ability of markets to respond to increases in consumer demand.

Product standards also work to restrict trade without actually violating the rules of GATT. Product standards covering emissions control and size of tomatoes, for example, exclude imports from particular nations, with the goal of protecting domestic producers and reducing balance-of-payments deficits.

Export subsidies are payments to producers of export goods that have the effect of reducing the cost of producing the export item. An example is the European practice of rebating tax payments to exporters when goods are sent abroad, thus enabling the producer to sell abroad more cheaply than in domestic markets.

Import quotas, product standards, and export subsidies distort comparative advantage and reduce the efficiency of international trade.

In the remainder of this chapter, we consider some of the recent controversies regarding free trade.

Self-Check

Use the following table to answer questions 1-3:

	Number of Units That Can Be Produced per Labor Day		
	Watches		*Cameras*
Albia	2	or	3
Verda	3	or	4

1. Which of the following statements is incorrect?
a. Verda has absolute advantage in the production of both watches and cameras.
b. Verda has comparative advantage in the production of watches.
c. Verda must give up 4 cameras to produce 3 watches, or $1\frac{1}{3}$ cameras for each watch.
d. Albia must give up 3 cameras to produce 2 watches, or $1\frac{1}{2}$ cameras for each watch.
e. All answers are correct.

2. Assume each nation has 50 labor days to use in production. If each specializes in the product in which it has a comparative advantage, total output will be:
a. 100 watches and 200 cameras.
b. 150 watches and 150 cameras.
c. 100 watches and 150 cameras.
d. 150 watches and 200 cameras.
e. None of the above.

3. In Verda, the cost of producing each camera is:
a. $\frac{3}{4}$ watch.
b. $2\frac{2}{3}$ watches.
c. 3 watches.

d. $1\frac{1}{3}$ watches.
e. 4 watches.

4. Which of the following will cause an outflow in the balance of payments?
a. General Motors sells a Cadillac to an Arabian Sheik.
b. A U.S. technician trains Brazilian computer programmers.
c. An Italian tourist takes his family to Disney World.
d. A Mexican subsidiary of a U.S. firm increases its income from sales.
e. IBM builds a plant in Belgium.

5. In recent years, our balance of trade has been:
a. Negative, because we import more than we export.
b. Positive, because foreign nations have imposed barriers on American-made goods.
c. Negative, because we have invested heavily abroad.
d. Negative, because of global demand for American grain.
e. Positive, because foreigners have bought stock in American firms.

6. The value of the dollar declines in relation to other currencies:
a. When foreigners buy gold from the U.S. Treasury.
b. When foreigners demand more dollars for spending in the United States.
c. When the supply of dollars increases in foreign exchange markets.
d. When exchange rates are fixed.
e. When foreign banks buy dollars.

7. Which of the following does not belong with the others?
a. General Agreement on Tariffs and Trade.
b. Hawley-Smoot Tariff.
c. European Community.
d. Most Favored Nation status.
e. Reciprocal Trade Agreements.

Theory in Practice

FREE TRADE IN CONSUMER MARKETS

We have described the benefits of trade in terms of comparative advantage. And we have suggested that barriers to trade reduce the benefits nations would enjoy from free trade. In this section we illustrate the benefits of free trade through use of microeconomic models before and after trade. Then we show the effect of a tariff that interferes with free trade.

Figure 15.5a shows a hypothetical demand curve for sugar in the United States. Figure 15.5b shows a similar demand curve for sugar in sugar-producing nations of Central America. The supply curves show that Central America's costs of production are lower than production costs in the United States. According to the supply curves, any quantity of sugar can be produced in Central America at a lower average cost than that quantity can be produced in the United States. Without trade, the equilibrium price of sugar is higher in the United States than in the sugar-producing nations of Central America.

With free trade, more American consumers will want to purchase imported sugar, shifting demand for Central American sugar to the right and raising its price. At the same time, demand for U.S.-grown sugar will shift to the left, reducing U.S. sugar prices. Demand curves will continue to shift until there

Figure 15.5 Markets for Sugar

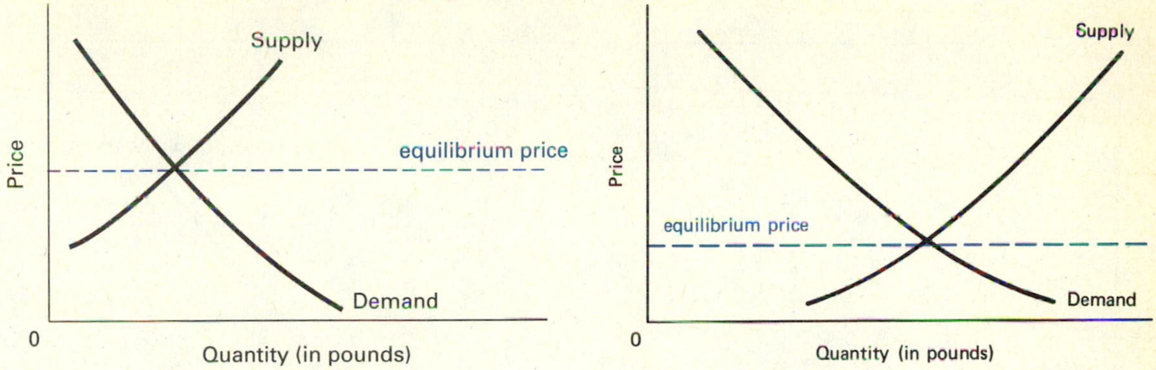

a. Market for U.S.-Grown Sugar **b. Market for Central American Sugar**

is no longer a price advantage in either market. Finally, all buyers will be satisfied at a price somewhere between the two extremes.

TEST YOURSELF

Pencil in offsetting shifts in demand in the two markets and mark the final equilibrium price for sugar.

Free trade will cause Central American nations to move toward specialization in the kind of production in which they enjoy comparative advantage. Likewise, free trade will cause the United States to move away from sugar production. U.S. sugar growers will suffer increasing unemployment. Often their transition to new jobs is slow and painful, but eventually U.S. sugar growers will find employment in kinds of production for which the United States has (or can develop) comparative advantage—perhaps electronic calculators, agricultural equipment, or technical services.

A tariff interferes with this adjustment process. The objective of a tariff is to reduce imports and protect U.S. producers from foreign competition. In the market for sugar, the effect of a tariff is to raise the price of foreign sugar. This is because the tariff is added to Central American costs of production, shifting the supply curve upward and to the left.

Figure 15.6 shows the addition of a tariff to the selling price of Central American sugar. Now any quantity of Central American sugar can be sold in the United States only at a higher price. U.S. consumers will be unable to shop freely in the lowest-cost market, and U.S. sugar growers will not be encouraged to move into more efficient employments.

When tariffs interfere with free trade, nations fail to specialize according to the principle of comparative advantage. As a result, total world output is lower and unit costs of production are higher than with free trade.

TARIFFS AND UNEMPLOYMENT

When a nation's workers face unemployment, they may insist on policies to increase employment at the expense of other nations. Such policies are called "beggar my neighbor" policies.

Following World War I, many nations had war debts to be paid. They tried to earn for-

Figure 15.6 Effects of a Tariff

A tariff artificially increases selling price. U.S. customers take advantage of low-cost Central American sugar.

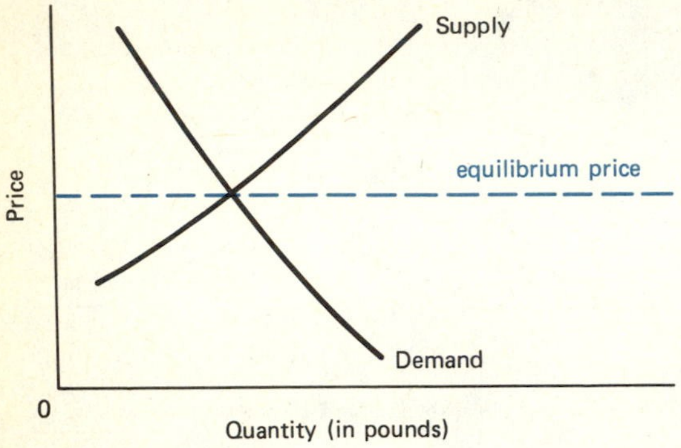

a. Market for U.S.-Grown Sugar

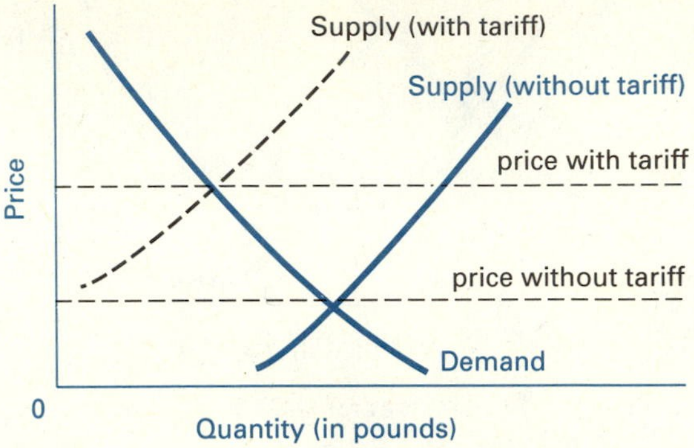

b. Market for Central American Sugar

eign currencies by selling more goods and services abroad. At the same time, they imposed tariffs to limit imports and achieve a balance-of-payments surplus.

Obviously, all nations cannot be successful in this objective. All nations cannot sell more to other nations and at the same time buy less from all of them. As a result of the attempt, however, trade declined, so that production fell and unemployment increased.

Many governments tried to "export" their unemployment by imposing still higher tariffs. The intent of tariffs was to avoid the loss of jobs, but the result was to spread unemployment more widely among other nations.

Tariffs can export unemployment, but a policy of high tariffs can backfire. When foreign workers cannot sell their products to U.S. consumers, they cannot buy the products of U.S. industries. High tariff barriers among industrialized nations in the 1930s contributed greatly to the high level of unemployment in the Great Depression.

Labor unions often favor a protective tariff to reduce competition from foreign producers. Support for tariff protection is particularly widespread in the textile and steel industries. Without a tariff or import quota, a lower-cost foreign producer would be able to undersell U.S. producers. According to the principle of comparative advantage, however, this is as it should be. The nation whose resources and technology are best suited for textile or steel production should specialize in that kind of production. U.S. workers should move into production for which the United States has comparative advantage.

When a particular industry is just getting started, it may need a protective tariff until it becomes well established. Otherwise, established producers abroad may be able to undersell it and drive it out of business. Such tariffs are called "infant industry" tariffs. Infant industry tariffs should be only temporary, however. As an industry comes of age, it should compete with foreign producers by operating at low costs and improving production techniques.

Other reasons are often advanced for tariffs (although the fundamental reason is generally to protect jobs). One reason is to encourage domestic production and avoid dependence on a foreign country for a strategic commodity: food, energy, or uranium, for instance. Unfortunately, a "strategic industry" tariff may protect nonessential production, too, since it is difficult to draw the line between essential and nonessential commodities. Before deciding to protect domestic suppliers, a nation should calculate the opportunity cost involved: the sacrifice of goods and services that could have been produced if high-cost production of the strategic commodity had not been protected.

THE MULTINATIONALS

The United States experienced a long period of surpluses in its balance of trade. Our agricultural products and manufactured goods were in great demand abroad. Many U.S. firms experienced inflows of currencies from the sale of U.S. exports. They used these currencies to build foreign plants or to acquire factories abroad. A firm that carries on productive operations in more than one country is called a multinational firm.

There are advantages to operating in several countries. First, goods manufactured in a foreign nation are not subject to that nation's tariffs or quotas; therefore, they can be sold more cheaply in the foreign market. Second, profits in foreign operations are not subject to U.S. income taxes until they are brought back to the United States. Third, multinational firms can arrange their operations to take advantage of differences in costs in many nations. They will use more labor in low-wage countries and satisfy their borrowing needs in low-interest countries. They might even shift profits into low-tax countries by reducing the prices of component parts made in one country and selling them cheaply to a branch plant in the low-tax country for final assembly.

The result of these advantages has been rising financial power and influence for multinational firms. Occasionally, multinational firms have been accused of attempting to influence a nation's political affairs.

Some nations are now taking steps to reduce some of the advantages enjoyed by multinational firms. The U.S. Congress has voted to reduce tax advantages on foreign income. Other nations are investigating earnings to ensure that multinationals cannot shift profits earned in one country to other low-tax countries. Also, the rise of wage rates in many formerly low-wage countries has reduced their low-cost advantage.

Some important multinationals with home bases in European countries are Shell, Unilever, Bayer, Volkswagen, and Nestlé. Japanese firms have also entered the multinational arena. Today Mitsubishi, Matsushita, Mitsui, Sony, and other Japanese firms own factories, hotels, office buildings, and restaurants in the United States.

Multinationalism has increased the interdependency of nations. It has encouraged production in low-cost areas according to the principle of comparative advantage. Furthermore, the income from U.S. multinationals operating abroad appears as an inflow in the U.S. balance of payments. The inflow of earnings from foreign investments has helped offset outflows of spending for imports. To the extent that multinationals enhance the efficiency of the global economy, they should be encouraged. But they should be subject to the same rules and regulations—tax and antitrust laws, for example—that affect domestic firms.

SUMMARY

1. The beginning of trade brought opportunities for economic progress through specialization and division of labor. Trade helped spread cultural, intellectual, and technical achievements.
2. Specialization replaces self-sufficiency. Specializing nations must be assured a free flow of trade if they are to realize maximum benefits from specialization.

3. Nations (or regions) specialize according to the principles of absolute advantage and comparative advantage. Specialization increases total output.
4. A nation's balance of payments records international transactions. The current account of the U.S. balance of payments has been negative for almost two decades. The long-term capital account has recently turned positive, as foreigners use their export earnings to make investments in the United States. The short-term capital account shifts from negative to positive, depending on interest rates in the United States and abroad.
5. U.S. dollars spent abroad can come back to the United States through increased exports or through foreigners' long- or short-term investments in the United States. Increased exports produce the most favorable results for U.S. workers and business firms.
6. A falling exchange rate for dollars as a result of market forces is called depreciation. Dollar depreciation can encourage greater exports and reduce a U.S. balance-of-payments deficit.
7. Tariffs reduce international trade and slow economic activity. Tariffs are sometimes intended to export unemployment. Recent agreements have aimed at reducing tariffs and other barriers to trade such as import quotas, product standards, and export subsidies.
8. Multinational firms are becoming an important part of international trade. Multinationalism enables firms to take advantage of low-cost resources and increases the interdependency of nations.

TERMS TO REMEMBER

absolute advantage: the ability to produce a good more cheaply than it can be produced in some other region or nation

comparative advantage: the ability to produce a good more cheaply in terms of other goods not produced

balance of payments: an account of financial transactions between one nation and other nations (international inflows and outflows of spending)

exchange rate: the price of one currency in terms of another

fixed exchange rate: the condition when currency prices are set at an established amount and maintained by Central Bank purchases and sales of currencies

floating exchange rate: the condition when currency prices are allowed to rise and fall according to supply and demand

depreciation: a fall in the price of a currency relative to other currencies as a result of market conditions

devaluation: a reduction in the price of a currency that results from an act of government

tariff: a tax on imports whose intent is to make foreign goods more expensive than domestic goods

TOPICS FOR DISCUSSION

1. The term *petrodollars* refers to outflows of U.S. dollars to pay for high-priced OPEC oil. In what three ways can oil exporters use their dollars? Explain the advantages and disadvantages of each use. Cite current examples of flows of petrodollars back to the United States.
2. Explain how floating exchange rates help correct deficits and surpluses in the balance of payments.
3. *Paradox:* The dollar is said to be "weak" when foreigners hold a large supply relative to demand. However, a weak currency may be an advantage to the U.S. economy. Explain.
4. Explain how opportunity cost is involved in determining a nation's specialization in trade.
5. List the advantages and disadvantages of tariffs, import quotas, and other barriers to free trade. On the basis of your list, what groups do you think are likely to support or oppose tariffs? Why?
6. Look up exchange rates for foreign currencies in the financial pages of your local newspaper. Using these rates, calculate the cost to a Mexican tourist of a night in a U.S. motel. About

how many pesos would you pay for a night in a Mexican hotel? Calculate in marks an approximate price for a steak dinner in Berlin. How many marks would a German citizen need for a steak dinner in New York?

ANSWERS TO TEST YOURSELF

(p. 338) With production of 150 units of machinery, Kant can produce only 125 units of food for a cost of 250 − 125 = 125 food units. Therefore, each unit of machinery costs $\frac{125}{50} = 2\frac{1}{2}$ food units.

(p. 338) At *A* total production is 100 units of machinery and 250 units of food; at B_2 total production is 200 units of machinery and 250 units of food. At *C*, total production is 400 units of machinery and 500 units of food, which is greater than the sum of production at *A* and B_2.

(p. 343) Efforts to reduce the money supply and increase interest rates may fail if higher interest rates encourage foreign holders of dollars to move them back to the United States.

(p. 346) The dollar price of essential imports also will rise, aggravating inflation in the United States and increasing production costs for U.S. importers.

FURTHER READING

Aho, C. Michael and Jonathan David Aronson, *Trade Talks*, Council on Foreign Relations, New York, 1985.

Bean, Charles R., "Economic and Monetary Union in Europe," *Journal of Economic Perspectives*, Fall 1992.

Bolluck, Richard and Robert E. Litan, "Down in the Dumps," *Brookings Review*, Spring 1992.

Dornbusch, Rudiger, "The Case for Trade Liberalization in Developing Countries," *Journal of Economic Perspectives*, Winter 1992.

Flam, Harry, "Product Markets and 1992: Full Integration, Large Gains?" *Journal of Economic Perspectives*, Fall 1992.

Friedman, Sheldon, "NAFTA As Social Dumping," *Challenge*, September/October 1992.

Karier, Thomas, "Unions: Cause or Victim of U.S. Trade Deficit?" *Challenge*, November/December 1991.

Krugman, Paul R., "Is Free Trade Passe?" *Journal of Economic Perspectives*, Fall 1987.

Levy, David A. "1990s: A Contained Depression," *Challenge*, July/August 1991.

Nivola, Pietro S., "Reflections on Regulating Unfair Trade," *Brookings Review*, Winter 1993.

Pastor, Robert A. "NAFTA As the Center of an Integration Process," *Brookings Review*, Winter 1993.

Reich, Robert B., "We Need a Strategic Trade Policy," *Challenge*, July/August 1990.

Schiefer, Jonathan, "What Price Economic Growth?" *The Atlantic*, December 1992.

Stern, Paula, "A Burdensome Legacy for the 1990s." *Brookings Review*, Fall 1991.

Wachtel, Howard M., *The Money Mandarins*, M.E. Sharpe, Armonk, N.Y., 1990.

Answers to Self-Check

CHAPTER 1

1. The basis for the economic problem is choosing how to use society's scarce resources (d). The other answers reflect problems that grow out of the problem of scarcity.
2. Scarcity imposes the problem of choice, so (a) is correct. Careful choices may result in full employment, which would be desirable in view of scarcity.
3. The correct answer is (a). Can you change each of the other answers to make it correct?
4. It is important of think of capital as a produced means of production. Money may be used to *buy* capital, but money itself is not capital. Your answer should be (b).
5. The market economy is a kind of economic democracy; it responds to "dollar" votes (d). A command economy is described in (b); a traditional economy in (c) and (e). All economies must make sacrifices, so (a) is never correct.
6. Opportunity costs may be measured in many units other than dollars: accomplishments, satisfactions, rewards. Your answer should be (d).

CHAPTER 2

1. The correct answer is (c). Perfect competition can exist only if all firms in an industry produce identical products. This is to ensure that no firm can charge a premium price based on product differences. (Of course, we don't have many examples of identical products in American industries. The best example is probably agricultural products.)
2. The correct answer is (d). Changing *one word* in each of the other answers would make that answer correct. Can you find the word in each?
3. Only (b) is correct. What is the key word that tells you (b) does *not* describe a change in supply?
4. Only (c) describes a change in quantity demanded. Identify the source of the shift in *demand* associated with each of the remaining choices.
5. The correct answer is (b). Only buyers who are willing to pay the equilibrium price are satisfied.
6. Answer (b) includes substitutes—for most palates! The other answers are complements.

CHAPTER 3

1. Consumer A's demand will not change much if price changes (d). Apparently A regards pizza as a necessity—no substitutes!
2. Only (c) has no clear substitute—and is not substitutable for other goods. Consumers either must buy (c) whatever the price, or will *not* buy (c) whatever the price.
3. Although (b) is affected *by* price elasticity of demand, it has no effect *on* price elasticity. Can you explain why each of the other choices does affect price elasticity?

4. The correct answer is (c). Can you change one word in each of the other answers to make it correct?
5. Only (a) is incorrect. In fact, a linear demand curve has an infinite number of price elasticities for every small segment of the curve.
6. The correct answer is (c). What principle of mathematics explains the relationship between the demand curve and total revenue from sales?

CHAPTER 4

1. Answers (a), (b), (c), and (d) are necessary payments to owners of productive land, labor, capital, or entrepreneurial ability. Answer (e) is not an economic cost but is described as economic profit.
2. Only (b) is correct. Can you change each of the other choices to make it correct?
3. The correct answer is (e). Explain why each of the other choices is incorrect.
4. The pizza parlor must be able to expand (or contract) quantities fairly easily in response to price changes. All answers are correct (e).
5. Only (e) precisely states the definition of average economic profit. The other choices are incorrect statements of other cost/price relationships.
6. The correct answer is (e). Can you explain why each of the other choices is incorrect?

CHAPTER 5

1. All answers describe the benefits of production under conditions of perfect competition (e).
2. The correct answer is (a). Answers (b), (d), and (e) would help reduce monopoly. (Can you explain why?) Answer (a) is more likely to cause firms to operate as monopolies.
3. Oligopoly occurs because high capital requirements prevent the entry of new firms. The established firms have similar cost and pricing policies. The correct answer is (d).
4. An important characteristic of monopolistic competition is the slight differences among products. Designs are changed often (d).
5. All of the practices mentioned favored large, established firms. They were a means of preventing new competition from getting a share of the market. All are forbidden by current laws when the effect would be to reduce competition (e).
6. Answer (d) is correct. A monopoly firm may lose revenue if it reduces prices. This is because it may not gain enough new customers to make up for the lower price.

CHAPTER 6

1. All answers are correct (d). Specialization, division of labor, and exchange will generally produce larger output on either a regional or a national level.
2. The employment level of a variable resource is based on its price and the market value of its output. Both (a) and (b) are correct, so your choice should be (d).
3. The correct answer is (b). Can you change one word in each of the other answers to make it correct?
4. The correct answer is (d). Often the ability to mechanize a production rocess enables a worker to produce more output per unit of labor time.
5. The correct answer is (e). Resource misallocations may be the result of government regulations and requirements that

have objectives other than efficiency, such as increased equality of income distribution or improved environmental quality.

CHAPTER 7

1. Only (a), an appendicitis operation, is included in GDP. Refer to the definition of GDP and explain why each of the other answers is incorrect.
2. The correct answer is (b).
3. The correct answer is (c). How could you change the question to make each of the other answers correct?
4. Only (e) would cause an increase in GDP. The others would cause GDP to fall. Which part of total spending (*C*, *I*, or *G*) is affected by each of the other answers?
5. Both (a) and (c) are correct, so your choice should be (e). The circular flow will stabilize only if total spending flows are high enough to purchase the entire output supplied by business firms.
6. The correct answer is (c). Show how each of the other answers can be changed to make it correct.

CHAPTER 8

1. *Marginal propensity to consume* is defined as the fraction of *additional* income that will be spent. Your answer should be (d). Can you explain how each of the other conditions would change your *MPC*?
2. All answers are correct (e). The economy will stabilize at the level of GDP at which total spending is equal to the value of output. However, this may not be a healthy equilibrium in terms of the wise and efficient use of our scarce resources.
3. You are respending a government expenditure. This is an example of the multiplier effect (c).
4. The hamburger chain is increasing its capacity in order to fill a higher demand. That is an example of an increase in investment (d).
5. The Queen is cutting spending to reduce aggregate demand and eliminate the inflationary gap. The correct answer is (b).
6. Congress wants consumers to spend more, shifting the *C* component of aggregate demand upward. Congress must believe there is a deflationary gap (c).

CHAPTER 9

1. The correct answer is (c). Highway construction, health, education, and welfare are large outlays of state governments.
2. When the federal *net* tax structure is considered, the only correct answer is (e). Each of the other answers is associated with other taxes. Can you identify each? Answer (c) would apply to the tax structure as a whole, including federal, state, and local taxes.
3. The correct answer is (a). Answers (b) and (c) would worsen the situations that fiscal policy is meant to correct.
4. Answer (c) is correct. Some of the other answers describe the disadvantage of discretionary fiscal policy.
5. The best answer is (d). Spending power redistributed as taxes is used to pay interest to bondholders only if all bondholders are paid at once.
6. The correct answer is (e). Give examples of (a) and (d).
7. Only (e) would be correct. All other choices would increase spending and add to the problem of inflation.

CHAPTER 10

1. The use of money *removed* the need for barter. Your answer should be (d).

2. Gold has many advantages as money, but ease of transporting and storing is not one of them! It is costly and risky to transport and store, so (c) is the correct answer.
3. The Federal Reserve does not deal with the public, but acts as banker for member banks and the U.S. Treasury. The correct answer is (a).
4. All answers are correct (d).
5. A major problem with monetary policy is the problem of persuading businesses to borrow during recession and discouraging them from borrowing during inflation. The correct answer is (c). Answers (a), (b), and (e) would be correct if one word were changed. Can you spot the word?
6. The best answer is (b). Trace the effects of each of the other policy actions.

CHAPTER 11

1. The correct answer is (d). Can you explain how each of the other answers would interfere with the free adjustment process between money and goods?
2. People on fixed incomes suffer from inflation as their *real* income falls (c). Borrowers and hoarders may make substantial gains in spending power. Cost-of-living clauses protect workers from inflation. And the government gains in tax revenues when prices and incomes rise.
3. Aggregate demand inflation results from a high level of total spending (d). Explain how each of the other answers would affect the general price level.
4. The monetarists believe that a steady increase in the supply of money in line with the average growth in production will keep prices stable. The correct answer is (b).
5. Incomes should rise only as much as the average growth in productivity (a). This would keep prices from rising.
6. All answers describe structural inflation, which may result from the power of large firms (e). Many economists have attributed our recent inflation to these structural changes in industry.

CHAPTER 12

1. All of the conditions stated would be true under the Classical assumption of perfect competition in the markets for labor and for goods and services (e).
2. During periods of unemployment, workers tend to lose their skills through idleness. The correct answer is (a).
3. Structural unemployment (c) is not easily corrected by government programs. Can you explain why?
4. The chief disadvantage of public-service employment is that it may interfere with hiring for private production. The correct answer is (c).
5. The only incorrect answer is (a). Your answer should be (e). Employers generally react to an expectation of wage increases by raising their prices, but they do not necessarily hire more labor.
6. Only (d) is correct.

CHAPTER 13

1. None of the answers is correct (e). Can you change each incorrect answer to make it correct?
2. Categorical aid programs are aimed at particular categories, or groups, of poor people. One of these groups includes the aged; others are the blind, the disabled, and dependent children. Cyclical poverty includes a broader range of persons unable to find work because of a downturn in economic activity. Locational poverty is confined to particular geographic or industrial areas. The correct answer is (c).

3. Most of the answers given are considered advantages of direct grants. Answer (d) might be considered a disadvantage if one assumes that the real causes of poverty can be determined and dealt with directly. However, the best answer is (c). Direct grants may have a disincentive effect, particularly if the government reduces aid dollar for dollar as income rises.
4. Direct grants and negative income tax payments would apply to the entire population. This would ensure aid to all poor people. Answer (c) is correct. These programs may, however, result in the problems listed in the other answers.
5. Answer (d) would be the incorrect approach to cyclical poverty. Can you change the answer to make it correct?

CHAPTER 14

1. The best sequence is shown in answer (b). Plentiful resources are necessary before an economy can produce enough to save. Saving permits investment in capital equipment, ensuring greater production in the future.
2. All answers are possible (e). The mature economy may select some combination of these possibilities.
3. All are limits to growth (e). The interaction among population, agricultural and industrial production, pollution, and resource depletion presents real problems for the global economy.
4. The correct answer is (e). If the sectoral theory is the best explanation of growth, policy should encourage investment in the primary sectors of the economy.
5. The answer is (e); both (a) and (c) are correct. Sales of export goods will cause an *inflow* of dollars into the producing region, so (b) is incorrect.

CHAPTER 15

1. All answers are correct (e). Can you explain why? (Look back at the definitions of absolute and comparative advantage and the explanation of computing comparative costs.)
2. After specialization, Verda will be producing 150 (3 × 50) watches and Albia will be producing 150 (3 × 50) cameras. The correct answer is (b).
3. The cost of producing any good is the other types of goods that must be given up. In Verda, the cost of producing 4 cameras is 3 watches, or $\frac{3}{4}$ watch for each camera (a).
4. With the exception of (e), every transaction would bring currency into the United States. When an American firm makes a direct investment abroad, as in (e), dollars flow out. This is a form of long-term capital.
5. The correct answer is (a). See if you can find the errors in each of the other answers.
6. In a free market for foreign exchange, the value of a currency fluctuates according to supply and demand. The value of a currency will decline when its supply increases (relative to demand) or when demand falls. The only correct answer is (c).
7. To answer this question you must know the provisions of each act and each policy. With the exception of (b), all actions were an attempt to increase free trade by removing tariff barriers.

Index

Page numbers in italics refer to charts, figures, and tables.